Farnborough
College of Technology
Library

This book is to be returned on or before the last date stamped below

Child's Play

EXPLORATIONS IN ANTHROPOLOGY
A University College London Series

Series Editors: Barbara Bender, John Gledhill and Bruce Kapferer

Child's Play

Myth, Mimesis and Make-Believe

L.R. Goldman

Oxford • New York

First published in 1998 by
Berg
Editorial offices:
150 Cowley Road, Oxford, OX4 1JJ, UK
70 Washington Square South, New York, NY 10012, USA

© L. R. Goldman 1998

Berg is the imprint of Oxford International Publishers Ltd.

Library of Congress Cataloging-in-Publication Data

A catalogue record for this book is available from the Library of Congress.

British Library Cataloguing-in-Publication Data

A catalogue record for this book is available from the British Library.

ISBN 1 85973 913 X (Cloth)
       1 85973 918 0 (Paper)

Typeset by JS Typesetting, Wellingborough, Northants.
Printed in the United Kingdom by Biddles Ltd, Guildford and King's Lynn.

For Colleen, Leon and Oscar

Extracts from a Huli (Papua New Guinea) sung narrative (*bi te*) which articulates the stereotypes of female beauty (*Bebogo Wane Pandime*) and male beauty (*Iba Mulu Lunguya*) respectively. The reiterated refrain of 'like you can't imagine' – a phrase that might well have served as an alternative title to this book – is echoed by Huli children in their make-believe play.

Narrator: Giame – Yaluba 1993

Huli agali mbira layago laro
There was one man there, I am saying
agali igini ibu one mende laya laro
This man's son had a wife, I am saying
ibu waneore mabura mabuage tebone laya laro
His young daughter was a third person there, I am saying
mabuage ogodege agali wane la tago tago o nabi laya laro
This young girl was not like any man's daughter, I am saying
kewa tangi urume ogoalebe toba hea laya laro
With string hats like you can't imagine, I am saying
hali kuni payada urume ogoalebe toba hea laya laro
With arm-bone bracelets like you can't imagine, I am saying
limale mabu urume pugu lalu togo lea laro
With feathered cassowary claws as nose plugs, I am saying
kewa tangi pugu pugu lea laya laro
Wearing these string hats, I am saying
baya wane purugu laya laro
This wonderful girl who was so good as to dazzle and confuse, I am saying
. . .
uyuguria handa tagi halu heria
While they were looking outside
gulu babu gulu barabu gulu pilipe pili logobe o lama igiri mbira ibiya
One boy came blowing these pan pipes
igiri ibiyaria ai ibiyabe toba hayagola
As the boy came she didn't know who was coming
wali biago ibu gi howa handalu heria igiri ale la tago tago howa nabi layago
When she saw him she was frightened because this boy was not like other boys
unduni hundu mandaru ogobialebe toba hea layago
With a wig coiffure like you can't imagine
ulu babu gulu barabu gulu ogoalebe toba hea layago

With cordyline leaves like you can't imagine
honagaga lagoli uru ogoalebe toba hea laya
With brown cassowary feathers fixed on his wig like a kneecap on a knee, such as you can't imagine
pulu yabe kindiru ogoalebe toba hea laya
With a flapping bag decoration like you can't imagine
geni ge haleru ogoalebe toba hea laya
With leg bands on the legs like you can't imagine
pagabua mano gu gau learu ogoalebe toba hea laya
With the apron ends making sounds like that made by pigs when moving, like you can't imagine
gelabo mandibu gugu ndibu learu ogoalebe toba hea laya
With the apron sitting tightly on each thigh like you can't imagine
agali igini ale tago tago nabi ibiniya laya
A person like this man's son couldn't be mentioned in the same breath as others, and he came
agali igini handaya howa nabiya laya
It wasn't possible even to look at this man's son
Iba Mulu Lungiya agali igini ndo
Iba Mulu Lungiya was not like any man's son
walirume bi labe naheaya
It wasn't possible even for women to talk to him
igiri hegene aube toba hea
This was a clever man like you can't imagine
amu daramabi biagoria dugu yalu tagira ibiyagola igiri labona agali iginila paliaba loa nabi nahea
When he came out of the red lake he was an utterly amazing man such that you couldn't tell another person to go and sleep with him

Contents

Foreword

Anthropologists have finally begun to embrace the topics of play, creativity and improvisation in social life (see Lavie, Narayan and Rosaldo 1993). Thanks in part to researchers with diverse perspectives such as Roy Wagner, Victor Turner and Pierre Bourdieu, adults have become 'active agents' who constitute, manipulate, interpret and invent culture. No such luck for children – at least not in anthropology. For the most part the importance of play, invention and imagination has been masked by mechanistic theories of socialization which continue to characterize this activity as imitation of and preparation for adult life. In anthropology the attitude remains one of mild amusement and only occasional study of children's efforts to 'play society'.

Laurence Goldman sets out to unmask this approach in *Child's Play* by arguing against approaches that treat play as an epiphenomenon and suggesting that the issues of realism and verisimilitude, referentiality and illusion, fact and fiction that one encounters in children's pretence make 'the case for privileging spontaneous play as a focus for attention [in anthropology] . . . both compelling and timely' (p. xvi). In other words it is time, finally, to see what can be learned from an in-depth study of children's pretence, and, in particular, how it is socially mediated and linguistically achieved (p. 3). It turns out that we can learn a lot about a range of issues of concern to both anthropologists and psychologists, issues such as the acquisition of language, the assimilation of metaphor, the development of abstract thought, relationships between language and identity and under-standing how children, as well as adults, make narrative sense of the world.

I have been waiting a long time for anthropologists to appreciate the value of producing richly detailed and 'thick' ethnographies of children's play. Recent exceptions to what has been a drought of studies include Goodwin's *He-Said-She-Said* (1990) and Lancy's *Playing on the Mother-Ground* (1996), but most anthropologists continue to neglect this topic. Goldman's achievement is to keep his focus on make-believe 'for its own sake' and this means that his study is packed (brimming) with ideas about ways to conceptualize as well as to study this topic. Even though his main concern is Huli (Papua New Guinea) children's make-believe, researchers concerned with other places, and even other issues, will learn a great deal from this account.

The focus of Goldman's research is on child-structured play – the play of children which they create 'on their own' and often 'out of sight' of adults. This emphasis is important because the literature has been dominated by studies of adult-structured play – games and sports introduced to children by adults or supervised and/or elicited by adults. Anthropologists are well positioned to examine child-structured play because of our focus on participant observation and our desire to understand events from our informant's point of view. Goldman makes good (even inventive) use of observational approaches in difficult field conditions and this allows him to compare and contrast 'naturally-occurring' play with 'fabricated' play (i.e. play produced for adults or in the context of adults). In particular his contrast between ways children think they pretend with how they actually do pretend has important implications for understanding the competencies that children display in play. This approach underlines the importance of examining play, as Vygotsy suggested some time ago, as an activity in which the child 'jumps above the level of his normal behaviour' (1967: 15), but it also strongly suggests that researchers need to pay more attention to the influence of context (especially setting type as well as participants and audience) on children's pretend productions.

Goldman locates his approach to play within a sociolinguistic/language socialization tradition by arguing for the importance of examining 'how fantasy is spoken' and how it is 'accomplished' as a conversational activity (p. 100). Following in the narrative tradition of researchers such as Jerome Bruner, he is also concerned with examining how behaviour is 'storied' and how 'narrative organizes the structure of experience' (Bruner 1991:21). In this regard, he is particularly interested in relating play to children's understanding of other imaginative genres, most importantly, stories and myths. This is one of the major achievements of his study because instead of just asserting that relationships between these genres exist, Goldman illustrates how, in specific instances, children understand, construct and transform these relationships in their play. This is most apparent in his discussion in Chapter 2 of 'double-play' when children pattern or overlay their fantasy talk with a storytelling genre (*bi te*) that is ordinarily used in the recounting of myths, folktales and legends. Here he clearly demonstrates links between make-believe play and myth as he shows how Huli children 'raid' and 'reinvent' cultural repositories of fantasy in respect to their themes, forms, motifs and performance (p. 143). This relates to one of Goldman's central arguments – the process whereby play serves as a 'passageway' between mimesis and mythos.

There are important by-products to Goldman's study as well. Students of play will appreciate his careful review and critique of past and present research on play and specifically his attempt to locate this topic in relation to a series of intellectual projects in philosophy and the long-term effects of these discussions on studies of play. I was also impressed with his inventive use of radio microphones in the recording of naturally occurring play events. As he notes, child-structured play is an exceedingly difficult and fleeting behaviour to 'capture' and perhaps his solution to some of the technical problems encountered in trying to record this activity will stimulate more researchers to collect this type of data. Finally, Goldman does the field of play, as well as child development studies in general, a great service by juxtaposing his research on Huli children's fantasy productions with the expanded corpus of research on this topic that exists for Western children. However, in making these comparisons, Goldman offers an important note of caution to researchers who want to make quick and often simplistic cross-cultural contrasts and generalizations. In his view it is still very premature to engage in superficial comparisons because of the paucity of research in non-Western societies. In this regard I should also mention that Goldman's study is one of the first projects to examine how children 'play society' in post-colonial contexts. There is much more to be done in this area.

Child's Play clearly illustrates the opportunities that a detailed and grounded study of children's make-believe play offers researchers for questioning as well as re-theorizing traditional approaches to the study of play, children, language and culture. At a time when anthropologists seem eager to examine the role of imagination in culture, as well as their own role in the 'imagination' of cultures, it is time to turn our attention to children who have much to teach us about this topic. If we do this, and Goldman's book is a good model to follow, then I believe that our ethnographies as well as our theoretical constructs will be enriched, to play with a refrain from the Huli poem cited in the epigraph, in ways 'like you can't imagine'.

Helen B. Schwartzman
Evanston, Illinois

Bibliography

Bruner, J. (1991), *Critical Inquiry*, vol. 18, pp. 1–21.

Goodwin, M. H. (1990), *He-Said-She-Said: Talk as Social Organization among Black Children*, Bloomington, Indiana: Indiana University Press.

Lancy, D. (1996), *Playing on the Mother-Ground: Cultural Routines for Children's Development*, New York: Guilford Press.

Lavie, S., Narayan, K. and Rosaldo, R. (eds) (1993), *Creativity/Anthropology*, Ithaca, NY: Cornell University Press.

Preface

Igiri emene bibi agoba kiruba mbola toladago agali ibinime ogonidagua au lole

Real men don't speak like children, or play the child games 'Which hand is it in?' or 'Mud balls'

In much the same way as the above Huli aphorism articulates a cultural idea that 'real Huli men' should not talk or play like children, so in anthropology a view has long prevailed that 'real anthropologists' do not study child play (Norbeck 1974; Schwartzman 1976, 1978; New 1994). Children's voices have thus by and large received only perfunctory consideration in ethnographies and the profile of child play as a topic within mainstream anthropology has been rightly characterised as 'minuscule' (Chick and Donlon 1992:236). Indeed, anthropological monographs about child play, let alone the specific genre of make-believe play considered herein, remain extremely thin on the ground.

Play analysts have suggested that such neglect is an outcome of the way academia itself, a quintessentially adult pursuit, perpetuates and embraces a socio-historical legacy which devalues infant interaction. Thus the most conspicuous facet of children's behaviour – their indulgence in 'play' – has often been typified as irrational, trivial, non-productive and decidedly something other than work. At first glance these Western attributions appear to resonate well with the implied dichotomy between serious and frivolous actions embedded in the above Huli adage.

But even in this more enlightened era where play is appreciated as the 'work' of childhood, the persistent reticence of anthropologists to engage the topic of child pretence remains somewhat of an enigma. I say this in the light of remarks made in the Introduction that models of child make-believe have long serviced theoreticians across the disciplines of philosophy, phenomenology, psychology and literary theory. These interests reflect a long-held view that in the imaginative play routines of children we encounter issues of realism and verisimilitude, of referentiality and illusion, and abstractly of the priority of the word in the accomplishment and commerce of fictional representations. Such concerns with humans as actors in, and authors of, their own fictions are profoundly anthropological in nature. Precisely because then this core boundary of the 'real and irreal' is, and has always been, central to the ontologies and epistemologies of all these disciplines, the case for privileging spontaneous pretend play as a focus for attention appears both compelling and timely.

Pretence is implicated in the development of understanding about others and others' minds, in the acquisition of language and the assimilation of metaphor, and in how children come to construct, experience and implement their models of the world. It thereby assumes a quite critical place at the interface between anthropology and psychology. Indeed, pretence emerges from this study very much as one modality of human existence, of what it means to be a social actor who practises culture. In this respect no apologies are made for borrowing the Heraclitean notion of a world enveloped by the ludic metaphor of a game. It seems from such observations that we can therefore no longer justify conducting our discourses about the related topics of symbolism, identity and mythology as somehow independent of cross-disciplinary research on, or indeed without making reference to, contexts such as fantasy play in which these phenomena universally prevail. The make-believe dramas considered within have a cultural iconicity because they instantiate shared symbolic frameworks and references, and they provide yet one more exemplar of how humans reciprocally adapt and exchange their world views through talk.

This work then is in part driven by a perception that in anthropology our understanding of non-Western pretend play is still very much in its infancy. And yet the topic of 'as if' play is, I believe, an area of potential and consequential effect for anthropology. Such ludic phenomena provide a unique window onto current interests about human imagination, about images of modernity, about how roles are imbued with distinct 'voicings', and about how these in turn get translated and transformed into mythic texts. Amongst the myriad ways in which anthropology has sought to locate itself in respect to understandings about the 'imagination', pretend play offers a unique and ethnographically grounded tangent along which to pursue such quests. If the capacity to imagine new possibilities, to indulge in subjunctive thought, is characteristic of cognitive development it is also (for all the above reasons) surely determinative of disciplinary progress.

Succinctly stated, the topic of make-believe play instantiates a *rapprochement* between a more ethnographically enlightened psychology and a more cognitively aware anthropology. In this vein I have quite deliberately set the analysis of Huli materials against the burgeoning backdrop of findings about socio-dramatic play amongst Western children. Whilst remaining sensitive then to the need to account for cross-cultural continuity and discontinuity, this book seeks to extend the scope of relevance normally displayed by cognitive psychologists. It therefore looks both to entrenched cultural practices that incorporate pretence between children, and between children and adults, as well as presenting an analysis of the how and why of 'myth' telling in Huli child play. This latter focus and its theoretic implications are foregrounded in the title of the book and can be briefly elucidated in terms of the following key question. If, as is accepted within, Huli children are making narrative sense of the world around them through their fictional representations and play, and indeed if in such collaborations they appear to approximate the mythic endeavours of Huli adults, then what conventional models of pretence scaffold such activity or are invoked by the children themselves?

What is offered by way of answer to this question constitutes the particular set of compromises represented by the chapters in this book. On the one hand these provide a case-sensitive look at the kinds of factors I felt impinged on consideration of this question within the context of Huli ethnography. On the other hand the chapters also highlight the central conclusion that in pretend play we witness behaviour which moves between *mimesis* and *mythos*. Play as pretence emerges very much as an imaginatively constructed and linguistically realised pathway between simulation and mythologisation. From this vantage point make-believe play is social poetry in the making. This work, however, is not offered as the complete story of this pathway, but, like the play texts children produce, is rather a heavily selective, editorialised, elliptical vignette of what such a mediation might look like.

Beyond the intellectual challenges posed by the topic of pretend play itself, the fieldwork for this project was a particularly pleasurable experience for two reasons. First, few adult onlookers fail to be impressed by the sheer levels of joyous engrossment and impressive achievement wrought by children engaged in fantasy play. The ease with which players enter into such collaborative ventures blissfully belies their complex communicative foundations; indeed, the more one analyses such episodes the more one ponders the question of how such play is possible at all. Second, the technical challenges posed by attempting to capture naturally occurring fantasy play episodes, often lasting less or no more than a few minutes, were daunting. Because of such difficulty the data one does manage to collect become especially rewarding.

In reflecting on how this interest in child play meshes with the previous *oeuvre* (Goldman 1983, 1988, 1993) concerning the intricacies of adult Huli disputing, it appeared to me that this was not just a sideways shift in topic. Among the many links it sustains to these works can be counted the fact that it is embossed with a signature approach that privileges the spoken word. It thus endorses a viewpoint that an understanding of collective make-believe has to be adduced from an examination of the language behaviour in which it typically inheres. As other researchers have perceptively noted, 'the saying is the playing' (Garvey and Berndt 1977; Schwartzman 1978). But there is more common ground between the books than acceptance of methodological precepts and simply being about 'Huli' culture and people. Pretence, like 'accident', is surely one of those little known and researched concepts whose tentacles of implication reach to all aspects of the anthropological enterprise. In this regard the book encapsulates a profound conviction that pretence is set to move from the periphery to the centre of disciplinary attention.

While working on this manuscript I have variously benefited from insights and comments on the play transcripts and other data made by my colleagues Dr Jeffrey Clark, Dr Jim McKay and Dr David Lee. Portions of the work were also presented at conferences held by the American Anthropological Association (AAA), the Association for the Study of Play (TASP), the International Conference on Language and Social Psychology, and various seminars held at the Australian National University and University of Queensland. A debt of gratitude is extended to the numerous participants who volunteered comments at these sessions but who remain formally unacknowledged. Special mention must be made of the unique contribution of Dr Michael Emmison, with whom I have co-published a number of articles on pretence, puppets and parlance, and who brought the formal rigour of conversation analysis to bear on the speech materials.

While in the field my understanding of Huli play was immeasurably enhanced by the people of Yaluba, all of the children whose voices appear in the book, and most particularly my longstanding friend and field assistant Yorobi Uga. Finally, I would like to record my thanks to Jill Pappos for her formatting skills on the tables and figures, to Carolyn Magerl once again for her incomparable illustrations, to Jim Smith of GEOID for his maps, to Kathryn Earle and the editorial team at Berg Publishers for their work on the manuscript, and to my parents for their continued support.

Transcription Conventions

( )	encloses interpolated comment or interpretation
(( ))	encloses description of action or voice features
( )	signifies a failure to retrieve utterance or transcriptionist's doubt
(1)	indicates a time-gap in seconds or parts thereof either within or between utterances
=	indicates a lack of interval between the end of one person's utterance and the commencement of the next turn
⟦ ⟧	indicates extent of voice features
{	signifies overlapping speech
> <	signals a faster delivery
< >	signals a slower delivery
::	indicates the degree of extension of a sound it follows
!	indicates an animated tone
↓ ↑	marks rising and falling shifts in intonation
emph	italic marks emphasis by speaker
CAP	capital letters mark increased volume of delivery
°	marks quieter delivery of surrounding talk
i-i	marks an arrested or cut-off utterance
→ ←	calls attention to a feature in the text
´	indicates low rising tone
ʹ	indicates high falling tone
. . .	indicates omitted speech

Abbreviations

ABIL	abilitative
BH	*Baya Horo* (ogre)
BT	baby-talk
DESID	desiderative
DEF	definitive
DL	dual
EMPH	emphatic
ERG	ergative
EFP	explicit fantasy proposals
EN	enactments
EV	evidential suffix
(F)	far
FUT	future
FN	fantasy negotiations
HORT	hortative
IGV	interrogative
(I)	immediate
IC	imaginary companion
IMP	imperative
IT	*Iba Tiri* (trickster)
l./ll.	line/lines
NEG	negative
OL	ordinary language
PE	performative evaluations
PEV	previous evidence suffix
PL	plural
PLYS	players
PR	prompts
PRES	simple present
PST	past
PTST	past stative
RP	remote past

SG	singular
STSTM	stative stem
SUB	subordinate clause
Ts.	transcript
UD	underscorings
yrs	years old
1:2	1 year and 2 months

Introduction

The first person he met was Rabbit.
'Hallo Rabbit,' said Pooh, 'is that you?'
'Let's pretend it isn't,' said Rabbit, 'and see what happens.'
'I've got a message for you.'
'I'll give it to him.'

A.A. Milne 1926

The Plea for Pretence

In the above epigraph Milne gives us a literary rendition of an everyday conversational practice of children. The players in this piece of fiction are projected as 'childlike'; they undertake changes of identity in a game of 'let's pretend'. Importantly, our ability to make sense of this passage is, like that of the players themselves, dependent on our shared knowledge about make-believe routines, about role playing, and also about the kinds of social information these representations incorporate. Moreover, and even though we may be quite unaware of the processes involved, our understanding further entails grasping not one but two quite separate transformations of identity. That is, both an oblique and silent transition of the animals (Pooh and Rabbit) to children, in addition to the more overtly signalled change initiated by Rabbit to some unidentified persona. Our experience of pretending is being tapped to help elucidate the meaning of this passage. Through this device of fantasy speech the author has similarly managed to project his internalised model, we might even say his ethnography, of child behaviour (cf. Frank 1981). Moreover, it is one partly centred upon conventional acts of pretending accomplished by quite conventional acts of talk. Simply put, the author portrays two child-animals developing a pretend scenario as a language-mediated interaction.

This book offers an anthropological account of precisely this kind of make-believe behaviour as a window onto the imaginal life of Huli (Papua New Guinea) children. But what is 'pretence'? What is thereby implied in an overture to 'let's pretend'? And what types of 'phenomenal world seem

1

drawn or implicated by proffered explanations or revocations that 'not really, I was only pretending'?

At the very least pretence involves a mental act of representation, the creation of an artefact that stands for or portrays some aspect or knowledge of the world. In pretence an actor conjures up an alternative, counterfactual state that is temporarily overlaid onto a conventionally understood 'reality' conceived as veridical. When two or more children cooperate on the basis of their culturally rooted and shared experiences to consciously transform an object, situation or action into a flexible signifier of some other pheno- menon – such as when a stick becomes the here and now of a medieval horse – they thereby engage in social pretend play. Pretence is therefore symbolic, referential and communicative behaviour. Whether manifested as a mentation, or more usually as some physical act, pretence invariably involves *acting as if* one thing was another. It therefore invariably involves the use of imagination (cf. Woolley 1995).

Now for pretence to occur one must grasp things on two levels and intentionally recognise the dual identity of some phenomenon. Most often this is signified by a renaming of an entity such that, as Austin so aptly expressed it, 'contemporary behaviour misleads as to contemporary fact' (1961:217). Pretence as a modality of play is here quintessentially an activity then which transforms. By such means children arrogate to themselves the power to recontextualise their experiences within a dramatic crucible free of the temporal-spatial and motivational constraints that normally attend such behaviours in non-pretend contexts. But how are these collaborative and consensual fantasies achieved?

Collective make-believe reposes, as was noted above, on a common set of understandings about, and a common system of reference to, a conven- tional world. The coordination of such as-if behaviour is thus only possible where there is a negotiated and nurtured distribution of what is commonly referred to as intersubjective knowledge (Göncü 1993). Players thus bring to the 'improvisational encounters' (Sawyer 1995:146) of pretend play at least two systemic forms of knowledge: (1) their typifications of cultural identities and roles, social events, ways of speaking and ways of acting; and (2) what they have internalised about pretend playing itself. To invoke both these resources of socio-cultural theme and cognitive model of pretence-making, children engender fictions or representations. They dissemble by recreating reality as an event. Through careful orchestration of gesture, posture, language, and often action on and with objects, their common understandings are partly reproduced, partly reinvented, and partly mandated. These 'events' come to relate to a non-pretend reality as an 'other' because of a predilection in our everyday acts of reference to talk about these players as being *in a world of their own.*

These fictions have then to be choreographed and stage-managed in a manner that compels children to 'become coplaywrites, codirectors, coactors and vicarious actors, without getting confused about which of these roles they or a playmate are momentarily adopting' (Bretherton 1989:384). Essentially the players conjoin word-pictures with action-pictures to produce a model of the world in the form of a narrative. To service such ends there appears to be a culturally invariable set of tasks which must be performed. That is, beyond the solicitation of other players to enjoin fantasy play, a rudimentary script or story theme has to be agreed upon, a possible range of transformations of props instituted, and the appropriation and assignation of roles carried out. So not only are these parodic constructions socially mediated, they are also linguistically achieved. It is not simply that to play one must say, but that in a more profound sense 'the saying is the playing' (Garvey and Berndt 1977:7; Schwartzman 1978). Moreover, the kinds of language choices children make in these contexts reflect their appreciation that the maintenance of such fictional dramas depends on adopting mutually accomodative postures. Structuring a pretend scenario and maintaining a common orientation as an 'equilibrated exchange of thought' (Stambak and Sinclair 1993:xii) provide a set of constraints on both what and how children talk to each other when engaged in make-believe play.

In the Western cultural context, social pretence often takes the following prototypical form. One or more players may initiate a pretend episode either (1) implicitly, by performing some action which is itself a token of pretence and which may carry the functional load of exhorting others to join in; or (2) explicitly, by a verbal proposal of the type 'let's pretend to x or y'. Players may then collaborate to 'set' the scene by mutual adjustment of a narrated history – 'let's pretend this happened and then that happened' – or merely start behaving within an appropriate role character. The pretence develops by means of acts, some of which are an inherent part of the unfolding drama itself – *in-frame* – some of which are about how that drama should be enacted and developed – *out-of-frame*. The tension between agreement and disagreement, between deferring to or disagreeing with ongoing definitions, is maintained by a series of checking procedures based on verbal devices such as questions – 'shall I do x?' – and clarification requests – 'I'm mother aren't I?'. By such means children monitor the appropriateness and acceptability of their proposals and pretend enactments. The environment becomes an altered landscape attuned to the prevailing fantasy, with its own special ecology in which players have a degree of 'referential freedom' (Fein 1987) to create their unique symbolic canvases.

These episodes of make-believe may last only a few minutes, or may develop as a series of vignettes which are thematically or sequentially aligned – that is, the scene may move from, say, a police station to a prison and thence to a courtroom. Equally the play may incorporate, or oscillate between, phases in which the children switch from social to solo or parallel (simultaneous but independent action) pretence, or between social pretence and social play or games. Like any other type of interaction the flow may be punctuated or terminated by various forms of breakdown, miscommunication and dispute. Furthermore, while most collaborative pretence occurs spontaneously, it can be subject to a degree of scheduling by the children themselves or by some supervising institution, or indeed be elicited by participating or non-participating adults and researchers. As soon as we attempt then merely to describe what goes on it all sounds so complicated. And yet we know children appear to produce such play in both an effortless and a seamless fashion.

In effect we have talking actors who process information to enact conjointly a social drama in ways that are for the most part not formally taught, are sensitive to constraints attendant on maintaining pretence, and may very well be structurally similar across cultures. While this is in and of itself an interesting field of inquiry, what has uniquely captured the imagination of philosophers and psychologists is the simple fact that these verbal performers are both sentient and semiotic beings. Analysts have taken their cue from the observation not simply that play is the predominant activity of early childhood, but that 'make-believe play is the most important manifestation of "symbolic thought" in the child' (Piaget 1962:169). Pretenders practise signification on a number of levels, in ways analogous to and showing a parallel evolution with language. They are able to entertain subjunctive premises and reason inferentially from these. Critically, any episode of social pretence reflects a prior reciprocal agreement amongst the participants to 'attend to the transformation without being misled by it' (Rapp 1984:141). The dissembling or lie is accepted *as if* it were true. In other words, for pretence to occur the pretender must have consciousness of its own as-if attitudinal stance towards phenomena, which *per se* constitutes that activity as pretence. We are reminded then that in pretending we witness some of the first manifestations of the child adopting an attitude towards its own knowledge.

The lavish attention now accorded pretence in psychology reflects this acute appreciation of its semiotic pre-eminence in the cognitive development of the child. Pretending is thus viewed as a defining moment in childhood but equally a topic fraught with problems about how best to conceptualise the pretending child's cognitive status. If for a moment we accept that definitionally the child must be aware that it is producing representations if it is to be pretending – otherwise there is no more than mere illusion, delusion, error or mistake – what does this imply about knowledge of the mental attitude of a co-player? Does pretence mark the emergence of 'the child's ability to interpret mental state phenomena' (Fein 1989:349)? Is the child not simply an interpreter of other minds but one who understands pretence *qua* mental state? Does this not, in the current jargon, evidence *metaknowledge* or the ability to *metarepresent*? And what is the relationship between knowledge of fictional and epistemic mental states: does pretending come before believing, does understanding of dreams and imagination come before pretence, does knowing the difference between the real and pretend serve as a foundation for understanding the real–apparent distinction? (Flavell et al. 1986).

Such questions as these go to the nub of current debates in psychology about the nature, role and place of pretence in child development. They reflect attempts to uncover a model of mind that underlies and accounts for a range of early proficiencies seemingly implicated in pretending; for example, that children can imagine 'mental states that they do not have' (Harris 1991:285), or manifest an early understanding of other minds. For the most part such inquiries endorse the position that pretence represents a 'zone of proximal development' (Vygotsky 1966:16), a behavioural domain in which children display skills not otherwise evident in non-pretence contexts. It may be that children operate at a higher cognitive level when pretending than in other milieus such as to constitute what is referred to in psychology as a decalage. Actors indulge in social pretence as young as 2 years of age but appear not to be aware that the mind performs acts of representation until 4 years of age. The mechanics of such postulated abilities continue to preoccupy researchers and we need to acquaint ourselves even at this early juncture with a few of the principal lines of argument.

As previously noted, when we pretend, we overlay one identity onto another such that both are immediately and simultaneously cognisable. Now in order for pretence to service or scaffold cognitive abilities to these 'sophisticated' (Ryle 1949; Lillard 1993b) levels two axiomatic functions are presupposed:

1 the capacity to engender a set of (a) *primary* representations directly anchored in and responsive to perceptual, aural or tactile stimuli; and (b) *secondary* representations which are partly parasitic on these, but which may make a primary representation an object of reflection, or may entertain or project ideas about absent and/or non-existent entities (i.e. the counterfactual);

2 the capacity to mark and retain a distinction between these two representational types to avoid referential abuse or semantic confusion – that
   is, being unsure whether a stick is a stick or a horse. The player 'stamps
   the play with the seal *ipse feci* as a safeguard from error' (Groos 1901:388).
   That this is not always successfully achieved is evidenced by junctures
   in a play dialogue when confusion occurs and disambiguation of realities
   is required.

There is broad agreement amongst analysts that pretence is predicated on
these quite fundamental processes. For example, the insistence that make-
believe (i.e. secondary) representations are *'quarantined . . . decoupled . . .
bracketed . . .* or *uncoupled'* (Fein 1987, 1989; Leslie 1987; Perner 1991) from
primary representations of reality appears to echo the philosophical
metaphors of 'insulation' (Austin 1961:201), 'disclaimers' (Ryle 1949:238)
or maps 'unhooked' (Bateson 1955; Miller 1974:35; Bretherton 1989) from
territories. Now leaving aside the issue of what specific mechanisms have
been posited to process such bifurcated representations, the question
remains as to whether it is necessary for a pretending child to have a 'theory
of mind' – always to incorporate the dispositions and beliefs of others as
part of the pretending child's mind set. Succinctly put, does the child
operate in pretence with representations of others' representations?

One school of thought has it that in order to participate in social pretence
children must understand that a partner is similarly simulating, adopting
an 'as-if' propositional stance towards the events portrayed. In addition
he/she 'must have similar information about you' (Garvey and Berndt
1977:7; cf. Woolley 1995). In part this approach reposes on a number of
arguments including, for example:

1 that a precondition of any form of deception is 'awareness of another's
   awareness on the part of the deceiver' (Mitchell 1986:3). The point is
   made that social pretence is a collusive fabrication in which no one is
   excolluded and in which everyone is aware of each other's attitude
   towards information about the fictional and conventional worlds. In
   effect, every player must have knowledge of others' fictional mental
   states;
2 that other minds' knowledge must underlie the adoption of, say, such
   reciprocal roles as mother and daughter in pretend scenarios;
3 an influential argument which suggests that the very ability to pretend
   is inextricably linked to the ability to understand pretence in others
   (Leslie 1987, 1994).

This last hypothesis is a somewhat different point to the more conventionally expressed arguments that 'in illusion play the real I is supplanted by the apparent I' (Groos 1901:388), or that such *taking the role of the other* (Mead 1934) plays a causal role in the socio-cognitive, affective and linguistic development of the self. Indeed, what is being mooted is that knowledge of other minds develops through knowledge of one's own mind, that 'the emergence of solitary pretence is yoked to the emergence of the ability to understand pretence-in-others' (Leslie 1994:221).

The critique of this mentalistic view of pretending adopts a more behaviouristic, activity-based stance which declares that very young children are capable of sharing another person's pretence without necessarily taking a view about that player's mental state (cf. Harris 1991; Perner 1991; Lillard 1993a, 1993b). Pretending from this perspective may not then be as complex or as advanced an activity as it seems. In responding to the key issue of what is involved in participating in social pretence these theorists contend that:

1 children only reason as to what others think on the basis of complex analogical and hypothetical premises;
2 there is a claimed difference between acting *as if x* were *y*, and *using x* to represent *y* (Perner 1991) which indicates the equivocal nature of the term *pretend*. Perner has thus argued that the former is not a symbolic but a substitutional process, that resemblance between objects is not representational, and that therefore 'acting-as-if provides an adequate interpretation of early pretend play' (1991:53). On this model social pretence is enjoined on the basis of simulated, copied or even ritualised behaviour – i.e. knowing what do to in some situational role – rather than necessarily imagining others' mental representations of the world;
3 subjunctive thought is not *per se* metarepresentational or symbolic but a different modality of representation that is recombinative of experience, and stands on the same level as primary representations.

Such arguments are consequentially entwined with problems about false belief, about deaf and autistic children's acquisition of a 'theory of mind' (cf. Peterson and Siegal 1995), and developmental sequences in terms of what the child can achieve in belief systems as opposed to, or as a precondition of, pretence capacities.

The evidence for what is thereby implied in pretending concerning a theory of mind – of whether pretenders 'participate in the mental states of another individual' (Groos 1901:300) – seems inconclusive at present (Lillard 1993b; Woolley 1995). But the questions being asked by child psychologists are both important and indeed parallel to those debated in such research fields as cognitive ethology, socio-biology and primatology. When looking for the ontogeny of pretence, and the role of deception in human evolution and social intelligence, analysts have asked to what extent non-human primates are natural psychologists, to what extent apes read minds (Dennett 1987; Jolly 1988; LaFrenière 1988), and to what degree do they display Machiavellian intelligence (Whiten and Byrne 1988). It is contended that because deception (and by implication pretence) involves self-awareness or self-objectification – seeing oneself through others' eyes – this had selective advantages in hominid evolution (cf. Groos 1901:300). It was noticed that such pretence, often of a mutual nature, appears anchored to play and is perhaps indexical of a capacity among non-human primates to indulge in imaginative thought.

Some of these issues are broached again later in this chapter and elsewhere in the book, so I shall here restrict myself to offering just a few comments. First, variations in the contexts from which readings are taken by psychologists – as between laboratory-elicited or naturally occurring data – intrude into the behavioural manifestations of children when they monitor other children. While I return below to the comparative merits of experimental vs. ethnographic paradigms, we should note that in the former case 'researchers may be learning more about what children think the word *pretend* refers to than about children's understanding of what is involved in pretence' (Woolley 1995:181; cf. Lillard 1993a, 1993b). Moreover we need to be clear that psychologists acknowledge metarepresentation – i.e. having thoughts about other players' thinkings – to occur in late childhood (perhaps after 4 years of age) but merely disagree as to its appearance at the onset of pretence sometime between 18 and 24 months of age. In these regards there would appear to be some relationship here both to the child's knowledge of what lies are, since these share certain family resemblances with deceptive practices like pretence, and the age at which children are able to *pretend to pretend*. When a person tells lies we learn about how she/he wants us to construe the factual state of the world initially through what we believe about the liar's state of mind in respect to her/his beliefs about the world. In both pretending and lying the performances are to some degree mimetic and parasitic on non-deceptive communication. Equally, in the behaviour of pretending to pretend is displayed children's cognitive model of pretence itself, which may or may not be structurally homologous with how they actually do pretend.

Second, the issue of 'when is a substitution a symbol' – or when is 'as-if' play symbolic – appears to turn (*contra* Perner) on two discriminable but empirically fused aspects of the relationship between an agent player and a playful situation; that is, on both what an agent is intentionally or wilfully conscious of when, say, utilising a pen as a spoon, and the degree to which this act draws meaning from contextual cues which index 'the pretend-edness of the activity' (Giffen 1984:87) – e.g. as when a pen is a prop at a pretend tea party rather than just something with which to stir liquid. This seems a point of no small import, since objects which function in fictional narratives embed 'stand-for' relationships at many levels, which often transcend the story itself and which speak about broader aspects of the play ecology and the pretend economy. For example, Schwartzman (1978) has argued that imaginative play relationships are not discontinuous with relationships between the same co-players in non-imaginative contexts, and that in effect there is some carry-over between the tenor of relationships, actions and their meanings across both contexts. Equally, children in such play are capable of using props as tokens of more than one recognised and discrete genre of cultural performance so that often there is more than a simple one-to-one substitution to be considered.

The above has merely served to highlight, from the perspective of cognitive psychology only, just some of the questions and debates which have currently propelled pretence into the forefront of academic attention. In the light of such issues we might say that pretence is recognised as the loquacious courier of childhood cognition, a pathway between the struct-ures of semiotic competencies and the slipstreams of their culturally encoded and shaped manifestations.

But from the perspective of mainstream anthropology it might at first glance be difficult to see how we could locate ourselves in dialogues that appear so specifically focused on issues about the mind. After all, if pretence is hard-wired in our mental architecture and part of the 'primitive informational relations' (Leslie 1987) conscious agents possess (such that 'pretend' cannot itself be transcribed by, or reduced to, some other, more basic modality of thought), then what price culture? Despite some very notable exceptions (discussed below) anthropologists have in fact shown only tangential interest in pretenders and pretendership. This paucity of programmatic research reflects a tendency to subsume such concerns within broader treatments of deceit or play as an enculturative mechanism. Opportunities to mount challenges to the implicit assumption of psycho-logical research, namely that what holds for white, European–American, middle-class infants is true in general of the 'human infant' (LeVine 1980), have largely been passed up. Similarly it has been *de rigeur* to note the tardiness of response to calls for either cross-cultural data on pretence skills (Schwartzman 1978; LeVine 1980; Kessen 1983; Göncü and Kessel 1984; Watson 1986:75) or interdisciplinary dialogue on the kinds of questions posed above. There is still very little information of a systematic nature on cultural differences in make-believe play, so that it is far from clear how such behaviour might in significant ways be culturally encumbered. The received impression is of a discipline in which there prevails a view that pretence play, like play in general, is an epiphenomenal product of diminishing anthropological significance (Chick and Donlon 1992) which has fallen prey to 'contemporary anthropologists' general lack of interest in children' (Toren 1993:461).

This study is an attempt to address such shortfalls. It is constituted as an anthropologically grounded inquiry into 'make-believe for its own sake' (Giffin 1984:75), and make-believe as predominantly refracted through the language-mediated exchanges that typify the personative performances of Huli children. Predicated on the saliency of investigating naturally occurring behaviour, and imbued by the belief that the topic of 'as-if' play is an area of potential and consequential effect for anthropology, it responds to the challenges articulated above by way of prolepsis. That is, the insights to be reaped by a micro-ethnographic perspective on social pretence as a distinct project of understanding must be a matter of gradual disclosure.

Perhaps the first disclosure to be made is the recognition that when pretence makes itself felt playfully and precociously in childhood it invariably instantiates a process by which these agents come to mythologise their experience and knowledge of the world. What they produce is only partially parasitic on reality – what Rapp spoke of as a 'dissimilar similarity' (1984:143) – because in play children manufacture a slippage between 'what was', 'what is' and the 'what if'. This paradoxical fusion of reality and irreality invests these fictions, understood in the etymological sense of 'mythological entities' (Vaihinger 1924:82), with a cultural iconicity. But they are also for their players a reflexive exemplar of how humans reciprocally adapt and exchange their world views through talk.

At this juncture pretence appears implicated in the development of understanding about others and others' minds, in the acquisition of language (Werner and Kaplan 1963; Vygotsky 1966) and the assimilation of metaphor, and in how children come to construct, experience and implement their models of the world. As Groos remarked concerning these social monads, one cannot help but be 'impressed with the incalculable influence of imitation on the whole psychic life of the child . . . as affecting their deeply rooted sympathies and antipathies, habits and convictions, all of which are deeply influential on the developing character' (1901:305). For all of these reasons make-believe assumes a quite critical place at the interface of a host of academic inquiries into the fictionalising modality of such artistic representation. It is a topic which has the potential not only to penetrate the 'integuments' (Sutton-Smith 1984) of disciplinary barriers, but most particularly further to revitalise the *rapprochement* between a more ethnographically enlightened psychology and a more cognitively aware anthropology.

Having said this, a second disclosure is made that this book does not promote these ends by attempting to solve the conundrums attendant on 'theory of mind' approaches. Neither does it seek to provide cross-cultural testing of a Piagetian, Vygotskian or indeed any other paradigm of cognitive development. Rather, it pursues a goal of culturally situating pretence within a broader picture of how narrative 'forges links between the exceptional and the ordinary' (Bruner 1990:47). The quest to defy imaginative construction, as imparted by the refrain 'like you can't imagine' in the book's epigraph, manifests as a device which does not simply frame narrative content and delivery in both Huli myth and make-believe play, but makes a profound statement about the incessant project of world reconstruction and understanding in Huli. In the very act of defiance is encapsulated the paradox of realising unrealisable desires (cf. Vygotsky 1966:7). Amongst the myriad ways then in which anthropology seeks to explore human imagination, pretend play offers a unique and ethnographically grounded tangent along which to pursue such endeavours. As acknowledged in the Preface, this study adopts a distinct viewpoint on this quest which provides the rationale for the substantive matters of the chapters and the peculiar set of compromises they represent. This viewpoint is imparted by the subtitle to the book and can be succinctly formulated in the following terms.

In their pretence play Huli children move between *mimesis* – part reproduction and part re-creation, part fidelity and part fantasy – and *muthoi* – the oral and poetic products of these emulative processes. Play as pretence thus emerges as an imaginatively constructed and linguistically realised pathway between simulation and mythologisation. This loquacious conduit of children's transformational activity is social poetry in the making. Such an interpretative slant presents as a finding drawn from examination of the following levels of data: the way in which pretend play intercalates with substantive and performative dimensions of Huli mythology; the way in which pretend play is continuous in this latter respect with the wider economy of child games; and the way in which pretendership is itself scaffolded by the ludic motivations and structures inherent in the cultural stereotypes of the ogre and trickster. These multi-layered relationships locate as well as explicate how pretend play is conceived to occupy the interstitial space between mimesis and mythos. This is not (*contra* Sutton-

Smith 1984:58) to reduce play to only a passageway to something more important, but rather to recognise in what the achievement of make-believe play consists. The posture taken is avowedly neo-Aristotelian, for reasons explained below, and it is important I foreshadow how the following chapters progress this theoretic stance.

The remainder of this Introduction is devoted to providing an historical, cross-disciplinary overview of the myriad ways in which pretence, and the problematical nature of its epistemological and ontological foundations, have fared throughout Western thought. The overview is necessarily restricted in extended detail. It is particularly concerned to chart what common ground has too infrequently been acknowledged to subsist between the approaches of philosophy, literary theory, psychology and anthropology in respect of make-believe play. The synopsis is intended to provide any newcomer to the topic of child pretence with an understanding that is both broadly informed and appreciative too of the fact that this topic has always uniquely engaged human thought. Whether as somehow a reflection of, or challenge to, so-called reality, models of child make-believe have always serviced debates about the phenomenological nature of the world. These synoptic vignettes provide then a backcloth against which to consider the Huli semantics of pretence, the particular forms of embodiment it represents, and some of its peculiar linguistic properties in respect to pretenceful producers, processes and products.

Priority has been accorded in this book to the analysis of social pretence in what Schwartzman termed 'child-structured play' (1983:201) – self-generated play which is neither inspired, instigated, supervised by nor undertaken in the presence of adults. Essentially, it is what children do and say when they are by themselves rather than in adult-designed contexts. Equally it explores the importance of speech as the primary vehicle for socio-dramatic play. But this compromise need not blind us to the recognition that children's life-worlds (Corsaro and Streeck 1986) inevitably reflect the milieu of total communication in which they developmentally progress their socio-cognitive skills. The ontogeny of pretence is partially embedded within the gamut of child–child and adult–child interaction. Chapter 1 focuses on some examples from what is the ethno-topography of pretence. Specifically it examines:

1 *child games* – and what kind of make-believe components are traditionally found in these. I have in mind here the fantasy components of Western analogues such as the routines of 'This little piggy' (Singer 1973). This line of inquiry also illuminates the pretenceful pathway to mythos because many of these Huli games are played out against the backcloth

of folklore in both their historical aetiology and mimetic models. Pretence emerges here as part of the ludic infrastructure of Huli games;

2 *caregiver–child* speech – some of the early language interaction of Huli baby-talk. The argument is made that in such practices we encounter the key feature of social pretence and its metaphorical underpinnings – i.e. the occurrence of renamings, the nominal predication of one identity onto another. Caregivers thus systematically introduce the pretend mode during the infant's early years (*contra* El'konin 1966; Fein 1975, 1981; cf. Haight and Miller 1992) through their everyday speech acts and nursery rhymes. While thus illuminating the socio-genetic origins of pretence, such renamings are also clearly implicated in the wider language economy of specialised argots used in mundane and magical cultural contexts. Across a range of these important practices we note the centricity of body imagery that further demonstrates how Huli perceive play and pretence as interdefinable modes of action.

Chapters 2 and 3 present an in-depth analysis of collaborative fantasy play in which the central perspective of social poets as myth makers is revealed in a somewhat different light to that in the previous chapter. When engaged in such verbal make-believe Huli children frequently pattern or overlay their talk with a storytelling genre (*bi te*) ordinarily employed in the recounting of myths, folktales and legends. Because children are invoking such genre conventions outside of their normal context they indulge in what I refer to as 'double play'. They thereby create make-believe interaction and then play again with their artefact by collaboratively constituting it as a simultaneous 'mythological narrative'. Most certainly while this is a form of heteroglossia (Bakhtin 1981; Sutton-Smith and Magee 1989) – the use of multiple voicings to index social roles – there is no direct Western analogue which precisely captures what is going on here. Though the behaviour of Western school-age children who adopt a sportscaster register (Hoyle 1989) while playing football comes close, in Huli the mythological register is by contrast directly overlaid onto dialogue even as it progresses in the first person – e.g. 'I'm doing *x*, and now I'm doing *y*.'

Huli children thus create fantasy play at two levels: that is, both at the level of some engendered imaginative episode in which they are interacting (for example, *hunting, road/house-building, hospitals, anthropologist–field assistant* or *spirit attacks*), and at a further level where they create a mythological narrative of this first game by pretending they are myth narrators of the ongoing action. The artefact then is simultaneously constituted as an 'as-if' form of narrative discourse. Players become enmeshed in symbolic play both at the level of the underlying (or primary) fantasy frame and at the level of the overlaying genre mode. This instantiating of themselves as myth creators and redactors has profound semantic and structural repercussions on how meaning is constituted in these contexts. On one level the findings speak directly about what Huli children count as prestigious emulation, and how these play artefacts *qua muthoi* symbolically institute their visions of the world. On another level they begin to circumscribe ways in which children's experiences of adult play become active in transforming their own pretence. This constitutes a bi-directional flow of influences because Huli children do not just internalise but become part of the culture as mimetic resource (cf. Corsaro 1992).

Chapter 2 in particular thus focuses on analysing these fantasy dramas in terms of the following interrelated tasks:

1 the provision of a typological matrix of utterance moves that is sensitive to the specific ways in which Huli children constitute their fantasy games as 'double-plays';
2 a preliminary consideration of the proportional incidences of selected grammatical forms – namely, exhortations, imperatives, interrogatives and inclusive pronouns – within each matrix category to assess what consequences follow from switching to this genre mode play. My concern is thus to assess whether cross-culturally children appear to employ a standard repertoire of speech routines to construct play talk consensually. Is symbolic play saliently similar across cultures?
3 the undertaking of a comparison of naturally occurring and fabricated pretence data to expose what cognitive models of make-believe play children operate with – that is, how children constitute their understandings of their own fantasy activities. What do they think they know about their own pretending?

Chapter 3 continues the discussion by examining how collaborative pretence texts illuminate the interplay between language and identity in both the pre- and post-colonial eras. Children's understandings of cultural roles are refracted through the players' cognitive and behavioural representations such that in fantasy play actors confront each others' definitions of an 'other'. Moreover, these pretence personae may themselves become objects of attention. That is, players, out of concern for aesthetic integrity, authenticity and internal consistency in role enactment, may undertake to repair each other's mimetic representations. Of particular interest here then are the speech resources used by children to signal their playful transformations of roles and props. The analysis focuses on (1) how roles are assigned and appropriated in pretend play; (2) the extent to which these processes are overtly or non-overtly signalled with some pretend lexeme; and (3) the gender-inflected patterns which emerge in the contrast between playing in a rural as opposed to an urban locale. We witness in this chapter how actors institute through discourse their shared understandings of what roles are and how roles present. By means of their symbolic behaviour children 'play society' (Furth and Kane 1992) such that their representations of personae must surely be recognised as part of the cultural beings of 'mother', 'father', 'doctor', etc.

Chapters 4 and 5 seek to reach beyond the specific confines of pretend play to examine the overarching mythical frameworks that present a similar shifting between the real and irreal. That is, over and above any thematic indexing of folktale characters, Huli pretend play is inextricably modelled by ways in which in myth the literal is embedded in the non-literal, fact implicated in fiction. The argument is made that in the Huli figures of the trickster and ogre are realised stereotypical models of pretendership in the image of which children play – in the sense of seeing themselves as well as being seen by others. These protean and perhaps universal emblems of human imagination are an integral part of the Huli fantasy economy as well as having loomed large in the history of anthropological analyses of myth. What might thus strike the reader as a diversionary tangent is from the perspective of this author a central part of understanding the cultural milieu of pretend play. Indeed, psychological considerations of monsters have invariably alluded not simply to how they reflect innate destruction fantasies, but to how such figures display the child's comprehension of reality–fantasy distinctions (Harris et al. 1991). Moreover, the regional data on tricksters in Papua New Guinea begin to suggest a previously under-played and ignored reading on this most studied of personae: that we are very much confronting a culturally standardised 'imaginary companion' (Mead 1934; Prentice et al. 1978). In effect, the comparative literature on these mythic characters has yet to come to grips fully with the child as audience, or with the child as creator and player with such forms in ways that, it is argued, were central to the classical vision of, say, the Cyclops. Because the mythic tapestries are underpinned by concern with physical and human impossibility – 'like you can't imagine' – these pretenceful figures of fun instantiate models of and for pretence. No apologia need then be proffered for these chapters, because they relocate the relationship between play and cosmology (Turner 1974) as well as reinforce the point that pretend play is enmeshed with children's understanding of fiction, drama and art.

This work then is in part driven by a perception that in anthropology our understanding of non-Western pretend play is still very much in its infancy. This ludic phenomenon provides a unique window onto current interests about human imagination, about images of modernity, about how roles are imbued with distinct 'voicings', and about how these in turn get translated and transformed into mythic texts. But these foci have a history and it is one we need to address.

Historical Overview of Pretence Theories

Whilst then 'pretence' has of late been accorded the status of a cardinal concept – such that it now stands at the confluence of several merging streams of critical thought across psychology, philosophy and literary theory – its intellectual roots are of course much older. Indeed we first engage the topic of pretence as embedded within the profoundly consequential notions of *mimesis*, *imagination* and *play*. The landscape of Western theorising from Plato to postmodernism is indelibly stamped with debate about these three overarching concepts. Needless to say a fuller treatment of these terms would require a much larger work and one singly devoted to these topics. Because of this my concern in the following sections is necessarily restricted to providing a broad outline of the salient contours of these traditions of thought as constitutive of the historical archaeology of pretence itself. As a preface to the synopses I want to foreground two points, one of which has been axiomatic in philosophical inquiry, the other having received a some- what more muted recognition in the literature.

First, the language of analysis, like the language of pretence, appears invariably to ground debate on the phenomenological duality between 'real' and 'irreal' worlds. Whether invoking or questioning ordinary language expressions – such as *'in a world of her own'*, *'out of this world'* or *'beyond imagination'* – what we might call the ontological otherness of pretence representations has been a key issue (cf. Gadamer 1975:103; Ehrmann 1968; Fink 1968). Most usually allusions to this bifurcation of worlds are encapsulated in dichotomies where 'reality' is privileged as a default setting. That is, an actor or author via some imaginative medium temporarily 'escapes' from, but ultimately returns to, a given world. Most conspicuously analysts thus frame their arguments in terms of such binaries as primary– secondary representations (Leslie 1987; Perner 1991), ingenuous/real– make-believe/pretence behaviour (Ryle 1949; Austin 1961; Rapp 1984), factual–fictional works (Fish 1980; Currie 1990), or untransformed– transformed (Gadamer 1975:102) phenomena. The complex mosaic of themes treated in the following sections are woven onto this fabric of dual worlds and the seeming paradox whereby, in fantasy play, one produces something that appears to exist both inside and outside the phenomenal world we conventionally understand or refer to as reality.

Second, and a little more surprisingly, throughout the history of theorising about these perennial issues of truth and representation, art and society, paradigms of child make-believe often served as both a prototypical and ontogenetic picture of how humans do and ought to exist. In other words, ethnographies of fantasy play were explicitly embedded within philosophic polemic. For example, in Plato's *Laws* child play was projected as both an important context for role socialisation (1970:1. 643) – also echoed by Aristotle (1962:1. 7:17) – as well as something potentially subversive of social order because of its inherent capacity to innovate and transform rules. Child play, Plato informs us, is 'the biggest menace that can ever afflict a state' (1970:1. 798) and anything but 'just a game'. Even the dramatic impersonations of child make-believe, which Aristotle later claimed to be the origin of poetry (1980:Book 4), carry the potential to infect with false ideas and habits 'of physical poise, intonation and thought' (1979:1. 395d). The 'madness' (ibid.) which results from imitating animals was considered non-didactic. The nexus of links established between play, morality and art was furthered in the Kantian doctrine of the sublime whereby play, such as that displayed by children, exemplified an autotelic rationale and self-realising finality – it embodied 'purposiveness without purpose' (*Zweckmässigkeit ohne zweck*). What is continued here is the movement from a model of how children play to the reification of play as a cosmic principle. This harked back to the prevailing notion in antiquity of a world governed by divine and often irrational beings much in the manner of children at play.

But even beyond questions about what metaphysical principles of being play instantiated – as for example Gadamer's claim that in 'children's delight in dressing up' (1975:102) is embraced the 'essence' (ibid.) of the phenomena represented – were the 'playing bears' conundrums of Ryle (1949) and Austin (1961; cf. Emmison and Goldman 1996, 1997). In their own linguistic games these writers argued that pretence illuminated the nature and language of imagination, action and intentionality. Child make-believe thus came to be seen as a process of symbolic reproduction that critically unravelled the problems associated with 'similarity' (Benjamin 1979), 'fiction' (Searle 1975; Currie 1990) and artistic process (Rapp 1984; Walton 1990) in culture. This unique capacity of pretence to unlock the workings of the human mind further explains its central place within some of the major psychological work of Piaget (1962), Freud (1959), Mead (1934) and Vygotsky (1966). Make-believe assumed the role of a fundamental explanatory concept in terms of which not just play but art, literature, existence and truth were grounded.

Philosophy and Phenomenology

Most certainly within philosophy one locates pretence as secreted within three major and interrelated projects of understanding:

1 *The role of imagination in human existence.* Analysts here have variously endeavoured to exalt or decry the imagination as a representational medium through which we experience, construct and make sense of the world. From Hume to Kant the idea that imagination was a precondition of consciousness, that in fact there would be no world to understand were it not for some prior imaginative construction, had been espoused. Pretence as one modality of imagining thus posed issues of the relationship of perception to image making and so ultimately of how knowledge, reason and truth are acquired. If imagination were indeed the filter through which humans engaged with their reality then mimetic activities like pretence, poetry and dramatic performance could provide an intimate geography of the world.

2 *The ontological status of representations.* Recalling issues broached above, Nietzsche formulated this question as 'What role does this performing being play in general Being?' (quoted in Vaihinger 1924:360). Because in pretence an intentionally feigned appearance overlays an otherwise conventionally fixed reality, creating its own unrealities of space, time, identity and meaning, questions about the correspondence or coherence between so-called originals and copies are raised.

3 *The aesthetic constitution of imaginal products.* Precisely because the philosophies of consciousness addressed not just the actual but the possible, the resultant models became permeated with idealisations of the poetic mind. Pretending as a dramatic act expressed the fictionalising capacity of artistic representation. Following Aristotle, Coleridge for example sought to define imaginal processes as 'metoptric' – transposing through rearrangement – rather than merely 'catoptric' – a mirroring of external reality. Indeed, this difference between reproduction and re-creation, the unadorned and the adorned, fidelity and fantasy, underscored historical shifts in the way mimesis itself came to signal a productive rather than a mnemonic paradigm for imagination (cf. Kearney 1988). Taussig reflects this sentiment when he notes that 'pulling you this way and that, mimesis plays the trick of dancing between the very same and the very different' (1993:129). Pretence then became one window onto the complex set of relations between art and reality, and between art and play.

These foci reflect a long-held view that in the imaginative play routines of children we encounter issues of realism and verisimilitude, of referentiality and illusion, and abstractly of the priority of the word in the accomplishment and commerce of fictional representations. Such concerns with humans as actors and authors of their own fictions embraced a theory of art which articulated the relation between poet and fictional voice, dramatist and dramatic character, author and persona.

Much of the early engagement of philosophy with caricature and dissembling had its roots in the Platonic concept of *mimesis* – 'to liken oneself to another either in voice or in appearance is to make a mimesis of the person to whom one likens oneself' (Plato 1974:1. 393c5). This is mimesis as impersonative art where the actor projects a self into a persona and a situation. Sometimes such imitation was conceived as harmless pleasure, as mere play and of 'no serious value' (Plato 1970:1. 667; 1974:1. 602). At other times literature and play (*paidiá* – 'of the child') as forms of artistic make-believe were pejoratively stigmatised as distorted copies of 'original' truths (cf. Spariosu 1982; Kearney 1988). Imitative arts like poetry were thus agencies of falsehood and deception, 'an inferior child born of inferior parents' (Plato 1974:1. 603). Plato's polemic was a philosophical attack on make-believe as anti-rational, a view quite out of character with the Hellenic view of art as divine in origin. Artistic representations were themselves copies of imitations of transcendent truths (Ideas, Forms) such that the mimetic imagination (*eikasia/phantasia*) was a third-hand, deforming lens on the world.

Nuances of 'copy' as etymologically reflected in *imag*-based (*imago, imitari, imaginari*) terms gave linguistic sanction over the years to a Platonic metaphysics which prioritised the physical original over the replica. Indeed the very semantics of the terms 'pretence', 'fictional' or 'literal' was conceived as being anchored to an 'implicit opposition between a phenomenon true to some extra-institutional reality and a phenomenon that is not' (Fish 1980:243). What Plato had to say about good mimesis became obscured by the lasting impact of privileging that which is imitated over that which imitates (cf. Derrida 1981) in a manner that was to dominate thinking for the next two millennia. What kind of cross-cultural representation such a metaphysics had, or indeed to what extent humans as language users invariably juxtapose their lexemes of pretence and reality, were questions yet to be asked or addressed.

In Aristotle's revisionist hands mimesis became much more than veridical reproduction. It now incorporated the innovative, hypothetical reasoning of 'as-if' thinking. Poetry was a mimesis of action, of universals – 'the sort of thing that (in the circumstances) a certain kind of person will say or do either probably or necessarily . . . this kind of speech belongs to that kind of person' (Aristotle 1982:Book 9). Poetry was less history and more dramatic creation of what 'might possibly or probably happen' (ibid.). The relationship of the mimetician to reality is now more oblique than in Plato. Freed from its slavish dependence on faithful reproduction mimesis becomes a poetics of the possible, a way of accessing reality through irreality. In this vein Aristotle recalled ideas of play as a 'rational' force (Spariosu 1982) and of the achievement of understanding through hypothetical reasoning, and perhaps too Philostratus' seminal observation that imagination was 'a wiser and subtler artist by far than imitation' (1912:79). In this vein Aristotle thus foreshadowed the notion that the mind in pretence is interpretative rather than replicative, that play is transformative not just simulative of reality.

Indeed the *Poetics* prefigured so much later thinking about representation across disciplines that at times it can appear as if all subsequent thought on the matter is no more than a postscript to Aristotle. The idea of the universal represented in the particular – of stereotypical knowledge structures – was formative in both the Kantian notion of transcendental imagination which imposed orderliness on nature, and in the cognitivist paradigms of 'script theory' – a mental structure which organises experience and social discourse. Similarly, the analyses of children's pretend play as 'dramatised performance' (Burke 1969; Goffman 1974; Forbes and Yablick 1984; Furth and Kane 1992; Sutton-Smith 1994:11, 1982, 1989; Sawyer 1995), the psychoanalytic concepts of catharsis, as well as the idea of the autotelic appeal of play itself are all *au fond* Aristotelian in origin. Equally, in anthropology the so-called 'performative turn' (Conquergood 1989; Palmer and Jankowiak 1996) with its declared emphases on adults as *Homo performans*, their relationships to experience as situated practice and poetics, are fundamentally neo-classical interpretations. Aristotle stands to these later thinkers as architect to mason.

Mimesis as a transformational process displayed truths, not just appearances, and was considered to offer 'the experience of learning things' (Aristotle 1982: Book 4, 1936:l. 30.6) – an early formulation of the cognitive, educational or social learning function of make-believe that dominates modern thinking on the subject. The pleasure of mimesis is essentially the pleasure of cognitive recognition – 'in putting one's self in the place of another, in the play of imagination and in the enjoyment of aesthetic effect' (Groos 1901:300). In these respects Aristotle, like Plato, recognised that dramatic illusion reposed on deception (*apate*); imitations engendered fictional personae who perform fictional acts in fictional worlds. Mimesis as an imitation of 'doings' (*drâma*; Aristotle 1982:Books 3, 9), of *praxis*, produced *muthoi*. These were plots that represented actions *by* actions and *in* actions. Most pointedly, Aristotle leaves us in no doubt of two principal facts about mimesis: first, that producers of myths using the medium of language are poets (*poiêtai*); and second that such activity is rooted in the make-believe play of children (1982:Book 4). As for Plato, for Aristotle humans were a race of imitators (*ethnos mimētikon*), or in Mead's (1934) terms, role-taking animals.

From an Aristotelian perspective then child fantasy play emerges as a dramatic mimesis of human behaviour; a mimesis in the sense not of bland reproduction, but of something transformed. The poetic products of mimetic behaviour are myths (*muthoi*) in this classical sense of constituting *speech, story, report, fable, fiction* or anything *said* or *told*. Aristotle thus bestowed a new critical edge on the notion of myth as phenomena 'shaped afresh', not the original material but the specific result of an act of mimesis. The sovereignty of performance was thereby proclaimed. More importantly, the idea was introduced that an original achieves its significance only through copies; they have their being only in becoming. On this note of ontological communion between original and copy Gadamer (1975) built his aesthetics of art as play, and Ricoeur voiced the truth that symbolic systems make and remake the world (1978:123). For these reasons the fictionalising modality of child pretence is both culturally and socially iconic. Such performances are never intended as veridical representations, real-world documentaries. Rather they present as distorted simulacrums, not copies but editorialised caricatures incorporating embellishment and exaggeration – 'dissimilar similarity' (Rapp 1984:143).

For any analysis of make-believe play the *Poetics* (Aristotle 1982) has then a *prima facie* claim on our attention as the earliest and best exposition of the way in which play models stand to reality as map to territory, or myth to event (Miller 1974; cf. Rapp 1984). As Lowes was later to express it, the imagination does not operate in a cultural vacuum: 'its stuff is always fact of some order, somehow experienced; its product is that fact transmuted' (1927:427). And in so far as psychologists and linguists are now embracing arguments which posit links between 'as-if' play and competencies across a range of fictional domains, they too express the Aristotelian truth that children in play make narrative sense of the world around them (cf. Forbes and Yablick 1984; Bruner 1990; Furth 1996).

The continuing history of imagination as it subsumed mimesis and play is one marked by vacillations between its incarnations as a cognitive faculty and as an artistic capacity (cf. Strawson 1970). In the former respect, and in the hands of Locke, Hume, Hartley, Bentham, Berkeley and others, the conundrums of how ideas, images and impressions relate to perception,

memory, consciousness and knowledge were spawned. These were questions about what kind of phenomena imagination invoked: a reactivation
of sensum, the image as a feint copy or trace? Hume above all was fully
appreciative of the imaginative grounding of reality as well as its
transpositional capability to confound nature in 'winged horses, fiery
dragons and monstrous giants' (1951:19). Indeed there were few moments
in imagination's history when discussion did not touch on perspectives
about the place of such myths in society.

But it was Kant and Coleridge who imbued the imagination with a new
agency as the inner draughtsman of the mind (cf. Kearney 1988). This was
an active, productive *forma efformans* interposed between percipient and
perceived, between the raw data of sensation and understanding. In a
defining moment in philosophical analysis this new idealism grounded 'the
objectivity of the object in the subjectivity of the subject' (Kearney 1988:167).
The imagination partook of a reality it sought to render intelligible. Imbued
with such agency, this 'shaping spirit of imagination' (Coleridge cited in
Richards 1960:151) left the passivity of British empiricism with its *tabula
rasa* mentalism to embrace the Copernican revolution of Kant, Fichte and
Schelling. The imagination was now empowered, its schemata acting to
synthesise manifolds and create coherent unities, and was a fully fledged
symbol-making faculty. Make-believe became the 'fancy' handmaiden to
the new intellectualism of imagination.

Both Kant and later Nietzsche thus continued the critique began by
Hume of a logocentric viewpoint – the notion of a single, founding, reference
culture or phenomenal domain. As we have seen, culture was now both
imaginative construction and permanent illusion (*schein*). Departing from
both the model of mimesis as founded on real-world referentiality, and the
idea that the texts of make-believe arise *ex vacuo*, representations were now
fundamentally intertextual in nature. A new trajectory was thus initiated
whereby eventually the copy – the mythos engendered through mimesis –
would be ontologically privileged over the original as all that is knowable.
So for Nietzsche ultimately all art and philosophy is founded on fantasy,
fiction and falsehood. There is an impossibility of knowledge without
falsification. The indispensability of fictions is proclaimed as the only basis
on which knowledge was possible. The will to illusion, to deception, is
deeper than the will to truth. And so the foundation of many modern
philosophies of play was fashioned. These were permeated by the idea that
the world in and as illusion is ultimately the kingdom of play – a *paradis
artificiel*. Play thus became freed from the shackles of reason and restored
to its trickster-like status, liberated even from dialogue about the relationship between mimesis and art.

Now while it would certainly be false to convey the impression that child play and pretence always clearly emerge as central foci in these projects of understanding – of the cognitive structure of imagination, of the existential status of imaginal products, and of the mythopoeic qualities of such representations – these inquiries nevertheless provided a nucleus of issues and terms which continue to shape modern approaches to make-believe. More directly, discourses on fiction became inextricably entwined with concepts of play.

Particularly relevant to the history of inquiry into child make-believe was this strain of thought in German idealism, which restored 'play' to the status it enjoyed in pre-Socratic, Dionysian metaphysics as both a cosmic first principle and a modality of human existence. The world, and the human actor, become encapsulated in a ludic metaphor. For example, Schiller's (1875) theory of art as play – 'man plays only when he is in the full sense of the word a man, and he is only wholly a man when he is playing' (ibid.:80) – was later adopted by both Spencer and Vaihinger – 'I recognised in the play of as if, the driving force of aesthetic activity' (Vaihinger 1924:xlv). But these formulations themselves drew inspiration from the earlier Heraclitean concept of play as an irrational force, of life as the interplay of chance events. Play was here indexical of the whole arbitrariness of 'being': 'Lifetime is a child at play, moving pieces in a game. Kingship belongs to a child' (Heraclitus 1979:Fragment 94). The world reflects by analogy the back-and-forth movements of a game. The elemental transformations of the cosmos occur 'as if' they were determined by a child in play. Children are lords of the universe because they control transformations of reality through their play. Play thus comes to assume the mantle of a primary mover in the universe independent of the consciousness or intentionality of any player. Here is the birth of the recurrent notion of the sovereignty of players (Fink 1968:24; Rapp 1984:153) over the world. Thus Sartre was to come to talk of the 'imperious and infantile' (1950:141) qualities of imagination as a willed negation of distance and time (cf. Huizinga 1955). In Heidegger these strands of thought are developed in terms of the notion that play defines man and not the reverse, and was enshrined in his concept of world-play (*weltspiel*). The essence of Being is the game itself. Play was now fully disconnected from the subjectivist projects of Kant as based in the *cogito* of Descartes. The player becomes played with rather than an agent of the play; play 'holds' the player so that it is no longer incarcerated in the subjectivity of its players. Play is seen as self-renewing, self-purposed, a cosmic logos. Both Fink (1968) and Gadamer (1975) proclaimed the sovereignty of performance itelf – 'play also exists' (Gadamer 1975:92), it is 'at play' and 'in play'. Importantly, the play concept is unshackled from the skeins of perception and consciousness.

With a more directed attention to child make-believe the anti-Platonic polemic is in full bloom. Imitations are not merely second versions, but 'the recognition of the essence' (Gadamer 1975:103). Far from the Platonic view that artistic representations are 'inferior child[ren]', it seems that in many respects 'the being of representation is superior to the being of the material represented' (ibid.). In this proclamation of the re-created world as the true or prioritised reality, the pretence world is rescued from its historical fate as the 'other'. Representations are not metaphorically but metonymically related to Being. Fink rhetorically poses this most profound of questions as follows: 'is the exotic land of irreality the consecrated place for conjuring up and rendering present the essences of all things that exist?' (1968:28).

If pretence was now firmly encased by imagination as 'play' itself (Rapp 1984), a more decisive rupture with, and dismantling of, the metaphysical opposition of real: irreal was made by Derrida's (1981) deconstructionism. As noted above, Sartre had posited that imaginal products were acts of negation, an essential nothingness next to reality. But in Derrida's hands issues about the corporeality of images seemed to pale against the fact that dramatic parody discloses reality as no more than perpetual allusion, a mimesis of mimesis – 'we are faced with mimicry imitating nothing' (ibid.:206). The process of parody and pastiche is at once commencement and completion point. The metaphysical illusion of an original presence is revealed, the imagination now no more than a parody of itself. But what Kearney has referred to at this historical juncture as the 'wake of imagination' (1988) was equally a time when pretence began to emerge from behind the masks of these projects of understanding as an object of independent attention in both philosophy and psychology.

In the modern analytic philosophy of Ryle and Austin, pretence, and most particularly the everyday language and semantics of pretence, were to have two critical moments of attention:

1 In Ryle's (1949) hands pretence continued to become subsumed within philosophic reactions to the Cartesian doctrine of mental copies, 'pictures in the mind', interiorised seeing. Ryle thus approached pretence by critiquing the notion that imaginary phenomena inhabit some sort of 'other-worldly' reality. Imagining was now more firmly anchored in make-believe, pretence, or 'as-if' thetic attitudes (Ryle 1949; Casey 1976). Rejecting a 'copy theory' of mind, imagining became a type of oblique narrative about the ingenuous or 'everyday' reality' (Berger and Luckman

1966:39). A child pretending to be a bear is narrating a story about real bears; pretence is thereby a commentary on non-pretence.

This is a view of make-believe naturally bereft of a cognitivist's plea for inner representations, 'interiorised play' (Piaget 1962). Such things were for Ryle pathological. The child's pretend performance and disposition are now the prototype case of 'imagining', which is behaviour not necessarily co-occurrent with, or underpinned by, any ghostly mental event. The pretender merely abstains, 'carefully and even artistically' (Ryle 1973:145), from really doing what is being copied. But even beyond problems about mentations in pretence, Ryle further left untouched the question of whether, when an observer pronounces a child to be make-believing he/she is a bear, this statement is made with or without reference to the child's state of mind.

2   Other analysts, however, drew insight from Austin's (1961) work on expressions of pretence and what is there implicated by way of doing/not-doing things. What puzzled Austin was the manner in which pretence is isolated or quarantined from 'really doing' some action. His seminal paper on the topic was a plea for pretence as part of the wider project of disentangling the synonymity of action descriptors like *rehearsing, imitating, mimicking, simulating, dissembling, impersonating, disguising*, etc. Because there are 'limitations' on pretence actions which should not be overstepped – a pretend bite should not feel like a real bite – we gain insight into relationships between doing, intending and seeming-to-do.

Speech-act theory thereby gradually introduced itself into puzzles about the ontology of fictional works. Fiction, as we learn in the next section, is not a property of some text but rather an attitudinal or propositional stance of *pretence* we take towards a set of discourses (Searle 1975; Ariel 1984). In pretence we suspend our conventional communicative intents of truth-telling, we 'simulate seriousness' (Marrelli 1994:254) as we dissemble some reality. These interests thus established pretence as both a primitive term of analysis and a productive mental operation grounding theories of literature, make-believe, play and being. For example, lying could now be legitimately conceptualised as a *'pretended* speech act of information' (Castelfranchi and Poggi 1994). In this sense pretending is a *mimetic* act, cloaking itself in the guise of a truthful informative act. Pretence and lying are subspecies of deceptive communication (cf. Bretherton 1984:37) in which some speaker/actor aims to make an addressee believe false knowledge. This achievement is, however, critically dependent on what a hearer thinks about a given speaker's mind. In lying then what a hearer believes about the world is gained en route through what is believed about a speaker's mind or attitude to the information about the world. But how does this analytical explanation separate lying from pretending? Must we have recourse to the intention to mislead? And is social pretence then not the shared understanding about other players' mental dispositions towards what they are producing for an audience?

The above overview is a highly condensed and partial look at the philosophic and phenomenological heritage of pretence theorising. It presents as a complex web of discourses about the paradigms of *play, imagination* and *mimesis*. Too unwieldy in themselves to offer either a cross-culturally sensitive or fine-grained understanding of pretence-making, they nevertheless set an agenda of questions and ideas which it has been difficult to escape from, difficult to ignore, and in many instances difficult to develop upon.

Literary Theory

That literary theorists succumbed to the influence of these philosophical debates is evident from their varied attempts to endorse positions which either dissolved the boundary between the real and the imaginary, or reconceptualised it as bridge rather than barrier. In many ways these analysts saw themselves as on a mission to rescue imagination from what Ricouer phrased as the 'shambles of the theory of imagination today' (1994:120). In this project they have espoused pretence as pivotal to the enterprise of understanding the role of fictions in life. 'One thing we could not have done without is the notion of make-believe' (Currie 1990:217). Indeed, both fictional and everyday discourse are themselves only possible on the basis of our conventionalised, mutual but ultimately arbitrary agreements. In other words, reference is understood as inscrutable because it is nothing but a 'language game' in Wittgenstein's terms. As Fish has so eloquently expressed it, 'shared pretence is what enables us to talk about anything at all' (1980:242). Imagination continues to bear the impress of anything that is pretendable, and human artefacts and processes of all kinds are reduced to the single capacity to indulge in shared pretence.

Those who subscribed to the idea of pretence as a bridge between worlds, such as Currie (1990), Walton (1990) and Searle (1975), thus went beyond the generality of pretence itself to fixate explicitly on child socio-dramatic play as *the* analogical model which articulates and enlightens about the nature of literature and art. Artistic representations, these analysts inform us, are like props in a game of child make-believe. Authors or artists extend overtures to others to enjoin a shared fantasy as projected by their representational props. Fictional spaces are created into which readers are invited by means of the inherent and implicit solicitations – '*let's say* x *is the case . . . let's pretend . . . let's treat it as if . . .*' – contained in the artistic product and communicative process. Play analysts frequently allude to these devices when treating the interrelationships between play 'texts' and play 'contexts' (Schwartzman 1978; Kelly-Byrne 1984; Sutton-Smith 1984; Wolf and Pusch 1985). In narrative theory the same functions are serviced by opening gambits such as '*Once upon a time*', which signal the overhearer to invoke an 'as-if' attitudinal posture (cf. LeRoy 1985:50). In these re-created worlds representation precedes perception as authorial voices covertly manipulate two worlds, 'one considered true, real and authentic, the other false, imaginary, and fake' (Marrelli 1994:254).

Fiction and non-fiction, as we observed above, become distinguishable on the basis of the stance adopted to given information. The author's pretended acts of reference carry a diminished responsibility in respect to what they assert about the conventional world. Writers, for example, pretend to make assertions so that puzzles about the ontological status of fictions are really puzzles about pretending. Such ideas encapsulate the belief that these forms of hypothetical thought are an entrenched part of how humans as culture makers classify and comprehend their phenomenological environments. In respect to the concept of pretence, literary theory betrays its indebtedness to the above philosophical debates as well the continuing power of the model of child fantasy play to serve as a critical tool of illumination. Less articulated is what this tells us about fantasy play *per se*, or indeed the human mind, both deep veins into the topic of pretence which have been almost exclusively mined by developmental psychology.

Psychology

In psychology, pretence play has dominated the more general history, literature and theory of play (cf. Rubin et al. 1983). While then a decade ago it was perhaps appropriate to pass comment that 'little is known about how children interact with each other during social imaginative play' (Göncü and Kessel 1984:6), the intervening years have witnessed a veritable explosion of interest in this topic. Most certainly for an unsuspecting anthropologist the sheer volume and breadth of such studies can appear daunting.

Collaborative pretence has been referred to by an array of terms not all of which are inconsequentially interchangeable. Most usually these terms incorporate some qualification of the lexeme *play*, such as 'dramatic/ imitative' (Groos 1901:300), 'sociodramatic' (Smilansky 1990), 'make-believe/pretend' (Rubin et al. 1983), 'symbolic/representational' (Piaget 1962; Feitelson 1977; Golomb and Cornelius 1977), 'fantasy/thematic' (Sutton-Smith 1972; Rubin 1980), 'non-literal/simulative' (Garvey 1974; Garvey and Berndt 1977), or more commonly 'as if/dramatic' (Sutton-Smith 1967; Stone 1971; Fein 1979). In general these studies have been oriented to how fantasy play is causally implicated in psycho-social development, or meets the stimulus-seeking needs of psycho-biological selves (Ellis 1973). Most prominently research has focused on the following kinds of issues: cognitive, affective and symbolic competencies (Werner and Kaplan 1963; Golomb 1977; Fein 1989); personality factors such as variability in individual levels of imaginativeness, playfulness, creativity or 'fantasy predisposition' (Klinger 1969; Singer 1973; Lieberman 1977; Singer and Singer 1977; Fein 1981; Görlitz and Wohlwill 1987); differences in styles of play as between object-focused and people-focused (Wolf and Gardner 1978); the evolution and acquisition of narrative and language capabilities (Rubin and Wolf 1979; Winner et al. 1979; McCune-Nicolich 1981; Garvey and Kramer 1989; Dixon and Shore 1993); psychotherapeutic and educational parameters of fantasy play (Fineman 1962); and sequential trajectories in play forms, such as Piaget's seminal cline from early sensorimotor (infancy 0–2) and socio-dramatic (pre-school 2–6) play to games with rules (childhood 6–8; Piaget 1962; Robinson and Jackson 1993). Socio-dramatic play has thus been treated as indexical of measured forms of maturity.

While then the scope of relevance has been anything but narrow this now burgeoning literature on social pretend play is characterised by a distinctive set of methodological practices and epistemological premises. These need to be highlighted for two reasons. First, fieldwork paradigms employed by anthropologists and psychologists can appear radically different in a way that can militate against the comparative utility of many of the findings. Second, such identifiable differences may further explain why attempts to fulfil the disparate expectations of a multi-disciplinary audience successfully are often fraught with problems. Succinctly stated, and in respect to fantasy play research, what can happen or be made to happen in a laboratory context is not always easily, or even desirably, reproducible in a non-Western, naturalistic play setting. With a high degree of brevity and generalisation I shall list three predominant trends in the fantasy play literature from psychology:

1 The geography of the play world is one predicated on the logical positivism of a directly knowable phenomenal world 'out there'. This

assumption remains in the literature almost impervious to critique, and presents as a direct realism that has dispensed with the need to engage in dialogue with, or even acknowledge the problematics of, phenomenological accounts. Juxtaposed with 'reality', the landscape of the play-world is metaphorically depicted in the demotic language of disconnection or displacement. Fantasy play is behaviour 'in the void' (Piaget 1962:32), and 'the opposite of play is not what is serious but what is real' (Freud 1959:144). Such play instantiates a movement, an 'increasing separation from the world of the immediate present . . . from the world of pragmatic action . . . to the world of imagined narrative action' (Rubin and Wolf 1979:27). Thus actors are overwhelmingly portrayed as 'escaping . . . departing . . . travelling [or] flying' (Winner and Gardner 1979) from, to or between the bifurcated realms of the real/ immediate/objective/mundane/literal/factual vs. pretend/fantasy/ symbolic/fictional (Mathews 1977; Morison and Gardner 1978; Rubin 1980; Field et al. 1982; Howes 1985; Sachs et al. 1985; Flavell et al. 1986; Doyle et al. 1992; Fein and Glaubman 1993; Garvey 1993a; Lillard 1993a; Walker-Andrews and Harris 1993;).

The pathology of play is transformed 'normal' interaction in which children create 'second realities' (Callois 1961:10; Simmel 1964:300; Schwartzman 1978:328; Bretherton 1984:37). Their texts are set against the context of the 'surrounding "real" world' (Wolf and Pusch 1985:67) that constitutes the default setting (Walker-Andrews and Harris 1993).

2   Along with such seemingly innocent phenomenology is a longstanding faith in the pre-cultural givens of cognitive development. The view prevails that while cross-cultural work may tinker with variabilities in contextual factors – for example, in the time allowed or space given to play, or in patterns of caregiver interaction – it appears impotent to subvert the generality of psychological laws of development fundamentally. As others have noted, the concept of 'child' in the discipline is an essentialist one; it is conditioned and determined by biological dictates, an homunculus – a miniature and plastic adult waiting for the imprint of culture (LeVine 1980; Kessen 1983; Wartofsky 1983), which is itself the invisible and uninvited guest at the analytical table.

3   Much of the existing knowledge of what Western children do and say in pretence is based on direct or indirect play proposals that researchers have made to children (LeVine 1980; Haight and Miller 1992:335; Lillard 1993b:366). Thus 'we do not know what children bring to social pretend play when left to their own devices . . . we need to observe them in their own naturally occurring activity' (Göncü 1993:195; cf. Klinger 1969:296; Göncü and Kessel 1984:6). It appears to me that this domain is one where

the debate about laboratory/experimental vs. ethnographic approaches has not outlived its usefulness (Laboratory of Comparative Human Cognition 1979). It is not simply that children in naturalistic settings may display competencies or understandings not otherwise recordable, but that, as we noted above in regard to 'theory of mind' research, interview formats frequently risk skewing the responses of actors to the selective saliencies of the experimenters. Furthermore, psychologists have here used the phrase 'naturally occurring' to denote adult-initiated, designed or facilitated play (Black 1992:217), and even talked of the 'naturalistic setting of a laboratory playroom' (Mathews 1977:212). Clearly there appears a vast chasm between the ways various social scientists view the constitution of naturalistic data.

How such problems impinge on research methodologies can be illustrated by the following observations. In order to provide a set of fine-grained, testable findings about age-related developmental clines, psychologists prefer to isolate particular age-groups of players when conducting their experiments. But in an indigenous, naturalistic environment such as Huli children's fantasy play, or indeed that of Zulu children (Furth 1996:58), groups are typically made up of players ranging anywhere from 2 to 11 years of age. Moreover, the play episodes may evidence oscillations across a number of distinct play types (see below), and/or incorporate solo, parallel or social play and/or teasing. What is therefore distinctively important for the anthropologist is almost detrimentally problematic for the psychologist.

Even where the experimental findings are bolstered by tests which measure for deviation in response, or which attempt to factor out subject bias, one nevertheless encounters a proliferation of coding schemas that often replicate categories using different names. For example, in the analyses of the speech acts used by fantasy players, what Black calls a 'self-statement' (1992:231) Giffin calls 'underscoring' (1984:82; cf. Chapter 2); what Field et al. (1982) describe as a distinct form of pretend play – 'announced fantasy play' (1982:504) – is elsewhere a particular type of enacted move variously referenced as 'formation statements' (Schwartzman 1978:237), 'overt proposals to pretend' (Giffin 1984:87), 'explicit mention of pretend transformations' (Garvey and Berndt 1977), 'invitations' (Göncü and Kessel 1984:9) or 'social bids' (Forys and McCune-Nicolich 1984:166). But these criticisms, I would be the first to concede, can appear churlish given that as yet anthropologists have contributed very little to the research profile on pretend play.

The hallmark of psychological investigations into socio-dramatic play is the attempt to get to grips with a very basic set of questions. What are the affective, linguistic and symbolic features of pretend play? What factors modulate the incidence, nature and role of such behaviour – for example, how and with whom does make-believe play first emerge or sustain itself? And what parsimonious model of mind (images, propositions) best accounts for pretence capacities and development?

In response to questions such as these a number of generalised findings have been made (see Fig. I.1 near here) which can be usefully summarised in terms of the following foci.

1 *Trajectories.* Pretend play appears to conform to an inverted U-shaped (Fein 1981, 1987) cline. It thus reveals itself somewhere around 12–14 months in the form of simulated behaviours – e.g. sleeping or eating, or the use of replica objects – performed out of their normal context – is at its height between 4 and 5 years and seems to decline thereafter. The Piagetian trajectory of superseding phases, from the repetitive behaviour of the sensorimotor stage to symbolic play to games with rules, is now better regarded as stages which overlap and exhibit parallel development.

2 *Props.* There is robust evidence that the introduction, kinds and substitutional patterns of props used in pretend play occur on a principled basis (Fein 1975, 1979; Mathews 1977; McCune-Nicolich 1977; Field et al. 1982). Moreover, such behaviour appears to proceed from reality play to object fantasy to person fantasy to announced fantasy play. What is being mooted here is that, as the child gets older, there is a correlative shift from play with material and prototypical objects in the child's immediate environment to an increasing reliance on and use of imaginary objects. The need for verisimilitude weakens as does the anchorage to proximal physical objects that demonstrate correspondence between prop and copied object in respect to tactile, shape or colour features. In effect, that developmental progress takes the form of an increasing ability to work with ideational schemas. A number of ancillary findings have been made appertaining to (a) the ability of children to discriminate the reality–fantasy status of objects which seems linked in part to the emotional valency of target objects (Morison and Gardner 1978; Harris et al. 1991); (b) the tendency of props in the first instance to function as passive recipients of a manipulator, only later being agentivised, which parallels the growth of abilities to *take the role of another* (Rubin et al. 1983); and (c) universal patterns such as that propounded by Erikson (1950) whereby object play progresses from the autocosmic (body) to microcosmic (play with other things) spheres.

3 *Play forms.* As foreshadowed above, a number of critical distinctions
   have been made which discriminate types of play forms. *Thematic fantasy
   play* describes the acting out of some specific fictional narrative – say,
   the story of Red Riding Hood – drawn from fairy tales, television, cinema
   or comics. *Replica play* refers to play in which children act as narrators
   who comment on the action of figures as well as take the perspective of
   these props. Equally, children may engage in pretend play on their own
   accord – *solitary* – with others – *social* – or simply alongside others, so
   that players are independently engaged in fantasy with mutual awareness but no mutual interaction – *parallel play* (see Figure I.1). Not only
   may a single play episode move between all of these forms but it may
   also evidence shifts between pretence and non-pretence (*social play*) play
   such as rule-based games. While the progression from solitary to social
   play thus occurs somewhere between 12 and 20 months it is less clear
   where the cut-off age is for solitary play, or indeed when children make
   a transition between social play and social pretence (Howes 1985).
4 *Roles.* Research (Garvey 1974; Garvey and Berndt 1977; Miller and
   Garvey 1984) indicates that the first roles undertaken in make-believe
   play are imitative and relational (i.e. kinship based) in nature, with a
   gradual progression to uptake of thematic fantasy characters. While this
   is certainly an important line of inquiry there has been little systematic
   work of a cross-cultural nature which might confirm or disconfirm such
   findings. Nevertheless, following the lead of Bateson (1955), it is argued
   fantasy play thus facilitates both learning of the concept of role (Sarbin
   1966) itself as well as role content in terms of linguistic modalities like
   speech style (Martlew et al. 1978; Rubin and Wolf 1979). Lately analysts
   have attempted to relate such trajectories to sex role reinforcement, status
   development, and friendship formation in peer groups (Black 1992;
   Doyle et al. 1992). One of the most interesting dimensions to role play
   research is what kinds of sequentiality are demonstrated by children in
   their linked fantasy episodes. Thus older children appear more capable
   of maintaining narrative threads across scripted adventures and
   evidence an increasing capacity to enact complex and combinatorial
   roles, such as acting as a mother, patient and doctor in the one scenario.
5 *Contexts.* What is the contributory influence of socio-cultural context
   on pretence behaviour? Does pretence, as Piaget (1962) claimed, develop
   regardless and is it the case that 'there is little evidence to support the
   claim that parents as a rule teach or model pretence for their children'
   (Fein 1981:1106, 1975; Fein and Fryer 1995:380)? Little by way of
   challenge has been forthcoming in respect of the former proposition,
   but much ink has been spilled rebutting the argument that caregivers

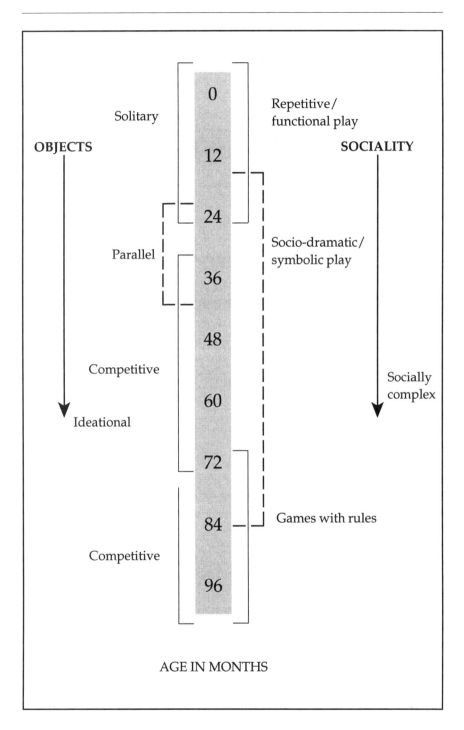

Figure I.1 Developmental trajectories in play

are not critical to the development of make-believe competencies. Mothers and other caretakers, along with peer familiarity, are seen as consequential contributors to children's fantasy play (Werner and Kaplan 1963; O'Connell and Bretherton 1984; Furth and Kane 1992; Haight and Miller 1992; Farver and Howes 1993; Bornstein and Tamis-LeMonda 1995), affecting duration, complexity, frequency, quantity and diversity of pretence interaction. This may either result from direct modelling, facilitation or elicitation, or derive from the routinely structured pretending inherent in games such as 'Peek-a-boo' or 'This little piggy' (Haight and Miller 1992; Harris and Kavanaugh 1993; Farver et al. 1995). Variability across cultures has been recorded in respect of the influence of cultural values and the particular types of relationship (e.g. sibling) sustained by caretakers (cf. Farver and Howes 1993; Farver et al. 1995) to child pretenders.

6 *Scripts.* Much of the intersubjectively shared knowledge that children bring to fantasy play is encapsulated in what are commonly referred to as internalised 'scripts' (Schank and Abelson 1977; Corsaro 1983; Mandler 1983; Bretherton 1984; Nelson and Seidman 1984; Fein 1987; Johnson 1990). These are organisational frameworks of conventional roles, speech, objects and causal patterns assimilated from everyday experience; that is, mental templates or schemata of generic features of the way things are and work. In pretend play these become operationalised to pattern partially the ongoing drama on the understanding that such 'scripts' are shared knowledge structures. Fein has expressed it best when she noted that, for example, a restaurant script contains an implicit injunction that 'this is a restaurant and everything we know about restaurants applies to actions we are about to perform' (1987:287). An event representation of a restaurant scene might typically be composed of such routine actions as entering, ordering food from a waiter, eating and departing. Pretend play transcripts, like those of many puppet shows (cf. Emmison and Goldman 1997), reveal players' orientation to such routinised sequences both in the manner in which actors may progress fantasy actions as narrated condensations of action – '*now I'm cooking, now I'm taking the food out, now I'm eating*' – and indeed in the out-of-frame negotiations when 'scripts' become objects of debate and dispute. Importantly, adherence to script theory does not *per se* entail the inference that there is a complete prediction of all action, that fictional events cannot be included, or that a thesaurus of make-believe behaviour can provide a complete compendium of children's knowledge about the world. While in psychology script theory as an explanatory tool continues to be refined, it is clear that it sustains links both with

ethnomethodological understandings of human interaction and indeed with Aristotelian ideas about plots and universals.

The more enlightened presentations of script theory thus instantiate a growing recognition that pretence behaviour, from whatever perspective we may approach it, has to be contextualised within the wider fictional economy of dreams, stories and artistic media to which children are exposed. Such neo-Aristotelian sentiments thus affirm the sense in which cultural, semiotic and poetic artefacts scaffold pretence competencies much as these very competencies themselves 'offer the child an initial entry into the world of fiction and drama' (Harris and Kavanaugh 1993:72; cf. Scarlett and Wolf 1979; Rubin and Wolf 1979; Lloyd and Goodwin 1995; Woolley 1995; Mead 1934).

The above discussion provides a synoptic overview of research findings on fantasy play which are clustered within at least three distinct approaches to the phenomena – that is, cognitive, psychoanalytic and communicational.

Most certainly *cognitivist* paradigms in the analysis of pretend play reflect intellectual debts to the seminal work of Piaget (1962) and Vygotsky (1966), whose interpretative stances are often contraposed. For Piaget play reflected the child's cognitive structures and the dynamic interplay of two broad categories of adaptive intelligence. Thus the relationship between thinking organism and environment is articulated in terms of equilibrium or disequilibrium between *assimilation* – by which the child subordinates and transforms reality to its own schemata and which furthermore predominates in play – and *accommodation* – by which the child bends its mental structures to meet reality. The pretending child practices signification as 'interiorised play' (ibid.:131), which ranges from transpositions of 'real life' to the creation of imaginary beings for which no model can be found' (ibid.). Symbolic play for Piaget indexed conceptual immaturity. This emphasis on the knowing subject and an attendant movement from solitary to social fantasy play was reversed in Vygotsky's (1966) work, where the sociogenetic origins of pretence became privileged. That is, Vygotsky started with the interpersonal and cultural origins of such behaviour (Duncan 1995). Pretence was now not only criterial of play itself, but grounded on a defining moment when a substitute object pivotally severed or dislocated the signifying word from the signified thing. Substitutions, renamings or 'word meanings' (Vygotsky 1966:13) draw the critical relationship between pretending and language acquisition so that, as we have had cause to note previously, such play is constituted as a 'zone of proximal development' (ibid.:16). This exposition was enmeshed with behavioural rationales about wish-fulfilment that were heavily indebted to Freud (see below).

The specific cognitive operations identified by pretence studies are frequently crystallised as follows (Fenson 1984; Gordon 1993): *decentration* – the progressive shift from subjective egocentric thought to mutually coordinated viewpoints, from self to other-referenced behaviour (Golomb and Cornelius 1977); *reversibility/conservation* – consciousness of the real and imaginal duality of self and others' identities (Golomb and Cornelius 1977) consequent on moving in and out of roles; *decontextualisation* – decreasing reliance on prototypical play objects used as props in pretend transformations; and *integration* – increasing capacity to combine and coordinate themes in ever more complex action sequences (McCune-Nicolich 1977).

On these theoretic foundations make-believe play has variously been claimed to offer a context of application for practice and consolidation of, be causally implicated in, or constitute a precursor or index of the following competencies: perspective taking (Mead 1934), hypothetical and causal reasoning (Johnson 1990; Singer 1973), combinatorial flexibility, divergent thinking and associative fluency (i.e. multiple uses of objects, cf. Dansky 1980), problem solving (Rubin et al. 1983; Christie 1982), and the ability to discriminate appearance from reality (Flavell et al. 1987; Taylor and Flavell 1984), in addition to a gamut of socio-affective skills.

Psychoanalytic approaches to fantasy play stress compensatory and cathartic functions as well as draw variously on notions of arousal and neurological stimuli theory (Freud 1959, 1961; Erikson 1950; Winnicott 1971; Berlyne 1969; Ellis 1973). Succinctly stated, what these studies posit is unconscious symbolism, so that play is conceived as indexical of sublimated desires, wish-fulfilment, conflicts and traumas. Play thus becomes a context for displaced aggression and a medium in which to master, manage and manipulate one's impotence and passivity in the face of real situations. As a diagnostic tool socio-dramatic play is of importance in clinical psychology as well as educational therapy.

A far more recent development has been the steady growth of studies which recognise pretend play as a distinct socio-linguistic achievement of interest not simply for the light it may shed on the acquisition of language and narrative skills, but because it presents as a unique configuration of *communicational* patterns between children (Fenson 1984; Garvey and Kramer 1989; Bretherton 1984; Garvey 1990, 1993a, 1993b; Göncü 1989, 1993; Lodge 1979; Ariel 1984; Auwärter 1986; Giffin 1984; Forbes et al. 1986; Kyratzis 1992; Goodwin 1988; Corsaro 1983, 1992; Furth and Kane 1992; Kane and Furth 1993; Forbes and Yablick 1984; Sachs 1987; Sachs et al. 1985; Verba 1993). Almost without exception these studies have operationalised the analytic notion of 'frames' (Bateson 1955; Goffman 1974), defined as participants' situational definitions of what is going on. When 'in-frame', communicated messages are themselves governed by other messages – metamessages – which inform participants how to interpret meaning. Within a pretend play frame then messages incorporate cues which reference the pretendedness of the activity, that 'this is only play' (Bateson 1955:41). This constitutes the subjectivity of play whereby 'the players know that play is only play' (Gadamer 1975:91; Spariosu 1982:13). As has been remarked on previously, actors also talk about the messages to be sent, which is characterised as 'out-of-frame' behaviour. The pretend frame represents a possible world, an alethic modality where truth is relative and contingent for that world. In this regard the 'in-frame:out-of-frame' division is not inconsequentially interchangeable with a 'real: unreal' opposition. Equally, the maintenance of such a fictional reality depends on cooperativeness and this is determinative of, as well as reflected in, the language of pretending, which is frequently typified as displaying a mitigated or accommodative style. In essence, such language-focused studies treat pretend play as an object of interest in its own right and are driven by the conviction that the way to progress understanding of such interaction is via the loquacity of pretence itself.

Anthropology

> The imagination . . . is an aspect of human experience that has generally been ignored or underrated in anthropology; perhaps because of a presumption that it was a fitter subject for introspective psychology or for a phenomenological philosophy.
>
> (Needham 1978:66)

Though still somewhat of a minority interest, the anthropology of play has a well-respected history and a contemporary profile maintained largely, though not exclusively, by the critical mass of scholars, annual meetings and publications of the Association for the Study of Play (TASP). In accordance with the theme of this book the following discussion is narrowly targeted on what anthropology has had to say about pretend play in particular, so that it is not my intention to provide any general treatment of play theory itself. This is both because the topic has been ably covered by others (cf. Schwartzman 1976, 1978; Berlyne 1969), and because it is far from clear that an understanding of fantasy play necessitates some prior global theorising about, or definition of, play itself.

Perhaps unsurprisingly, paradigms of play within the discipline have largely reflected the changing analytical frameworks found in the history of anthropology. Thus the earliest engagements with play were those of evolutionists and folklorists interested in the material culture of toys, string-figures, and patterns of diffusion across cultures. But like psychology, anthropology too was heavily influenced by the philosophical heritage linking culture, aesthetics and play (Huizinga 1955; Callois 1961) as variously encapsulated in what are referred to as the four classical play theories:

1 *Recapitulation.* Associated with Hall (1906) and Gulick (1898), this mooted that the play stages of children recapitulated the bio-cultural history of development of the species. Child play was a rehearsal of ancestral activities, an instinctual, atavistic legacy which reproduced the sequential epochs of the history of culture – an 'ontogenetic rehearsal of the phylogenetic hierarchy' (Rubin et al. 1983:697).

2 *Surplus energy.* In this play as a fundamentally goalless activity utilised energy not otherwise spent in subsistence (Spencer 1873). This hydraulic model assumed finite levels of energy, a compulsion to expend, and a presupposition about instincts and competitive activity.

3 *Recreation/relaxation.* Almost diametrically opposed to surplus-energy principles, this theory interpreted play as recuperation. In other words, play was engendered by a deficit not an abundance of energy (Lazarus 1883; Patrick 1916).

4 *Practice/pre-exercise.* Play is here conceived as an instinctual, adaptive mechanism that allows for the practice of adult activities. This theory has of course its roots in early Greek thinking and was subsequently embellished in the work of Groos (1901), who has been generously cited throughout this Introduction. Play as practice allowed for the assimil-ation of adult culture including games and sports.

These theories were grounded on mono-causal explanations, were pre-dicated on the functional maintenance of a biological rather than social organism, and were typified by a tendency to ignore the content of play as something secondary or epiphenomomenal in nature (Ellis 1973). At the same time, and most particularly in the case of the work of Groos, they contain a repertoire of observations that continue to spark controversy and debate.

Subsequent investigations of ludic behaviour were dominated by structural-functionalism and a naive form of socialisation theory. Play thus continued to be considered as mimetic and preparatory of adult life, an enculturative mechanism. The child was seen as having to be moulded into a competent adult, so that the end-product of socialisation was predetermined, with play servicing an envisioned destiny. The passive child was an empty vessel into which culture was poured (Benthall 1992). But even within a framework of anticipatory socialisation, occasional glimpses, as Schwartzman (1978) reminds us, of the relationship between pretence and imagination can be found in ethnographies. For example, Fortes talked of the Tale (Africa) child's mimesis as 'never simple and mechanical reproduction' (1970:55), while Raum similarly noted for the Chaga (Africa) that the children's 'performance is a free reconstruction of more or less imagined happenings . . . [in which] much of the subject matter of imitation is in fact relayed through the mechanisms of speech only' (1940:104).

The more enlightened models of socialisation empowered children as agents in their own enculturation, and in the construction of their own peer culture (Corsaro 1992; Sawyer 1995; Schieffelin 1990; Wartofsky 1983). In play children produced texts that were metasocial commentaries, stories 'they tell themselves about themselves' (Geertz 1972:26). But the influence of such theorising has not been profound in respect of what anthropology has delivered by way of ethnographic insight into the cross-cultural dynamics of pretend play. While generally anthropologists have remained aloof from the definitional quandaries – the 'linguistic waste-paper basket' (Millar 1968; Mook 1994) – of the 'play' concept, by contrast with play in general, fantasy play has an almost invisible history and research profile. Most certainly one notes that some analysts have perceived pretence as the canonical modality of play (Norbeck 1974:1; Schwartzman 1976:291, 1978; Rapp 1984:152; Dundes 1974), and that there is evidence of a belated recognition that we witness in pretend play primordial forms of metaphoric thought processes (Fernandez 1974; Stross 1975; Bamberg 1983). In make-believe play, these analysts argue, is to be found the ontogeny of symbolic competencies, of the ability to 'see as'; not simply primordial metaphors such as the 'manifestation of the child's deep interest in the animal world' (Groos 1901:302; cf. Fernandez 1974), but a realisation that 'our ability to act out a fiction rather than to recognise a fact lies at the base of human sociability' (Dundes 1974:135). Notwithstanding these noticings we still know very little about what role culture plays in child pretend play.

Because of this lack of information, the few anecdotal accounts there are of make-believe play within the cross-cultural literature have assumed an importance for play theorists that is, to be blunt, quite out of proportion with the levels of ethnographic detail or reliability offered. Anthropological interest here has been less in addressing issues such as 'what model of mind can best account for the development of pretend play' (Göncü 1989:341) than in perhaps assessing questions such as these:

1   What is the universal status of children's fantasy play, and what saliently
    similar patterns does such interaction evidence?
2   How is it implicated or enmeshed in patterns of socialisation?
3   Are subsistent cultural variations in pretence play systematically linked
    to, or determined by, identifiable cultural practices or institutions?

There are as yet no clear answers to these questions and much disagreement
exists about the validity of available findings. Reported observations of
imaginative role play include, but are not limited to, the Fang (Fernandez
1974; cf. Groos 1901:302–3), Zulu (Furth 1996), Kpelle (Lancy 1996) and
Talensi (Fortes 1970) of Africa, the Kaluli (Schieffelin 1990) and Wogeo
(Hogbin 1946) of New Guinea, the Tzeltal of Mexico (Stross 1975), the Chaga
of Tanzania (Raum 1940), the Alorese of Indonesia, the Taira of Okinawa
and the Tarong of the Philippines (cf. Christie 1982). However, far more
attention has been devoted to instances where make-believe play is
supposedly absent or where it appears quantitatively and qualitatively
impoverished by comparison with the norm for Western children. Thus
analysts who indicate the low or non-existent status of representational
play cross-culturally (e.g. Feitelson 1977; Golomb 1977; Fein 1979; Pan 1994;
Sutton-Smith 1972) – what Schwartzman called the 'deficit hypothesis'
(1984:49) – repeatedly invoke the ethnographic cases of the Nyansongo, a
Gusii community in Kenya (LeVine and LeVine 1963:173), Egyptian (Silwa)
village children (Ammar 1954), Manus children of New Guinea – 'their
play was the most matter of fact, rough and tumble, non-imaginative
activity imaginable' (Mead 1930:96) – 'disadvantaged' Middle Eastern and
North African immigrant children (Smilansky 1968), and positively dangerous generalisations that 'such is the way the New Guinean plays . . . children
are not required to play make-believe' (Ebbeck 1973:322). In effect the
argument was mooted that fantasy play may vary not simply across
cultures, but in response to whether pretenders were from low or high socio-
economic and/or migrant statuses. Apart then from what anthropologists
might make of fantasy play as a cultural universal, there were implications
for educators, who pointed to the need for play training to promote or
facilitate cognitive growth in these types of case.
    The impact of the above findings was thus quite dramatic. It suggested,
for example, that the developmental cline in cognitive and behavioural
phenomena portrayed by psychologists, which linked play to growth in
symbolic reasoning, might not be universal and that other forms of social
interaction might be invested with the functional load normally carried by
socio-dramatic play. Moreover, this would indicate a need to theorise along
the more familiar axis of what does and what does not apply in so-called

modern/traditionalist or Western/non-Western societies. In this vein, for example, Sutton-Smith (1972) suggested that such data pointed to a distinction between 'ascriptive' and 'achievement' game cultures which lay along an evolutionary continuum. In the former kinship-dominated social systems, play was imitative, focused on realistic props, hierarchically choreographed, and non-transformational in the sense of reinventing reality through counterfactual thinking. In a remark that can appear almost nonsensical in the light of previous discussion, Sutton-Smith suggested that 'imitative play is not imaginative' (ibid.:299). Children in these societies, he argued, have a conversational style that is coercive and directive – 'bring me this, take that away' (ibid.). By contrast, in the 'achievement' game cultures of Western societies players adopt multiple fictional roles, may introduce dialogue between characters in solitary play, and coordinate behaviour to produce their pretend worlds cooperatively.

These theoretical musings were not, however, well received in the subsequent literature (cf. Eifermann 1971; Fein 1981; Schwartzman 1976, 1984). This reflects in part a plethora of discrepant results achieved in follow-up studies, in part the possibility that situational and methodological factors impinged on the early findings – the use of non-naturalistic settings – and in part the more mature realisation that until children's make-believe play is firmly placed on the culturally relevant agenda of anthropology all such speculation is likely to remain premature.

To substantiate the above assessment it is worth taking a closer look at the much-cited case of the Manus, and their claimed 'lack of imaginative play' (Mead 1930:94), because while it highlights problems associated with early ethnography it at the same time poses some intriguing lines of comparative inquiry. Mead depicted Manus adult culture as bereft of any imaginative models (e.g. folktales, myths, games, riddles, puzzles) for stimulating pretence behaviour in children. This reflects, she argued, an overly empirical or matter-of-fact proclivity in the language, which is described as similarly lacking in imagery or metaphor (ibid.:102) that might stimulate child imagination. Indeed, imaginative explorations are discouraged by the children themselves and the very idea that Manus children might actually want to hear stories 'seems quite fantastic' (ibid.:98). Revealingly, Mead interprets one Manus child's use of the pidgin *grease* to gloss an act of pretending to grate coconuts – a term which Mead renders as 'deceit or lie' (ibid.:103) – as exemplifying the cultural condemnation in Manus of make-believe behaviour.

There are a number of criticisms one might easily make of Mead's account. The characterisation of Manus language, or indeed any language, in such terms would not be acceptable to most socio-linguists or anthropologists. Furthermore, a close reading of Mead's materials does evidence episodes of mimetic play around compensation payments, domestic role playing, house building, food preparation, etc. (ibid.), all of which are perfectly continuous with themes and scripts observed for other Melanesian societies such as the Huli or Kaluli. This kind of internal inconsistency as found in such early sources parallels those noted by Schwartzman (1978) for fantasy play in Ammar's (1954) ethnography of Silwa children and the results obtained in LeVine and LeVine's (1963) work on Gusii.

Perhaps more critical for the arguments of this book is the point that the passage of inference from an introduced term like *grease* to a cultural attitude is not quite as simple as Mead assumed. First, psychologists of lying have indicated that anything counterfactual in a young child's environment may be labelled a 'lie' in ways that are otherwise non-conventional uses of the term from an adult's perspective. Second, we would certainly need to know more about the folk-taxonomy of make-believe in Manus, because *grease* may import here the sense in which Manus children understand lying and pretending as semantically quite similar activities. After all, both activities are oriented towards fabricating second realities and, as we have seen above, lying is itself parasitic in some socio-linguists' eyes on pretence-making. These reinterpretations of what Mead recorded seem particularly plausible in the light of the following observ-ations. In the pretend play of Huli children, players may sometimes explicitly underscore their make-believe activity in the following manner:

(Ts. 17: ll. 296–303)

1	Mogai:	*ai hagira biamabe*
2		shall we build a fence?
3	→	*ina hawa tindule e ala godamabe*
4		we pretend false garden first dig-1PL-(I)HORT+IGV
5		shall we dig a pretend garden first?
6		*ai godalu ina hagira ala biamabe*
7		or shall we make a fence first before digging?

In this extract Mogai (girl 9–10) issues a number of overtures about what kind of pretend themes might be enacted. In line 3 she references the fabricated nature of a 'garden' by contiguous placement of two pretence markers, *hawa* ('trick'; a morph also present in *hawalanga* 'cat's-cradles'; see the list of 'Traditional Huli children's games' in Chapter 1 and *tindule* ('lie/falsehood'). As part of the Huli lexicon of deceit (cf. Goldman 1993) the occurrence of these two terms illuminates Huli perspectives on the semantic proximity of lying and pretending. Furthermore, it does so in a manner that supports the alternative reading of what Mead suggests is going on in Manus speech and attitudes to pretence. Succinctly put, the Huli term 'lie' has a penumbra of meanings which include the concepts of 'false/pretend', so that the occurrence of *grease* in a Manus child's speech might just as probably have imported this kind of connotation. In effect, this contra-case for the universality of fantasy play cannot be accepted without reservation.

Notwithstanding these remarks, in positing relationships between the scaffolding nature of adult narratives, fantasy games, and indeed the natural metaphorical 'play' in language form and use, Mead critically identified a correlative set of phenomena that is widely recognised and attested to by most play researchers today. While furthermore it seems intuitively plausible that cultures which place emphasis on oral story telling to children stimulate imaginative play (Singer 1973), though doubtless all cultures do this to some extent, we as yet appear a long way from measuring, knowing how to measure, or indeed offering any predictive statement about cultural variation along such a continuum.

In some senses one comes away from this overview of anthropological perspectives on pretend play with the impression of a discipline caught between acceptance of the Aristotelian links between pretence, play and dramatic art – 'all poetry is born of play' (Huizinga 1955:129) – and acknowledgment of its enculturative efficacy – 'the store of culture must be acquired by each individual anew. Play does much to make its attainment possible, and, above all, dramatic imitation play' (Groos 1901:398).

The Body of and in Pretence

Importantly we learn from these synopses that pretending is fundamentally a mimetic, and therefore parasitic, form of artistic behaviour. As its etymological root of *prae-tendere* (Latin: 'stretch forth'; cf. Austin 1961) betrays, pretending involves the imposition of one representation over or 'in front of' another. This mental act need not of course realise itself in some physical action, nor need the pretence representation, even where conceived of as some faithful copy, actually correspond to an original. It may be that the pretender has a genuinely false concept of the reality being portrayed. Successful social pretence, however, relies rather less on correspondences between copy and original and rather more on shared understandings about others' mental dispositions as to what is transpiring. In this regard a produced state of the world is always footnoted with a reference to actors' attitudinal stances towards that information, such that pretending has an inextricable propositional foundation.

The mental architecture of pretence, as well as its language and analysis, seems anchored to some type of bifurcation that separates modalities or representations of reality. Across the disciplines covered in the above overview we note that pretence emerges as 'a biologically preprogrammed activity' (Flavell et al. 1987:817). From Aristotle (1982:4) to Groos (1901), from Huizinga (1955) to Benjamin (1979), the ontogeny of humankind's mimetic and artistic behaviour has been located in the 'common competence' (Furth 1996:59) of child pretend play. But how well do these theories, exclusively Western in origin and formulation, sit with the perspectives of pretenders from other cultures?

The passageways of ordinary language and etymology as routes to enlightenment here (*contra* Turner 1974) seem a particularly useful commencement point when coming to grips with the semantics of pretence (*tingi ha*) in Huli. As a bridge to the next chapter, in which I examine the anatomical centricity in child games and renamings, I want to look at the make-up of the key Huli words for 'play' and 'pretence'. *Tingi ha* is a type of verb displaying what is known as an adjunct-plus-verb constitution (cf. Goldman 1993):

A [adjunct]	P [plus]	V [verb]
tingi	+	*ha*
(body)		(be/placed/inside)

The Huli term for pretence thus morphologically and semantically parallels the English verbs (*im*)*personate* and (*em*)*body*. To the fore is the sense of *passing into another body*, of *corporealisation*, of taking on a new identity, all of which are at the heart of Huli mimetic ideology. Such meanings are further encapsulated in the way in which the Huli term *tingi* and *dongone* (skin) can, like the English 'body', be used metonymically for 'person' – *dongone/tingini alego haruago* – 'like all those skins/bodies there' (Goldman 1988:22;l. 762, 1993:289). Moreover, there is a significant parallelism between the Huli terms for 'pretend' and 'play' which points to yet a further set of intercultural homologies, in the sense that both these central lexemes are semantically grounded in body parts:

tīngi	**PRETEND**	:	**PLAY**	*gìni*
tīngi	**BODY**	:	**HAND**	*gí(ni)*

The Huli concepts of play and pretence seem then semantically structured by anatomical tropes and are in one sense in accord with the Western notion that bodily action is often the identifying component of pretence-making (Woolley 1995:176). Now as Huizinga has remarked, the English word 'play' derives from the Anglo-Saxon *plega, plegan*, a 'rapid movement, gesture, a grasp of the hands, clapping, . . . all kinds of bodily activity' (1955:58; cf. Turner 1974:65). Play is something close to the body (Plato 1970:l. 653) and the hand is the metonymic instrument by which it achieves realisation. Indeed, in the absence of props in pretend play, younger children often use a body part to represent missing or imaginary objects (Overton and Jackson 1973).

There are a number of points I want to draw from these linguistic parallels. Aside from any question of the validity of theories (e.g. see above on Erikson and Freud) which identify the body as the primordial super-toy or super-symbol, it appears that in Huli metaphysics the body is conceived as an expressive or instrumental canvas for consciousness and action. What is here instantiated is a complementarity in the pathways of pretence and play that bears directly on the emergent and prevailing viewpoint of Huli pretending previously articulated. That is, there is a coordinate homology between the way in which *pretence* mediates *between mimesis and mythos* as both an 'embodied' experience and a loquacious conduit – i.e. as both body and voice – and the way in which *play* as the 'handiwork' of ludic agents ontologically defines the self. In Huli ideology *play* and *pretence* are etched within the same corporeal image, and conceptualised as merographic (part–whole) and mediatorial modalities of self-realisation. Play realises pretence in the way 'hands' (*gi*) extend and manifest 'bodies' (*tingi*). This is what is critically apperceived about play and pretence in the Huli folk model, and what constitutes a metacode of their ethno-ludology.

But we are not quite done with terminology. While the interpretative stance that pretence is a pathway between mimesis and mythos is to be taken in the rest of this book, it still remains to nail the philosophical point made above about 'play' and 'self-realisation' in a manner that is not too abstractly formulated. Now in the Huli language there are two tonally contrastive verbs:

gíni – **STRAIGHTEN, TIDY**   *gìni* – **PLAY**

(cf. Appendix 1: Ts. 2;l. 107–8)

In Huli, tone operates in a systemic manner to mark the senses in which the derivationally related terms of some single polysemous lexeme 'are similar and yet different' (Goldman 1983:43). To take one example, *yári* – 'cassowary' and *yàri* – 'decoration' are tonally contrastive and yet index the semantic association between adornment and bird feathers. In the case of the two tonally apposed *gini* terms a relationship is drawn between the 'hand' and any act which 'straightens, makes right, fixes, or causes to be in a proper state'. The Huli term 'play' is thus directly analogous, for example, with the African Basotho lexeme *bapa*, which has the meaning of 'making things . . . commensurate' (Adams 1980:151) in the explicit sense of creating an identity. The common corporeal trope to pretence and play thus also emphasises the idea that through play the actor achieves a 'straightening of the self', the actor achieves subjecthood. To pretend play in Huli is the way the child (and possibly the culture) realises its humanity (cf. Furth 1996).

Unlike the English adjective *pretend* the Huli *tingi* cannot qualify objects, so that the idea of a 'pretend garden', as we noted above (Ts. 17: l. 3), has to be rendered by a word drawn from the extensive repertoire of deceit terms, such as *tindule* ('lie, false') or *hoge* ('joke, trick'). Pretending is performative, something you do in Huli. As we have had occasion to remark (p. 2), in English one may revoke an act in terms of its consequential readings about intentions by simply saying 'not really, I was only pretending'. This linguistically implied bifurcation of the *real* vs. the *pretend* worlds is also comparably marked in the Huli language. So in Huli one can say *henene bini tingi habe* – 'pretend it really was done'. The contrast between *henene* ('truth, real, genuine') and *tingi* ('pretend') is that between an essentially ephemeral transformative state or act – of passing but not staying in another body – and 'real' as something that is permanent and 'stays'. The morphological root of the Huli term for 'truth/real' is *hene* from *ha* – 'to be/stay'. To make reference to a pretend house one might use the expression 'not a real/true house' (*anda henene ndo*), which signals that it is the kind of house that lacks permanent representation. It seems therefore that Huli conceptualise the bifurcation of real vs. pretend less as one between types of worlds, and more as one between the way in which phenomena exist within a world.

Without refusing then to countenance a comprehensive fear, as entertained by philosophers of illusion, that the Huli like others might be permanently deceived by their senses, it seems to me that we need at this initial juncture to indicate the perhaps universal contrastiveness of such lexical pairs as 'real and pretend' and their appositional and co-occurrent place in various speech acts. Notwithstanding two thousand years of philosophical wrangling it may very well be linguistically impossible for us to escape incarceration within a pretence–non-pretence prism. In Huli the internal metaphysics of pretending suggest ways in which actors conjure possibilities as transformative, but fundamentally impermanent and transitory, forms of being. Pretence may create socio-poetic landscapes but it leaves no permanent mark as a landscape feature. In some ways there is a juxtaposition here between the realities of truth as 'permanence' and empirical verifiability, and the realities of pretence as 'eternal flux'. And it is in the context of this semantic opposition that Huli may pejoratively contrast, as articulated by the adage quoted in the Preface, 'real men' and 'men who play child games'. The latter make no effective contribution, leave no lasting impression. In the philosophical imagination of Huli, pretence behaviour is situated within this nexus of meaning that contraposes ontological conditions of 'staying' with conditions that are essentially expressive, as well as reflective, of the ongoingness of things. One of the arguments taken up later in this book is that there is a cultural image, a face, to this kind of paradoxical shifting of reference frames. The shared subjective reality of pretence in Huli seems very much the refracted image of self that is the 'trickster' Iba Tiri. Child pretence presents itself to both children and adults as 'in the trickster mould' – a mask that portends, portrays and professes the permanence of illusion.

Chapter 1

Naming and Gaming

Huli

Question: *I ambologo beraria minaribe?*
                Where did you get that baby?

Answer: *Hai/Anga maneha beraria minaru*
                I got it from the top of the banana/pandanus tree

[Huli caretakers frequently identify heard but unseen frogs in the bush as 'babies'. When a newborn arrives, the above response references the frogs mentioned on previous occasions.]

Anglo-Australian

Question: Where do babies come from?

Answer: I found it under the gooseberry [mulberry] bush/in the cabbage patch/the stork brought it.

Ethnographic Context

The above conventionalised question–response sequences speak directly of attitudes to truth-telling and of the social expediency of pretence between caretakers and children. Such cultural routines do more though than register an intercultural coincidence. They surely display universal problems associated with children as *Homo interrogans* – their responses to a new arrival, the symbolism attached to newborns, and the problems that confront adults when accounting to younger others for their existence. That cultures should have engendered broadly comparable and fossilised speech sequences attests to a perhaps ubiquitous recognition that the unvarnished facts of procreation may hurt children. We understand from the mere existence of these routines that certain types of knowledge are 'classified' in nature, and thus compel culturally shaped and pretenceful responses. Children are socialised *through* pretence as much as *to* pretence by the 'play sequences' (Anderson 1986:332; cf. Furth 1996:10) of adults' lies, lullabies, threats, teases and stories. Such seemingly mundane interchanges have the power to open up the sub-cultural world of caretaking as one predicated upon deception and false promise. These sensitise the child to the dissonance between someone's presentation of the world and the way the world otherwise seems (Marrelli 1994:263; Goldman 1995). Significantly, this question–response sequence is in Huli as in Western cultures remembered as knowledge communicated predominantly by female caregivers.

In this chapter my concern then is to present a preparatory backcloth to social fantasy play in Huli by examining the culturally patterned, or 'ready-made', set of analogic renamings found in 'baby-talk', nursery rhymes and lore, and child games. In the talk for and by children speech play (*bi gini*) becomes, as it were, a prolegomenon to the speech of play. But why choose these particular exemplars of interaction? The answer lies in part with the fact that such a triangulation of phenomena permits me to display the interrelationships between pretences as acts of 'renaming', the wide spectrum of behavioural forms in which these inhere, and the critical links that are thereby established to the mythopoeic levels of adult culture. The following analyses of socio-dramatic play given in Chapters 3 and 4 are thus situated within a continuum of practices lying along the vector from mimesis to mythos. But there is more to the rationale than mere contextualisation. The presentation adheres to well-established findings in socio-linguistics that implicate the modelling behaviour of nursery lore, of 'adult–infant baby talk and dandling interaction' (Kirshenblatt-Gimblett 1976:177), and of child peer lore, in the development of metalinguistic awareness about speech aesthetics and communicative competence. That is, such behaviours are significant in the acquisition of a culture's structuring poetic structures.

But while speech play is more often considered with respect to its patterns of rhetorical and mnemonic efficacy, its contributory role in how language and narrative lessons are learnt – thus indexing how 'speech play is instrumental to the acquisition of adult verbal art' (Sanches and Kirshenblatt-Gimblett 1976:105; cf. Goldman 1983) – and equally as a gauge of the importance of language itself in the culture, the focus here is somewhat different. The question being addressed is how these resources manifest, and are secreted within, a pervasive set of pretence practices and rationales. Inasmuch as such speech exchanges appear anatomically focused – as both semantically and linguistically about 'body and hand' – they articulate (for reasons explained in the previous chapter) an ethno-ludology of 'pretending and playing'. Children's games, as well as the games played with children, provide the analyst with a special arena for rethinking the relationships between pretence and its role in knowledge acquisition and communication. This is not to claim that all there is to ludic pretence is enculturation, but rather to explore the manner in which it is both generative as well as expressive of Huli culture.

As an apt introduction to the ascribed values of speech in Huli it is useful to unpack from the comparison of routines cited above some further insights. As primordial symbols of fertility or familiar locations, banana and pandanus trees seem figuratively comparable to the mulberry bush or the nurturing nuances evoked by a stork carrying a sling (no doubt suggested by storks' habit of nesting in human abodes throughout Europe). Such fecundity derives from their status as staple ancestral foods, which implicated them in a host of traditional rituals associated with a person's physical and spiritual well-being. For example, following birth the placenta (*nu to* – 'umbrella bag') and part of the umbilical cord (*lumbi* – 'one long') were planted in a pandanus tree to ensure promotion of growth. Similarly, repossession of a lost soul involved a rite known as 'planting the pandanus seedling' (*anga wai hangaga*), in which a knotted tuft of hair known as the 'hair umbilical' reattached the subject to its shadow. Moreover, as we will see below, pandanus metaphorically signify 'penis–male–fertility' in Huli nursery lore (Table 1.1 below D.6) repeatedly figuring in mundane medical pathologies and folklore. Thus the cure for snoring (*ka*) involved creeping under a pandanus root system and making a false pretence; the snorer directs the snore 'You wait here and I'll come back soon!' while departing in the belief that the snore is forever and hopelessly entrapped.

Similarly, bananas are symbolically important as a source of baby nutrients as well as leaves which provide the first waist-apron (*mandibu*) of the child. But beyond such superficial continuities between these Huli and Western sequences there is also one quite explicit discontinuity. In Huli the newborn is presented as a transformation of a 'frog' rather than simply an accidental find or disparately located body. Noteworthy here is the culturally specific message encoded by 'frogs' (*mbola*) as quintessential symbols of loquacity that figure prominently in language development practices described below. Importantly then for Huli children the new arrival is received as a metamorphosis from frog to child; the baby has already passed through another identity when it arrives in the world. And it has done so by virtue of an act that will later come to be appreciated as a necessary pretence. Equally germane to the topic of this chapter is that the newborn's presence is perhaps less importantly that of a new 'body' than that of a new 'voice'. For Huli personhood, as is the case for other Papua New Guinean cultures, is one proclaimed and constituted through talk (cf. Goldman 1983, 1993).

The Huli people (see Figure 1.1) live in the Southern Highlands Province of Papua New Guinea and now number over 90,000. Their territory is

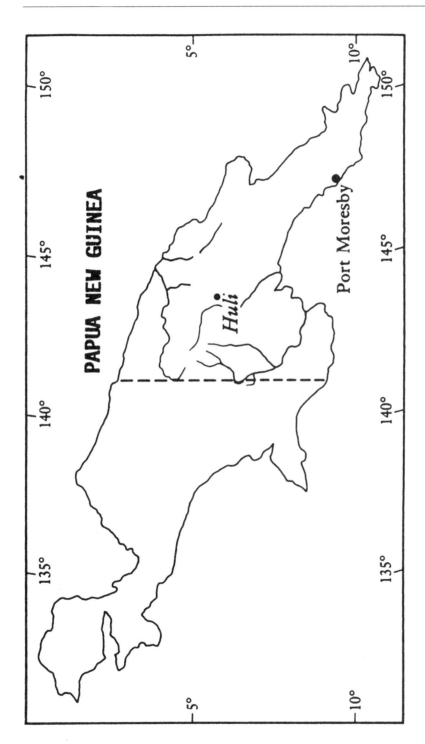

Figure 1.1 Huli region – Papua New Guinea

administratively divided between the sub-districts of Koroba (in the north) and Tari (in the south), both of which support government stations. Though the major concentration of people inhabit the Tagari river basin small communities are spread as far as Tanggi in the north and the relatively isolated populations of Homa, Pauwa and Baguale in the south-west adjacent to Lake Kutubu. While a degree of uncertainty surrounds the prehistory of the Huli, on the basis of linguistic and mythological evidence it seems likely they formed part of a north-west migration from the Kutubu region pre-dating the introduction of sweet potato. In the pre-contact era there were well-developed trade routes, intermarriage and ritual collaboration between Huli and their various cultural neighbours such as the Duna, Enga, Ipili, and peoples of the Bosavi-Strickland (Etoro, Onabasalu, Kaluli, Bedamini) region (Biersack 1995). Trade items included black palm for bows, bird of paradise feathers and beaks for decoration, Tigasso tree-oil, string, salt, axes, shell and sago.

First contacted in the early 1930s, the Huli with their 'girlish mops of brown hair adorned with flowers' (Hides 1936:81), who live in 'farmhouses . . . without villages' (ibid.:78) and have a 'pantomime language' (ibid.:83), have witnessed rapid, if unevenly spread, social change. One finds small contingents of police, various government personnel, large trade stores, schools, market sites, air-strips, hospitals and local, district and village courts on the two government stations. Most of the major population centres are linked by negotiable tracks and the main highway from Lae is routed through Hagen to Tari and Koroba. Outlying communities may be serviced by local aid-posts, small trade stores, schools and a range of denominational churches, though certainly in these marginal areas change is less easily noticeable. Most Huli now claim nominal conversion to some form of Christianity but traditional beliefs and fears about spirits (*dama*), witchcraft (*wali boleme*) and sorcery (*toro*) remain firmly entrenched. With sustained contact since the mid-1950s, the major large-scale fertility rituals of Tege (Glasse 1968) and Dindi Pongo (Goldman 1979, 1983; Frankel 1986) have long since disappeared, as has the Haroli bachelor cult. This last secular institution was intimately associated with the male cultivation of body, spirit and growth of the elaborate coiffures for which the Huli are justly renowned. For it is the Huli as 'wig-man' that, through sustained exposure in Western media travel brochures, journals, newspapers and advertisements, constitutes the people as the generic 'face' of indigenous Papua New Guinea culture.

By far the most dramatic development of late in this region has been the increasing pace of oil, gas and gold exploration, which, at the time of writing, seems set to alter fundamentally the traditional systems of social organisation, land tenure and leadership. The newly perceived values which land represents has thus engendered a frenzy of inter- and intra-clan disputes, a wholesale change in the way these are negotiated, and a consequential diminution of traditional leaders' powers, now devolved to their younger, university-educated and English-speaking sons or relatives. Notwithstanding this, and despite the widespread use of tinned fish and rice, the Huli remain predominantly subsistence farmers, utilising a bush-fallow technique devoted to sweet-potato cultivation. There are no marked seasonal changes and thus no annual horticultural cycle. Sweet potato is supplemented by sugar cane, bananas, pandanus, various leaf vegetables, and less commonly wild game like possum, snake, cassowary and pig (either domesticated or wild). Indeed pig husbandry continues to play a vital economic role as a standard of wealth, providing items of exchange in bride-wealth and compensation payments consequent on disputes and war.

In terms of their descent structure the Huli conform to the polygynous–patrilineal systems typical of much of the Highlands region. They are divided into named exogamous clans (*hameigini* – 'father–sons'), each of which has a primary locus of ritual and territorial interests referred to as their *dindi kuni* – the bone land. Because of the implications of cognatic kinship, multiple-parish affiliation and residence were tolerated with people maintaining gardens in several parish areas. The typical constitution of a parish, often named after the clan which claims tenurial precedence, is one composed of varying subsidiary clan segments who relate to a 'core' of agnates (*tene* – 'source, bole') through matrifilial connections, and who are collectively known as *yamuwini* ('women placed'). These latter units may in turn have accreted other segments who are *yamuwini* to them but non-related 'others' (*wali haga*) to the core. At the higher levels of inter-clan relationships we find both phratries and often clans who strategically position themselves in terms of this binary schema of primary host (*tene*): guest (*yamuwini*). Both individuals and clans may hold multiple-category statuses and a portfolio of interests in land by reason of longstanding residence, rights in perpetuity, and genealogies which reflect ancestral marriages and descent from some host female clan agnate. Irrespective of region or historical time, these principles of social organisation have been constant. But this is not to ignore the dynamic potential for manipulation and recasting of relationships: 'actors in these systems are engaged in processes of continual reanalysing and reassessing linkages, so that perceived agnatic or cognatic definitions are not irrevocable one-time models . . . structure in this sense is a "becoming", not a "being", in accordance with, and sensitive to, agendas that are frequently politically motivated' (Goldman 1993:23).

The residential pattern is one of scattered households with Huli men and women still continuing for the most part to maintain separate abodes, tend separate gardens, and cook and consume food largely in the privacy of their own homes. These practices reflect culture-specific (and to a lesser extent region-wide) beliefs about cross-gender interaction. These are pervaded by an ideology which articulates the dangers associated with the physiological functions and products of female sexuality. Thus most forms of inter-sex behaviour were hedged by taboo and, in the pre-contact era, governed by elaborate purificatory and protective rituals. Similarly, the division of labour is typified by sex-role differentiation. Women are primarily involved in tasks of tending pigs, weeding and child care while men undertake major labour projects concerned with garden clearing, fencing and house construction, and dominate politico-legal affairs. Young children normally live with mothers but once boys reach about the age of 6 they take up residence with fathers or other senior male relatives, such as brothers or father's brothers. This reflects an ideology which posits a gendered differentiated trajectory of male growth that, for a period, must avoid the depleting and injurious affects attendant on intimate association with females. Power domains, as between domestic/private (*anda*) and public/epideictic (*hama*), are thus coordinate with a male/female dichotomy. While this accords with themes of sexual dimorphism and asymmetry commonly noted in the literature on Melanesian societies, the intensity of beliefs about pollution in Huli and their consequent behavioural repercussions are somewhat atypical. Stigmatic dogmas encompass then a consistent set of ideas about the relationship of women to defilement, disorder and dispute. Female sexuality was traditionally adumbrated in terms of toxicity and contagion, which underscored disparities of social power between the sexes, as well as the semantic and linguistic derogation women were subject to. This was inherent in the lexicons of anger, dispute and shame, in labels of unit (residence/descent) structuration, and in the form and substance of genderlects.

Over the last decade, and almost without parallel amongst the more than 700 other cultures indigenous to Papua New Guinea, Huli has been a mecca for anthropologists, film makers and steady streams of tourists. More theses have been produced and published, more films made, and more articles written from a wider spectrum of interests (disputes, language, prehistory, gender, fauna, archaeology, religion, mining and ecology: cf. Ballard 1995: 401–8 for a comprehensive bibliography) on the Huli than for any other people in Melanesia. There are no doubt complex factors which account for such interest, including the relative size and location of the population within the Southern Highlands, and most particularly the mythological tenor and depth of the Huli's preoccupation with narrativising all aspects of their world and its history. This is a culture which, atypically for the region, has not only genealogies that are regularly more than twenty generations in depth, but aetiological traditions that uniquely adumbrate a sacred geography which both conceptually and (in the pre-contact era) practically encompassed a conglomerate of neighbouring cultures in common fertility rites. Because of the extraordinary depth of materials available (cf. Glasse 1968; Goldman 1983, 1988, 1993; Goldman and Ballard 1998; Frankel 1986; Ballard 1995b), I have forsaken a lengthy introduction to Huli culture and restricted myself to those principal traits least documented and directly involved with child rearing and the operative dynamics of social pretend play.

Rhyming and Renaming Structures

Talk (*bi*) and knowledge (*mana*) are the two pervasive and complementary idioms in which Huli conceptualise both relationships and identities at successive levels from the interpersonal to the inter-clan and inter-tribal. They juxtapose as active and quiescent dimensions which express not just ideas about cultural authenticity and difference, but the very concept of historicity in Huli: '*ina mama mamalinaga mana ogome mo mbiyaore kemagoni* – the *mana* of our ancestors makes us one people.' Identities then are thought of as composite profiles or mosaics of both 'speech' and '*mana*'. While these may often be highly specific to the 'holder', they nevertheless fall within distinctively named categories. These reflect Huli concepts of cultural homogeneity and constitute an integrative force within the society. That is, for example, despite variability in the specific forms of child rearing rites across Huli such knowledge and behaviour is classified under the general rubric of *waneigini mana* – children's lore.

Male and female children are symbolically contrasted in terms of a pair of assonant symbols: *Danda* (bows) and *Damba* (brideprice pigs). The 'bow' signals a developmental trajectory for a boy in accordance with parental aspirations that he will provide support in war, in talk, and with chores demanding strength. By contrast 'brideprice' expresses a perspective on a girl that reflects both her outgoing status at marriage and the degree to which she represents a source of incoming wealth to her family. Irrespective of these gender-inflected values the Huli system of upbringing, as expressed in life-stage rituals, has always been targeted at promotion of physical strength (*hongo*), early independence (*anda anda bira*) and loquacity (*bi*). The picture that emerges of pre-contact practices is one where the achievement of such ends was seen as partly dependent on relationships to, as well as the capricious will of, supernatural progenitors, and partly related to performances of developmental spells and rituals (*gamu*). After birth mothers would thus regularly perform *hongo helo gamu* ('to make strong spell'), and co-participate in rites such as *ma hiriya* ('taro roasting') or *Kebe haria/balimu pudaga* ('tracks of Kebali/cutting Balimu [*Melastoma*]': cf. Goldman 1983), which invoked an ancestral model of subsistence reliant on non-domesticated food species. Similar practices continued throughout the first years of an infant's life, with *gamu* recited for new aprons (*mandibu gamu*) and hair cutting (*mbalupa*), or intestinal tract illnesses which necessitated religious rites propitiating spirits (eg. *nogo wandia/kebe wandia*), or secular rites based on the properties of clay (*dindi dongoma*) or pandanus (*anga lo tibaga/tini hubua*).

The point to be drawn from these kinds of historical data is that the early childhood of a Huli infant was one in which it was repeatedly exposed and sensitised to occurrences of ritualised speech forms. These incorporated metaphoric structures of meaning drawn largely from avian and faunal domains, and were replete with the kinds of eulogistic renamings described in more detail below. Simply put, the child's linguistic diet was critically, if only partially, an ingestion of lessons about synonym use. Examination of spell texts reveals that the child's identity was temporarily etched and transformed 'as if' it were a bird, a plant or a possum. In this process the desired qualities would be imbued through the efficacy of speech acts that were inexorably pretenceful in nature. So 'role taking' by others on behalf of the child was one dimension of pretend behaviour to which children were regularly exposed. To give one example, the property of independent movement was instilled in 'making strong *gamu*' by projecting an image of the child as a 'wasp' flitting between plants and thus capable of 'flight' (*yaga/di*):

Spell 1.1: *Hongo Helo Gamu*
Kabua Ainya – Yaluba 1977

Dangi mone harane di	/	*Walu mone di*	/	*Diya Mone di*
wings of the grass wasp, fly	/	wings of the mud wasp, fly	/	wings of the wasp, fly
yagibi / *yagama*	/	*ya pudu pudu*	/	*ya banga banga*
fly / fly	/	flap your wings	/	flutter your wings

This central theme of 'wasp flight' is reiterated in the verse by minor substitutions in location terms followed by poetic play with the verb *'yaga'* to produce non-conventional synonyms like *yagibi* and *yagama*. In much the same way children were imbued with loquacity by the conjuring of images of loud raucous birds, while growth spells talked of a body that swells (*pururu*), sprouts (*piago*), thickens like a clump or grove of plants (*te*), hardens (*dai*) and is in the process of joining together (*nguai nguai*). Creating multiple identities for the child, as imaginal transformations in the tropes of spells, was then a significant feature of developmental practices and ideology.

As previously noted, the well-being of the physical body was intimately related to possession of one's spirit (*dinini*), so that prevention of spirit loss by a child was, and still is, of vital concern to caretakers. After sitting with a baby caregivers will lightly brush the ground on standing to ensure the spirit returns to the child's body. Similarly, a small horizontal fringe of hair is left on children's heads to cover the fontanelle, through which one's spirit may escape after, say, major fright. Traditionally it was necessary to perform *galai/hagari gamu* ('widow spells') after the death of a spouse for two months to protect the child from the inimical effects of a deceased's spirit. What we witness in the following spell text is the manner in which the performer projects herself *into the persona* of a dead husband, voicing lines in the first person 'as if' she were the dead man fulfilling the fantasy aspirations of a widowed wife – that, for example, the deceased 'distance' himself from her children:

Spell 1.2: *Hagari Gamu*
Anya Imane – Yaluba 1977

1		*Humbirininaga Ayeri doro haro*
2		In Ayeri for the land of dead souls, I am warming myself
3		*Hayeri doro haro*
4		In Hayeri I am warming myself
5	→	*Ligari . . . Bawari . . . Beme . . . Bererome . . . Emema . . . Uruaga . . .*
6		*Yamo wane yango ha*
7		In Yamo your girlfriends are staying
8		*Hulu . . . Adoba . . .*
9		*I baya homani iraga haro*
10		I am climbing the Baya tree
11		*homanungu iraga haro*

12		I am climbing like the possum
13	→	*dagi yali . . . andi duru . . . gwai manoni . . .*
14		*bali inaga hangu hangu*
15		child my separate
16		my children are separated
17	→	*bawali . . . niyali . . . odali . . . odoma . . .*

Many of the structures we will encounter in the materials to be considered in this chapter are manifested in the above text. In ll. 1–5 the speaker takes the perspective of the deceased other who is journeying to the land of dead souls (*humbirini*) 'warming' his now cold corpse. The same thought is repeated for several lines by substituting the initial place name Ayeri with a sequenced run of rhyming place names (→ Hayeri, Ligari, Bawari, etc.), all of which lie along the route of the migrating shade. In lines 6–8 the speaker now assumes her primary identity as widow entreating the deceased to 'make friends' with other female spirits. A second switch is made at ll. 9–13, where the speaker again takes the role of the other analogically projected as a possum climbing up trees much as the spirit must climb to *humbirini*. But these are not conventional Huli words because *homanungu* and *dagi yali/andi duru/gwai mano* are respectively poetic synonyms for possum (*tia*) and the *andira* (*Nothofagus*) tree. A single statement is repeated by either (1) substitution of a single term drawn from an enumerative list of appellations from the same semantic domain; or (2) substitution by a renaming using a poetic synonym precisely, as illustrated in ll. 14–17, where '*bali*' is successively replaced by *bawali/niyali/odali/doma*, which are all assonant/alliterative synonyms in a predefined set replacing the ordinary-language word for baby (*gambolo*).

We are presented in the above with a poetic speech form in which a caretaker oscillates between speaking from the perspective of the self and an other – in which the speaker pretends to pass into another persona. Not only did adults present as interlocutors who would take on the role of the child as a transformed body, but they also presented as actors capable in their spells of assuming a number of distinct perspectival roles. The child as audience comes to internalise and assimilate not simply the form and place of multi-labelling within the speech economy but the essential fusion, if not fun, of poetic/dramatic and pretenceful practices as a structured means to achieving ends.

Talking then is an important activity in Huli and their consciousness of and attention to language is partly indexed by one of the most complex verbal art systems yet reported for the region. This embraces a gamut of distinct genres distributed between male and female speakers, a host of specialised ritual and secular vocabularies described below, and pervasive occurrence of three discriminable eulogistic repertoires (*bi mone, mini mende* and *kai mini*) found variously in political oratory (*damba bi, malu*), spells (*gamu*), mourning laments (*wali o*), courting songs (*dawe u*), ritual chants (*bilagu, gereye*) and both fictional (*bi te*) and factual (*tene te*) narratives. Moreover, there is almost no domain of cultural knowledge that has not in some part encoded truths within conventionalised, pre-formatted speech forms known as *pureremo*. All of the above are invariably structured by the artifices of sound play broached above – assonance, alliteration, reduplication, parallel syntax, enumerative lists based on rhyming terms – as well as distinct patterns of refrain, and punctuational and prosodic contours.

By way of introduction to these speech play forms I am going to select for brief attention the single domain of weather/time ditties or rhymes. I have in mind here Huli child analogues of Western forms such as 'Rain rain go away come again another day', or 'It's raining, it's pouring, the old man is snoring'. In Huli such rhymes do not fall neatly within the discrete categories of either nursery lore or child lore, being commonly employed by both adults or children to, or in the company of, other children.

Huli chart the movement of the moon (*ega*) in two blocks of fifteen days. The standardised depiction is given as follows:

Hombene angi	*hombene ibule*
On the twelfth day	it will come out on top
halene angi	*hale howa hama ibule*
on the thirteenth day	it will come silently listening
dene angi	*de howa yalu ibule*
on the fourteenth day	having opened its eyes, the moon will come
nguini angi	*ngui higi bu yalu ibule*
on the fifteenth day	with squinted nose it will come

(on days 16–24 the moon is 'on top of the hill' (*dindi hombene*))

nguira (15 +)	
pini angi	*pi lole*
on the tenth day	it will fall down
beane angi	*bea nge lole*
on the eleventh day	it will break
hombene angi	*homolebira*
on the twelfth day	it will die

The constituent lines of the rhyme reflect a bipartite structure which counterposes the initial temporal phrases (ie. days) with a second phrase whose lexical and semantic structure is determined solely by the phonological similarities between its governing verb and the numerical morph. In other words, the sequence of sound similarities between the counterposed terms in a line constitutes speech play. This is evident both from the recognised morphemic parallels of 13, 14 and 15 and 'ears' (*hale*), 'eyes' (*de*) and 'nose' (*ngui*), and from the non-derivative terms:

pini	(10)	*pi lole*
beane	(11)	*bea lole*
hombene	(12)	*homolebira*

This kind of intentioned play with sound, the marked interest in the morphophonological level of speech patterning, is particularly prominent in both children's games and the whole gamut of chants/rhymes they use to talk about or influence the weather. One notes in these performances a pronounced rhythmic cadence or tonic movement with low rising over the inital statement, then a marked caesura that divides it from the second part, which in turn is high falling and correlated with emphasis on its message content:

Rhyme 1.1: *Ni Ibu Lalu* – 'to say "Come sun"'

Example 1.1:
Dagiwa (boy, 4 yrs) – Yaluba 1993

Example 1.2:
Paul (boy, 4 yrs) – Yaluba 1977

ni ibu	*naribu*	*auwa ko*	*aluba debene*
come sun	(wind)	bad (dark) greens	good (light) greens
pularia	*pangaria*	(Cruciferae)	(Amaranthaceae)
(wind?)	doorway	*pulai*	*longai*
aluba	*debene*	blows	blows (*kai*)
greens (*Amaranthaceae*)	good time of day	*hiribu*	*naribu*
dabu	*dendebe*	wind (*kai*)	wind (*kai*)
pandanus platform	sweet	*auwa ko*	*aluba debene*
maguba	*mbirini*	bad (dark) greens	good (light) greens
sickly	meat		
ayege manini	*ngo nole*		
Areca palm tree on top	I left to eat		
ni biri biri labe	*ni pudu*		
sun shine quickly	sun rise up		

Examples 1.1 and 1.2, drawn from the same locale but from periods almost two decades apart, reveal perhaps unsurprisingly that such standardised

ditties clearly undergo change over time. Notwithstanding this, both verses in the main juxtapose phrases which share sequences of phonological similarity in either the initial or terminal segments of words. Additionally, there is a more complex layer of metaphoric structuring in the oppositions of (1) the two species of greens which contrast as 'dark' – an unwanted state – and 'light' – the desired state – in colour; and (2) the semantically opposed notions of 'something sickly' with 'something good' like meat. Beyond these properties the rhymes are replete with eulogistic (*kai*) synonyms for 'wind' (eg. *hiribu, naribu*) that present as minimal rhyming pairs.

Rhyme 1.2: 'Call for rain' Nabili (girl 11) – Yaluba 1993		Rhyme 1.3: 'Call for rain to stop' Handabe (boy 6) – Yaluba 1993	
giwili	*gewali*	*pobo bia*	change to mist
cane	cane	*poboanda bia*	change to mist
ngue te	*daria te*	*poboda bia*	change to mist
many worms	many lizards	*narogo pobo nguliya*	
mu gege	*himu gege*	I'm eating and I'll give you mist	
sand cover/multiply	dust cover/multiply	*duguarogo pobo nguliya*	
waru gege	*gutagali ni muni gege*	I am pulling out food and I'll give you mist	
mud multiply	sand multiply on Tagali river	*emene ko be taguabi ede ibirago*	
		The small ashes are plenty and coming	
pandani gege		*hamaga tolo bu holiya*	
dead leaves multiply		I am spitting at you	
		[then spits on ground as insult to rain]	

Rhymes 1.2 and 1.3 provide more examples of similar patterning along both phonological and semantic axes. In Rhyme 1.2 'rain' is invoked by means of images associated with the observed natural consequences of 'wet' weather such as a build-up of mud, silt and sand and a proliferation of worms and lizards. These ideas are adumbrated by phrases with parallel syntactic structure. In Rhyme 1.3 cessation of rain is a wished-for state conjured up by images of mist as the aftermath of rain – initially with collocation of corrupt poetic synonyms built on the ordinary Huli term for mist (*pobo* → *poboanda, poboda*) – and later the 'rising mist' associated with cooking, or the concept of 'dryness' in ashes. All of these patterns are replicated in a further range of nursery lore rhymes used by caretakers for when the sun goes down, for the morning mist, and for the fall of dusk. That children are known typically to utilise these same resources is evident from the various adult speech practices to them. Thus caretakers may

reprimand or tease children who do not answer questions, or respond to some other solicitation, with standard sequences that employ a set of rhyming nonsense terms:

ngaraga laya	she/he said '*ngaraga*'
karaga laya	she/he said '*karaga*'
kurugu laya	she/he said '*kurugu*'

Such routines explicitly recognise the fact that this type of verbal corruption is highly typical of children's speech interactions. In essence we begin to appreciate the economy of names – plurality, poetic structuration, metaphoric or analogic bases – that typifies forms of adult speech both to and for the child. There is not only a pervasive occurrence of renamings which impregnate rhymes, but a deliberate exploitation within these of sound and semantic dimensions. Such a diversity in the range of materials examined above merely reinforces the point that exposure and access to the ritualistic speech of fiction, drama, oratory, etc., is a matter as much of familiarity with their grounding in renaming structures as of appreciating their *in situ* relationship to circumscribed contexts. Without wishing to prioritise particular practices as causally implicative for pretence competencies, there seems good reason to foreground baby-talk as one of the more critical conditioners.

Huli Baby-Talk

'Baby-talk' (hereafter BT; cf. Ferguson 1964, 1977) is generally recognised to be a special register employed by adults and older children in talk to babies, and sometimes to animals. It has variously been referred to in the literature as 'nursery speech/language' (Jakobson 1962; Bynon 1968; Austerlitz 1956), 'caregiver speech' (Ochs 1982) or 'hypocoristic speech'. While a conventionalised and institutionalised part of adult speech, BT differs in systematic and discernible ways from normal adult conversation. The small corpus of anthropologically oriented studies of BT (Ferguson 1964; Crawford 1970; Sabar 1974; Casagrande 1948; Kelkar 1964; Dil 1975; Blount 1977; Rūķe-Draviņa 1977) all attest to a register that is pervasively simplified, adjusted, attuned or accommodated to the child's psycholinguistic competencies. Typically, where adult speech is treated as the source from which BT derives, the diacritical features are regarded as eminently suitable for use with people of low communicative ability and hence as a propaedeutic to language learning. Very much as was found to be the case for imaginative play, the universal status of BT remains somewhat of a contentious matter (cf. Ervin-Tripp and Strage 1985) and particularly in regard to the special inventory of lexical items that often typifies such registers.

For the most part the phenomenon of BT has been analysed in terms of lexico-semantic patterns, paralinguistic features, derivation processes from conventional adult terms, and its function as a simplified register in language development. Despite the historical importance of anthropological studies of BT in the development of language-acquisition research, the response to sustained pleas (Ferguson 1964; Hymes 1964; Schieffelin 1979) for cross-cultural data has been somewhat pedestrian. The low analytic priority accorded such study by mainstream anthropology in part reflects the way children are perceived as marginalised occupants of mundane space, but is also a failure to appreciate fully how such data can transcend narrow linguistic interests into simplicity parameters, or the matching of input features with consequential variations in language acquisition. There is a need then to articulate ongoing relationships between inter-child, inter-adult and adult–child communicative behaviour, to specify how 'culture' impinges on the acquisition of cognitive and linguistic skills, and thus how BT is integrated with communicative patterns elsewhere in the speech economy. As Ferguson (1977:230) has remarked, the interesting and important questions about BT – such as 'why BT words have the forms they do and are used in the way they are' (Bynon 1977:255) and why BT lexicons extend over an invariant set of semantic fields – can only be answered with reference to specifiable socio-cultural considerations.

The argument to be pursued here is that this type of linguistic social-isation practice reflects prevalent ideologies about language learning and children's developmental trajectories. Moreover, because BT is predomin-antly a 'pretend' code, and one structurally homologous with the broader canvas of synonym patterns we have been examining in this chapter, it is both directly and developmentally implicative in shaping pretence competencies in Huli. The meaning of BT is not exhausted then by its contextualised uses but rather appears to convey structured information about pretence- making. It stands as an expressive symbol drawing analogical correspondences between the fictive texts in which it inheres and their membership of a class of pretend parlances which narratively re-present the world.

As noted above, the importance attached to talk in Huli is reflected in a host of functionally differentiated lexicons employed across both sacred and secular speech situations. The existence of so large a number of synonym sets seems attributable both to (1) the prevalence of contexts and themes of concealment that compel speech disguise and (2) the place renamings have in aesthetic and poetic art forms. Very briefly these vocabulary sets can be usefully detailed as follows (cf. Goldman 1983).

1 *tayenda tu ha* – 'forest language' – consists of over 300 lexemes employed to trick forest spirits while hunting or collecting pandanus in primary bush areas. The language is a barrier (*tu*) between inimical spirits and humans, since the former cannot understand the special cant and thus cannot read people's intentions. The vocabulary, standard across the whole of Huli, includes non-related suppletive forms, derivations by mutation or deletion from ordinary language (hereafter OL) terms (eg. *dogone* (OL, 'skin') → *yongone*), as well as OL terms given new but unrelated meanings (cf. Pawley 1992). Normal Huli verb suffixes and syntactic structure remain unchanged. Similarly, the agglutinative logic of everyday Huli is retained:

raining [OL] *dalu* (rain) *ibira* (coming)   → *erene* (water) *aremo lara* (come/go)
tears   [OL] *de* (eye) *iba* (water)   → *hangarine* (eye) *erene* (water)

but in the interests of economy a multititude of normally distinct words are encompassed by one 'forest' term by virtue of their perceived common semantic features:

[OL]	[Forest]	[OL]	[Forest]
iba (water)		*bayua* (carefully)	
pu (urine) } *erene*		*tigabi* (correct) }	
kuyama (lake)		*baya* (good)	*hangarine*
dalu (rain) }		*mini* (mind) }	
		daliga (above)	
		li (high) }	

2 Sacred vocabularies are used in Haroli, Kebeanda and Tege are associated respectively with the bachelor cult, pig oblations to progenitorial ancestors like Kebali, and fertility rituals. Specialists within these cults would utilise full lexical replacements for conventional terms: eg. tongs [OL] *pero* → [Tege] *lebolaki*, talk [OL] *bi* → [Haroli] *guyu*.

3 Apart from other contexts like cooking or illness where synonym substitution occurs, the Huli have three distinct eulogistic lexicons tied to songs, spells, laments, narratives and politico-legal speech. These are:

(a) *mini mende* – 'second names' – substitutions that retain full genus and species differentiation for animals and plants. In some cases there is a complete replacement of a given term – eg.[OL] *dalu* (rain) → *ginane* –

while other synonyms utilise ordinary language terms that signal special semantic features; for example, [OL] *wanekui* (forehead, lit. 'daughter's bone') → *homa embo* (lit. 'one skull'). Some OL words then have both a *kai* (see (c) below) and a 'second name' analogue: eg. [OL] possum (*tia*) → [second name] *dulu baya*, [praise term] *homanungu* (cf. Spell 2: 1. 11). These 'second names' are also used as penthonyms to make an oblique reference to dead kinsmen, since mentioning their OL name is thought to invoke the dead spirit.

(b) *bi mone* – 'good words' – where the substitution may incorporate an extra lexeme that semantically qualifies the host term in some way – eg. [OL] *wali* (woman) → *mandi wali*, in which *mandi* (*Euphorbiaceae*) denotes the leaves women are said to pick in the land of the dead (see further explanations in Chapter 5). The replacement term may also constitute a suppletive form with or without independent OL meaning: eg. [OL] *porage* (Echidna) → *dindi pubu* ('comes and goes in the ground'). Such renamings often occur in pre-formatted speech forms such as proverbs, as is the case with the *bi mone* term *dumbi yalu* (forehead; [OL] *wanekui*: cf. Goldman 1983:233) in the following adage:

Inaga **dumbi yalu** *bi te wandarirunaga halepange aledago mbira agi lolebere*
Your forehead is shining like the pearlshell necklace of girls in fictional tales, so have you got something to say?

[Used when someone approaches with a smile on his/her face as if he/she is about to convey good news. The forehead is the locus of 'truth' in Huli culture and an anatomic register of affectivity and truthfulness.]

(c) *kai mini* – 'praise names' – quite distinguishable from the above two renaming classes in that for each OL term there may be as many as seven equivalent *kai* words. These synonyms form bound sets that have a predetermined sequential pattern. Choice of the first member in any paradigmatic set allows an audience to predict the sequence of utterances that follow in the verse in which they appear. A pronounced feature of these sets is name pairing on the basis of shared phonological shape, much as already found in Spell 1.2: line 17 above for the praise analogues of 'baby' – *bali, bawali, niyali, odali, odoma*.

[OL]	[*kai* set]
beard (*angari*)	*dirini waiyabe – wambo waralo – wabulu waiyabe*
baby (*gambolo*)	*bali – bawali – niyali – odali – odoma*
children (*waneigini*)	*gili – gawali – barina – bangale*
cowrie shell (*dange*)	*puluni – pulumagi – ilini – gilini – dodane – dagini*

Again many of the *kai* synonyms may reflect specific semantic features of their OL analogues. For example, the *kai* for 'wig' is *abu abai*, where the OL term *abai* denotes the spotted cuscus (*Spilocuscus maculatus*), the fur of which is used to adorn coiffures. In effect a single referent such as a 'pig' may have anything up to fifteen different synonyms distributed amongst the above lexical sets.

What emerges from this summary overview of the distinct lexicons used by Huli is that poetic form is here grounded in the mechanics of synonym substitutions and metamorphoses of sound shape. But the point to be emphasised is not simply the range of sound play devices incorporated, or necessarily their complex metaphoric bases, but rather that to be a competent communicator in this culture demands an understanding of the structural and discoursal salience of renamings. While there are probably few cultures without some similar renaming forms, it is the sheer extent and number of these sets in Huli which appear singularly noteworthy. In one sense the whole artistic empire is built on the foundation of appellative transformations. There is in this culture a marked and unremitting attention to synonym usage, which, as a distinct cultural trait and pretence paradigm, one might expect to be reflected somehow in the language socialisation practices.

Baby-talk uniquely engages our attention in this context because of its axiomatic links to metaphor. Metaphor, as we have previously noted, is a way of understanding and experiencing one subject or domain in terms of another. A metaphoric attribution is fundamentally pretenceful because, as Aristotle noted long ago, it is 'the extension of a name from that to which it usually belongs to some other object' (Fernandez 1974:123; cf. Lakoff and Johnson 1980). With metaphor we think 'as if', we conceptualise as 'seeing as' (Bamberg 1983) – an imaginal imposition of meaningful relations. Like play, metaphor constructs make-believe worlds (Stross 1975).

Now one characteristic of early language use in pretenders between 1:2 and 2:5 is the occurrence of what are known as *lexical overextensions*, in which words come to designate referents outside their conventional range of application. So, for example, *mushroom* may denote *umbrella*, or *moon* a *grapefruit*. While a proportion of these usages are often misnomers or category mistakes due to overly broad or immature categorisation, research (Hudson and Nelson 1984; Mendelsohn et al. 1984) suggests a high incidence of such usages are analogic stipulations. The child is intentionally underscoring comparisons between conventional and unconventional referents by this naming practice. There are a number of points of intersection between overextensions, BT renamings, and identity transformations found in fantasy play which signal why it is that we need to contextualise play behaviour in this fashion. Overextensions, as a spontaneous, innovatory and unprompted behaviour, are counterpoised in Huli by the shared ludic symbols of BT as standardised pre-formatted 'renamings'. Both kinds of analogic operation are cognitively continuous with the pretence transformations of objects and roles children process in their solo and collective fantasy play. They are all situated forms of 'as-if' manipulation with names and attributes. In recognition of this analysts have targeted pretend play as *the* resource for illuminating the bases on which overextensions are constructed, namely, whether they proceed on physical (shape, colour, texture, number, etc.) or functional correspondences between objects brought into a tropic relationship. Equally, all such modalities of renaming imply the child's capacity to maintain the real and imaginal duality of some referent, to make 'side-by-side' comparisons through symbolic acts for pretenceful purposes.

Baby-talk, as described below, emerges as a context in which there is pretend play with analogy and as such stands as a precursor if not precondition to the symbolic play of collaborative make-believe. Along with the routines in which it is embedded it appears as a conversational milieu through which children are exposed to conventional symbolisations. If BT does provide a carefully graded curriculum of information about the mother tongue (Snow 1977), it does so in part as a pretenceful practice constitutive of knowledge that reflects and is coordinate with conventions applicable elsewhere.

The consciousness in Huli of the presence of many of the generally reported features (Snow and Ferguson 1977) of BT registers – exaggerated intonation contours, nursery tone (*Ammenton*), slowed speech, clarified pronunciation, shorter mean length of utterances, use of reduplication and diminutives (eg. doggy, itsy-bitsy), high incidence of imperatives, questions, repeated use of certain sentence frames, a set of special lexical coinages and a semantic content that has experiential immediacy for the child – finds realisation in the independently labelled activity of *gange bi*. In a restricted sense, the phrase refers to the special lexicon presented in Table 1.1 below. However, it is also understood to embrace more widely the early utterances of children and the gamut of games and nursery rhymes used in caretaker–child interaction. One may speculate that, in accordance with findings explained in the last chapter about tonally contrasted terms, the word *gange* is etymologically related to *gange/gahenge* meaning 'raw/unripe'. Men profess ignorance of *gange bi* but many clearly remembered words when questioned, and taped sequences of fathers interacting with children showed their speech to retain the prosodic and redundancy features normally associated with this register.

There is an extensive range of practices and beliefs linked to ensuring speech production in Huli children, all of which express the importance caretakers attach to language development within the culture. Fathers are prohibited from eating snakes until children say their first words, perhaps because ingestion, through some analogic process of sympathetic trans-ference, would rob the child of the capacity to talk. People whose speech is ineffective are proverbially said to be like 'snakes who merely extend their tongues without always biting' – *nogombi bo napole yamo hege tomia bere* (cf. Goldman 1983:215). To encourage sound production mothers daily tap babies' mouths with the open palm. From the following recorded text of a spontaneous play sequence between a mother (M), her baby (B) and his two brothers (who mockingly pretend to hit the baby), we gain a good insight into prototypical BT behaviour:

Text 1.1: (M: (Dalu's wife), B (Mai – boy, 12–15 months))
Yaluba 1984

[Mother lifts the baby on to a fence while holding his hands as he stands]

1	B:	*a↑e:*
2	M:	*a↑e:*
3		(2)
4		*a↑e:*
5		*a↑e:*
6		*Ma↑i↓O* (1) <u>*mai mai*</u>
7	B:	*aya*
8	M:	*a:ya*
9		*a↑e::*
10		((staccato delivery))
11		*hiya hiya hiya hiya*
12		stand stand stand stand
13		*ae ae ae ae ae*
14		*w↑o↓o*
15		*igiri wahe* (1)
16		old boy (has the sense of 'what a big boy to stand up')
17		*w↑o↓o igiri wa: HE:*
18		old boy
19		*igiri wa:↑HE ibu o w↑o↓o*
20		old boy, come on
21		*a↑oo:* (2)

22		((staccato delivery))
23	→	*handa bia handa bia handa bia handa bia*
24		dance, dance, dance
25	B:	*a↑e:*
26	M:	((high pitch))
27		*a:↑e:: (1) a↑e a↑e*
28		*a↑e: la*
29		say 'ae'
30		*la*
31		say
32		*a↑e:: (1) aya (.) la*
33		say 'aya' ('aya' occurs as one synonym for 'mother')
		((the two brothers begin to tap the child on his legs while the mother holds him. This pretend hitting continues throughout the next exchanges as the mother encourages the child to strike his brothers))
34	→	*a a*
35		hit
36		*ba ba ba*
37		hit hit hit
38		*ba la*
39		say 'hit'
40		*AG↓i:: agi*
41		what what
42		. . .
43		*pu la*
44		say 'go'
45		*puda↑ba:* (said on behalf of the child to his brothers)
46		you all go away

As we will see in the next chapter, the features found in this vignette of early language interaction become internalised as a 'model of speech exchange'. The model is reproduced by children when role playing mothers and/or children. So in what does this prototypicality consist? Many of the turn sequences are constructed from the spontaneously produced sounds of the child itself (ll. 1–2, 7–8, 25–6). The repetition by the mother of these referentially meaningless sounds – a manipulation of sound play – is typified by exaggerated intonation and increased loudness (ll. 17–19, 27), and lengthening of vowel sounds (ll. 9, 17, 40). In attending to the phonological shape of the child's utterances the mother can thereby establish her repetition as an awareness of turn-taking between them, as a model of conversation itself. Significantly, the child is variously prompted to repeat terms that are framed with the imperative construction 'say *x*' (ll. 28–32, 38, 43–4). There are two points to be made concerning this feature: first, the model is applied to meaningless sounds as in l. 28, as well as conventional Huli words; and second it parallels findings made, for example, among the neighbouring Kaluli whose ɛlɛma routines of 'say after me' are claimed to socialise the child into the modality of assertion (Scheiffelin 1990; cf. Goldman 1991). Equally, mothers may take the perspective of the child, as in l. 45 where she talks to a third party 'as if' delivering the baby's speech, marked by rising intonation and vowel lengthening. The mother treats the baby as a responsible interlocutor. One notes too the high incidence of repetition in utterances (ll. 11–12, 23–4, 37) and the incorporation of BT (→) terms. Significantly, there is switching here between BT (l. 34) and ordinary language words (ll. 36–8) in adjacent utterances, which suggests less some inconsistency of BT employment than a motivated attempt to instil understanding of synonymity between the terms. Some insight is gained here then into both the typical form that interaction takes between caregivers and infants and the particular way in which Huli mothers promote awareness of BT substitutions.

The Huli have a number of conventional practices aimed at improving late language developers. One such action involves obtaining a frog and lightly tapping the child's lips, teeth and tongue (organs associated with articulation and all of which can metonymically stand for 'talk') while chanting spell-like phrases. The rationale behind this practice involves, as noted above, the cultural association of frogs and talk. Their species names – *Nge, Engo, Gara, Guarere, Mbola* – compose reduplicated onomatopes for their respective calls. Furthermore, the link between talk and frogs is evident in colloquial phrases like 'laugh like a frog' (Goldman 1983:185: l. 391, 177: l. 38) or *mbola magini to ho wuwa*: 'the frog's throat was expanded', which denotes readiness to speak by analogy with the frog's vocal sac, which balloons with air to amplify sound. In the ecological domain frogs and noisy birds are contrasted in terms of a speech/speechless distinction with non-vocal animals like snails and leeches. For example, a parent will admonish children to be quiet at night by saying *Gindi gangadela bi nimu ladaba*: 'Stop talking and be like the snails and leeches', or to the child who cries a lot *Ega Umiale u la ho wiabo mangaba*: 'You are crying like an owl (Papuan Frogmouth – *podargus sp.*), stop it!'

A particularly significant feature of Huli BT is the occurrence of a small inventory of special lexical coinages that are used in everyday talk (as above), as well as in nursery rhymes (*kai*), verbal play routines, and young children's games. The BT lexicon is presented in Table 1.1 and is consistent with others I have recorded for the neighbouring Duna and Fasu, suggesting an endemic practice in the Southern Highlands region. The salient character-istics can be summarily given as follows:

Table 1.1 Huli Baby-talk Lexicon

Adult Speech Term	English	Baby-Talk	Literal Meaning
A. 1 *Hina*	Sweet potato (*Ipomoea batatas*)	*Amu namu*	–
2 *Du*	Sugar cane (*Saccharum officinarum*)	*Hambu*	lips
3 *Tiabu*	Highland pitpit (*Setaria palmifolia*)	*Habu*	–
4 *Anga*	Pandanus	*Haboli*	–
5 *Lini*	Fruit	*Haboli*	–
6 *Gereba*	Rungia (*Rungia klossi*)	*Abuda*	–
7 *Tigibi*	Water dropwort (*Oenanthe javanica*)	*Abuda*	–
B. 1 *Puya*	Snake (generic)	*Nē*	–
2 *Tia*	Marsupial (generic)	*Auwi*	–
3 *Huru*	Rat	*Auwi*	–
4 *Nogo*	Pig	*Ani nani*	–
5 *Wena*	Fish	*Mena*	–
6 *Yago*	Frog	*Gago*	–
7 *Gau*	Lizard	*Au*	–
8 *Haiya*	Tadpole	*Gagua*	–
C. 1 *Iba*	Water	*Dada*	–
2 *Pu*	Urine/Urinate	*Dada hambira*	'fetching water'
3 *Ti*	Excreta	*Dē/Dī*	–
4 *Ta*	Defecate	*Ega bara*	'hitting birds'
5 *Wali wahe/yomo*	Old woman/female cognate (+1 gen.)	*Bama*	–
6 *Agali wahe/yomo*	Old man/male cognate (+1 gen.)	*Mama*	–
7 *Ni*	Sun	*Aba*	'father'
8 *Ega*	Moon	*One*	'wife'
9 *Dange*	Cowrie shell	*Gange*	–
10 *Ira*	Fire/anything dangerous	*Nē*	–
D. 1 *Hale*	Ears	*Hale nano/ kope nainya*	'mushrooms'
2 *Gi/Ge hondone*	Fingers/toes	*Gi/Ge goloma*	'short digits'
3 *Gi*	Hand	*Ame/Dabi*	–
4 *Ngui*	Nose	*Iba gendo*	'water source'
5 *Ge*	Leg	*Be gauni*	'new bamboo'
6 *Wi*	Penis	*Anga*	'pandanus nut'
7 *Hamba*	Vagina	*Mbare/mburu mbare*	'water insect (?)'
8 *Here*	Buttocks	*Nanombe*	'mushroom'

Table 1.1 Huli baby-talk lexicon (*continued*)

Adult speech term	English	Baby-talk	Literal meaning
9 *Haguene*	Head	*Hubi gaiya/ mambu*	'taro'
10 *Manda iri*	Head hair	*Gulu abai*	'marsupial fur'
11 *Andu/Andu ibane*	Breast/breast milk	*Amu*	'mother/dearest one'
12 *Gi/Ge*	Hands/legs	*Hariagani*	'roads/tracks'
E. 1 *Bira*	Sit	*Baba la*	–
2 *Palia*	Sleep	*Abu la*	–
3 *Mali*	Dance	*Handa handa bia*	–
4 *Waya*	Wash	*Dada bia*	–
5 *Ba*	Hit	*Ah Ah bia/da bia*	–
6 *Gali*	Baby	*Ambolo*	–

1   In terms of extensiveness, the lexicon falls within a quite typical rage of 30–70 items (Casagrande 1948; Lewis 1974:65; Dil 1975:20).

2   Huli words are always of the open-syllable type so that vowel endings in the BT do not here constitute an identifying feature as among the Bengali (Dil 1975) or Latvians (Rūķe-Draviņa 1977).

3   It is possible that the incidence of /u/ in word final position, or indeed in word medial position where it is often lengthened, has hypocoristic status, replacing other alternatives in both BT and adult speech. Thus many adult terms having clear affective nuances – for example, breast milk (D 11) – end in /u/, while others often undergo change in contexts where there is a premium on heightened emotional significance. *Ainya/ ama* 'mother' is mutated to *Amu/amuli* in death laments, nursery rhymes and talk to children.

4   As in all other reported BT lexicons, reduplication occurs (as in A1, B4, D7, E3, E5, or as duplicated consonant + vowel forms E1, E4, C5, C6, B6) that is not immediately related to its occurrence in adult speech. Precisely the same occurs in the Fasu BT words wash ([OL] *hea dabu* → [BT] *dada*) or eat ([OL] *nis* → [BT] *mama*). Moreover, there is little avoidance here of difficult sounds such as one might expect in the case of nasalised vowels (A7, C3) which occur in adult Kanada but not Kanada BT (Ferguson 1977:217).

5   With the notable exception of B5, B6 and B7 all the Huli BT forms are full lexical replacements. Unlike all other cultural systems reported, it is not possible to derive these Huli words – through phonological processes of mutation, gemination, deletion or reduplication – from

conventional adult words. No rewrite rules can be constructed such as those given for Berber (Bynon 1977), Japanese or English (Ferguson 1977). This is consistent with findings above about the structure of synonym replacements elsewhere. With respect to B5, B6 and B7, these were among the terms elicited from informants and appear to support the suggested distinction between central and marginal (Bynon 1968: 111) – or core and peripheral (Rūķe-Draviņa 1977:243) – members of any lexicon. That is, B5, B6 and B7 present as candidates in the 'marginal' class (idiosyncratic usages restricted perhaps to particular caregivers and families).

6 Many of the BT forms represent words functioning as exclamatives, imperatives, interrogatives and declaratives.

7 Confirming Ferguson's (1977) predictive hypothesis about BT verb forms in verb-final languages, we find no words derived from adult verbs, no reductions to the imperative form, and no use of colourless auxiliaries, eg. *bia* ('make-do'; E3, E5) or *la* 'cause to' (E1, E2), which is not already a feature of the adult analogues.

8 Precisely as for the Commanche (Casagrande 1948) term for fire, some Huli words refer both to an object and to its associated qualities, eg. B1/C10 *ne* ('snake, fire, danger').

9 The occurrence of certain idiomatic phrases as in C2 and C4 has parallels in other BT lexicons; for example, the Latvian (Rūķe-Draviņa 1977:243) usage 'go to the sleepy manor' for 'go to sleep'.

10 With respect to the domains covered – body parts and functions, foods, animals, kin terms, everyday actions – Table 1.1 confirms the extent to which these areas of experience represent a near-universal set for BT representation. The presence of these categories cross-culturally undoubtedly suggests their experiential primacy for the child, forming part of the 'here and now' (Snow 1979) content of the semantically concrete speech used by caregivers. Penis and vagina appear in all reported lists, and the cited Huli parts (D1–D12) correspond exactly to those found in Gilyak BT (Austerlitz 1956:264).

The constellation of features outlined above demonstrates the degree to which Huli BT is quite regular along phonological, lexical and semantic axes. While thus incorporating all the 'kitchy-koo' (Brown 1977:5) characteristics that identify this register, the BT lexicon also reveals one quite dramatic difference in respect to the body names that makes this a critical case as an example of cultural variability and patterning in caretaker's speech. Moreover, this difference is integrally related to what has earlier been said about the metaphysics of play and pretence. It is not the occurrence of body parts *per se*, or their percentage proportion of the total items covered – Huli 28 per cent, compared with Gilyak 21 per cent, Bengali 17 per cent and Zakho 22 per cent – but rather the fact that this semantic sub-domain has been systematically structured in terms of a corresponding set of environmental forms. The renamings are analogic – 'extensions of words to unconventional referents for the purpose of making a comparison' (Hudson and Nelson 1984:338) – and based on perceived physical resemblances – leg ↔ bamboo, ear ↔ mushroom – as well as symbolic associations, as in the concept of 'fertility' linking penis and pandanus in D6.

Unlike the low incidence of suppletive forms in Gilyak BT whose origins are unknown (Austerlitz 1956:276), the *gange bi* terms of D1–12 (like those of C2, C4, C7–8) are all conventional adult words. Not only is this element of systematicity quite unique in the cross-cultural literature, but it does not occur anywhere else with significance in the domains covered by Table 1.1. They are thus clearly not ad hoc survivals, or loan words from neighbouring languages, but a culturally motivated and constructed set which has to be explained in these terms. Now the degree to which D1–12 is semantically ambitious throws some doubt on the idea that BT is consistently simplified to facilitate learning. The single motive of addressing a child on his/her own psycho-linguistic level – and the related theory that BT originates in the talk of children (Kelkar 1964; Dil 1975; Brown 1977) – seem quite inadequate as an explanation of the analogic renamings of D1–12. Explanation has to take into account what is being learnt from such interaction and what communicative intents are encoded. In this vein the BT terms have adaptive significance for (or are functionally appropriate in) sensitising the child to the kinds of complex multi-labelling typical of adult communicative competence (as outlined above) through the medium of pretence. It is not reading too much into this register to suggest that in many ways it is a 'pretend' code. The use of BT promotes metalinguistic awareness about the place of pretending as a language experience because it disembodies name, meaning and referent, in a manner that allows for a metaphorical masking of a given reality. The substitutions in this body sphere are not arbitrary selections but repose in a fundamentally important way on layers of metaphorical meaning inherent in the paired terms themselves. Moreover, in connections to be traced more fully in later chapters, this elaboration of body renamings and imagery mirrors the structure of identities presented by all manner of frightening figures, such as the ogre and trickster, used in social control routines in Huli.

On another level, the pragmatic intention behind a caregiver's performance is made transparent as an activity that is essentially fun, essentially 'play'. The predetermined set of substitutions involve speech play, a lesson in the ethnography of speaking but, more to the point, a lesson in the ethnography of pretence. In a literature which widely reports folk rationalisations of BT use as primarily 'pedagogic' (Austerlitz 1956:260; Bynon 1968:108), the Huli express a different slant. Huli mothers consistently responded to my request for rationales of BT use with *turu helo* – 'they will be happy.' I would argue that Huli caregivers see themselves more as entertainers and pretenders than language teachers. In stark contrast to the Kaluli, who, seemingly alone amongst Southern Highlands' societies, are reported not to have a BT and indeed ascribe counterproductiveness to such practices (Schieffelin 1979, 1990), Huli do not feel BT impairs language maturation: *ibini manda bialu lolebira awe* – 'when they come to understand then they will say [adult words] later.' None of this must be taken to imply that an absence of BT can be consequentially correlated with a deprivation of 'pretence' socialisation. Rather, it is to implicate, for this culture, a dimension of interactional significance hitherto underplayed, and one that highlights lines of connection to pretence practices in other contexts. Moreover, it is a site where indigenous rationales are seemingly in accord with the analyst's theorising.

This ambience of pretence is to the fore in the varied occurrences and uses of BT. Caretakers everywhere cannot survive by virtue alone; pretence allows them to get things done and is at a premium when they must survive the critical moment of separation from children to attend to other matters. They will entice, cajole, promise, reward or pretend in order to 'secure cooperation' (Merlan and Rumsey 1991:226). Sometimes a caretaker will feel a child's head and announce *mambu gangade de la* – 'the taro is not ready, cook it!', or if a child scratches its eyes *abanaga iba angibu* – 'those two lakes (ie. eyes) belong to your father [leave them alone].' Often a mother will place a bag on an infant's head and recite a variety of food names as she is about to leave, eg. *ani nani honole* – 'I'll carry pig', or on returning may recite a *gange bi* rhyme:

Rhyme 1.4: Ago's Mother
Yaluba 1993

→   *ainyeli amale amu hambu yidogo*
    mother mother breast milk (BT) I am carrying
    andalu dewali wane
    daughter of this many persons
    igiri dewali wane
    daughter of many boys

> *agira dewali wane*
> daughter of how many boys
> *amu o ala ibu*
> come quickly for milk

For slightly older infants caretakers may leave a bag close by to give the illusion that they are still physically present, pretend that 'someone is stealing a pig', or leave a tied bundle with strict instructions not to open it, knowing that the child will be absorbed in puzzlement or will use the time to disobey blatantly. Most frequently caretakers will engage in a game of *gi daga* ('counting fingers') very much in the style of the Western play of 'This little piggy', where there is an inbuilt element of make-believe (Singer 1973), a blueprint of pretence-making:

> *Gi Daga* (each line is coordinated with the counting of a finger)

> *ogo yago honole*
> I'll bring this frog
> *ogo gau honole*
> I'll bring this lizard
> *ogo bombo honole*
> I'll bring this lizard
> *ogo gonalia honole*
> I'll bring this beetle
> . . . [other animals matched with fingers] . . .
> *ogo nde ugurilime yalu pene mbira no honole*
> If the ants are pulling something (eg.pig) I'll carry it for you to eat
> *i ha*
> so you stay

These mundane interactions are of course reciprocated with children equally making pretence with their caretakers, and again there are standard rhetorical forms in Huli for such behaviour. If a parent asks a child to fetch sweet potato from a garden the standard riposte is **mambu laribe?** – 'did you ask me to get taro peelings?', while if asked to fetch water the response is **puya** – 'did you ask me to get snakes?'

What needs to be stressed at this juncture is the developmental membrane that links these kinds of situated pretences, the renamings found in BT and other language interaction, and the whole gamut of child games and fantasy play. All these interlinked, intersecting practices – what might be called the rhizome of pretence – are grounded in the calculus of culturally entrenched synonym conventions. The materials presented here are thus selective lines of articulation, sacred sites in the ethnographic geography of deceit, in which the core transformational act of 'applying another name with its own imported nuances' is realised. Their connections and disconnections merely capture the rhizomatic configuration of pretence itself. One telling demonstration of this ramification of anatomical analogy occurs in the child game 'see and say' (Table 1.2), where the precise images drawn by BT lexemes are rendered highly familiar (cf. Strathern 1975:190 for a similar Melpa game). Participants in the game take turns in asking each other to identify or locate the appropriate body parts denoted by each agricultural play symbol. Example 1.3 is an elicited episode while Example 1.4 is from a taped naturally occurring sequence following straight after socio-dramatic play. As is often the case, the exchange becomes an occasion for spontaneous teasing, as the child who was unable to provide a correct response calls the questioner a 'trickster'. Leaving aside for now what is thereby implied in such an appellative attribution (see Chapter 5), we can note the metaphoric continuity with BT terms in respect of visual concordances – teeth → fence, lips → war drains – and perhaps even deeper levels of analogic meaning. For example, forehead → cleared place draws together concepts about truth and places where 'truth' emerges outside for public consumption:

Table 1.2 'See and Say' [*Handa Laga Bia*]

Conventional Huli	English	Play Term	English
Ne	Teeth	*page/hagira*	Fence
Manda	Hair	*ugu tigibi*	Dropwort
Ngui	Nose	*homa*	Dead body
De	Eyes	*iba kira*	Two lakes
Wi	Penis	*ani/dene*	Thorn/point
Pindu	Vagina	*iba haiya/mbare*	Tadpoles
Hale	Ears	*hale nano*	Mushrooms
Gi hondone	Fingers	*duria pira hamene*	Five or ten brothers
Haguene	Head	*nano ombe*	Mushrooms
Hambu	Lips/mouth	*wai gana*	War drains
Ngui haria	Nostrils	*uli kira*	Two holes/caves
Andu	Breasts	*pongone kira*	Two flies
Wanekui	Forehead	*hama mbira*	A cleared place

Example 1.3 Elicited sequence – Yaluba 1986 (cf. Goldman 1986a:203) PLYS: A (boy, 13 yrs), B (boy, 9 yrs)	Example 1.4: Yaluba 1993 Transcript 26: Tape 9: 220–44 PLYS: Handabe (boy, 6–7 yrs), Hiyabe (boy, 8–9 yrs)

(Following a fantasy play sequence the two boys indulge in a brief game of *'handa laga bia'* which develops into mild teasing.)

B: *Ina anime teneni nano mbira*
  da tagihowa ngago handa
  there is one thorn inside and
  one mushroom growing
  outside, look
A: (laughing)
  wi ogoda
  this penis

B: *Duria pira hameneme mbira kago*
  handa
  these five or ten brothers are
  there, look!
A: *ira kagobe*
  all these pieces of wood?
B: *Ndo*

  No
  i kegoria dege ka
  close to you
A: *ge ogobe*
  these legs?
B: *ndo*
  no

  . . .
  i gubalini naragoni
  it's eating your heart (ie. in front of you)
  gi mbira ogo ge mbira ogo
  this hand and foot

Hiyabe: *tauwa lina kira bedago la*
           there are two flies there so
           guess
Handabe: *i manda nabi ina la*
           I don't know so you tell
Hiyabe: *ina loabe*
           shall I say?
           ah:: galu hombeni andu kira
           beda
           the two breasts on the chest

           wali andu benio::

           women's breasts
Handabe: *iore iba tiridago wa ha*
           you really are an Iba Tiri so
           shut up

Whatever else may be learnt from such encounters – as for example turn-taking, role differentiation or analogic task-oriented behaviour – the pleasure in the language game services cognitive skills of make-believe.

As Strathern noted for Melpa, 'it must provide some kind of means of entry for a child into the adult ways of using veiled speech' (1975:190). The role of such play in nurturing language development is well recognised (Bruner 1983), but here it is the culturally specific types of transformation connected with the body that have a luminous presence. If play reflects the culture in which it occurs then in Huli the body is the super-toy, super-trope and super-symbol of pretence. The saliency of body lexemes here is contrastingly paralleled by the centrality accorded to kin terms in Bengali culture. There the flair 'for elaborate naming and nicknaming' (Dil 1975:14) of kin is perfectly mirrored in the extensive range of BT kin terms. But while cultural variation in particular parts of the BT lexicon (Ferguson 1964:112) is expected, the differential elaboration need not of course be systemic across caretaker–child contexts or in multi-labelling structures. That it is in Huli suggests a development of the argument about pretend rationales in yet one further direction.

Examination of the conventional anatomical nomenclature (cf. Goldman 1986a) suggests an ontogenesis in these kinds of pretenceful interactions which provide a generative logic of body classification and terminology. Such a theory is quite consistent with suggested links between analogic renamings and figurative language (Hudson and Nelson 1984), as well as play theories relating play to language evolution and proliferation (Ratner and Bruner 1978). But what is the evidence for such speculation?

The Huli anatomical classification has no intermediate taxonomic levels, few paradigmatic sets exhibiting inclusion relations – so that body-part terms cannot be organised or described in respect to hierarchical or contrastive relations – and no recognition that certain parts constitute connective links between body levels. Lexemes for internal organs do not reflect knowledge of physiological functions and any prior assumption of formal taxonomic arrangements is inappropriate for this lexicon. The patterning of this nomenclature does not reflect a special concern with illness or the need to make fine-grained identifications of pain/illness loci. Rather, what is culturally salient about the body is not some schema of relations between parts, but the imagery, symbolism and poetry of sound that inheres in the terms and their uses. Over 65 per cent of the 118 body terms recorded are descriptive (imagistic) rather than specific. In other words, there is a high incidence of natural imagery, of analogy, of metaphoric transfer:

pupils	–	eyes' sons (*de igini* – as for Latin)
kneecap	–	hat/cap of knee (*lagoli tangini*)
lungs	–	leaves (*duni*)
heart	–	fruit (*lini, gubalini*)

Not only are the same principles adhered to in the eulogistic analogues –
eg. heart (*lini*) → [*Kai*] *wandari wali* (girl woman) – but Huli personal names
appear to reflect similar figurative emphases (cf. Glasse 1987). It is the axis
of analogy that is the most distinctive feature of conventional anatomical
labels. For some clues as to why this domain should be replete with
descriptive terms it is instructive to examine a little more closely aspects of
their phonological structure.

The presence of rhyme in the lexicalisation of body parts indicates
deliberate ludic manipulation, reflecting the fact that their primary contexts
of use are not illness prophylaxis or therapy, but rather folktales, spells
and narrative genres. They are good to say and many form invariant
rhyming sets, poetic syntagms such as the following ubiquitous sequences:

nuni/ayuni/buni/yabuni/abene/tombene/tini/lilini
omentum/spleen/liver/arse/fat/stomach/intestine/kidneys

tombene/endolobane/tibane/dugutabane
stomach/rectum/colon/small intestine

Body appellations then represent ludic material *par excellence*, and in both
an evolutionary/developmental and a logico-operational sense the nomenclature appears determined by common semantic and lexical patterns
already encoded or realised in child play/pretence routines. The logic of
Huli body names seems prefigured in pretence parlance (of both child and
adult), expressing again the metaphoricity of meaning making and
ultimately of make-believe itself. Children become sensitised at an early
age to a set of ethno-poetic devices that recur through their language-
making life. Talk about the body, across a range of contexts, reveals a
remarkable congruency of constitutional patterns. In the light of such data
I would disagree with Ellen that 'perception and classification of body parts'
(1977:347) is assimilated by children before semiotic uses. The structure of
many of the caretaker–child routines examined here suggests rather the
primacy of analogic over taxonomic information. So in one sense looking
at child behaviour reverses the normal order of priority, by which analysts
commence with what is known about the adult as a way of coming to
comprehend the child. This privileging of the 'other' may need to be
reformulated.

There is yet one further context in which the types of body centricity
and their BT synonyms I have been discussing make a unique appearance.
This is the field of nursery lore and rhymes. The presence of BT here is not
in itself exceptional, and there are indeed well-documented cases from

Latvia (Rūķe-Draviņa 1977), Bengal (Dil 1975) and the Kurdistan Jews of Jerusalem (Sabar 1974). These rhymes serve a number of purposes, from sleep-inducing lullabies to eulogistic incantations seemingly manifesting some '*Funktionlust* – pleasure in activity itself' (Bruner 1983:47). Importantly, they provide entry into cultural expectations about adult roles in addition to a locus of affective images. Furthermore, it is often claimed that many of the motifs and themes in the rhymes reflect social-structural and cognitive characteristics of the society in which they occur. For example, the theme of long life is linked in Zakho to the incidence of high infant mortality (Sabar 1974:327).

Huli nursery rhymes are also known as *kai* and sung exclusively by women at any time of the day and not necessarily with any soporific intent. Thematically many of the rhymes differ according to the sex of the addressed child and appear to manifest two distinct but interrelated ideas. First, a fantasised scene is conjured with prospective wish-fulfilment based on conventional roles for males and females. Boys are linked with actions concerning building drains, picking nuts, ringbarking trees, the hunting of possum, the making of bush huts and decoration; females with garden digging, carrying heavy loads, fetching water, foraging for frogs, rats, etc. These gender-inflected patterns are explicated by way of the functional importance attached to specific body parts for the two sexes. Second, and more simply, the beauty of some body part is extolled through invoked imagery, or the child 'praised' as the son/daughter of a range of kin, or as a descendent of 'fertile' land.

Now the structural schema of these *kai* is one of pronounced syntactic and semantic parallelism such that, precisely as noted above, component lines differ in the minimal respect of having one-word synonym substitutes. An idea expressed in the first line is repeated for several lines following which there may be another transition point with a second idea, which is again repeated using stock renamings. This semantic redundancy, as I have previously remarked, conceals the fact that these substitutions – their sequential relations, pronounced pairing and distinctive rhyme patterns – constitute poetic verse form for the Huli. This structure applies not just to *kai* but to the whole range of female verbal genres like laments (*wali o*) and mouth harp (*gawa*) verses. In Rhyme 1.5, a *gawa* verse, an insult is delivered to young boys, pictured as always 'pretending' they are richer than they really are, with the two main statements of l. 4 and l. 9 repeated with no fewer than eleven *kai* analogues for pig (*nogo* – l. 3). Rhyme 1.6 is a nursery rhyme in praise of a female child's body which invokes the metaphor of a 'strong tree trunk' – the body should 'be like' this in order to perform heavy chores. The verse is built on precisely the same foundations where poetic synonyms replace ordinary-language terms for bag (*nu*) → *waro, warali, mamai,* umbrella leaves (*to*) → *yubili, yubele, dumale, gurubu, gebai,* and grass skirt (*hurua*) → *tandai*:

	Rhyme 1.5 Mouth harp (*gawa*) verse Yaluba 1993	Rhyme 1.6 Nursery rhyme for daughter's body Yaluba 1986
1	*Wi ale tingi hagaya*	*Ainya waro hongo irane*
2	pretending always to have goods	be a strong trunk for string bags
3 →	*ti lawini nogo hini ale*	*warali hongo irane*
4	your boyfriends are looking after pigs	be a strong trunk for bags
5	*hibuna hini ale*	*wagali hongo irane*
6	*agora hini ale*	*yubili* (umbrella) *hongo irane*
7	*awaiya hini ale*	*yubele hongo irane*
8	*parili mindibi ale*	*tandai* (skirt) *hongo irane*
9	it was dark from so many pigs	*gurubu, gebai mamai hongo irane*
10	*pagabua mindibi ale*	
11	*payaba mindibi ale*	
12	*dibulu dibai dawai damona mindibi ale tingi hagaya*	
13	they were pretending they had so many pigs it was dark	
14	*i lawini hea ale tingi hagaya*	
15	your boyfriends were pretending there	

On the one hand these inter-genre continuities reinforce findings about the child's exposure to structuring poetic structures. On the other hand they also alert us to the point that as a resource for understanding key cultural values, and the way certain types of knowledge about role expectations are inculcated or promulgated, nursery rhymes are surely amongst the most neglected type of ethnographic data attended to in Melanesian anthropology. For an understanding of Huli caretaker–child interaction they hold a multi-dimensional significance. The majority of more than sixty sample texts collected are targeted specifically on body parts. Caretakers will dandle, hold, caress, massage and address body parts when singing, and rhymes have been recorded (cf. Goldman 1986a, 1987) for the nose, ears, legs, penis, head, hands and eyes. Children will frequently join in the verse as they come to recognise its predictable pattern. Importantly, there appears a gradation of complexity in themes broached such that the older the infant the more the verse may approximate a mini-narrative ranging over themes like recent events, wars, etc. Precisely as was noted for Text 1.1: ll. 34–6, BT analogues are often juxtaposed in adjacent lines with ordinary-language terms, illustrated again in Rhyme 1.7, which articulates how a boy will use his 'hands' (cf. Table 1.1: D.3) when mature to wield axes and cut trees. Equally, the verse theme may not only talk of pretence but constitute the performative speech act as 'pretenceful' in nature. In Rhyme 1.8, a mother attempts to induce a smile from her son by disparaging his sister, pretending she is worthless and lazy:

Rhyme 1.7 Nursery rhyme for boys' hands Yaluba 1993	Rhyme 1.8 Nursery rhyme insulting a sister Yaluba 1993
→ *Dabi ogome* with these hands	*Gula wali iginime bulebira laruguni* a Gula woman's son will do everything
→ *gi goloma ogome* with these hands	*Gendole wali, Ibanda wali, Eganda wali* a Gendole's woman's son . . . Ibanda . . . Eganda
Gede dibule ayu he will cut with an axe in Gede *gendele dibule ayu . . . ibugu . . .* *ibanda . . . eganda* in Gendele . . . Ibugu . . . Ibanda . . . Eganda he will cut *ala amule inaga ayege dibule ayu* he will cut my pandanus in Ala Amule	*biango one i ngubi o* this smelly dog's wife *magubi o nenege handaga* this sickly sister will just visit people only *manga o biraga* she will refuse to do any work and just sit around

These last verses introduce a final thematic tangent on the whole field of Huli renamings and one-element substitutions. They begin to shed light on how it is that the Huli, like all their regional neighbours, learn the vast repertoire of both place and kin names required for use in almost all speech genres irrespective of gender. Female caretakers inculcate these through their *kai* rhymes collocating names of kin (siblings, and relations at both first ascending and descending generations) in rhyming enumerative sets (Rhyme 1.9: *Habia – Habialu – Harigi . . . Matialu – Matiabe – Mai*), or designating the candidate child, by means of the same strategy, as a son/daughter/grandson/granddaughter of places (Rhyme 1.10: *Limbabu –*

Limanda – Eganda – Kamianda) on which there are mushrooms, swamps, cassowary, pandanus and other sought-after food. Such verses may further incorporate the totemic species of the clan to which the child belongs, as in 'daughter of a pig' for a female agnate of Doma clan. Children as young as 3 were observed in their own company reciting parts of these *kai*, perhaps as self-amusement, but perhaps too as part of fantasised role play, taking the perspective of a mother. This issue of modelling through mimetic performances of oral genres is taken up in the next two chapters in detail, so it is sufficient here merely to indicate that these rhymes scaffold knowledge of the relationships between pretence, parlance, poetry and personae. Rhyme 1.9 gives a relatively simple example of a set of male siblings for a young boy, while Rhyme 1.10 describes mother's brother's places which will cause the child to get muddy when visited because of their fecundity:

Rhyme 1.9 Nursery verse for 'brothers' Yaluba 1993	Rhyme 1.10 Nursery verse for MB land Yaluba 1993
Habia hamene	*ale wane maganeru*
brother of Habia	daughter of these mother's – brothers
Habialu hamene	*Limbabu waru bane baguni*
Harigi hamene	in Limbabu your thigh and calf will get muddy
Habialu hamene	Limanda . . . Eganda . . . Kamianda . . .
Matialu hamene	*abeni lolebira lumbini lolebira*
Mai hamene	we'll say the sides and umbilical will get muddy

But this landscape of nursery lore and BT does more than merely promote metalinguistic awareness of what kind of sedimented levels pretence strategies occupy in the commerce of communication. They contain the elements with which children continue to practise playing. As a closure to this section, as well as a link to the next which explicitly deals with games, it is instructive to note that kin/place names figure in a host of guessing games much like the 'see and say' scenarios discussed above. Text 1.2 was recorded at night between Habia and Habialu (named in Rhyme 1.9) just prior to their going to sleep. It is an excellent example of the interactionally managed way in which appellations come to service ludic intentionalities amongst Huli children:

Text 1.2: (A (boy, 6 yrs), B (boy, 7 yrs)
Yaluba 1993 – Dalu's house

A: *Wandari ainya igiri ainyala lababe*
we'll guess the mother of the girl and boy
>i ala la<
you talk first

B: *i ala laro*
you first I'm saying

A: *o umm (4) wandariore kirago la*
there are two girls so you say (who they are)

B: *o agoha yagi*
on which side?

A: *o larobe*
can I tell?

B: *<berabu ainya>*
Berabu's mother
(3)

A: *AINYA ina ala laga biri*
mother, you got it quickly
(2)
i la
now you give the clue

B: *°kaiyame giname°*
Kaiyame Giname (now name the mother)
.
.

A: = *uru aniwali*
they are from which place?
(2)

B: *ede garai*
over there in Garai

A: *ogo ago haga lone la dai bia*
where did they used to stay, you say it again
((tape intertupted))
.
.

A: *eh*
yes
habe mbira tabera mende mandira ainya tebone umm:: gulungu wane (2) gulungu mbira (2) habe mende umm abago iya ainya mende eh dauni eh:: (1) handabe lone la dai buliya
Habe is one, Tabera two, Mandira's mother three uh Gulungu's daughter,
Gulungu is one

Habe two umm what's-her-name our mother is two eh five (1) wait, I'll say it all again
(5)

B: *o i loliya i manda bedegoore l-lai ha*
I'll say so you finish saying all yours that you know

Playing Games with Pretence, Proverbs and Parables

One of the key arteries in the body of Huli pretence that feeds into the vast organ of fantasy play and compels, if only briefly, some attention is that of child games. Indeed, far more than socio-dramatic play, the topic of games has always engaged anthropologists in ways previously outlined in the Introduction. In one sense the inventory of Huli games presented in the lists below are no doubt deserving of much fuller and more separate treatment than is possible in the context of a book avowedly focused on pretend play. While some of these ludic forms are discussed in more detail in other chapters, I want to narrow my present comments to four particular aspects of the repertoire, which relate both to what has been said in the preceding sections and to what is to come in the expanded consideration of fantasy play itself. I consider then what can be learnt in respect of: (1) the pattern of game terms and imagery; (2) inherent practices of pretence in the game performances; (3) the extent to which the games are mimetic of adult behaviours; and (4) the links they sustain to the panoply of mythological/cosmological themes, texts and talk which further articulate the viewpoint about passageways *between mimesis and mythos*. Huli games do not exist within some insulated interactional vacuum, and they are not somehow impervious to explanations of their aetiology, or indeed the culturally inscribed history in which their forms are frequently etched. Moreover, they cannot be decontextualised from the plethora of routinised speech formats alluded to above, because the pathway between simulation and mythologisation is as much a linguistic as an imaginative construction. The principal aim of the present discussion is to substantiate and entrench the adopted viewpoint as a way of foregrounding the continuity between what Huli children do (predominantly not exclusively) in games, and what Huli children do in their fantasy play. Both myth and play speak to actors and analysts alike in the language of symbols. Indeed, as has often been noted, myths endure 'only in play' (Stone 1971:4).

In respect of the four aspects discriminated above, I make the following observations.

1 Much as is found cross-culturally for game appellations, eleven (see list of 'Traditional Huli children's games' below: 1–8, 15, 28–9) of the

twenty-nine game terms recorded are reduplicative in nature. Moreover, their English analogues are frequently structured in precisely the same manner:

> *hawanga polanga*
> *pendo pendo*　　} 'roly-poly'
> *mbili gili*

In some cases the name is onomatopoetic in the sense of replicating a particular 'sound' heard (29), but in other cases considerable manipulation of the OL terms has occurred to derive a rhyming game name; for example, in (28) *dugulano* from '*dugua*' and *begelano* from '*beregeda*', or in (1) and (3) non-conventional suffixed forms of OL lexemes occur. Precisely as was found to be the case with both the BT and body lexicons, these terms make good talk and this explains why, for example, they are particularly chosen for rhetorical speech forms such as the adage noted in the Preface, which combines *agoba kiruba* (1) and *mbola toladago* (4). In most cases these game terms are recognisably based on words that semantically convey the action of, or some participating gesture in, the game, such as in (3) where 'spinning around' recalls the spinning motion of hands when weaving string bags or string aprons. Of course it would be false to convey the impression that this list reflects an exhaustive compendium of game interactions in which we find sound play of this type. There are indeed many sequences which, for example, approximate to Western pretences of 'now you see it now you don't'. In the routine below utterances are coordinated with non-verbal gestures which make an offer and then retract it. A clenched fist is produced while uttering the first term of a pair, and the hand is subsequently opened to reveal an empty palm on utterance of the minimally distinct antonymic form. The sound symbolism of the paired phrases iconically marks opposition:

ogolabo	*tegelabo*
these two	not these two
ogoda	*nogoda*
this one	not this one
mba	*mba tau*
let us go	let us not go
au	*hau*
here it is	nothing here
bole laya	*ega bole laya*
'I'll hit you' he said	'I'll hit a bird' he said

Small changes to the phonemic structure of the first OL terms signal antonymy, producing words that (with the exception of the last phrase) ordinarily are nonsense terms. In these kinds of verbal pretences there is an eventual revelation of the masked reality. The pretender's illusions, as both Goffman (1974) and Gilsenan (1976) have noted, are usually 'taken in the right frame' and the dominance or superiority of A over B is evanescent.

Traditional Huli Children's Games

Game Terms   **Term Structure**

1 *Agoba Kiruba*   [*ago* (which?) + *ki* (two)]
Similar to the Western game of 'which hand is it in?' One player conceals a stick in one hand, folding the arms, and the other player has to guess which hand the stick is hidden in.

2 *Kamu Namu*
Similar to the Western game of 'blind man's bluff'. One player closes his/her eyes and attempts to tag another participant who then takes a turn as a 'blind' catcher.

3 *Wangarere Hongorere*   [*wanga* (weaving, spinning motion of hands)]
Players spin their bodies around to induce a state of dizziness, after which they may fall to the ground.

4 *Mbola Tola*   [*mbola* (frog) + *to la* (fill up)]
Players fashion a hollow pit in a lump of clay with the elbow and then spit into the hollow. Before throwing the ball onto the ground players used to say: '*gugu malibu ho we dodo we*: the Malibu bird shouts loudly and whistles' in the belief that this would result in a larger explosion.

5 *Mbilayu Pilayu*   [*pila* (fall over)]
Rough and tumble, wrestling

6 *Hawanga Polanga*   [*pola* (scatter)]
'Roly-poly'

7 *Mbili Gili/Gili Gili*   [*gili* (drag)]
Players make sledges from banana/nut tree stems and then drag them to the top of a hill. They make the hill slippery by pouring water down it and then slide down the hill. Informants stated they would often pretend they were on canoes (*tali*) in various Huli rivers.

8 *Pendo Pendo*   [*pendo* (roll)]
Players roll down hills or along the ground, often clasping a small log.

9 *Tia Abi Nogo Abi*   [*tia abi* (compensation for possum), *nogo abi* (compensation for pig)]
Two players link arms to form a seat while a third player sits or lies across in the middle of the seat. The players intone a chant while raising

and lowering their arms before finally dumping the prone player on the ground on the last utterance of '*wea*'. The two following examples of chants show changes over time:

(a) [elicited from memory – c. 1940]: *Yawa* (ferns): *Dindiwa* (mushroom) / *Muni* (anus): *Timuni* (anus)

(b) [observed; 1993]: *Amu ibira aida* (who is coming there?) / *De ngole* (looks up to see): *Deni ngole* (putting it on the eyes) / *Gua ambu* (?): *Gula gula* (feather decoration) / *Gula ambu* (praise term: feather decoration): *Gula gula* (feather decoration) / *Dabura wabu* (praise term): *Dabu dabu* (things in the hand) / *Pora anda* (?): *Yali yale* (holding) / *Bai iba* (tree sap): *Tanke iba* (tank water) / *Balu* (hitting): *Baboraya* (?) / *Wea*

10 **Tiari Nogo**   [*tiari* (divination) *nogo* (pig)]

A form of 'wheelbarrows' where one player holds the legs and lower body of another player, who then walks on his/her hands. The action is physically reminiscent of the way in which a half side of pig was traditionally placed on a platform in *Tiari* forensic divination and the end of the platform was then held and shaken by the diviner.

11 **Baya Horo Dawe**   [*mali/gereye* (celebratory dances) of *Baya*
Gereye/Iba Tiri Mali/   *Horo* (ogre) or *Iba Tiri* (trickster)]
Wai

Players mimic ceremonial dances. They take dried berries and place them in pandanus nut leaves, which are then tied as a bundle to create a rattle. Often they clap hands against holes in logs to simulate a drum sound. They may also adorn themselves with *angiyeli* (*micanthus floridulus*) ferns.

12 **Baya Horo Ibira**   [*Baya Horo* (ogre) *ibira* (is coming)]

One player decides to dress up as an ogre. He/she ties a piece of string around the nose, tongue and chin, and places a bent stick into each nostril. Two boar's tusks protrude from the mouth, and the head or body is dressed with ferns and feathers. The intention is to frighten children who are crying in the expectation that they will forget the temporary absence of their parents.

13 **Tiari, Berolo, Halaga**

All three terms reference traditional Huli divination procedures which were often copied by children as play forms. In the event, for example, that a child blames another for smelling, stealing or defecating, all candidate culprits are represented by a finger on the chosen diviner's hand. The diviner may then spit into the middle of the palm before shaking the hand to see along which finger the spit moves, thereby indicating the guilty party.

14 ***Iba Tiri Ge Koya/Pero***   [*Iba Tiri* (trickster) *ge* (legs) *koya* (deceiving)/
                                          pero (tongs)]
A blade of grass is obtained and progressively split into a figure 'N'
and then a figure 'X' to give the illusion of two legs or a pair of tongs.

15 ***Puda Bambuda***   [*puda* (cut) *bambuda* (fill up)]
One or more players will obtain some *payabu* (*cordyline fruticosa*) leaves
and then place some well-chewed *gereba* (*rungia klossii*) leaves on it
before making a bundle of them both. The bundle is then squeezed in
the fingers or exchanged with another player while silently wishing
for some desired object like an axe, oil, shell, feather, etc. The players
might further agree as a joke to pretend to eat the bundles.

16 ***Gambe Ya Ira Ya***   [*gambe* (pitpit)/*ira* (stick) *ya* (hold)]
Four or more sets of different-size sticks are made and the object of the
game is to amass a whole set. Each player passes unwanted sticks
behind his/her back to other players until she/he gets a full set of the
desired-length sticks.

17 ***Gi Hamua***   [*gi hamua* (possum claws/leprosy)]
One player crosses the fingers over each other on each hand and says
to another child: '*i ainya yago mbola minalu heria iba poragola howa nogo
hina ogo miabe nabene ogo miabe*: while your mother was collecting frogs
in the river she drowned so you give this much sweet potato to the
pigs and have this much for yourself.' The twisted fingers represent
amounts of sweet potato.

18 ***Guriya Ku***   [*guriya* (hoop pine) *ku* (tight)]
Players enter the forest and swing on the tree vines. Traditionally, as
they were about to jump they would shout, '*guriya ku ku*: rope tighten,
tighten.' When swinging to one end they would say, '*ale ale ale*' and
when returning utter, '*ango ango ango*'. Players now talk of going to
particular destinations as if they were 'flying' on an aircraft.

19 ***Bendele Gini/Pele gono***   [*gini* (playing) *bendele* (bending)/*pele* (let go)
                                          gono (trap)]
One player obtains a long stick, then bends and plants it while hiding
in the bush. The other players will look for the secreted player and
when close the first player will let the stick unbend so that it hits one
of the other players.

20 ***Kundu Pai***   [*kundu* (hide), *pai* (surprise)]
Peekaboo

21 **Throwing games**
    (a) *Waru gini*: mud throwing
    (b) *Gambe kodaya gini*: throwing the tops of pitpit
    (c) *Poge li*: throwing the fig-tree fruit

(d) *Hongo li gini*: throwing beads

(e) *Danda timu*: shooting with pitpit and kunai-grass bow and arrows

(f) *Dagi wai*: fighting with the curled ends of ferns

22 **Dolls**

Players would obtain some mud and then fashion a full head with ceremonial wig out of the clay and decorate it like a Haroli (bachelor-cult initiate) coiffure.

23 *Tia Yo/Biango Tiala*   [*tia* (possums) *yo* (swinging)/ *biango* (dogs) and *tia* (possums)]

One or more players assume the roles of possum and dogs who chase them up trees. Once tagged, players reverse their roles.

24 *Handa Laga Bia*   [*handa* (see) and *laga* (say)]

A guessing game in which one player will allude in the conventional terms of the game to some phenomena and ask the other player to guess where on the body that particular phenomena is to be found. For example, 'fences' represent 'teeth', 'lakes' represent 'eyes' (cf. Goldman 1986a).

25 *Tele Gini/Wai*   [*gini/wai* (playing/fighting) *tele* (spinning tops)]

A row of five small wooden stakes is placed by two players at opposite ends of a rectangle in the earth. Each player takes turns to knock out an opposing marker with his/her own spinning top. Conventional terms apply according to how many markers are left. In descending order these are: 'five..four..axe..bow..mother's string bag'. 'One string bag' signals the bagging of all markers. In Foi the game is called *sugu*, and the rows represent villages between which a state of war obtains.

26 *Iba Paya Dugua*   [*iba* (water) *paya* (close) *dugua* (open)]

One or more players stop the flow of water in one location while another blocks water further along its stream. They then unblock and block again to test if the water collapses the makeshift dam.

27 **Hand Games**

(a) one player clenches a fist while another pinches the top skin to produce the response of '*mmmm*';

(b) one player obtains a stick and then pretends by sleight of hand to push it through a finger or through his mouth as a trick.

28 *Dugulano Begelano*   [*dugu* (pull out) *be(re)ge* (turn around)]

Players pretend to cook one of the participants in a fire, leaving the last one to burn, and then act out a scene where compensation is demanded by the parents of the dead child.

29 **Pu Abu**   [sound of the whirling toy in the wind]
A flat piece of wood is fashioned and a hole made in the end, to which
is tied a piece of string, and the player whirls this around so as to
produce a continuous humming sound. Another variant of the toy is
made from a bowed piece of wood and grass.

Introduced games observed at Yaluba

Game Terms   **Term Structure**

1 **Wena Be Garo**   [*wena* (fish) + *be* (can) + *garo* (car: pidgin)]
Using a long stick at the end of which is attached a horseshoe-shaped
piece of tin, the player will 'drive' a tin lid which is called the 'car'.
Alternatively, a piece of bark is used to drive a hoop made of cane.

2 **Mbira Kira**   [*mbira* (one) + *kira* (two)]
A game of tag involving two or more players. Some players will hide
while another player shuts his/her eyes while holding onto a stick and
then counts to fifteen. The object of the game is to discover a hidden
player, call his/her name, and then touch the stick before she/he
does.

3 **Butterfly Ainya Abala**   [butterfly (pidgin) + *ainya* (mother) + *aba*
                                  (father)]
Involves two or more players who seek to increase the distance between
horizontally placed sticks on the ground, thus increasing the level of
difficulty involved in stretching the steps between the markers. The first
player who sets the marker sticks is called 'mother'. One variant on this
game is known as **Pegi** [pegs: pidgin], in which players attempt to
traverse ground between two sticks before being tagged.

4 **Ira Hangaga**   [*ira* (stick) + *hangaga* (planting)]
Two players each with three sticks take turns to 'plant' their sticks at
the corners, or in the middle, of intersecting lines of a rectangle drawn
on the ground so as to achieve three sticks in a row. A more complicated
version of the game allows the use of diagonal lines and is known as
Hariga Dewa [*hariga* (roads) + *dewa* (many)] (cf. Goldman 1995).

5 **Wada**   [*wada* (water: pidgin)]
A complicated form of 'hopscotch'. Players throw personal tokens (*tubi*)
and move between segments of a box-like structure drawn on the
ground. This is executed with either one or both legs according to the
place at which the tokens lands after being thrown or moved by kicks.
Players take several rounds to finish the game, as a tally (*bebeli*) of
completed circuits is kept.

6 *Marblo*   [*marblo* (marbles: pidgin)]

Players flick marbles against markers to gain possession of competitors' marbles. There are many versions of this form of game.

Traditional Huli Cat's Cradles

Habolanga/Hawalanga (Cat's-cradles)	Glosses
(a) *Hari maga*	Lightning
(b) *Hali biangola*	Possum and the dog → dog eats the possum
(c) *Homane hangane*	Jawbone of a skull
(d) *Gulina pini* → *lini kira deda*	Roots of a pandanus → bears two fruit → disappears
(e) *Tele Tele haba*	Eggs of Tele Tele (White-shouldered fairy-wren) bird
(f) *Tele Tele igini*	Children of a Tele Tele bird
(g) *Dange dole*	Bearing fruit of shells
(h) *Ega palia* → *ega bayadagoni*	Bird sleeps → bird gets shot
(i) *Mbagua haraba* → *baya*	At the gateway to oil → caught
(j) *Yari haba*	Cassowary eggs
(k) *Hari*	Mountain
(l) *Ega abuage pada* → *beregeda yarini beregeda* → *nogo u*	The sulphur-crested cockatoo sleeps → it turns over → its decorations change → it makes pig shout
(m) *Puya*	Snake → runs away
(n) *Hai daga* → *hai unguara*	Bananas → pick bananas
(o) *Hina garaya*	Crooked sweet potato
(p) *Tagali togo*	Bridge across the Tagali river
(q) *Mali komia* → *wali heba*	Komia dance → dancing with women
(r) *Hai page*	Stealing bananas
(s) *Au nu*	Big string bag
(t) *Wai*	War → shortest side will pay compensation
(u) *Anga daga*	Bearing pandanus fruit
(v) *Anda tauwanda*	Pandanus leaf house
(w) *Ayu arela wai*	The axe and the stone war
(x) *Yaluba gai*	Bent Yaluba tree
(y) *Iba Tiri mali*	Iba Tiri's (trickster)dance
(z) *Iba Tiri ti*	Iba Tiri's excreta: the player simulates a conversation between Iba Tiri and a human:

'Iba Tiri is sitting but he used to jump to the other side. "Iba Tiri, you are shitting there!" "Not me!" Iba Tiri says and he jumps to the other side.' (The player makes the knot which represents excreta move along the string).]

(z1) *Iba Togo*   Bridge across water

[→ indicates the figure undergoes transformation]

2 Many of the games incorporate high levels of make-believe most particularly in respect to role transformation, much as was found to be the case for some of the caretaker–child interactions. Taking 'pretend journeys' (7–8, 18) involved imaginal role taking often as an adult or, in the post-contact era, as a 'driver' of cars or planes. Other games more explicitly designate the roles to be taken as for tricksters and ogres (11–12), or hunters and hunted animals (23). Object transformations in which some physical token presents as a 'pretence' phenomena, and in which some conjured state of the world is fostered, occurs in (17) fingers of a leper's hand as 'sweet potatoes', (15) bundles as 'food' or 'wished-for-items', (22) representative objects, the cat's-cradle forms listed separately, and (10) where the familiar 'wheelbarrows' draws an analogy with the platform and pig used in forensic divination. Such representational overlays may be fused to the kind of speech play artifices we have been examining, as is the case in (9). This game recalls the way in which compensation payments are built up and then dissipated, so that the physical acts of lifting and lowering signal changes in compensatory amounts. One of the players will tell the child to be manipulated: *i ainya abalame ogoria paliabe layago palia*: 'your mother and father said "sleep here" so sleep.' Despite over five decades of change, the rhyme structure remains anchored to the same prosodic contours (rising on *abi* and every second phrase) and phonological speech play elements:

	Tia ↑ *Abi*	(1) *Nogo* ↑ *Abi*
(Elicited *c.*1940):	*yawa* (ferns)	*dindiwa* (mushroom)
	muni (anus)	*timuni* (anus)
(Observed 1993):	*amu ibira*	*aida* (who is coming there?)
	de ngole	*deni ngole* (looking to see)
	gua ambu (?)	*gula gula* (feather decoration)

gula ambu	*gula gula* (feather decoration)
dabura wabu	*dabu dabu* (things in the hand)
pora anda (?)	*yali yale* (holding)
bai iba (tree sap)	*tanke iba* (tank water)
balu (hitting)	*baboraya* (?)
WE ↑ A:::	

The striking impression made by the range of games is not simply their inherently pretenceful nature, but the sense in which despite the competitive constitution of many games, such as the ubiquitous 'spinning top' (25), there is no enduring one-upmanship among consociates. As Burridge noted for Tangu games, questions of 'who wins who loses' are inappropriate because 'equivalence' (1957:88) not disequilibrium was the appropriate outcome. In the same vein, pretenders suffer no lasting status; their social biographies are not etched in terms of some prestige/nonprestige label because pretence presents as temporary illusion not permanent monument of truth.

3 and 4 These dimensions to the game inventory are best dealt with together because they both articulate the myth:make-believe relationship. Of the games (9–14, 25, 28) which appear to mimic non-child behaviour directly, (11, 12, 14) stand out in respect of the links they sustain to the supernatural figures of both the trickster and the ogre. No other personae from the vast pantheon of deities in Huli come in for this kind of game treatment because no other spirits are defined to anywhere near the same degree as Baya Horo and Iba Tiri. Here players attempt to engage a 'larger-than-life' reality projected by a mythological world populated by figures of 'unearthly beauty or strength' (Bettelheim 1975:57). Child imagination is fed, by means of *muthoi*, what is quintessentially characteristic of the ogre and trickster as like-minded players. They are uniquely woven into the fabric of Huli play culture, thematically structuring everyday games as well as child pretence play. More to the point, such games are enmeshed with parable and proverb. While discussion of these two figures – their emotionally charged nature and opposed positive and negative valences – is reserved for separate treatment in Chapters 4 and 5, it is possible to note the refraction of this broader oral tapestry in another game domain.

A partial list of 'Traditional Huli cat's-cradles' is also given. Significantly, the category term *hawalanga* is itself etymologically 'pretenceful', being constituted of the morphs *hawa* ('trick, pretend') and *langa* ('arrow barb') to render an image of strings as the various 'barbs' which extend from an arrow. These figures are both visually representational and also 'event' associated. Many of these three-dimensional figures move and transform so that more often than not they require either the assistance or presence

of another person. These interactants thus either (1) facilitate transformations (indicated by →) in the figure by taking over or moving strings;
(2) are used as dupes in a joke (*hawa*); or (3) simply constitute overhearers
of the narratives which may accompany a given performance (eg. (z)). I
want to emphasise that in Huli many of the string-figures are correlated
with parables that provide a supportive context of folklore explanation for
a given representation. The string-figure becomes a symbol of cultural
history. These aetiological tales are frequently told when first showing
children a given figure so that again the game becomes a conduit for
movement between mimesis and mythos. While I will have more to say
about the 'trickster' forms (y–z) in Chapter 5, the following examples further
instantiate and illustrate the kinds of mythical resonances I am alluding
to:

String-figure: [w] – the 'axe and stone war'
Informant: Alembo (Pi clan)
Tari – August 1993

The axe and the stone were sleeping together in a house which had a roof made
of pandanus nut leaves. The axe did all the work such as chopping trees and
providing firewood while the stone never did anything. Then one day the axe
got angry with the stone who never brought anything and said 'you never bring
firewood' and told it to sleep in another house. They got angry with each other
and started to fight and from that time on they became enemies. If you try to
cut stone with an axe the axe will break.

String-figure: [b] – the 'possum and dog'
Informant: Degondo (Koma clan)
Yaluba: June 1977

The dogs (*biango*) and wallabies (*hali*) used to be friends and sleep in one house.
But the wallabies used to do all the hard work while the dogs were lazy and
used to sleep all the time. One day a lone wallaby returned to the house and it
was empty and so they started to insult the dogs in the absence. But they were
overheard by one of the dogs who was still sleeping in the corner and he told
the other dogs when they returned in the afternoon what he had heard.

*Ngui iba gi hamua hororo hea ti mondoni to paya bialu hene dawa mini guya mini
hangunaga keba hea*

Nasal mucus (insult for dog), leprosy, mushroom (looks like leprosy), shits on the garden surface, gets the cooked things and only eats all the time, they (dogs) are lazy.

They have been insulting us he told them. When the wallabies and tree kangaroos returned there was a big war and that was when the dogs first tasted possum blood which they thought was sweet. They had been good friends before but from that time they became enemies. Some possums ran away and climbed up the trees but the ones on the ground were killed. The ones on the trees continued to insult the dogs and called them lazy, called them names, told them all they did was stay around men for food and defecate on the gardens. 'We will stay on the trees and it will be difficult to kill us, and we will stay near caves.' The dog smells possums quickly because from that time they have been enemies.

The narratives do more, though, than draw lines of connection between game representation and myth. Many such parables are further articulated in both lore and game transmission contexts, with adages, sayings and proverbs often used to compose idiomatic insults between children: for example, (1) 'you don't work, you are like a dog that just carries its hands in a bag: *biango ko erebi mbalue ni kego biabe nabialu hene gi no ha hono*'; or (2) 'you are like the dog who shits in the middle of the garden (ie. does not know what to do and waits to be fed): *biangome mondo dombeni ti to werebe.*'

This is a universe which, at least in narrative, presents to children as agonistically constructed and where the texture of interaction is predominantly one of deceit and pretence. Games are part of the complex repertoire of cultural artefacts which inflect this world view and which symbolically are played out against the supportive backdrop of cross-genre explanations and resonances. In over eighty sayings collected, more than three-quarters were accompanied by exegeses in terms of stock parables known throughout Huli (cf. Goldman 1983:245). Such lines of meaning referral and reference can be extremely complex, with allusions made in political rhetoric to adversarial situations via the idiomatic pairings of 'fire and water' (cf. Goldman, Duffield and Ballard 1998), 'dog and snake', 'axe and knife' or 'flea and cockroach'. Fables of this type, and most particularly those involving animals, have long been known to occur across the Highlands region (cf. Wagner 1978:91). However, as told to children they are in Huli invariably transmitted with their associated proverbial form. One is particularly struck in the following example parables by the pretenceful curvatures of experience they must radiate for children:

Proverb: *Galowaba pubu i ki i ki*
            'the Galowaba possum says "your two grubs – my two grubs"'
            [Said by one person to another if they don't get enough pigs or share
            of a bride price.]

Fable: The Galowaba possum used to collect the tree grubs and the male
            would fold one in half pretending to give the female two by hiding
            the fold and saying 'your two' and now 'my two grubs' as he took
            two grubs for himself.

Proverb: 1 *Hali anda yawi bule padebe?*
            'are you sleeping because tomorrow you are going to build a
            wallaby house?'
            2 *Kadia ibu anda biyagola Hali anda yawi yawi bule lalu heneyale kebe
            lolebira*
            'when the Kadia says he's going to build a house then the wallaby
            says "I'll do it tomorrow" so is that you?'.
            [Said to someone who procrastinates about an endeavour.]

Fable: The kadia possum builds a new house when the old one gets bad.
            When the wallaby sees this it used to say, 'I'll build mine tomorrow'
            and then goes and stays in the old house of the kadia. The wallaby
            had all its fat squeezed to the bottom by the dog (see above parable)
            in their war. Its hands are small and always paining which is why it
            carries them up. When they get better it will make its own house.

Proverb: *Andaya Porege harebe?*
            'are you (acting deceitfully) like the *andaya* and *porege*?'

Fable: The tail of the Andaya (tree kangaroo *dendrolagus dorianus*) was under
            the ground and he pretended to Porege that he had no tail. He said
            to Porege (echidna *Zaglossus bruijni*), 'Can you see my tail?' Porege
            thought it was true that Andaya had no tail, so he cut off his own to
            be like him. When he had done this the kangaroo said to him,
            'Brother you have done a good thing!'

The diversity of materials considered in this chapter is a celebration of
an ecology and linguistic economy invested with pretenceful intentions. If
the medium of pretence is the message, it is one that unremittingly pursues
its objectives through deployment of and dependence on intentional
category violations – renamings. These appellative and phenomenal transformations – the very stuff of myth and make-believe – occur in culturally
shaped ways to provide a vision of Huli fabrication that is literally as well
as figuratively an *embodiment* of play and pretend meanings. What we must
take away from the present consideration is perhaps less an understanding
of the myriad and institutionalised behaviours of pretence, no doubt
implicated in the development of the psycho-linguistic capacities of fantasy
players, than their meaning as practices which occupy the interstitial space

between mimesis and mythos. Between spell rhyme and imagined, wished-for state, between nursery lore and tropic body, and between game form, name and narrative history, the analogical motivation to re-present phenomena in the image of an other is palpably evident. They compose a connective skein through which children access and create structured information about the world. The parables and proverbs provide then both a closure on one tangential entry point into the complex modality of pretence, and an opening onto the unique way in which Huli children re-enact their movements between mimesis and mythos in their social fantasy play.

Chapter 2

Pretend Play

[Ts. 17: ll. 91–103. Ayubi (girl, 8–9 yrs) and Mogai (girl, 9–10 yrs) hide inside a house while Joy (girl, 7–8 yrs) pretends to be a 'spirit' about to haunt their home.]

Ayubi: I am the dog
Mogai: we are saying you can be the dog later
          dogs used to be able to see spirits
          come here Ayubi
Joy: (hooting noises characteristic of spirits)
Mogai: *dama ogo ha holebirago handabiya ibu* the spirit will be here so come over
          here and let's see
          be tiabe agalebe toba headago or maybe it's a possum like you can't
          imagine?

Introduction

In both this and the next chapter I explore collaborative pretend play as a particular kind of conversational activity. My declared interest is in the relationship between how talk constructs, negotiates and sustains such fantasy productions, and how this speech articulates, for analyst and actor alike, the pathways from simulation to mythologisation. These considerations thus form a bridge which crosses backwards to the enactment of games as imbued with mythically defined traditions of pretence, and forwards to the specific models of agency, exuded by the ogre and trickster, which scaffold the transformational behaviour of Huli children. But this equation of make-believing with myth-making, the Aristotelian notion that poetic products of mimesis 'shape afresh', gains a new critical edge or resonance in the context of Huli children's social pretend engagements. On the one hand, the evidence indicates these social poets reconfigure their experiences of the world in saliently similar fashion to Western child pretenders. On the other hand, they do so in 'unlike' fashion shaped by the culturally given repertoires of how fantasy is 'spoken'. We need to review here then precisely how Huli pretend play is in this respect 'unlike'.

In their imaginative play routines Huli children will frequently overlay their ongoing fantasy talk with an invoked storytelling genre known as *bi te*, normally reserved for adult narrative performances of myths, folktales and legends. That is, while making appropriate contributions to the planning or enactment of some chosen theme – be it hunting, hospitals, road-making or spirit-killing – they render their speech 'as if' it was also the constitutive lines of some sung myth. The children thus create fantasy play at two distinct levels: first, at the level of some engendered imaginative episode in which they are role playing, and second at a further level where they play again with their make-believe artefact by collaboratively re-presenting it as a simulated 'mythological narrative'. Players are thus enmeshed in symbolic play both within the underlying (or primary) fantasy and at the level of the overlaying genre modality. By thus redefining their ongoing role – say, a 'doctor' – as simultaneously both myth creator and redactor, the pretenders wreak profound semantic and structural reper-cussions on how meaning is constituted *in* these plays, what readings are taken *of* the play *qua* play, and what is thereby implied about children's cognitive ability to mesh pretend identities. Huli children appear to be 'playing with the playframe' (Bretherton 1989:384) not simply as a means of blurring reality and pretence, but as part of their incessant project to 'shape afresh' even their own play experience. This process is aptly referred to herein as 'double-play'.

Why and how Huli children double-play in this fashion are questions variously addressed in the discussion below. Certainly by importing a set of external oral tradition conventions to overlay one imaginative creation onto another, the fantasy enactments are performed subject to the support-ive context of folklore. In addition to the autotelic appeal of such ludic acts, double-play perhaps also speaks directly about what Huli children count as forms of prestigious emulation. Being able to imbue a narrative with authentic cadence and pause structure solicits the admiration of co-players as both audience and speech interactants. Equally, it may signal an understanding that these play artefacts *qua muthoi* symbolically institute visions of the world. Pretend players thus emerge as symbolic *bricoleurs* appropriating their play resources but also thereby instantiating diffus-ionary processes across behavioural domains. Within the cultural economy of make-believe, double-play exposes how porous the boundaries are between the component fantasy frames. Children's experiences of adult play and make-believe, as perceived dimensions of *bi te*, thus become active in transforming the character of their own child-structured play. In later chapters this argument is developed by suggesting the bi-directional nature of such influences. In other words, child actors do not merely internalise, but become part of, the culture as a mimetic resource. From this perspective, mythic traditions such as that of tricksters present an arena for analysts to reconceptualise the links between child and adult fantasy behaviour – they compel us to consider a child-centric viewpoint.

While then I am primarily concerned to explore the substantive nature of double-play, the issue of eliciting children's own cognitive models of pretence is not left untouched. I argue below that transcripts of contrived play elicited by an attentive and inquiring overhearer are likely to be illuminating in this respect. That is, in the very process of 'pretending to pretend' players are predisposed to exaggerate, emphasise and make explicit what they regard as criterial features of collective make-believe play. Fabricated play exposes what actors consider cognitively salient about pretence-making as they attempt to reproduce their models of artificiality for a non-participant audience. These findings represent inferences drawn from comparison of both fabricated and naturally occurring pretence play in which there are marked discontinuities between the relative incidences, and occurrence rates, across the range of conversational moves delineated below. The analysis of these two quite distinct data bases reveals what similarities and differences exist between how children *do* in fact structure fantasy episodes, and how they *think* they structure these same episodes. The methodology employed, as described in the next section, has then profound implications for the role and importance assigned to elicited data in ethnographic and psychological analyses of socio-dramatic play.

The approach adopted herein is informed by three distinct guidelines.

First, analytic priority has been accorded to what Schwartzman termed 'child-structured play' (1983:201) rather than the 'adult-structured' pretences examined in the previous chapter. The focus is squarely on what children do and say when they are by themselves; that is, in self-generated play which is neither inspired, instigated, supervised by nor undertaken in the presence of adults. This engenders a quite distinct set of research foci; in particular, how do children collaboratively constitute and display their understandings of their own make-believe enactments, and how does one elicit such models of pretence?

Second, the discussion deliberately evades (at this juncture) the problems previously alluded to as associated with bifurcated-world models that commonly shape discourse about pretend play. Play is not here presented as displaced or transformed 'normal' interaction. Rather, like other re-searchers (cf. Bretherton 1984; Giffin 1984; Forbes et al. 1986; Garvey 1993a; Furth 1996), I operate with typological schemas cast in terms of 'frames' (Goffman 1974; see Introduction). These are participants' situational definitions, players' intersubjective knowledge that tells them what they are doing is only 'play' – an index of the pretendedness of the activity. Most importantly, the 'in-frame: out-of-frame' division is not inconsequentially interchangeable with a 'real: unreal' opposition. I argue that this latter approach allows us to demonstrate more sensitively how children establish and enact relationships across distinctly conceived domains through their discourse in 'as-if' play. In this context it is important to appreciate that double-play, as defined above, is quite different from either Goffman's notion of 're-keying' – that 'radically reconstitutes' (1974:45) interactional definitions – or Corsaro's notion of 'embellishment' (1992:165), which is an intensification of the primary fantasy frame. Most certainly in double-play an activity meaningful, say, in terms of the frame playing doctors, is transformed or transcribed into a 'mythical performance/narrative about doctors'. But in double-play the subsistent primary activity continues *at the same time* as the narrative game is enjoined and continues to retain its own meaning. This is best conceived as two texts rather than privileging one as text and the other as sub-text. Within the frame 'pretend play' are, one might say, two sub-frames of pretend 'doctor' and pretend 'narrator-audience'. It is this phenomenon of playing at two levels which is not successfully captured by these other proposed categories.

Third, pretend play is recognised here as a distinct sociolinguistic achievement which sheds light both on the acquisition of narrative skills, and on the unique configuration of communicational patterns children employ in these pretend engagements. The strategies by which child pretenders collaborate to sustain their precarious and ephemeral illusions are only capable of being studied through their very loquacity. To gain an understanding of the discourse accompanying child-structured make-believe, in the context of those issues broached above, I have focused on the following three interrelated tasks:

1 provision of a typological matrix of utterance moves that is sensitive to the specific ways in which Huli children constitute their fantasy games as double-plays;
2 a preliminary consideration of the proportional incidences of selected grammatical forms – namely, exhortations (HORT), imperatives (IMP), interrogatives (IGV) and inclusive pronouns (1DL/1PL) – within each matrix category to assess both what consequences follow from switching to genre mode play, and how best to conceive the overall character of the play discourse;
3 a comparison of naturally occurring and fabricated pretence (ie. 'pretending to pretend') to expose what cognitive models of make-believe play children operate with; that is, how children constitute their understandings of their own fantasy activities.

Ethnographic Data and Method

The persistent neglect of children's pretend play in anthropology can only partially be attributed to doubts about how such research intercalates with other levels of data so as to constitute a theory-building part of the discipline. It also reflects problems about how one actually goes about investigating naturally occurring socio-dramatic episodes. After all, such play tends to be extremely fleeting in nature, the actors are highly mobile, and the physical presence of an adult observer is unacceptably intrusive or, at the very least, exerting an influence which itself requires measurement and assessment. In these respects, moreover, there are few programmatic guidelines that might assist such research endeavours.

The data examined in the next two chapters were collected between June and September 1993 and consist of thirty transcripts of audio-recorded play episodes. Initial fieldwork was conducted in the border Huli community of Yaluba, where the ethnographer's house was sited between a number of other households which included children between the ages of 4 and 11. This was the same parish and location in which I had continued to conduct fieldwork over the last two decades and so an understanding of the nature of my presence had already been formed by the community. Before commencement of the study I had noted that a group of players often congregated around an old dilapidated house, some ten metres from my own hut, and could thus be both unobtrusively observed and recorded from within my own house. After consultation with the children's parents, but not in the first instance with the knowledge or permission of the children, their make-believe talk was tape-recorded. In this task I variously employed a long-range microphone as well as a number of radio microphones, the signals from which were received on, and hence recorded from, an FM radio. Acceptable results could be achieved provided recording levels were constantly monitored and the radio frequency band constantly tuned to ensure the best reception from the radio microphones. The drawback of this method, for the lone fieldworker, is that it is not always possible to maintain visual contact with the players and it is acknowledged that an audio-visual replay would have been infinitely preferable. However, in its own way this would have presented even more of a technical challenge for a researcher determined to ensure a minimum of obtrusiveness.

In all instances no other adults were present and the children were quite unaware, for reasons explained below, that their activities were being monitored in this way. The researcher was thus initially totally reliant on the whims of the children to conduct their play within the sound field constructed around my field residence. At various other times parents agreed to allow me to place these radio-microphones in their house to record late-night child conversation. The constitution of the fantasy play groups reflected their residential proximity to me so that the corpus of texts records a distinct group of dramatic personae. Over a two-month period I would have averaged no more than perhaps one episode every three days. The median duration of these socio-dramatic vignettes was 7.84 minutes, with a range from 1.49 minutes to 19.19 minutes. By comparison with other fieldwork topics then it is evident that it can take a long time to build up a reasonable data bank, given the chance nature of such behaviour occurring in a targeted locale. At the same time the very rarity of capturing such naturally occurring phenomena imbues the data with a unique significance for, and insight into, make-believe play. After two months the children were informed of the recordings and were invited to assist in the process of transcription. In addition to adherence to principles of informed consent, involving the child players in the preparation of final translations was vital on account of various inaudible passages encountered, and most especially the use of child cant that was unknown to the ethnographer, the ethnographer's assistant, or indeed most Huli adults.

Once the children had been exposed to the play recordings their sensitivity to my interest and research saliencies rendered natural play discourse in such contexts difficult to obtain. A series of elicited pretend play episodes was then initiated, in which the choice of venue and theme was the children's. Additionally, further recordings of supposedly spontaneous pretence occurred where the researcher was physically in view of the players and which were used as a control sample on the prompted sequences described above. As detailed in the following sections, the structural contrasts between the natural and fabricated pretence episodes were so marked as to indicate that indeed one was dealing with two quite distinct sets of data. To ensure further the data did not overly reflect peculiarities of the chosen field-site, or indeed idiosyncrasies of the play group being monitored, I shifted locale during the course of the study from the outlying community of Yaluba to the township of Tari, where again precisely the same procedures were adopted. This allowed for both checks on the typicality of the corpus collected, and assessment of the continuities and discontinuities in theme, roles, and script development in the rural vs. urban contexts, examined further in Chapter 3.

A brief comment about the transcripts seems judicious here, though a more detailed discussion of the problems attendant on translation and transcription procedures can be found elsewhere (cf. Goldman 1993). Transcripts are as much a product of the reading as they are a product of the writing. The notion of a definitive representation of some speech event is as chimerical as a definitive reading, for the idea that a transcript can serve as a transparent medium through which to access meaning is an illusion. Ethnographers are interpolators who construct the reality of their texts, from which the ethnographers cannot be alienated or 'devoiced'. The transcripts then should not be perceived as 'hard', objective, impersonal data but clearly theory-laden edifices reflecting the selectivity and inter-pretational discretion of their manufacturers. As always, the author must ponder the question 'What to leave in, what to leave out?' in a balancing act that attempts to avoid making the texts unreadable, unmanageable and unpublishable. This is especially critical both where an author addresses a multi-disciplinary audience, and where that audience is likely to be composed of undergraduates and non-academic readers as well as research scholars. In attempting to narrow the disjunction between the 'taped' representation and the original 'real' conversation, the compromises reached here have been guided by the above defined tasks of interpretation. To minimise criticisms of gross distortion or decontextualisation, the reinscribed fantasy talk is rendered in sufficient detail to allow others, whether native speakers of Huli or not, to pose further questions about the data.

While ideally a transcript extract may include vernacular, interlinear, literal and free translation lines – even perhaps indicating tone, voice, quality, speed, amplitude, stress, intonation, gaze, gesture, etc. – such an annotated text runs the risk of encumbering and obscuring, rather than clarifying, the principal arguments forwarded within. While conceding then the consequent loss of communicative channels, the trade-off in terms of the paramount need for accessibility was considered acceptable. In respect of the presentation of texts, those conventions commonly utilised by conversation analysts have been adopted, and where the discussion did find aspects of the verbal performances noteworthy, then other detail has been appended to the rendered extracts.

Bi Te: Storytelling Genre Mode

Bi te are legends, myths and tales told usually at night by men or women to an audience of other adults and/or children. Such oral literature may relate events as historical fact (*tene te*: 'origin stories'), or blend in the one tale both fact and fiction. Transformations from fact to fiction are character-istic of the way Huli construct and construe their historicity: *tene te mani mo bi te holebira*: 'a source story will later become a folktale.' In these respects Huli narratives do not easily fall into discrete categorial classes, nor do they always clearly segment time as between recent and remote past. Recognition cues for audiences include conventionalised openings, names of places, people and rivers (Huli have distinct appellations for fabled places and lakes), and stylised descriptive sections of stories often referred to as *pureremo*.

Regardless of thematic content, in their most stylistically appreciated form bi te are performed in a distinctive and melodic recitation style referred to as *bi mo* ('good style'). Poetic conventions include the use of parallel repetition, context-specific synonym substitutions, and various rhyme devices such as alliteration and assonance (see Chapters 4 and 5). Such storytelling occasions may last anything from a few minutes to several hours, and many Huli have region-wide reputations as famous *bi te* practitioners. Adopting a *bi mo* style, as against a less embellished prose delivery, both imbues the performance with aesthetic merit and invests the artefact with a heightened degree of authenticity that reflects back on the speech prowess of the performer.

Narrative conventions include a topic framework that is constantly repeated throughout the story telling. Statements are thus bounded in a cellular structure sometimes commenced by a phrase or lexeme (eg. *nde nigureni*: Figure 2.1) that functions to announce forthcoming information,

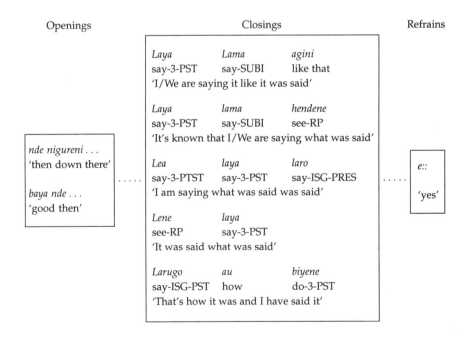

Figure 2.1 Bi te structure

but which itself adds nothing to the story line. More importantly, each cell is terminated by an obligatory phrase which signals the fact that the information given has been reported in the past by someone else, as well as marks the present act of assertion. That is, occurrences of 'said' are frequently metanarrative markers. These parenthetic functions are communicated by inflected forms of the verb *la* ('to say') which can sometimes be terminated by a sustained holding of the vowel /ɔː/ (Goldman 1983; cf. also Text 2.2: ll. 1, 8, 10, 12 below).

Storytelling in Huli is not a monologic but a dialogic structure of discourse exchange. The framing gambits listed in Figure 2.1 not only segment slices of story information, but are sequentially implicative devices in their own right. They signal the boundary of, or an end to, an utterance or turn at talk, cueing the audience as to when to make an appropriate response. Listeners are therefore enjoined at the start of narration (under sanction that the narrator's parents might otherwise die) to acknowledge verbally their continual monitoring of the talk by appropriate refrains which consist solely of the monosyllabic assent lexeme *e* ('yes'). Typically this is nasalised and extended, and acts to finalise both metre and that exchange cell of information.

It is these blueprints of 'fantasy' talk which children access and appropriate from other children or adults. They form part of the communicative ecology of childhood. There were certainly no observed occasions on which such genres were formally taught to them, and indeed children as young as 3 were able to simulate *bi te* talk. By invoking this genre mode, as a thematically undifferentiated form of narrative performance, players pattern their extended dialogue exchanges of fantasy play as a simulated storytelling event. By contrast with 'real' *bi te* performances, all participants are able to take turns at being narrators and acknowledgers. That is, when players make their own in-role contributions to a script as, say, a driver or doctor, formatting the speech with the appropriate narrative cadence, they in turn become myth redactors. The underlying fantasy game is, however, predicated on event scripts drawn largely from outside the *bi te* genre. Moreover, because the discourse format of *bi te* is dialogic in nature, switching to genre mode both constrains players' turn-types and alters the allocation of meaning to utterances. The overlay creates a separate context in which children share multiple levels of understandings about their play texts. Speakers remain simultaneously constituted in the two identities of make-believe actor and story narrator. Statements, commands, insults or teases (see Texts 2.2–3) must thus be contextually interpreted as moves of a narrator progressing a fantasy story. The speaker achieves a measure of distance or alienation from the direct impact of the talk he/she makes. While then a further set of behavioural licences is appropriated by speakers when in genre mode, the overhearing child audience, who also have twin identities as make-believe characters in some story as well as listeners of the *bi te*, are thereby compelled to make explicit their tacit approval and acknowledgement of others' play moves. The genre switch imposes a communication code wherein players' utterances are constituted as solicitations of agreement or solicitation responses. The collaborative nature of joint make-believe is thereby deferred to, and displayed by, this culturally specific form of double-play.

Two issues are immediately raised by the finding that Huli children invoke *bi te* conventions to format their fantasy play. First, what perceptions do actors have of their play creations as aesthetic or mythological artefacts? Second, why have children structured their play with this genre as opposed to some other genre form (cf. Goldman 1980, 1983)? In response to the former question, children engaged in double-play do not instantiate a viewpoint about the factual or fictional nature of their story talk; the invocation is purely one of form, not theme. Such importation of *bi te* format out of its normal performative context is rather a play with speech resources, which is mythic in the precise sense of expressing the symbolic importance of *bi te* in Huli culture. The fantasy play is simply a projection of narrative authenticity onto the primary conversational exchanges. In this sense children could be said merely to refabricate the already 'fabricated world' (LeRoy 1985) of myths, legends and folktales. The choice of *bi te* as against some other genre appears in part accounted for by the above facts and in part related to the following predisposing factors. Research on the solo and social play of Western children (cf. Rubin and Wolf 1979; Scarlett and Wolf 1979) has long indicated the connections between such make-believe activities and the development of storytelling capacities and narrative roles. In delivering a genre mode performance, children appear to establish the sense in which their story productions create 'dramas' (Forbes et al. 1986) that instantiate perceived identities between myth and make-believe. In other words, their speech activity socially enacts their understanding of their engagements as passageways between *mimesis and mythos*.

Bi te is the only non-gendered genre associated with fantasy topics and clearly its prominence in Huli life makes it a prime source of imaginative stimulation for children. What needs to be appreciated though is that since double-play is not adult initiated, modelled or supervised, or otherwise encouraged by adults (though it is adult inspired), we must suppose that it does have an autotelic appeal for its oretic practitioners (cf. Nelson and Seidman 1984). Such appeal no doubt reflects the humour wrought by the incongruity of blending, for instance, an ongoing fabricated scene between road builders and government inspectors with a simultaneously presented and culturally authentic piece of myth telling. This surmise is supported by both the observation that many of these pretend episodes engender laughter among the players, and indeed what is known cross-culturally about the production of humour. Thus while Huli double-play provides an illustrative example of a culture-specific patterning in socio-dramatic interaction, close analogues of such overlaying processes exist within Western cultures. For example, Robin William's rendition of a line from Shakespeare's *Macbeth* in the film *Dead Poets' Society* is an instance in which a primary ongoing script becomes transformed by simulation of a familiar speaking style (ie. identifiable as belonging to the cinematic Western hero John Wayne) to produce humour based on the incongruity of such juxtaposed voices. Similar forms of double-play are of course a staple resource of comedy impersonators and advertisers alike, all of whom may package an underlying conversation into a fantasised artefact that draws variously on other public and familiar communicative models.

Now none of this should be taken to suggest that child pretenders do not also import other speech genres into their mimetic play. However, such instances of heteroglossia are most usually while in-role and are thus reflective, not transformative, of the primary script being enacted. They instantiate the perceived relationships between identities and speech forms. Not only are such occurrences infrequent, by comparison with *bi te* invocations, they can also engender oppositional turns of disagreement. In the example in Text 2.1 Nabili calls into question the appropriateness of Dagiwa's use of a 'pig chant' in the context of an already ongoing play script. She thereby alludes both to the incongruity of two fantasised scenes that are mutually unrelated, and to Dagiwa's lack of orientation to the shared make-believe play. His inexplicable behaviour is formulated by invoking the 'trickster' image (cf. Goodwin and Goodwin 1987).

Text 2.1
Ts. 19:ll. 228–40

[Dagiwa (boy, 4–5 yrs) and Nabili (girl, 10–11 yrs) were engaged in constructing pretend houses when Dagiwa decided to mimic a scene he witnessed two days prior where men carrying pigs for a funeral chanted a 'pig song' (*Nogo U*).]

Dagiwa: ((pretends he is carrying a pig on a stick and begins to chant the appropriate genre *Nogo U*))
           <u>ale</u> ↓ <u>ho</u>:: <u>ale</u> ↓ <u>ho</u>:: <u>ale</u> ↓ <u>ho</u>::

Nabili:	*i mbirali homaragola larebe*
	did someone die and that's why you are singing that?
Dagiwa:	*e* (4.1) *ale* ↓ *ho::* *ale* ↓ *ho::* *ale* ↓ *ho::*
Nabili:	>*O AGILE LALU KA*
	what are you going on about?
	iba tiri ↑ *harebe*
	are you becoming Iba Tiri (a trickster figure)
	mbirali homo ngagola lagago
	we only used to say that when someone is dead
Dagiwa:	*ale* ↓ *ho::* *ale* ↓ *ho::* *ale* ↓ *ho::*

The point to be drawn from Text 2.1 is that no such opposition moves were recorded for the multiple instances of double-play where *bi te* protocols are similarly overlaid without warning. This suggests that child players have a good understanding and tolerance of this type of transformative behaviour in make-believe scenarios – they acknowledge it as a conventional reshaping.

To gain a preliminary understanding of how genre switching operates in socio-dramatic play it is instructive to examine briefly a related type of verbal pretence. In Text 2.2 two boys are engaged in a teasing episode that lasted for over eight minutes. The repartee consists largely of statements about fictitious people reported to have said 'let's go' (a stereotypical speech line in *bi te* narratives). The speech play is conducted almost exclusively in the genre mode (hereafter marked by text shading).

Text 2.2
Ts. 2: ll. 1–16, 66–75

[Dagiwa (boy, 4–5 yrs) and Handabe (boy, 6–7 yrs) had been seated in the reasercher's hut for some time when they spontaneously engaged in the following speech play episode. The researcher had retreated to another room to monitor the recording.]

1	Dagiwa:	<*ya:ma iba mba laya (.) na doma biniya laya* ↓ *o::*>
2		Yama said let us go, he drank and crossed the river it is said
3	Handabe:	*hundiale iba na doma biniya laya:::*
4		Hundiale drank and crossed the river it is said
5		*gubale o bedago ibugua mba laya::::*
6		Gubale ((Dagiwa's father)) over there he said,'Let's go'
7	Dagiwa:	<*hagame ibugua mba laya::*>
8		Hagame he said,'Let's go'

9		*gubale ibugua mba laya::=*
10		Gubale he said,'Let's go'
11	Handabe:	*=ibu mba nale*
12		he didn't say,'Let's go'
13	Dagiwa:	*E-↓E: gubale:=*
14		yes, yes Gubale
15	Handabe:	*=guBE: gubale ndo la::::*
16		don't say Gube, Gubale
17		. . .
18	Handabe:	*dagiwa dandabu ibugua mba laya o::*
19		Dagiwa and Dandabu he has said,'Let's go'
20	Dagiwa:	*digima dibima dagiru mba laya o::*
21		Digima, Dibima, Dagiru have said,'Let's go'
22	Handabe:	*wagiba wagima wagalu mba laya o::*
23		Wagiba, Wagima, Wagalu have said,'Let's go'
24	Dagiwa:	*e:::*
25		yes
26	Handabe:	*wamili bamili wandabe >ibugua mba laya< ↓ o::*
27		Wamili, Bamili, Wandabe he has said,'Let's go'

In the extract in Text 2.2 players construct a fantasy narrative through turn-taking episodes in which they play with 'sounds' – the prosodic and segmental possibilities of name shape often by addition of nonsense syllables. They collocate minimally distinct appellations (ll. 15–27 eg. *wagiba, wagima, wagalu*), and deploy repeated syntax throughout. The inclusion of the name Gubale (l. 5), which denotes Dagiwa's father, intrudes an element of teasing into the exchanges. Oscillations in storytelling roles as between narrator and listener occur (ll. 18–27) so that, for example, Dagiwa progresses the narrativised tease as well as acknowledges in conventional fashion (ie. e:: ll. 13, 24) the story line produced by Handabe. This serves to validate co-production of the genre fantasy as a transformed exchange of insults. What distinguishes this routine from other 'back and forth' verbal teasing is that the importation of the genre is wholly responsible for the sequential placement and shape of a turn such as that in l. 24. We note too that in addition to the sustained vowels on the sentence final verb 'say' and /ɔ:/, even disagreement about what should and should not be said is framed as discourse within the narrative (ll. 11, 15). By contrast with the *bi te* structure delineated above in Figure 2.1, there is a noticeable absence here of metanarrative verbs. Reports on make-believe characters' speech are not recursively marked by past forms of the verb 'say', and the explicit performative 'I/we am/are saying' is omitted. I suggest that the contextual displacement of this genre renders metanarrative marking redundant, as the message 'we are simulating a mythological narrative while playing' is cued by other linguistic and situational factors.

The developed awareness of the potentialities for further speech play within the fantasy frame, as embracing both myth telling and tease-talking, leads the players to begin substituting the human names with special vocabulary sets. First, expletive terms (Text 2.3: 1. 1) normally used to express anger towards dogs – *dondogoli, ngui iba* ('nasal mucus'), *habogumbi, habidogo* and *bandagoli* – are substituted so as to make it appear humorously as if dogs were the story-tellers; second, child argot terms for substances or fluids which 'spread around' – *watagelo/watagulu, padagolo/padagulu, luru/laralo, pedogolo/bedogolo* (ll. 20–9) – occur. We note both the scatological nuances of these latter terms and their structural make-up as rhyming pairs.

Text 2.3
Ts. 2: ll. 111–18, 180–9, 196–205

1	Handabe:	= *e-e e ndo dondogoli ngui iba umm ngui iba habidogo dondogoli*
2		>*emarume mba laya o::*<
3		yes, yes, yes no Dondogoli, Ngui Iba, Ngui Iba, Habidogo,
4		Dondogoli those have said, 'Let's go'
5	Dagiwa:	*e::*
6		yes
7	Handabe:	*o nde::*
8		then
9		. . .
10	Handabe:	= *handabe ema aleya LAYA E:::* *abago dagiwa*
11		he is like Handabe it is said, { what's-his-name Dagiwa
12	Dagiwa:	*e::::*
13		Yes
14		*ne haria ira peloabe!* (1.2)
15		can I push this stick into your mouth
16		*ne haria ira pelaya::*
17		he pushed the stick into his mouth
18	Handabe:	*o nde dagima*
19		then Dagima . . .
20	Dagiwa:	*ti unu biago pudu payabiya:::*=
21		the shit was spread everywhere
22	Handabe:	= *ndo au pudulu paya biama piya::°>pudulu paya biama<°*
23		no, that something was spread, spread, everywhere and he/it
24		went

25	Dagima:	*e:::*
26		yes
27	Handabe:	*watagalo paya biama (.) watagulu paya biama (.)padagala*
28		*paya biama*
29		something spread everywhere, something spread everywhere, something spread everywhere

In the exchanges in Text 2.3 speech acts of teasing are packaged and performed within the narrative conventions of *bi te*. Once again we find the stereotypical response acknowledgements of 'yes' (ll. 1, 5, 12, 24), and utterance openings of 'and then' (l. 7, 18) so characteristic of this genre. Note also how at l. 14 Dagiwa breaks out of the genre mode to request permission playfully to invade Handabe's mouth, switching immediately back in the next utterance to assume the perspective of a narrator who reports his own action in the third person – 'he pushed the stick into his mouth.' What we will find in the materials below is that adopting a genred mode does not constrain the speaker to shift necessarily from first-person to third-person perspectives. The overlaying *bi te* genre here structurally formats the speech exchange so that the play of teasing is again played with to engender an ongoing narrative of the interaction. But such fantasy play is clearly also an opportunity for children to indulge in what is peculiarly childlike about their engendered communications through use of special cant.

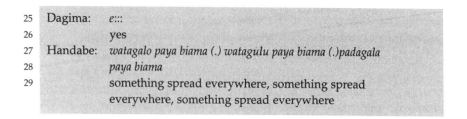

	Non-Fantasy Frame	**Fantasy Frame**
Non-genre mode	Fantasy negotiations Performance evaluations Explicit fantasy proposals Prompt	Enactment Underscoring
Genre mode	—	Enactment Underscoring Fantasy negotiations Performance evaluations Explicit fantasy proposal

Figure 2.2 Matrix of socio-dramatic play moves

The extent to which players will operate a genre switch either within or across play episodes appears (at this stage of my analysis) to vary unpredictably. What is clear, however, from the above extract is that Huli players are capable not only of switching genres but of making conversational moves that are sometimes related to, but not an essential part of, the fantasy dialogue (ie. are in non-fantasy frame). In the construction of a typology of play moves it was clearly important that account be taken of the incidence and structure of such transformations. The matrix presented in Figure 2.2 draws on categories proposed by Giffin (1984), Garvey and Berndt (1977), Auwärter (1986) and Schwartzman (1978), all of whom acknowledge a critical distinction between acts performed within an assumed role, and other acts that are 'about' this acting in role or use of props, etc. The typology is further discussed below. Notwithstanding this lineage, I have more sharply delineated the frame membership of the moves rather than conceive them as lying along a continuum according to whether they reveal or conceal 'pretence' (cf. Giffin 1984:79). All speech acts in or about pretence reflexively comment upon the make-believe nature of the interaction. The matrix then reflects the culturally specific way in which Huli children construct their 'as-if' play. Non-fantasy frame moves which are not performed in a genred mode are, in Goffman's terms, 'a stream of signs which is itself excluded from the content of the activity but which serves as a means of regulating it, bounding, articulating, and qualifying its various components' (1974:210). Where the same moves are, however, uttered in a narrative register, then they fall within a fantasy frame. The quadrant defined as 'genre mode/non-fantasy frame' must perforce remain empty since the very use of any genred speech here would immediately constitute that talk as 'fantasy frame' behaviour.

Table 2.1 presents the distributional frequencies for each of the discriminated move categories (occurring in either genre or non-genre mode) for three distinct groups, A, B and C, of make-believe transcript. These groupings were composed to ensure like was compared with like, as well as help illuminate what cognitive models of pretence children employed when simulating socio-dramatic play. Furthermore, to identify more precisely (1) how genre switching affects the primary discourse structure, and (2) what discontinuities between natural and fabricated pretence subsist, each move category was broken down to show incidence rates for pre-selected grammatical features. These features were chosen on the basis of available comparative research (cf. Goodwin 1988), albeit among English-speaking actors, as most likely to prove rewarding. Table 2.2 takes an illustrative transcript from each of the groups A, B and C to indicate the range of incidence rates for utterance categories that may be compared with

Table 2.1 Distributed frequencies for selected features

		Non-fantasy frame			
		Fantasy negotiations	Performance evaluations	Explicit fantasy proposals	Prompts
Distribution profiles	A[1]	12[2]	3	3	3
	B	6	4	4	–
	C	23	–	1	3
Inclusive 1DL/PL forms	A				
	B				
	C				
Imperatives	A	14	20	–	84
	B	21	–	–	–
	C	18	–	–	50
Exhortations: (I)mmediate/(F)ar	A (I)	–	–	54	–
	A (F)	1	–	30	–
	B (I)	–	–	25	–
	B (F)	–	–	25	–
	C (I)	2	–	50	–
	C (F)	–	–	–	50
Interrogatives	A	29	36	35	–
	B	21	–	–	–
	C	35	–	50	–

[1] *Groups: A (Ts. 5, 6, 8, 13, 15, 17) is constituted of make-believe play in both genre and nongenre mode (total moves = 830).*
B (Ts. 11, 12) consists of make-believe play in part elicited by ethnographer (total moves = 109).
C (Ts. 9, 16) represents the absence of any genre mode make-believe play (total moves = 119).

Fantasy frame						
Non-genre mode		Genre mode				
Enactments	Underscorings	Enactments	Underscorings	Fantasy negotiations	Performance evaluations	Explicit fantasy proposals
50	8	13	5	1	<1[3]	2
46	8	17	12	2	1	–
62	11	–[4]	–	–	–	–
	4		9			
	35		–			
	20		–			
18	–	5	–	5	–	–
15	–	21	–	–	–	–
11	–	–	–	–	–	–
3	–	8	–	–	–	31
6	–	14	–	–	–	30
3	–	13	–	–	–	–
10	–	13	–	25	–	–
4	–	–	–	–	–	–
10	–	–	–	–	–	–
10	<1	7	–	28	–	17
12	–	10	–	25	–	–
13	–	–	–	–	–	–

[2] *All figures are expressed as whole percentages*

[3] *<1 represents an averaged computation*

[4] *A – represents the nonoccurrence of the specified phenomenon*

Table 2.2 Distributed frequencies for example transcripts in groups A, B and C

| | Non-fantasy frame | | | | Fantasy frame | | | | | | |
| | | | | | Non-genre mode | | Genre mode | | | | |
	Fantasy negotiations	Performance evaluations	Explicit fantasy proposals	Prompts	Enactments	Underscorings	Enactments	Underscorings	Fantasy negotiations	Performance evaluations	Explicit fantasy proposals
A [Ts.6]	5	5	5	–	20	2	40	6	7	5	5
B [Ts.11]	2	–	–	–	40	8	20	24	4	2	–
C [Ts.16]	9	–	–	3	81	7	–	–	–	–	–

the group averages shown in Table 2.1. In the next section I define the move categories and examine what aspects of their relative occurrence rates deserve comment.

Socio-Dramatic Play Moves

Underscorings

These are statements which verbally foreground definitions of specific actions or states of being that are often conjointly produced or signalled by non-verbal means as well (cf. Black 1992; Schwartzman 1978; Giffin 1984; Smilanksky 1990:19). They function to alert a present or imagined over-hearing audience to the development of the enacted fantasy script. The majority of underscoring statements occur as first-person performatives – 'I'm doing *x*' – and give a narrative reality to the acts or definitions expressed. As such, these tokens are an important resource with which players choreographically direct and progress their versions of the engendered fantasy, since often speech substitutes for non-verbal action. In Text 2.4, where players pretend to lay animal traps, the underscoring moves of ll. 1 and 18 effect a transition from non-genre (conversational prose) to genre mode.

Text 2.4
Ts. 11: ll. 7–17, 63–8

[In the researcher's presence, Hiyabe (boy, 8–9 yrs), Mai (boy, 8–9 yrs) and Megelau (boy, 11–12 yrs) create pretend possum traps at the bole of an old tree in the forest. The actions were performed for the ethnographer's benefit and the participants were fully aware that their speech was being recorded for later transcription.]

1	Hiyabe:	→ *ah i ogoni- ogoninaga i o bero* ↑ *go:*
2		for that (possum) I'm building a trap here
3	Mai:	*ani yagua* (1) *ani yagua i nde libugua* ↑ *bi* ↓ *a::=*
4		if that's the case if that's the case you two do it there
5	Hiyabe and Megelau:	{ *e::::* }
6		Yes (refrain as in *bi te*)
7	Hiyabe:	*=e:::*
8		{ yes (refrain as in *bi te*)
9	Megelau:	*= e:::*
10		yes (refrain as in *bi te*)

11	Mai:	*ai I nde ogoha berogo*
12		so I am building it here
13	. . .	
14	Mai:	<*ti ndoda i h(h)aliru yagamaru (.hh)ogoha dama pu bialu ti*
15		*anda ogo (.) bigi bigi bialu tini ogoha (.) poradane (.)*
16		not in yours, possums and birds used to go in here and
17		they used to build their own houses and.
18		→ *o ↑ gono ↓ wero::>*
19		now I am placing a trap
20	Hiyabe:	*e:::*
21		yes (refrain)
22	Megelau:	{ *e:::*
23		yes (refrain)

The storytelling cadence and typical extension of sentence-final verb-vowel signal a double-play situation in which further progressions of the fantasy in this mode must conform to *bi te* format. Thus what remains heard but unanswered in the underscoring statement of ll. 11, compels explicit acknowledgement in ll. 5–10 and ll. 20–3; contributions are being constrained by conventions of the overlaying genre form. The refrain responses of ll. 20–3 confirm acceptance of a transformed fantasy play, as well as support the proffered enactment of double-play. This dialogic schema of solicitation–response becomes as it were a conduit for players' reaffirmations of the collaborative nature of their make-believe play. The double-play underscores the joint reproduction of the primary play as also a simulated mythological narrative, and the register is used regardless of whether the utterance is a directive as in l. 4, or a disagreement as in l. 14. The fact that the players even in their 'pretending to pretend' executed genre switching in this manner reveals once more how recurrent such transformations are among Huli children. Again, unlike normal *bi te* performances where roles of narrator: audience are fixed, in this context they are constantly oscillating. If then the genre switch appears to make verbally explicit what may otherwise be implicit or non-verbally signalled, what evidence might be adduced to suggest that tacit understanding of such metacommunicative functions exists among fantasy players in Huli?

In line with arguments advanced previously, I contend that such cognitive models of make-believe are particularly exposed when children fabricate pretence for overhearing adults. In elicited exchanges fantasy actors explicitly display what they consider salient about pretence-making and how they perceive their own activity with regard to coordinating shared fantasy meanings.

Text 2.5
Ts. 11: ll. 25–41

1	Hiyabe:	*agua i nde ega haria bulu bulu lama o porada::go:*
2		good in mine the birds used to flock in and out and now the
3		hole going there
4	Mai:	*i nde-i nde-i nde gabiago ogo ha bulu bulu lama o poradago nde*
5		in mine then, in mine in mine the gabiago birds used to flock
6		in through the hole there
7	Hiyabe:	*oh i nde i nde*
8		oh in mine in mine
9	Megelau:	*oh i nde i nde*
10		oh in mine in mine
11	Mai:	*>hariga o ngagome abago bero<* (2.1)
12		with the hole that is there I am building something
13		*i nde gabiago ogoha* (.) *i nde mbira ogoha anda piya dago::*
14		in mine one bird – in mine one bird went inside
15	Hiyabe: →	*gono weramago*
16		we are putting traps
17	Megelau: →	*ina nde gono weramago*
18		we are putting traps

In Text 2.5, also taken from the prompted play of Ts. 11 (see Text 2.4), players utilise the repeated opening phrase of 'in mine' (*i nde*) (ll. 1, 4, 7, 9, 12) to sustain an extended sequence of talk where complementary definitions are given out, rather than directed to, co-participants. The repetition marks the activity 'as one in which parallel courses of action' (Goodwin 1988:75) take place such that players share and display their orientation to the same fantasy constituents. However, it is the actual degree of extension and structural cyclicity (ll. 11–14) through the transcript that signifies how artificiality is both perceived and reproduced by players.

Text 2.6
Ts. 11: ll. 95–109

1	Megelau:	*inaga ogoha ↑ gono wia ko::*
2		I left my trap there
3	Hiyabe:	*e* (.) *inaga ↑ gono wia ko::*
4		yes, I left my trap there
5	Mai:	*inagabi ogoha gono wia ko*

6		I left mine there too
7	Megelau:	*libu agoha gono wini*
8		where did you place your trap?
9	Mai:	*o gono wia kogo*
10		my trap is placed there
11	Hiyabe:	*i wane gono wero::*
12		I'm still making my trap
13	Mai:	*i wane gono werebe::*
14		are you still making the trap?
15	Hiyabe:	*e::*
16		yes (refrain)

In Text 2.6, which occurs only a short time after Text 2.5, further parallel repetitions occur in ll. 1–5 but are here augmented by both some directed questions about another player's activity (ll. 7, 13) and a genre switch at l. 11. This atypical predominance of parallel repetition and seemingly redundant questioning exposes players' perceptions of the need in fabricated pretence to mark their joint engrossment. Deference to the cooperative nature of make-believe activity must be displayed to both other co-players and outside observers. It is precisely this exaggeration of showing and indexing one's cooperative orientation that reveals what children believe is significant in pretence-making, what they think they do when pretending rather than what they do when pretending to pretend. In other instances of underscorings which solicit agreement or acknowledgement, this deference is grammatically signalled by interrogative forms marked by the verb-final question suffix (cf. Goldman 1986b) -*be*, as in Text 2.7:

Text 2.7
Ts. 17: ll. 638–41

[Ayubi (girl, 8–9 yrs) during a fantasy game in which players were taking the roles of spirits (*dama*) and humans]

Ayubi: *ina gana walu kogo*
        I am here digging the drain
→ *ina   gana   walu   kogobe*
        I+ERG drain dig-SUB2 be-1SG-PRST+IGV
        am I here digging the drain?

In this context it is highly significant that players often choose to underscore their actions with the inclusive 'we', as in Text 2.5: ll. 15–18, that again works to acknowledge co-authorship in establishing shared fantasy worlds:

ina	*nde*	*gono*	*weramago*
we	then	trap	place-1PL-PRES+DEF

we are putting traps

In fabricated pretence play, then, our intuitive observation that players place undue stress on verbalising their performance or play states is confirmed not simply by the manner in which co-players repeat and question, but in the statistical predominance of underscoring statements. In Table 2.1 the gross averages of group B (ie. elicited play episodes) underscorings are noticeably higher than those of the naturally occurring discourse of group A. Although I acknowledge that the sample texts are indicative only, Table 2.2. presents a good illustration of the range of discrepancy found in the aggregate incidence rates of underscorings: that is, the contrast between 32 per cent (Group B: Ts. 11) and 8 per cent (Group A: Ts. 6). Moreover, a similar order of difference characterises the relative preponderance of inclusively marked (ie. 1st PL/DL forms) performatives – i.e. those with 'we' – as a proportion of the total number of underscorings computed: 35 per cent for group B as against 13 per cent for group A. These significant differences in the occurrence rates of underscorings and 'we'-marked performatives for elicited play conversations provide evidence that players operate here with finely etched models of precisely how artificiality is produced and reproduced.

Although by no means common in the data base, underscorings can occur which explicitly reference not simply the make-believe nature of the activity being undertaken, but the extent to which this may exceed the bounds of human imagination as 'beyond belief':

Text 2.8a
Ts. 13: ll. 220–3

[Nabili (girl, 10–11 yrs) during a make-believe session in which actors were pretending to dig gardens and plant sweet potato.]

Nabili:	{ <°*mabu goda* ↑ *ma*°>
	let's dig gardens

→   *ina*   *hiriribi*   *wa*   *berogoni*
    I+ERG   unimaginable   dig   do-1SG-PRES+DEF
    I am digging a frighteningly big one

Text 2.8b
Ts. 17: ll. 541–6

[Mogai (girl, 9–10 yrs) in the same play episode as Text 2.4 above]

Mogai: . . .

→   *ira biagoniore hiriribi deledogoni*
    I have made a fire like you can't imagine

    . . .

→   *ai   e   hawa   godarogoni . . .*
       garden   pretend   dig-1SG-PRES
    I am making a pretend garden

Text 2.8c
Ts. 17: ll. 385–6

Ayubi: →   *aube   toba   hea   mbira   deloleberogo*
              how+IGV   ignorance   be-3-PTST   one   bear+CAUS-1SG-FUT
              I am going to bear fruit like you can't imagine

The point to be made here is that it is not just the cadence and dialogic nature of *bi te* that overlays socio-dramatic episodes, but also (as I argue in later chapters) narrative motifs such as 'like you can't imagine'. There are clear analogies to be drawn here between Huli *bi te* and the status of magazine, radio, movie and TV themes and characters as a source of stimulation for pretence play among Western children. In Huli the oral literature medium is less a source of routine scripts to be re-enacted, or even a set of dramatic roles to be assumed, and far more a resource of speech patterns that can overlay ongoing play scripts.

Significantly, underscorings also occurred in the solo dramatic play transcripts where discourse was equally patterned by storytelling conventions. Children here enacted roles 'as if' there was an overhearing audience of which they too were members:

Text 2.9
Ts. 4: ll. 87–102

[Dagiwa is alone and dragging a flattened tin to which he has attached a length of cane to form a pretend 'vehicle'. He is piling small shavings of wood onto the tin which he pretends are passengers and goods, and is dragging the 'vehicle' around his caretaker's house. Observation and recording were made from inside the researcher's own house adjacent to his play area. Dagiwa adopts the *bi te* register for his narrative.]

1	Dagiwa:	*ummm o nde (3.3)° poragoni::: (1.2) porago:ni°:: (4.8) poragonidagua*
2		*poragonidagua poragoni::*
3		then, its going along, going, going like this, going like this
4		*ai ↑ nde (.) tigua ogoni hadaba*
5		and then, you all stay here
6		((some wood shavings are placed to the side))
7		*ti nde (.) hama ogoria hadaba::*
8		you all then, stay here on the clearing
9		((fixes the shape of tin carrier))
10		(32.7)
11		. . .
12		*agua agua agua agua*
13		going like this, like this, like this, like this
14		*be duni uru wia ↓ be::*
15		put those leaves on ((the car))
16		*be duni uruni (.) hili yalu laro ::: .hhhh e::::*
17		gather those leaves together, I am saying, yes
18		*ede biag ↓ o: (.) damu dai bule: (.) nde (.) kira biago libu pora o ma*
19		to come back and pick that one up, those two they are going, o let us go
20		. . .
21		*ai garo haiya lo wa ↑ hara (.) garo tinihangu ↓ pelo e:*
22		it's getting loose on the car, on the car only themselves will go, yes
23		*agali maru nde (.) ogo hangu nde pelaro*
24		some of those men, I am letting them go
25		*ogoria ogoria ogoria hh hiyu hiyu helaro*
26		here, here, here, I am standing them up, standing them up
27		*mbira hangu, kira hangu, tebira hangu*
28		only one, only two, only three
29		*kira hangu kira hangu nd ↓ e:: (.) au biyadago::*
30		only two, only two, it has been done like this
31		*ogoria nde (1.6)*
32		here then
33		*eh-e-e-e::: (8.4)*
34		*hina mbu uru nde (.) kedo wa haro*
35		those sweet potato peelings I made, I am throwing them away
36		. . .

37	*maru nde: garo* (1.7) *tebira ibu nde- tebira nde: garoni biri yalu pelaro .hhh e::*
38	some people ((on the)) car, three ((passengers)) then, three I am letting sit on
39	the car
40	*ti mani damu dai buwago halimu nde::*
41	I'll come back to get you people later, you all stay
42	*hali mu hali mu e e ↓ e ↓ e::: nde nde::* (2.4)
43	stay, stay

In this piece of solo replica play Dagiwa constantly metamorphoses between a number of quite distinct identities. In l. 1, for example, a narrative statement is made about the movements of the pretend car in the role of story-teller. Immediately in the next line he changes perspective (ll. 4–8) to that of the vehicle driver directing his make-believe passengers to remain where they are. This kind of switching is replicated in ll. 12–19, with the difference that here Dagiwa directs himself as outside choreographer to gather the strewn leaves which are his prop passengers. Now at l. 16, just as in l. 22, Dagiwa self-acknowledges his own genred talk with the conventional assent form 'e', which also occurs in l. 33 as an extended sequence of 'yes' utterances. So in effect he assumes multiple identities as story-teller, actor (car driver), production manager and story audience, structured in part by the overlaying genre form. While appearing to exit temporarily from his make-believe game of 'car driving', in the sense that he is now talking about the play environment, props and his role in their organisation, Dagiwa nevertheless remains well within his fantasised narrative frame of *bi te*, commenting upon and even underscoring (ll. 23, 25, 34) his own actions. Unlike the replica play of Western children, the narrative register compels the speaker to adopt a dialogic conversation with himself while simultaneously slipping between being both an in-role player (driver) and a myth redactor.

These data might seem once more to indicate a real contrast between Huli and Kaluli (cultural neighbours) children. In addition to the now questionable claim that Kaluli do not have a BT (see Chapter 1) register, Schieffelin also records that Kaluli children 'rarely engage in monologues. Talking to oneself . . . is considered "different" and incomprehensible' (1990:99). While it is clear though that Kaluli children do engage in solo fantasy play (ibid.:225) with scripts that are indeed very similar to those invoked by Huli actors, Schieffelin maintains they are not done for an overhearing audience. Now leaving aside the question of what kind of theatrical space the child constructs for itself when engaged in solo fantasy play, it may be that the discontinuities in occurrence of monologues accompanying play do indeed reflect quite different language socialisation ideologies, or differences in the nature, role and place of 'narratives' in the two cultures. Equally, however, there is evidence to suggest that egocentric speech is perhaps more common than Schieffelin has suggested, since Ernst (personal communication) reports observing play monologues for both Onabasulu (Lowlands neighbours of Kaluli) and Kaluli on the Onabasulu border. But beyond the comparative problems posed by such accounts, clearly on the evidence given above Huli children in solo play do create an imaginary audience, albeit one of which they may constitute themselves a part. In this regard Gadamer's denial of 'artistic' status to child play on the basis that it does not 'represent for someone . . . is not aimed at an audience' (1975:97) seems quite wide of the mark. While certainly Huli children 'play for themselves' (ibid.:98), they do so within a make-believe theatre that is a contextually inalienable aspect of 'myth telling' in the culture.

Prompts

Prompts are non-fantasy frame moves which instruct players as to 'how to act and what to say while temporarily abandoning the play identity' (Bretherton 1984:28). As has been noted for prompting among Western children, Huli children may also signal such moves by a distinct lowering of voice (indicated by '°') to mark off such utterances from the ongoing stream of fantasy talk:

Text 2.10
Ts. 13: ll. 88–97

Nabili: (pretending to kill Dagiwa the possum)
           ai i baro
           I am killing (it)
           (laughter from all players continues in the background)
           homolebira
           it will be dead
           (to Dagiwa)
 →   ° *homo wia homo wia*°(2)
           you die (pretend to die), you die

Text 2.11
Ts. 17: ll. 55–61

Mogai:	→	° *ai i gedai*	*ibida pu*
		you (Ayubi) run	away now
Ayubi:			{ *BIANGO I NDODABE* (1.9)
			I am the dog aren't I?
Mogai:	→	° *ai u u lama pu* (.) *joy poradagua* °=
		you (Ayubi) go shouting like this (dog sounds), after Joy

Where prompt-like statements are made in a genre mode they have been coded as enacted directives since they remain within a fantasy frame. Significantly, prompts were absent from the transcripts of contrived make-believe play (see Table 2.1), which perhaps tends to suggest that they have a diminished cognitive significance within the models of pretence held by children. That is, in 'pretending to pretend' the orientation is towards replicating or reinventing for an audience only the fictive reality, not the out-of-frame choreography which otherwise accompanies fantasy making. This finding of marked discontinuities between natural and fabricated make-believe seems further strengthened by the correspondingly lower incidence of fantasy negotiation moves in group B (fabricated pretence) transcripts as evidenced from the figures in Tables 2.1 and 2.2. These moves, which negotiate props, roles, settings and actions (discussed below), are likewise concerned with socio-dramatic choreography. Prompts are invariably issued as imperatives and there was a complete absence of any interrogative forms, as can be seen from Table 2.1. In point of fact the true rate of occurrence of prompt imperatives is 100 per cent; the distribution figures simply representing an averaged total after computing the absence of prompts in two transcripts.

Explicit Fantasy Proposals

While sometimes children simply engage in fantasy play without any overt marking of the passage, at other times players may solicit such behaviour by an explicit fantasy proposal of the type 'let's do *x*.' Analysts have variously referred to this phenomenon as 'formation statements' (Schwartzman 1978:237), 'overt proposals to pretend' (Giffin 1984:87), 'explicit mention of pretend transformations' (Garvey and Berndt 1977), 'announced fantasy play' (Field et al. (1982:504), 'invitations' (Göncü and Kessel 1984:9), 'social bids' (Forys and McCune-Nicolich 1984:166), and 'stage-managing'

(Wolf and Pusch 1985:83). Explicit fantasy proposals (EFP) are used to initiate interactions across frames, or propose new intra-frame activity shifts.

In respect to the coding criteria employed, I discriminated between statements which proposed some thematic development of actions that were normally linked sequentially or consequentially – as in Text 2.12: ll. 5–13, where 'cooking', 'eating' and 'extracting food' represent a condensed script of 'pig feasting' – and statements that indicated a quite novel entry into extended fantasy play, as in Text 2.12: l. 1, which proposes a genre shift:

Text 2.12
Ts. 12: ll. 41–51

[Dagiwa and Handabe were engaged in make-believe play involving the cooking and dissection of a pig. The ethnographer was present during the play and they were aware that their conversations were being recorded. Handabe's sing-song cadence on ll. 5–13 is marked by diagonal shading.]

1	Dagiwa:	→	*ai nogo u lama*
2			ai pig shout say-1PL-(I)HORT
3			ai let's make *nogo u*
4			( ) (1min 9secs)
5	Handabe:		*ai dawahowa birama*
6			ai cook+ABL sit-1PL-(I)HORT
7			let's cook and sit
8			*ai nama*
9			ai eat-1PL-(I)HORT
10			ai let's eat
11			*ai duguamiya*
12			ai pull out-1PL-(F)HORT
13			ai let's pull it out

Although EFPs constitute a very small proportion of total verbal interactions – only some 3 per cent across both fantasy and non-fantasy frames in Table 2.1 – they are particularly revealing of the organisational ethos and structure (cf. Goodwin 1988) that prevail within socio-dramatic play groups. Within the EFP category the total absence of directives in the form of imperatives contrasts with the extremely high clustering and incidence of exhortations. The averaged computations screen the fact that apart from two EFP statements which were declaratives, all other counted instances of EFPs were exhortations of the 'let's' type.

Goodwin (1988) has argued that the English analogue 'let's' imparts, in the context of Western children's play, an attenuation of directness by virtue of the fact that such gambits (1) are future-oriented proposals rather than immediate directives; (2) include both speaker and hearer as potential agents – similar to the inclusively marked underscorings noted above – and (3) resonate with the egalitarian nature of play interaction. They are, one might say, co-operatively oriented locutions. However, inferences concerning the discoursal efficacy of exhortations from seeming identities of form alone cannot be made *simpliciter*. They are problematic inter-linguistically because of discontinuities in the range and nature of syntactic choices in the relative speech economies, and intra-linguistically because there is no isomorphism between linguistic structure and semantic force. Coerciveness must thus be gauged not just from form but from patterns of selection and the manner in which exhortatives are embedded in EFP discourse.

The EFP utterances in the play texts are not accompanied by any proffered accounts which might function here to mitigate their directive force. However, a significant incidence of question-form exhortations can be observed in Table 2.1. In many of the transcripts, where EFPs were coded the percentage of interrogatively marked 'let's' phrases invariably exceeded 50 per cent. So why are these 'let's' statements so often formed as questions? I contend that one nuance of this syntactic choice is that such fantasy transformations are presented as requests for confirmation and that this functions independently of whether the EFP is in genre mode or not. Notwithstanding the above caveats about inter-linguistic comparisons and inferences, this finding appears cross-culturally significant given that parallel results have been given for Western socio-dramatic play speech (Giffen 1984:87; Garvey and Kramer 1989:378; Garvey 1990:207). As Garvey (1993a) has argued, the mitigated style of fantasy play speech here reflects the situational need for collaborative communication if there is to be any fantasy play at all. The interrogative form of EFPs suggests self-effacement (Lodge 1979), deference to addressee, agreement, conciliation and a request for confirmation.

Text 2.13
Ts. 17: ll. 296–303

1	Mogai:		*ai*	*hagira*	*biamabe*		
2			ai	fence	do-1PL-(I)HORT+IGV		
3			shall we build a fence?				
4		→	*ina*	*hawa*	*tindule*	*e*	*ala*	*godamabe*
5			we pretend false garden first dig-1PL-(I)HORT+IGV				
6		→	shall we dig a pretend garden first?				
7			*ai*	*godalu*	*ina hagira ala*	*biamabe*	
8			ai dig-SUB2 we fence first do-1PL-(I)HORT+IGV				
9			or shall we make a fence first before digging?				
10	Ayubi:		*e*	*hagira*	*ala*	*biama*	
11			yes fence first do-1PL-(I)HORT				
12			yes let's build a fence first				

In Text 2.13 alternative EFPs are suggested in Mogai's turn which solicit a response in l. 10. Each statement verb (ll. 1–9) is suffixed by the question marker -*be*, while in l. 4 the speaker references the make-believe nature of the joint activity by contiguous placement of two explicit pretence adjectives, *hawa* ('trick') and *tindule* ('lie/false'), drawn from the folk-taxon of deceit (cf. Goldman 1993:247). As was remarked upon in the Introduction, such lexemes qualify the objects of acts rather than the process of pretending itself. As is discussed in more detail in the next chapter, this appears consistent with the fact that Huli children in fact use very few explicit markers of pretending. There were no occurrences at all (even though such a linguistic choice is possible) of any exhortation literally framed as 'Let's pretend' or 'Pretend that', which would unambiguously reference the pretendedness of the activities. Non-actuality is thus clearly being signalled by the combination of devices such as the content of an exhortative act, the accompanying non-verbal behaviour and the context itself. But 'misunderstanding of interpretational frame occur[s], and exchanges devoted to clarifying the real or pretend status of referents' (Garvey 1993a:253) do arise and demand disambiguation, as evidenced in Text 2.14. Here Megelau has given his tin-fish car to Hiyabe as a 'prop' payment. But Hiyabe, who had always wanted one of these toys, is unsure, or tests out, whether Megelau is 'really' giving it to him, or just giving it in the context of the ongoing fantasy play. This may then indicate a juncture in the play when frames are blurred, though equally it may simply be that Hiyabe seizes the moment of ongoing 'out-of-frame' negotiation to indicate to Megelau an earnest desire for the toy:

Text 2.14
Ts. 8: ll. 447–68

[Megelau and Hiyabe are playing 'road-building', in which Megelau as a government officer gives as payment for Hiyabe's work his tin-fish car, which is to be treated 'as if' it were money.]

Megelau:	*ai ti (.) ai muni biago nawiyagola i garo (.) eberegoni i hawanaga i ho wa halu gerogoni (.) be*
	ai they – there is no money so my car – the pretend one I am giving to you (as payment), all right?
Hiyabe:	*e*
	yes
Megelau:	*i ngirugo i mo yabe=*
	so I gave it (the car) to you and you take it away
Hiyabe:	*=e*
	yes
	. . .
Hiyabe: →	*<garo ogoni i ho wa ↑ halube ai yamo ngere>*
	am I going to have the car for good or just for nothing now?
	((am I going to really have this car or is it just for the pretence?))

Text 2.15 is a particularly interesting occurrence of the above phenomenon since here the response of Dara to an EFP is an oppositional turn that proposes an 'alternative' (Garvey 1993a) fantasy script. Despite such disagreement, not only does Dara choose to genre switch at this time, thus initiating double-play, but the opposition is itself framed as an interrogatively inflected statement of desire.

Text 2.15
Ts. 6: ll. 112–17

[Dara (boy, 5–6 yrs) and Dagiwa had been playing a form of hop-scotch when Dagiwa terminates the game by moving off and suggesting to Dara they initiate a pretend sequence of 'killing and cooking pig'.]

Dagiwa:	*ogoria bia ↑ ba:: ↓ be* (7.4)
	here do-1DL-(I)HORT+IGV
	shall we do it here?
	nogo bo pialu dawababe?
	pig kill go-SUB2 cook-1DL-(I)HORT+IGV
	shall we kill and cook pig?

Dara:	→	*tiaru (.)*	*ina*	*agua*	*buabe:*
		possums	I+ERG	how	do-DESID+IGV
		possums; can I tell you how it will be done?			

What we note is the mitigation of potentially conflictual utterances by strategic choices of syntactic form, most especially the use of question suffixes. Most of the turns in which alternatives were proposed within the planning phases of pretence play were similarly marked in ways that are discernibly different from dispute speech in non-pretend contexts. The questioning format of EFPs does then introduce an element of tentativeness as children create a shared understanding of how the play will progress. Such response solicitations maintain their discourse functions despite ongoing transformations in the primary play frame.

I suggest that such conversions to genre mode may, however, further serve to soften the directive force of EFPs by invoking a communication code recognised as purely informative, playful, and for delectation only. Thus while it is quite possible for exhortations to have the illocutionary force of a command, notwithstanding their grammatical form, the speaker as *bi te* narrator gains a measure of distance from, or diminished responsibility for, any associated coercive nuances. Similarly, in those oppositional turns where speakers voice disagreement, denial or rejection of the previous speaker's turn – what Lein and Brenneis termed 'inversions' (1978; cf. Brenneis and Lein 1977; Brenneis 1988; Maynard 1985; Boggs 1978) – the genre switch lessens the impact of such conflict, thus diminishing the chance of possible breakdown in the play. For example, in Text 2.2: l. 11 when Handabe rejects Dagiwa's statement his use of the genre mode reconstitutes the inversion as plainly playful. Similarly, in Text 2.16 the genre mode EFP in l. 1 is not treated as necessarily establishing Nabili's control over play progress but as an entreaty to others to invent a narrativised fantasy jointly. The utterance triggers compliance in the form of response repeats (ll. 3, 7, 9) by co-players, who thereby partake and declare their agentive responsibility in the fantasy frame:

Text 2.16
Ts. 13: ll. 212–21

1	Nabili:	*ai ina mabu goda ↑ ma::*
2		ai now let's dig gardens
3	Dagiwa:	*mabu goda ↑ ma::*
4		let's dig gardens

5	Nabili:	>*i mabu ogoreni godaliribe*<
6		is that the place you used to dig gardens? (laughter)
7	Dagiwa:	*goda* ↑ *ma*::
8		let's dig
9	Nabili:	{ <°*mabu goda* ↑ *ma*°>
10		let's dig gardens

There are important parallels here with findings made on extended play-centred dialogue among Western children. Nelson and Seidman (1984), for example, identify 'holding' strategies used by peers to share topics with co-actors who repeat the content of each other's talk, and thereby affirm the collaborative nature of fantasy making much as we find in Text 2.16.

Importantly, Huli exhortations have an immediate (I) and far (F) distinction in accordance with whether the mooted action is to be carried out immediately or a little while later, and the suffixes are also inflected for number as between 1DL and 1PL to produce the following four forms: (1) (I) 1DL -*ba*, 1PL -*ma*; (2) (F) 1DL -*biya*, 1PL -*miya*. At this juncture no significance is attributed to the statistical incidences of (I) and (F) occurrences in Table 2.1.

Performative Evaluations

This category of utterance moves addresses the appropriateness, the quality and the 'how' of actions. Like any speech act, performative evaluations (PE) can function in a variety of ways such that they may not always constitute an exclusive category. Frequently they have 'prompt-like' efficacy in the play context. In Huli PEs tend to be marked by the interrogative adverb *agua* ('how') and may be self (Text 2.17) or other (Text 2.18) directed:

Text 2.17
Ts. 11: ll. 79–81

Mai: *ai kome i nde gono werogo*
       I am not placing the trap properly

Text 2.18
Ts. 6:ll. 126–38

Dagiwa:	→	*agua biaga MANDA BIDO*	
		it used to be done like this, I know how to do it	
Dara:		*eh (.) iba ogoreni dalira lowabe::*	
		is it said the water is flowing down here?	
Dagiwa:		↑ *be*	
		alright?	
Dara:	→	*eh ogonidagua nabibe*	
		don't do it like that	
		((they start to put a row of small sticks in the crevice))	
	→	*ai agua bia agua bia*	*agua bia:*
		do it like this do it like this	do it like this
Dagiwa:			{ *e=*
			yes

Notwithstanding the fact that the majority of such utterances occur as either declaratives or imperatives, Table 2.1 indicates the presence of a fairly high proportion (36 per cent) of interrogative forms within the PE category:

Text 2.19
Ts. 5: ll. 112–15

[Dagiwa and Hoyali (girl, 5 yrs) had been involved in a sequence of pretend play episodes which had moved from a doctor–patient script to a 'pig-cutting' theme (see Chapter 3).]

Hoyali:	*INA NOGO PODARO*
	I am cutting pig
	ogoni <u>*ndodabe*</u>
	this no-DEF+IGV
	it is like this isn't it?

This is an important finding because negative evaluations are inherently conflictual and always hold out the possibility that the play will occasion real dispute. Apart from the genred inversions discussed above (see also Text 2.18), most of the other incidences of denial or rejection were accompanied either by some demonstration of 'how *x* should be done', a proposed alternative – 'not x but y' – or some explanatory account – 'not x because y'. All of these strategies for expressing opposition, as well as others such as jocular insults, serve to mitigate open hostility, helping maintain orientation to the play. That players are well aware of the efficacy of such linguistic choices is suggested by those data where children enact a pretend dispute. In these fabricated argumentative routines, players tend to rely on a returned repetition of some accusatory statement or an escalation of the insult, two cross-culturally prevalent tactics in children's arguments (Brenneis and Lein 1977). In Text 2.20, the players replicate their model of how adults would argue about the issue of work payments, which we can see consists of counter-accusations of deceit:

Text 2.20
Ts. 8: ll. 403–14

Hiyabe:	*ke hara*
	he's lying
	garo hariga (.) *ina bu ha lo hewagola tigua bidaba lewane*
	I worked on the road and was resting; 'work' I said
Handabe:	>*KE HARA KE HARA IBU NABI HENE!*<=
	he's lying, he's lying, he didn't work and just stayed
Hiyabe:	= *ke hara*
	he's lying
Handabe:	{ *iname*
	we
	iname hangu bini o bedamagoni ndobe
	only we built it, us here isn't that the case?

Comparison then of pretend disputes with expressed opposition in the planning phase of fantasy play can be revealing of children's knowledge about what kinds of speech exchanges are likely to provoke 'real' dispute. They index a mitigated style of response or opposition which demonstrates again that Huli pretenders speak in saliently similar ways to that found typical of Western child pretenders.

In the above context it is significant that for group A the true occurrence rate of question-form PEs, given their absence in two of the six transcripts, was 55 per cent; no occurrences were recorded for group B (fabricated pretence) or C transcripts. There are two observations worth making here. Even if we accept that many of the interrogatives may be rhetorical in nature, their high incidence rate does appear to offer some insight into how it is that child players share, construct and convey meanings and ideas within the make-believe context. The solicitation–response sequences are crucial in this regard. Moreover, what may be a significant absence of PEs in fabricated pretence episodes suggests perhaps that players' models of make-believe appear oblivious to the functioning or occurrence of PEs in real pretence. The finding here is in accord with what has been previously remarked upon for prompts and fantasy negotiation moves. Performative evaluations signal approbation and disapprobation of other children, displaying how seriously a player takes his/her engrossment in the script. Questioning formats here may prompt acknowledgment of these facts by co-players. In fabricated pretence, by contrast with real pretence, players concentrate on communicating to an outside audience their conceptions of 'fabrication'. However, this appears discontinuous with the structural realities of what really goes on in 'as-if' play. Performative evaluations, like prompts, thus either are felt unimportant in the constitution of fantasy, or alternatively have a low cognitive salience in children's understandings of their make-believe play.

Enactments

Enactments (cf. Giffin 1984:81; Forbes et al. 1986:258; Black 1992:229) are constitutive moves in the fantasy frame which comment on, direct or define the 'state of play' – ie. states and actions. Such moves can be made while a player has taken on a specific role in the script or when assuming the voice of a narrator talking about perceived events. As is evident from the gross percentages of Table 2.1, enactments make up the largest category of utterances, with a mean distribution rate of between 50 per cent and 65 per cent of total moves computed. Across the three delineated groups A, B and C the incidence rates for imperatives, exhortations and interrogatives remain remarkably constant.

As we saw in Text 2.12 above, enactments enable players to develop situational definitions rapidly by verbal means alone. These frequently simulate the natural sequential order of actions that obtains in some non-fantasy context. The transcript data suggest that Huli children, much like their Western counterparts, often operate with event scripts or vignettes of social action. These scripts (cf. Bretherton 1984; Nelson and Seidman 1984) are assimilated from everyday experience and are modified for the purposes of socio-dramatic play. Enactments play a major part in progressing story lines as condensed scripts on topics such as 'pig feasting', 'spirit (*dama*) visitations', 'hunting', 'road building', 'car driving', 'making gardens' or 'playing white administrators (*honebi*; see Chapter 3)'. Enactments of this sort are not just good play resources thematically, but also good speech play materials. In the form of exhortations, enactments which consist of enumerative lists are frequently imbued with rhyme (marked by underlining) and sing-song cadence (marked by diagonal shading) as in Text 2.12 (repeated here in part) and 2.21:

Text 2.12
Ts. 12: ll. 41–51

Dagiwa:	*ai nogo u lama*	←	'let's say pig shout'
Handabe:	*ai dawahowa birama*	←	'let's cook and it'
	ai nama	←	'let's eat'

Text 2.21
Ts. 13: ll. 100–3

Nabili: *ai dawama (.) duguama* ←
let's cook it, let's take it out (after it has been cooked)
dugu nama (3) ←
let's pull it out (after cooking) and let's eat

Fantasy Negotiations

Fantasy negotiations (FNs) are employed by players to demonstrate their continual orientation towards organising make-believe interactions in respect of (1) roles, (2) props, (3) actions and (4) settings. Such interactions are often referred to by analysts as the 'set-up' phase (Forbes et al. 1986:256), 'stage-managing' (Wolf and Pusch 1985:73), 'emplotment' (Garvey and Kramer 1989:367), 'setting the scene' (Smilansky 1990:19) or 'building-up' (Auwärter 1986). They are stipulations which plan for make-believe in respect of procedural or preparatory behaviour. Moreover, they foreshadow fantasy enactment and as such are considered non-fantasy frame interactions. Where, however, they occur in genre mode they become part of the overlaying fantasy structure. Notwithstanding this definition, it would be false to convey the impression that all instances of such negotiations can be unambiguously coded.

Text 2.22
Ts. 17: ll. 1–18

Mogai: >*ai hondo ha hondo ha*<
        wait wait
        ai dama ai hole
        who is going to be *dama* (the spirits)?

Ayubi: *dama nahole*
        there isn't anyone to be *dama*

Mogai: *dama joy ina ha*
        Joy you become *dama*

Joy: *eh*
        what?

Mogai: °*joy*°
        Joy

Joy: *agua-agua buliya*
        what-what will you do?

Mogai: *joy i̯ dama*
        Joy, you are *dama*

For example, while Text 2.22 clearly portrays co-players negotiating their pretend roles at the commmencement of play, in Text 2.23, where actors are engaged in pig feasting, Handabe in ll. 5–10 may be talking as if he were an adult male who merely reaffirms the cultural norm that women receive pig's intestines to clean and eat (cf. Goldman 1983:94). This problem of not always being sure whether a player is talking in-frame or out-of-frame is one many analysts (cf. Verba 1987:24) of pretend play have passed comment on:

Text 2.23
Ts. 12: ll. 79–92

1 Handabe: *AGUA!*
2   like that
3   *ege unugua abago buleni*(2)
4   don't do that with the stones
5   →   *tini* (.)° *halu pubelo dugu nguliya*
6   I'll pull out and give you (Hoyali) the (pig's) intestines to go
7   and wash (Huli custom is that women receive this part of the
8   pig's anatomy for themselves)
9   →   *i walidago*°

10			you are a woman
11	Hoyali:	→	° *ibe*°
12			me?
13	Handabe:		°*tini halu pu*°
14			go wash the (pig's) intestines

What determined the coding in this instance was both the marked low volume in which the utterances are made by Handabe (ll. 5–9), typical of out-of-frame pronouncements, and Hoyali's question response (l. 11) to the allocation of an adult female role. This suggests that Hoyali heard Handabe's utterance as a role negotiation move rather than an in-frame declaration. While in accord with the kind of interpretative principles adumbrated by conversational analysts, and what is referred to as the 'sequential implicativeness' of a turn's talk (Schegloff and Sacks 1973), coding and counting utterances is often an inexact science. Many of the decisions taken – for example, not counting repeated comments in one turn – have been left unexplained, while other utterances represent complex category mixes.

Table 2.1 suggests a not insubstantial proportion (average 28 per cent) of FNs are formatted as interrogatives and indeed we noted the particularly high presence here of (1) verbs inflected with the desiderative suffix *-a* (cf. also Text 2.15) and (2) question-tags within the FN category. Desiderative constructions when formed as interrogatives operate to request permission and thus constitute yet another linguistic gauge of 'attenuated directness' homologous with the interrogative patterns delineated above.

Text 2.24
Ts. 6: ll. 147–50

Dara:	→	*iba*	*ndo*	*lo* ↑ *abe* (.)		*hurua*	*lo* ↑ *abe*
		water	no	say-DESID+IGV		grass-skirt	say-DESID+IGV
		can we say it isn't water ((a creek)) can we say it's a grass skirt?
Dagiwa:		*e*					
		yes					

Text 2.25
Ts. 17: ll. 465–78

1	Mogai:	*Ina*	*plan*	*yaruda*	↑ *loabe::*
2		I+ERG	plan	hold-1SG-PST+DEF	say-DESID+IGV
3		one plan		I have, so can I tell it?	
4	Ayubi:		{ *ina gana daligaore*		}
5			a much higher drain		
6	Mogai:	*ayubi!*			
7		Ayubi			
8	Ayubi:	*e*			
9		yes			
10	Mogai:	*ina plan bu yarudago* ↑ *loabe::*			
11		I have got one plan so can I tell it?			
12	Ayubi:	*e::*			
13		yes			
14	Joy:	{ *e::*			
15		yes			

Both Text 2.24 and Text 2.25 illustrate fantasy negotiations which have been embellished as genre mode moves. The interrogatives compel the culturally appropriate response of '*e*' (Text 2.25:ll. 12–15); its absence becomes noticeable, so that the request of Mogai is repeated in l. 10 exposing again the dialogic structure of cooperative make-believe. It is not just the fact that Ayubi had failed to respond to the solicitation of l. 1, but that in doing so she had failed to acknowledge the genre shift to double-play as well.

In this vein it seems equally significant that nearly 75 per cent of all tag-questions in the data occurred within the FN category. The most common negative checking tag in Huli is *ndodabe* [Text 2.26], very probably a compound of *ndo* (no) + *da* (contraction of *dagoni* (that one)+ *-be* (question suffix)). 'It is never neutral with respect to speaker's belief as to the truth of the statement made. It always asks for confirmation or is rhetorical' (Goldman 1986b:366). Examples of tag-questions in this context are contained in Text 2.11, 2.19 and 2.26:

Text 2.26
Ts. 9: ll. 120–1

Mai: *i garo-i garo yaga ogo*   ↑ *ndodabe* ←
       this is my car which used to be driven isn't it?

In this category of pretend play utterances, devices like tag-questions and other interrogative forms reiterate findings made above that the speech register used is very much a 'mitigated' one that seeks the acknowledgement and agreement of other co-players. The language reflects the structural constraints that are an inherent part of simply maintaining a piece of fictional drama. Equally, they also reflect the peculiar nature of double-play in Huli.

Conclusions

Establishing and maintaining pretence contexts makes demands on co-players both in terms of the kinds of scripts they choose to instantiate and in terms of the way they conduct their talk. Sustaining such play sequences requires children to coordinate their discourse and negotiate their shared fantasy models if such play is not to disintegrate. Double-play as I have described it here services these ends by providing the primary pretence dialogue with a format of conversational exchange that can endure, since oscillations between narrator and audience roles occur without limitation. My concern in this chapter then has been to explore the use of talk in the collaboratively oriented enterprise of building imaginative contexts. In respect of the discourse structures exhibited in double-play, the types of verbal moves I have discriminated and the correlational parameters chosen for analysis – exhortations, interrogatives, imperatives and inclusive number marking – reveal some of the fundamental mechanisms through which Huli children show deference to the ethos of equivalence and exchange. Most particularly I have noted the high incidence of interrogative forms as a prime facet of how players establish and negotiate their fantasy contributions.

But children clearly also bring their conceptual representations of such events to play: cognitive models of their own pretence and indeed their models of adult fantasy making. Their experiences of adult play and fantasy – as inherent dimensions of what *bi te* symbolise for Huli child culture and child–child discourse – become active in transforming the character of child-structured play. Such models are employed on, and indeed can be elicited from, occasions where players are prompted to reproduce fantasy play for a present and overhearing adult audience. They orient interaction to what they consider salient and stereotypical of pretence-making in a way that exaggerates such criterial features. This finding is an inference drawn from the marked disparity in incidence rates of certain types of moves discussed above, and demonstrates the heuristic value of the methodological contrast between naturally occurring and fabricated make-believe play. The analysis of these two distinct data bases has pointed out discontinuities in the way children *think* they pretend and how they actually *do* pretend in a manner that would appear to have profound implications for the role and importance assigned to elicited make-believe data in such research. In all of these respects my findings reflect and support the hardly novel notion that make-believe play is, in complex ways, culturally encumbered; that through play children live or, to borrow an idiom from feminist discourse, 'exist' their culture and history in their own culture making and interpretation.

As previously commented upon, most of the research on verbal fantasy play has been conducted in the context of white English-speaking children, and there are indeed few detailed studies of make-believe play from a cross-cultural perspective. It would thus be wholly premature in my opinion for anthropologists to conjecture in any general manner on variations in capacities or dispositions for make-believe behaviour across societies. Notwithstanding this, the interpretative task undertaken in this book is of a quite different order. It consists of attempting to establish and integrate relationships among layers of data to show diffusionary processes across frames. In this endeavour the drawing of links between make-believe play and myth will inevitably attract attention as forms of symbolic behaviour. But this myth: make-believe relationship is, as we have seen, multidimensional. The cultural repositories of fantasy are raided and reinvented by children not just with respect to themes, but also with respect to aspects of form, motif and performance. Double-play is thus one index among many of the prevailing viewpoint, which unfolds throughout this presentation, that Huli children in their fantasy play present as social poets who move between mimesis and mythos. Children thus sculpt their symbolic environments as scavengers of form and theme in a manner that exposes the kinds of porosity between fantasy frames I wish to explore.

While Huli double-play provides a unique and illustrative example of a culturally encumbered model of child pretence play, the point to be pursued in later chapters is that the very play itself is similarly fashioned by the models of agency depicted by characters in the mythical domain. So the scaffolding nature of *muthoi* is not limited to formatting the pretend speech, or even providing a repertoire of themes or scripts, but in an important sense it provides the rationale for 'pretending' itself. One is struck, in this context, by the noticeable presence in the transcripts of explicit moves predicated on the 'suspension of disbelief' – players attempting to engage a larger-than-life reality (see especially Texts 2.8a–c). This motif is frequently signalled by such adverbs as *hiriribi* ('frighteningly') or *gibidege* ('enormous') or constructions such as *aube toba howa* ('like you can't imagine'). Such cognitive predispositions are naturally enshrined in mythological worlds populated by stock figures of 'unearthly beauty or strength' (Bettelheim 1975:57):

> *pulu yabe kindiru ogoalebe toba hea laya*
> With a flapping bag decoration like you can't imagine
> *geni ge haleru ogoalebe toba hea laya*
> With leg bands on the legs like you can't imagine
> . . .
> *Iba Mulu Lungiya agali igini ndo*
> Iba Mulu Lungiya was not like any man's son
> *walirume bi labe naheaya*
> It wasn't possible even for women to talk to him
> *igiri hegene aube toba hea*
> This was a clever man like you can't imagine

Huli imagination is thus fed by means of *bi te* the need for the extraordinary in social life. It is woven into the very fabric of child culture and child pretence. The massive presence of such routine formulae in make-believe and mythological play emphasises again the permeability of boundaries between sectors of the make-believe economy, as well as the links sustained between the ordinary and exceptional.

But before I consider such arguments in more detail I want to turn in the next chapter to consider the particular aspect of identity-making in socio-dramatic play. Leaving aside issues about ultimate reference points for play itself, the focus will be on the specific roles children adopt, their interactional origin, and the extent to which these identities are constructed by, as well as constituted as, language practices.

Chapter 3

Changing Roles

> The poet should be a maker of plots more than a maker of verses, in that he is a poet by virtue of his imitation and he imitates actions.
>
> Aristotle 1982:1451

Introduction

In my Introduction I argued the case that in the pretence play of children we engage the relation of social poet to fictional voice, of dramatist to dramatic character, and of author to persona. In examining such behaviour we thereby address issues of realism and verisimilitude, of referentiality and illusion, and most centrally of the priority of the word in the commerce of representation itself. As players assign, appropriate and negotiate identities within this fictionalising modality they mimetically reproduce not just social characters, but characters embedded within frameworks of prototypical events and actions. These schematic frames, which represent stylised everyday situations – inclusive of roles, actions, props and routine locutions – also represent shared knowledge. Perceptions of the sequential properties of activities, both temporal and causal, inhere in these social 'scripts', which, as we shall see below, service child play as both objects of mutual attention and cognitive resources brought to the drama. Children's play, it was argued, was in the Aristotelian tradition the mimesis of personae engaged in action rendered as and through *muthoi* – plot-structures (scripts), narrative, speech or story. In part real-world documentary, in part elliptical hypothetical vignettes, these scenarios do not so much falsify the world as offer up a way of 'seeing it as'. This is pretending as an imaginative modality; this is pretending as making narrative sense of the world; this is pretending as constructive of iconic, and often ethnic, caricatures.

Because these worlds are constantly changing and evolving, examining the transformative behaviour of collaborative pretence can provide a quite unique window onto cultural identities in post-colonial contexts such as that of Huli. Moreover, it is a perspective that is uniquely child engendered.

Children by means of their symbolic behaviour 'play society' (Furth and Kane 1992; Furth 1996) such that their representations of personae must surely be recognised as part of the cultural beings of 'mother', 'father', 'doctor' or whatever. The pretences of identity are representational refractions of what roles *are*, and what roles *mean*, in child culture. Because these personative performances are predominantly texts of verbal interaction, we encounter the manner in which children enact their recognition of the relationship between language and identity. What we witness is how actors institute through discourse their intersubjectively shared understandings of how roles present as distinct 'voicings'. Pretence here stands as a commentary on non-pretence. But there is more to the analysis of sociodramatic play than just perceiving change. Psychologists have long attested to the fact that any kind of social learning of role behaviour is critically dependent on actors' capacities to process their knowledge through suppositional 'as-if' reasoning as practised in fantasy play.

In this present chapter then I am concerned to examine in detail the specific interplay between language and role. Pretence identities are refracted through the players' cognitive and behavioural representations such that in the dramatic crucible of social make-believe actors confront each other's definitions of an 'other'. Moreover, these pretence personae may themselves become objects of attention. That is, players out of concern for aesthetic integrity, authenticity and internal consistency in role enactment may undertake to repair each other's mimetic representations. Of particular interest here are the speech resources used by children to signal their playful transformations of roles and props, and the extent to which my findings are continuous or discontinuous with those reported for Western fantasy players. In contrast to the presentation of primary materials in the previous chapter, I shall here anchor the analysis of role transformations to just one complete play transcript. Rather than this text being secreted in an appendix, it is presented within the body of the chapter so that the onus is on the reader to familiarise himself/herself with the text before engaging with the discussion below.

Make-Believe Play Transcript 3.1
Ts 5, Tape 4: ll. 200–89
Extract Time: 6.25 minutes
Dagiwa (boy, 4-5 yrs), Hoyali (girl, 4-5 yrs) –
Yaluba
July 1993

[*While outside the fieldworker's (Goldman's) house the two children began to play spontaneously with my two feet, treating them as if they were child patients in a hospital. I was initially reclined on the ground with the right leg bent, and the left leg crossed over the right so that the foot dangled over the side of the right knee. On each foot was a running shoe with a hard rubber sole. A tape-recorder was hidden inside my shirt. In the short space of six minutes the play text evidences almost seamless transformations of identity and context from hospital rooms to cutting up pigs to anthropologist–assistant to mother–baby feeding.*]

((Dagiwa and Hoyali each begin to pull at the shoe laces and variously examine the rubber bottom of the shoe))

1	Dagiwa:	*i andu mia*
2		give your breast (to the shoe-child)
3	Hoyali:	*i andu mia*!
4		you give your breast (to the shoe-child)
5	Dagiwa:	*.hhuh ai mende mia ahh*
6		give the other one (breast)
7		*ai mende mia (1) halu mende mia*
8		give the other one (breast), do it again
9		(6.4)
10		((Hoyali continues to press her chest up against the sole of the shoe,
11		while Dagiwa continues to play with the laces))
12	Hoyali:	↑ *AI:::::::*
13		(15.3)
14	Dagiwa:	*ai ogoni (.) i govman kebe*
15		all right are you (Hoyali, pretending to be) government (hospital
16		staff)?
17	Hoyali:	°*e*°
18		yes
19		(5.5)
20	Dagiwa:	((addresses the foot-patient))
21		⌈ ((deep voice)) ⌉
22		⌊ *IBI TIgi barabe* ⌋
23		are you also sick?

24	Hoyali:	°*ogo ya (.) ogo ya*°
25		hold this one (foot) hold this one
26		((takes foot in hands and places it down on ground))
27		*ogoria berelaro*
28		I am letting it (the foot-patient) stay here (on the ground)
29	Dagiwa:	*ai ogo- ogobi tigi* ↑ *bayabe*
30		has this one also been sick, eh?
31		(1.1)
32		*be*
33		⎰ well?
34	Hoyali:	⎱ *e*
35		yes
36	Dagiwa:	°*ini yene nahabe*°
37		don't hold onto it (the foot-patient)
38		(12.8)
39	Hoyali:	*ai ogobi (.) ai ogo tigi baya*
40		this one has been sick
41	Dagiwa:	((pretends to give the foot-patient an injection))
42		<*mili biba haya*>
43		the injection is finished
44		(2.2)
45	Hoyali:	((holding other foot))
46		⎡ ((high-pitched voice and lilting intonation)) ⎤
47		⎣ ↑ *oo* ↓ *aa: ge hime wa ka* ⎦
48		ooahh it's tiring (holding the baby) on my thighs
49		(4.5)
50	Dagiwa:	⎡ ((gruff voice)) ⎤
51		⎣ *o tigi benedago .hh harudago bero* ⎦
52		it's been sick so I am looking after it
53		((coughs)) (1) *ogoria tigi* ↑ *bayabe*
54		has this one been sick too?
55		((feels parts of my leg))
56	Hoyali:	*nde*
57		yes
58	Dagiwa:	*e::* >*yes yes*< (pidgin) ((coughs))
59		yes, yes yes
60	Hoyali:	*ai mende ogo tigi* ↑ *bara*
61		this one (foot-patient) is sick too?
62		*be*
63		isn't it?
64	Dagiwa:	°*e*°
65		yes
66		⎡ ((deep voice)) ⎤
67		⎣ *ogoni hangugo* ⎦

68		⌈ that is all ((the treatment)) ⌉
69		⌊ hhhh <ag::ua> = ⌋ =
70		good, that's it now
71	Hoyali:	=AI::
72		(((14.6) they play with the foot-patients))
73	Dagiwa:	*ibi tigi bayabe*
74		has this one been sick too?
75	Hoyali:	*urubi tigi baya ↑ be*
76		have all these been sick?
77	Dagiwa:	⌈ ((gruff voice with slight sing-song cadence)) ⌉
78		⌊ o:: yes yes <nambout>((pidgin)) ⌋ =
79		yes yes
80	Hoyali:	= ( )
81	Dagiwa:	*ah yes* (pidgin)
82		yes
83	Hoyali:	((laughs continuously))
84		(4.8)
85		*i tigi barabe*
86		are you (foot-patient) sick?
87	Dagiwa:	*ndo* (.) *yamo*
88		no, nothing
89		*inaga gam<u>bolo</u>* (1) *i wane gambolo* (.) *eh taba ↑ henedabe*
90		your baby, is your little baby girl being carried?
91	Hoyali:	*ai*
92		who?
93	Dagiwa:	*i*
94		you
95	Hoyali:	*e*
96		yes
97	Dagiwa:	*e hiya* (.) *hondo ha* (1.9)°*hiya la*°
98		stand up; wait, say (tell it to) 'stand up'
99	Hoyali:	<hi::ya>
100		stand up
101		(2)
102	Dagiwa:	*HI ↑ YAO*: (.) (coughs) *au loleni*
103		'stand up' you should say it like this
104	Hoyali:	*HI ↑ YAO*::
105		stand up
106	Dagiwa:	⌈ ((deep gruff voice)) ⌉
107		⌊ *darasinibe* be ⌋
108		are there shorts? ⌠ well?
109	Hoyali:	⌡ e
110		yes

111	Dagiwa:	⌈ ((gruff voice)) ⌉
112		⌊ *o ngago* ⌋
113		they are there then
114		(23.3)
115		((Dagiwa leaves Hoyali and focuses his attention on a small banana
116		stump left in the ground nearby, which is treated as if it were a
117		new patient. Hoyali moves to join him))
118		*ogobi tigi bayabe*
119		is this one (stump-patient) ill?
120	Hoyali:	*o ina-ina nili barogo hondo ha*
121		I-I am giving it (stump-patient) an injection, wait
122		(3.2)
123		*ba mende beda*
124		give it a second injection
125	Dagiwa:	⌈ ((gruff voice)) ⌉
126		⌊ *ai ina nili baro* ⌋
127		I am giving it an injection
128	Hoyali:	((plays with the remaining strips of banana leaves on the stump as
129		if they were strips of pork))
130		*ogo ( ) nogo nogo nogo (.) nogo*
131		this ( ) pig, pig, pig, pig
132	Dagiwa:	((takes up a stick and pretends it is a car))
133		*garo: garo ge °wialu pelaro°*
134		car, I am letting the wheel of the car ((mark the dust))
135	Hoyali:	*INA NOGO PODARO*
136		I am cutting pig
137		*ogoni ndodabe*
138		it is like this isn't it?
139		*nogo podara: podara pod'- po'*
140		he/she is cutting pig, cutting, cut-cut
141	Dagiwa:	*poda hende*
142		cut it, I'm watching
143		(3.8)
144		*ogoni abago (.) hai hengeda*
145		somebody planted the banana stem
146		(14.5)
147	Hoyali:	((continues to pretend to cut the pork-leaves))
148		*alendo podarogoni AGALI↑ DA::*
149		I am cutting (pig) in the afternoon – the man
150	Dagiwa:	⌈ ((staccato delivery)) ⌉
151		⌊ *yu sum sumting* (pidgin imitation) ⌋
152	Hoyali:	⌈ ((high-pitched voice)) ⌉
153		⌊ *yu sum yu sum misum* (pidgin imitation) ⌋ =
154	Dagiwa:	= *yu sum yu sum sum* (pidgin imitation continues)

155	Hoyali:	⌈ ((high-pitched voice)) ⌉
156		⌊ *sum misum* (pidgin imitation) ⌋
157	Dagiwa:	⌈ ((slight sing-song cadence)) ⌉
158		⌊ *honebi bi bedaore larua* ⌋
159		the talk of white administrators is there and you are saying it
160		*ai::sum* (pidgin imitation continues)
161	Hoyali:	*i sum sum* (pidgin imitation)
162	Dagiwa:	( ) (pidgin imitation)
163	Hoyali:	*i i yorobi lowa*
164		I am Yorobi (ethnographer's Huli assistant) it is said
165		*i yorobi*
166		I am Yorobi
167	Dagiwa:	*i*
168		⌈ you
169	Hoyali:	⌊ *i*
170		me
171		*i sumting sumti' sumti'* ((pidgin imitation))
172	Dagiwa:	⌈ ((deep gruff voice)) ⌉
173		⌊ <*yoroBI*> ⌋
174		Yorobi
175	Hoyali:	*Y↓O::*
176		yes
177	Dagiwa:	°*yo hongo howa nalabe*
178		don't say 'yes' strongly like that
179		*ina hengeore labe*°
180		⌈ you say it softly ⌉
181		⌊ ((gruff and deep voice)) ⌋
182		<*yorobi*>
183		Yorobi
184	Hoyali:	<*yes*> (pidgin)
185		yes
186	Dagiwa:	⌈ ((deep gruff voice)) ⌉
187		⌊ *ah yu cum yu sup* ( ) (pidgin imitation) ⌋
188		you come here
189		(3)
190	Hoyali:	*HONABI*
191		anthropologist
192	Dagiwa:	*yu cum* (pidgin imitation) ( )
193		you come
194	Hoyali:	((while sitting with Dagiwa at the banana stem she peels off some
195		bark leaves and offers them to Dagiwa as food in the manner of a
196		mother feeding a baby))
197		*ai nogo na*
198		eat this pig

199		(4.1)
200	Dagiwa:	((pretending to speak like a child with its mouth full – nasalised
201		voice))
202		*ai < nde nogo ogo nde yabehedabe laro >*
203		I am saying it is possible to hold this pig
204		*e:::::* (noise of pretence ingestion like a child)
205		(4)
206	Hoyali:	*ogo ne hea ne hea ne hea ne hea* =
207		this one (child) has teeth, teeth, teeth, teeth
208	Dagiwa:	*e-e-e:::::* (makes noises of pretence ingestion like a child)
209	Hoyali:	*na na*
210		eat, eat
211	Dagiwa:	*e-e-e* (noises of pretence ingestion)
212	Hoyali:	>*ai ogoni*<
213		that's all now
214		(1.3)
215		*na*
216		eat
217	Dagiwa:	*e-e-e::* (pretence ingestion)
218	Hoyali:	*na*
219		eat
220	Dagiwa:	*e-e-e* (pretence ingestion)
221	Hoyali:	>*ai ogoni ogoni*<
222		that's all, all
223		(1.3)
224		*na*
225		eat
226	Dagiwa:	*e-e-e* (pretence ingestion)
227	Hoyali:	>*ai ogoni ogoni*<
228		that's all, all
229	Dagiwa:	*OGORIA POdama ibu ibu nabiabe*
230		don't cut on this side of the tree
231	Hoyali:	*na*
232		eat
233		(1.8)
234		>*ogoni ogoni*<
235		that's all, all
236		((breaks out in laughter))
237		>*AI NA*< (.) *AI NA*
238		eat, eat
239	Dagiwa:	<*ini na*>
240		eat it yourself
241		((recording discontinued at this juncture as Dagiwa wanders off to
242		his house))

Objects and Roles

Figure '3.1 presents both the sequential pattern of changes, and textual junctures at which they occur, of both (1) role transitions for Player 1 (Dagiwa) and Player 2 (Hoyali); and (2) the object-props used in Make-believe play transcript 3.1. In other words, it is a schematic representation

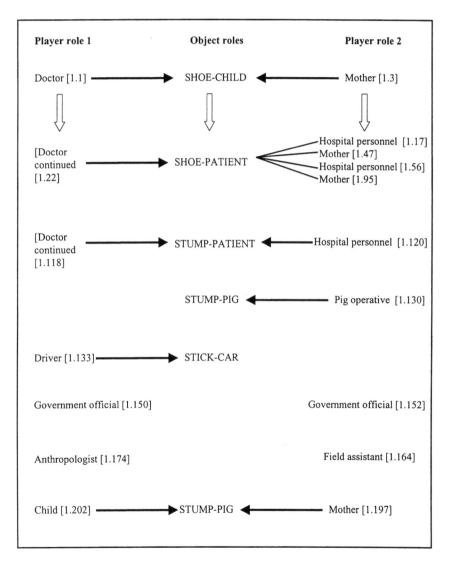

Figure 3.1 Schema of object and role transformations in Make-believe play transcript 3.1

of the complex interweaving and interdependence of thematic, role and physical object components in this one pretence routine. As an aid to discussion, we might usefully isolate here four distinct episodic phases of the fantasy play:

1   in which the parties exhibit joint focus on an animate other represented first by a shoe, and then by a tree-stump, while enacting a hospital-patient script;
2   in which there is a temporary disengagement of actors from this shared orientation to indulge in parallel role play involving respectively pigs and cars;
3   the re-engagement of the players in coordinated play, which instantiates linked scripts concerning government officials and anthropologist–field assistant. Importantly, we note that these scripts are not dependent on anchor supports in terms of any material objects other than the talk itself;
4   a recycling of the stump-pig prop within a quite new script of mother feeding infant.

The objects used in the play are thus revealed as being imbued with more than one pretend role as they undergo a series of transformations: sometimes inanimate (shoe) to animate (child/patient), sometimes inanimate (stump/stick) to inanimate (pig pieces/car). The degree of prototypicality shown in terms of the conceived analogies between strips of pig meat and stump shreds (high), or hospital patients and shoes (low), is of less concern here than the nature of how these pretend stipulations are made in the play. Significantly, this function is often processed implicitly by acting on, acting with, or referencing the object within a pretence role. In this context, there is a noticeable absence at the start of the episode of any overt marking of object transformations – players do not pronounce 'this x will be a y'. In effect, the shoe-child is constituted by the invocation of a category-bound activity associated with the directive 'give your breast' (l. 1). That is, the child inferentially constructs 'shoe-child' from knowledge of what is entailed by Dagiwa's use of 'breast', and is expected to tailor her actions to that make-believe identity. Similarly, the stipulations shoe-patient and stump-patient are implicit in Dagiwa's diagnostic questions (l. 22, l. 118) in his assumed role of hospital doctor. Role-appropriate biological conditions, like lactation and sickness, selectively indicate how the inanimate object is to be treated, and what sets of complementary identities are thereby implicated. The presence of a 'shoe-child patient' entails the role pairs doctor–patient and mother–child. There is an intersection of these two relational pairs of identities within the action sequence. Clearly though the pretence object shift from shoe to stump-patient is not motivated by the same concerns and appears merely improvisational. By contrast with these implicit designations, the props stump-pig and stick-car are more overtly indexed by the actors' declarative statements (l. 131, l. 134) which explicitly designate the pretence object.

Now an intriguing feature of the role stipulations found in Make-believe play transcript 3.1 is that they too are largely designations which are inferentially invoked within the context of pretence speech. Thus the directive 'give breast' in l. 1 tacitly appropriates the role of doctor for Dagiwa, as well as assigns the complementary object roles of patient (shoe) and 'mother' (Hoyali). In Phase 1 we may note two points of direct inter-cultural comparability. First, as is the case for Western children between 3 and 4 years, the initial social exchange is often a pretence locution (Forys and McCune-Nicolich 1984:168), rather than an elaborated out-of-frame negotiation, about who will take what roles. Second, Hoyali exhibits coordination between the two relational pairs of mother–child and doctor–child, adopting in the latter guise the same role content and script as Dagiwa of 'giving injections'. In respect then both of the manner in which fantasy episodes commence, and the incidence of role-sharing (ibid.:188), Huli players appear to behave in ways quite typical of the social pretend play of Western children.

Most importantly the players clearly invoke a range of indices of social identity that frequently combine both linguistic and paralinguistic resources. The adopted identities as transducers are, we might say, imbued with distinct 'voicings'. For example, Dagiwa's portrayal of a 'doctor' relies partly on voice features and intonational patterns – deep, gruff voice (ll. 21, 50, 66, 77) – and partly on his interspersed injections of pidgin words as markers of role authenticity and integrity (ll. 58, 78, 81). Hospital doctors and nurses in Huli are invariably non-Huli personnel who speak English or Pidgin. In parallel fashion, Hoyali implicitly manages a sequence of transformations between mother and doctor by mimicking the lilting high-pitched tones of a fatigued mother sighing at the weight of her child on her lap (ll. 46–8). By the age of 4 Huli children have already internalised the kind of speech patterns examined in Chapter 1 and can mimic motherese and conventional caretaking behaviour. Only at ll. 91–6 does Hoyali's task of multiple role coordination falter slightly in response to Dagiwa's assignation of her 'mother' identity. At this juncture the players have to make a detour from the ongoing pretence, stepping outside the frame, to clarify their respective statuses collaboratively in the ongoing fantasy script.

Notwithstanding the change in object-prop from shoe to stump, the players maintain dramatic continuity in the doctor script by recycling the actional components of patient examination and injection. The brief hiatus of Phase 2, in which the pretenders engage in parallel play, appears as a transition juncture between the post-colonial roles of doctor and unspecified government officials. It is as if there is a moment of pause in the play in which the players have temporarily abandoned the flow of the hospital script, and in which there is a breakdown of mutual orientation towards a common theme, and are independently seeking other ways in which to instantiate a new fantasy script. Hoyali pretends that some leaves are strips of pig meat while Dagiwa genre switches to begin a narrative about his new stick-car. What we note is that Hoyali does not engage with the primary script of 'car driving' in which Dagiwa is involved, but does take up the implicit solicitation contained in the overlaying genre of l. 133. Thus while continuing to pretend to cut pig meat, Hoyali herself genre switches at l. 139 so that her action becomes reported as part of a 'myth' narrative in the third person – 'he/she is cutting pig'. The peculiar property of double-play in this context is that it is then possible for players to co-pretend on one level – i.e. making mythical speech – while seemingly engaged in independent parallel play on another level. So double-play offers up the possibility of choosing which of the multiple scripts one co-produces with other players. The quite profound implication of this finding is that the behavioural categories commonly used in the analysis of child play, as discussed in the Introduction, should not be seen as necessarily mutually exclusive forms but may, as in a cultural situation like that of the Huli, co-occur. One can seemingly be engaged in parallel play while simultaneously also engaged in social pretend. As noted in the previous chapter, the potentiality for double-play is always there in Huli make-believe. Though it seems to occur unpredictably its signals are unmistakable and its invitation rarely refused.

The transition to Phase 3 is signalled by adopting pidgin lexemes with a distinctive staccato delivery (ll. 150–61). Despite their engagement within these roles Dagiwa at line l. 159 nevertheless clarifies the nature of their mimesis as that of playing colonial administrators. But what is particularly interesting in Phase 3 is that this parodic interchange of colonial voices appears not to be anchored to any specific thematic structure such as typified previous episodes. In other words, the children are simply 'talking like white adminsitrators' for its own intrinsic reward rather than necessarily enacting a particular storyline. The speech is the social action. Other than the fun of speech imitation the players are not in a defined, complementary relationship mutually oriented to a given actional script. It may be then that this too becomes an object for repair, as Hoyali extends and redefines the play as that between the identities of anthropologist (myself) and field assistant.

Phase 4 is a coda which essentially loops back to Hoyali's stipulation of stump-pig and the identity of a 'mother' who commands her infant to eat. The standardised script of continual promptings by a mother to a child is here humorously terminated by the rebellious counter of the child to the mother that she 'eat it' herself. What is suggested by the above is the critical dependence of concerted roles on their embeddedness within social scripts. Even where the script is the *mythos*, pretenders may play again with this artefact to constitute it simultaneously as a piece of authentic mythical narrative. We note both that misunderstandings of role assignment, and indeed lack of a mutually shared theme for developing a fantasy play, may occasion repair and clarification sequences between co-players. Equally significant is that players have well-defined understandings of how 'roles in contexts' should *sound*, and it is to this point that I now turn.

This claim that role appropriation, assignation and switching are predominantly carried out implicitly and paralinguistically has of course been reported for analogous Western play sequences (McTear 1985:205; Sawyer 1995:141; Harris and Kavanaugh 1993). But what is uniquely illuminating in Make-believe play transcript 3.1 is the evidence it provides of how actors both conceptualise the relationship between language and identity, and moreover utilise this very knowledge to repair misrepresent-ations of such roles. That is, understandings of 'voicing' become objects of conversational attention in the fantasy play and are revealing of just what kinds of role models the child brings to socio-dramatic play. Two specific instances of this phenomenon in the play text merit closer attention:

Example 3.1

97	Dagiwa:	*e hiya* (.) *hondo ha* (1.9)°*hiya la*°
98		stand up; wait, say (tell it to) 'stand up'
99	Hoyali:	<*hi::ya*>
100		stand up
101		(2)
102	Dagiwa:	<u>HI</u> ↑ <u>YAO</u>: (.) (coughs) *au loleni*
103	→	'stand up' you should say it like this
104	Hoyali:	<u>HI</u> ↑ <u>YAO</u>::
105		stand up

At l. 97 Dagiwa issues a prompt – marked by quieter voice (°) quality to indicate a non-pretence locution – which is repeated verbatim in the next turn by Hoyali. However, at l. 102 Dagiwa rejects her rendition as a misrepresentation (but not a misapprehension). He thereby exhibits his concern for representational accuracy in role performance in regard not of *what* Hoyali says, but of *how she says it.* Dagiwa next provides an authentic model which emphasises the need for forcefulness to be shown by a 'mother' directing a child, and Hoyali subsequently obliges with a repaired utterance at l. 104. This whole correction sequence relies critically on Dagiwa's ability to *metarepresent* by matching Hoyali's representation of 'mother commanding infant' with his construal of some referent model. Dagiwa orients to 'what should have happened' (Perner 1991:7) with respect to the paralinguistic dimension of role voicing.

Whereas in Example 3.1 Hoyali's voicing was perceived as too deferential for a mother, in Example 3.2 her voicing is by contrast evaluated as too assertive for a field assistant (Yorobi) responding to an anthropologist (Goldman). With due humility, I am at a loss to explain how such a model of my interaction with my field assistant was engendered, since it is incongruous with my own representations of my communication style. Perhaps the children simply perceived my status as within an ethnic category of 'outside administrators' all of whom exhibit analogous speech styles. The patterns are refashioned to mould and to mirror a stereotypical caricature. A remarkably similar mimetic episode, where the anthropologist again becomes a source of fantasy play amusement, has been discussed by Schwartzman (1976:291) for the Yoruba studied by the anthropologist Bascom.

Example 3.2

172	Dagiwa:	[((deep gruff voice))]
173		[<yoro*BI*>]
174		Yorobi
175	Hoyali:	Y ↓ O::
176		yes
177	Dagiwa: →	°*yo hongo howa nalabe*
178		don't say 'yes' strongly like that
179		*ina hengeore labe*°
180		you say it softly
181		[((gruff and deep voice))]
182		[<yor*obi*>]

183		Yorobi
184	Hoyali:	<*yes*> (pidgin)
185		yes
186	Dagiwa:	⌈ ((deep gruff voice)) ⌉
187		⌊ *ah yu cum yu sup* ( ) (pidgin imitation) ⌋
188		you come here
189		(3)
190	Hoyali:	*HONABI*
191		anthropologist

The forceful response of Hoyali to the anthropologist's (Dagiwa) summons of l. 174 again initiates a correction sequence with an out-of-frame performative evaluation (ll. 177–80) about production, followed by a recycling of the summons–response sequence (ll. 183–5) precisely as was the case in Example 3.1. Hoyali's much slower and quieter recycling (l. 184) manifests the acceptable level of deference which the children perceive to be appropriate in the modelled relationship of a Huli fieldwork assistant responding to a white anthropologist. In both the extracted examples no attempt is made to tamper with speech content in terms of the actual words used. Rather, status differentials between mother–child and anthropologist–field assistant are signalled by vocal qualities. The passages thus exemplify violations in construals of voice authenticity and as such represent a breakdown of intersubjectivity. That is, the representations of the players with respect to some role appropriate locution are not in alignment. The context-sensitive need to maintain collaborative pretence compels the parties to make a detour from the ongoing fantasy talk to perform what is referred to in conversational analysis parlance as an 'other-initiated repair' (Garvey 1993a, 1993b; McLaughlin 1984). The examples testify to a longstanding methodological truism that the norms and models which social actors have and use are often best viewed, and most transparent, when there is some 'hitch' in the ongoing interaction.

How far then are the discoursal features and patterns of Make-believe play transcript 3.1 typical of the transcript corpus and what degrees of intercultural similarity can be discerned? These forms of role stipulation have previously (see Chapter 2) been identified as types of 'fantasy negotiation' (FN). They are conversational moves with respect to *roles, props, actions* and *settings*, which foreshadow and organise the impending make-believe. As such analysts have regarded them as standing outside the ongoing frame of pretence itself and have variously categorised them as part of stage-management. The finding was made in the last chapter that one-third of all such fantasy negotiations were formatted as interrogatives, and that indeed 75 per cent of all recorded tag-questions in the data corpus occurred within this category of FN locution. Succinctly put, talking about who is going to do what, where and when, involves a high degree of question-asking rather than directing or commanding.

In this chapter I examine only the parameter of FN utterances concerned specifically with how the children *appropriated* roles for themselves, and *assigned* roles to other co-players. Table 3.1 plots the distributive frequencies for role claim and assignation with respect to the following three correlational dimensions:

1   the grammatical form of the initial locution in which some FN occurred – ie. declaratives, imperatives, hortatives, and specified interrogative forms such as tag-question (tag-q), yes/no, question (YN-q) and question-marked exhortations (cf. Goldman 1993);

2   the dissecting axis of whether these FN locutions were expressed *non-overtly* or *overtly*. For example, where the role identity was inferentially invoked from a pretence locution such as 'give your breast' (l. 1), rather than being explicitly designated, this was coded as non-overt. Thus at l. 126 Dagiwa says, 'I am giving it an injection' which non-overtly establishes and self-assigns the role of 'doctor'. By contrast, where the role name is stipulated, the locution was coded as overt. So for example, at l. 163 Hoyali says, 'I am Yorobi', which immediately appropriates a distinct identity as a play role. In some instances the grammatical form of such utterances, in conjunction with other sequential indices, suggest a coding of 'declarative' while in other cases the appropriating locution may be presented in a tag-question form:

Ts. 3: l. 36
iya honebi igini ndodabe
we are government officials aren't we?

---

3   the respective genders of pretenders in role appropriation, and the gender of assigning speaker and assigned hearer in role assignments. Table 3.1 thus provides a complete spread of same-sex and cross-sex possibilities in role assignation tasks. Similar computations for the significance of gender were performed for the tables presented in the previous chapter, but in those instances no gross disparities between male and female fantasy players emerged.

Table 3.1 Distributive frequences of overt/non-overt fantasy role negotiations

		Non-overt								Overt				
		Declaratives	Imperatives	Exhortations	Exhortations-q	Tag-q	Y/N-q	Sub-total	Totals	Declaratives	Imperatives	Tag-q	Y/N-q	Sub-total
					Interrogatives							*Interrogatives*		
Role appropriation	Male	73	4	7	5		11	93	39 ⎤ 52	100		100		7
	Female	79	7	14				85	19 ⎦					15
Role assignation	Male → Male	21	16	21	37		5	83	12 ⎤	25		75		17
	Female → Female	7	46	30	17			52	12	27	18	27	28	48
	Male → Female	27	27	33	20		20	88	9				100	12
	Female → Male	9	22	65	4			96	15 ⎦ 48	100				4

All figures expressed as whole percentages

It should be emphasised both that I am aware role designations can be made by non-verbal means, though these are not analysed here, and that, irrespective of the grammatical form such FN utterances take, they always to some degree solicit the agreement of others. Players are thus aware of the risk that disagreement and conflict in such negotiations can result in a breakdown of the collaborative pretence.

Table 3.2 displays the responses of other co-players to these role assignations in accordance with the cross-cutting axes described above of grammatical form and overtness of the locutions used. These responses have been categorised according to the following coding schema:

1 whether in the absence of an identifiable verbal response a role-appropriate action (RAA) followed. That is, while no verbal acknowledgment of acceptance of an assignation may occur, the actor may accept the role by simply performing an appropriate action, as Hoyali does in pressing her chest to the shoe in Make-believe play script 3.1;

2 whether the response took the form of some minimal acknowledgement like 'yes' (MA). For example, at l. 14 Dagiwa seeks to clarify the identity enacted by Hoyali, who gives a minimally positive response;

3 whether a role-appropriate locution (RAL) followed a particular role stipulation. It may be that while accepting a role assignation the actor both performs an appropriate act and speaks in an appropriate manner that can be taken as a token of his/her acceptance;

4 whether there appeared to be no uptake (NU) of the role suggestion, which here might include any form of disagreement or opposition. Table 3.2 thus presents some indication of how children tailor their responses to the pretend role negotiations of their fantasy partners.

The main findings with respect to Tables 3.1 and 3.2 can be summarily stated as follows.

Table 3.1

1 With regard to the relative incidence of role appropriation vs. role assignation it appears players self-select their identities at about the same rate as they assign them: ie. 52 per cent: 48 per cent.

2 With respect to the degree of *overtness* in FN locutions, an averaged computation reveals that roles are non-overtly signalled 83 per cent of the time. Quite clearly then explicit designation of make-believe identities has an extremely low incidence rate, so that Make-believe play

Table 3.2 Distributive frequencies of responses to overt/non-overt fantasy role negotiations

		Non-overt							Overt			
		Declaratives	Imperatives	Exhortations	Exhortations-q	Tag-q	Y/N-q	→	Imperatives	Declaratives	Tag-q	Y/N-q
M → M	RAA	75	50		63			17	100		100	
	MA		50		12		66					
	RAL	25		100	25		33					
	NU											
F → F	RAA		33		100			13	100	100	100	100
	MA			60								
	RAL	100	66	40								
	NU											
F → M	RAA	50	66	7	100			13	100			
	MA			53								
	RAL	50	33	40								
	NU											
M → F	RAA		60	60				0				100
	MA		40		33		66					
	RAL			40	66		33					
	NU											

All figures expressed as whole percentages.

RAA = role-appropriate action

MA = minimal acknowledgement

NU = no uptake

RAL = role-appropriate locution

script 3.1 appears quite representative of the manner in which Huli children process identity transformations in make-believe play. A simple in-role locution, or action with a prop, is sufficient to carry the communicative intent of both assigning and appropriating roles, without the need always to produce explicit markers of such transition.

3   Within role appropriation there appears to be a marked contrast in the incidence of interrogative forms for males and females. Indeed, a cumulative average over the table reveals males utilising question forms some 4.9 times more than their female counterparts. Conversely, females averaged twice as many uses of imperatives as males. Now it may be that this pattern is not representative for other types of FN communications concerned with, say, props, actions and settings. However, two factors may contribute to the statistical configuration found. First, the average age of the female players was 8.4 years, as compared with males at 6.8 years, so that it may be that older players employ less explicit question asking. Equally, the degree of familiarity between players may also operate to influence speech form. Noticeable is the fact that in non-overt role negotiations male to male (42 per cent) interrogative use matches male to female (40 per cent), but that female to female (17 per cent) is significantly greater than the incidence of female to male (4 per cent) occurrences. Again, the higher age of the female actors when playing with younger boys appears to result in less interrogatively marked locutions.

4   The average incidence of interrogatives across Table 3.1 is 37.4 per cent, which is broadly comparable with the one-third incidence reported for all FN moves discussed in Chapter 2. Nevertheless, with regard to the axis of overtness we can note an absence of any tag-questions in the non-overt sector of Table 3.1. Confirmation seeking by tags seems most likely to occur where there is some explicit designation of the role, or where there is a need for role clarification as in the above cited example.

Table 3.2

1   As other analysts have reported in their studies of Western children, attempts at 'role claim and assignment do not always gain ready acceptance' (Lloyd and Goodwin 1995:267), and in my data base such non-uptakes accounted for an averaged rate of 10 per cent. No clear distributive patterns emerged at this stage which might predict such responses.

2   Disregarding responses to particular question forms, there does appear to be a significant difference in the degree to which female and male

players verbally respond to fantasy role assignations. Table 3.2 indicates that females were likely to make a verbal response to an FN move 52 per cent of the time compared with 39 per cent for males. Although this is a restricted vector of comparison, in that I am only here considering fantasy negotiations in respect of *roles*, the incidences may be indicative that Huli girl players, like their Western counterparts, are conversationally more active in these play contexts (cf. Duveen and Lloyd 1988:93; Black 1992; Sachs et al. 1985).

3 Most of the replies to tag-questions and yes/no-questions were in the form of minimal responses. This contrasts markedly with the case of exhortation-questions, where actors tended to respond with either an appropriate action or an appropriate pretence locution. Solicitations of the 'let's pretend' type, even where marked as an interrogative, appear then simply to initiate pretence, as is the case with Pooh's response (in the cited extract in the Introduction) of 'I've got a message for you' to Rabbit's exhortation to 'let's pretend'.

Levels of Overtness

In examining the verbally encoded indications of how players appropriate and assign roles in social pretence, the transcript data suggest Huli children do not significantly differ in their practices from those reported for their Western counterparts. Thus even allowing for the problems which naturally attend interlinguistic comparison here – discontinuities in types of syntactic choice and expression of modal auxiliaries like gotta, wanna, could've – cooperative pretence seems not to depend on actors having to instantiate transformations of roles or objects through *overt* proposals. We find then only occasional acknowledgements of 'the pretendedness of the activity' (Giffin 1984:87) in the sense of actors relying on explicit phrases which incorporate the terms *'pretend, play, make-believe'* or their equivalents. As analysts of Western children's play have commented, players move in and out of fantasy roles predominantly by means of implicit markers (Göncü and Kessel 1984:10; Dunn and Dale 1984:150; Sutton-Smith 1984:56). This no doubt reflects in part the acceptance by actors that an 'as-if' preface to behaviour can be assumed by all (Giffin 1984:86). There is a shared understanding that actions are for the most part to be taken as pretenceful documents. Equally, the low incidence of overt pretends also indicates the efficacy and embeddedness of paralinguistic signals about roles, objects and themes. The attainment of intersubjectivity in social pretence appears then to proceed in quite analogous fashion in both cultural contexts.

Research on Anglo-American children, however, has indicated that they appear to increase their use of overt pretends between the ages of 4:4 and 5:7 years (Lloyd and Goodwin 1995; Garvey and Kramer 1989). In effect, the research suggests that occurrences of the cognition verb *'pretend'* (1) are rare in pre-school children, and rare in directives given between children and caregivers; and (2) seem to be a linguistically late adoption given that social pretence behaviour occurs at least by the age of 3. Moreover, when overt pretends do appear they are unequally distributed across the kinds of make-believe speech functions we have been examining in both this and the previous chapter. Overt pretends tend not to bracket roles and props – 'this is a pretend *x*', or 'pretend to be *y*' – but more commonly reference dimensions of the fantasy setting (Lloyd and Goodwin 1995:265).

Now these findings do contrast with those drawn from the Huli data, where, as I have had occasion to note previously, only six occurrences of any overt use of *'pretend'* across the transcripts were noted. These were distributed as follows: one occurrence of the verb *tingi ha* to reference the playful behaviour of the children, and five occurrences of the pretend adjectives *hawa, tindule* ('make-believe, joke, lie, false'), all of which qualify *objects*, as in Example 3.3:

Example 3.3
Ts. 17: ll. 298–9, 545–6

[Mogai (girl, 9–10 yrs)]

Mogai: → ina   hawa   tindule   e   ala   godamabe
               we   pretend   false   garden   first   dig-1PL-(I)HORT+IGV
               Shall we dig a pretend garden first?

           . . .

      → ai   e   hawa   godarogoni . . .
               oh   garden   pretend   dig-1SG-PRES
               I am making a pretend garden

How may we account for this simple intercultural discontinuity: i.e. that in Huli play texts produced by children between 5 and 10 there is no dramatic increase in overt pretends? Lloyd and Goodwin (1995) have attempted to explain their results as showing the possible responsiveness of children's play dialogue to fantasy narrative structures learnt in school. Most particularly they had in mind the way in which these narratives specifically mark types of pretend–real distinction. A high occurrence of overt uses of 'pretend' in scene-'setting' may reflect formulaic openings in stories, such as 'once upon a time', which are then operationalised in the children's own fantasy games. This would, however, fail to explain the low occurrence rates of overt pretends in Huli, since children are exposed to oral narratives well before the age of 5, and equally are well aware of many of the cues regarding how the narrative information is to be understood in respect of its historical or fictional character. Moreover, there is no analogous marking of object transformation in Huli stories which could similarly explain why Huli children use pretence adjectives mostly for *props* and not role claims, assignations, themes or scene-setting.

Perhaps one possible explanation for the differences may lie in the previously made observation that much of the existing knowledge of what Western children do and say in pretence is based on direct or indirect play proposals that researchers have made to children (Göncü 1993:195; LeVine 1980; Haight and Miller 1992:335; Lillard 1993b:366). These skew the responses to the selective saliencies of the experimenters, so that more naturally occurring data might reveal a higher degree of convergence here rather than difference.

Another possible explanation lies with the different ways in which the mental-state verb *'pretend'* is used in Huli and English, and indeed the different narrative styles used by players to construct fantasy scenes. In English texts players frequently establish events and situations that have previously occurred, and which might have current relevance, by bracketing their suggestions with a 'let's pretend' gambit (cf. Giffin 1984:87; Lloyd and Goodwin 1995:267), or using the past tense to mark the unreal/irrealis (Lodge 1979; McTear 1985); for example, 'let's pretend you went on holiday and fell down a cliff and the police went searching.' Groos gave a pertinent example of this kind of pre-fantasy narrative: 'then let's say that I am a thief, and there is a whole roomful of cakes, and the door is shut, and I cut a hole in it and take all the cakes away, and you are the policeman and run after me and get all the cakes back again' (1901:307). Now in Huli this kind of scene-setting that is verbally narrated prior to pretence enactment was not encountered. Children constructed past-event components of the scene as they went along. Reports of past actions or states of affairs occurred most usually as fictional utterances of speakers while in their roles (Example 3.4: l. 7), or within prompt directives to other actors (l. 9) in a stage-managing voice (Kyratzis 1992):

Example 3.4
Ts. 20:ll. 107–13)

1	Mogai:	((in the role of a mother talking to others about the actions of
2		riot police))
3		*anda delaragoni:*
4		they (the riot police) are burning the houses
5		(10)
6		⎡ ((high-pitched lilting voice)) ⎤
7	→	⎣ *anda delayagoni* ⎦
8		they have burnt the houses
9	→	*ai ° libu anda biago delayago bare mbireni handa dai buwa libu anda biago delara*
10		*ladaba °*
11		they have burnt your houses, look back from the slope of the mountain
12		and say, 'they are burning the houses'

Representations get shared amongst Huli child pretenders largely through the inferential work that is done by actors from the conversational cues provided in previous turns, and thus without the need for extended history-telling. Whether this difference is a further reflection of the common tendency to genre shift in Huli fantasy play, so that again 'history' is subsumed as part of mythical narrative, cannot yet be determined given the paucity of cross-cultural research into these topics.

Choosing Identities

In addition to these issues of how it is that players signal to each other what roles they have taken, and what roles they expect others to assume, are questions about the gendered nature and origin of the roles themselves. What can be said in respect of whether and when children understand their fantasy identities as gender specific, and what kind of impact has been wrought on this dramatic process by social change?

The problem facing an analyst is quite how one designates the gender of any appropriated or assigned role. Simply expressed, when a female Huli player plays 'gardener' or 'hunter', does the player see herself as a gender-differentiated or undifferentiated gardener? How far do other co-actors share the identity representation? Can an otherwise stereotypical male role – eg. a riot policeman – be fictionally female in scripted episodes? Table 3.3 is an initial attempt to provide answers to some of these questions.

It lists a full configuration of the roles that appeared across the corpus of transcripts that formed the data base of this book. Nevertheless, the kind of determinations represented in Table 3.3 are not mooted as necessarily unambiguous, but relied on two coding rationales:

1   conversational passages where *disambiguation* of this matter occurs; that is, where the players themselves seemed to be grappling with the very issue of gender itself;
2   conventional gender inflection in roles, by which is meant that 'female' is a default gender setting for a 'mother' role in Huli.

These coding rationales require some further explanation. The incidence of disambiguation sequences is strikingly low in the data, which suggests that unless otherwise marked, the player retains his/her gender identity in the character role. Thus in the following text example Ayubi's (male, 8–9 yrs) assumed status as a 'male gardener' is validated by Mogai's (female, 9–10 yrs) gnomic utterance – 'yes, men used to dig drains' – that presents a model of gender appropriate labour for Ayubi:

Example 3.5
Ts. 17: ll. 653–9

Mogai:	→	*ai e ogoria* (1) *>molo molo godamiya<*
		all right let's dig a small round garden
		hawa e be (.) *hawa e*
		a pretend garden? A pretend garden
Ayubi:		*e gana=*
		a garden drain
Mogai:		*=e*
		yes
Ayubi:		*ina gana warogo*
		I am digging a drain
Mogai:		*e* (.) *agalime gana waganego*
	→	yes, men used to dig drains

In Example 3.6 below Handabe's (male, 6–7 yrs) utterance at l. 4 reconfirms both that Hoyali (female, 4–5 yrs) is in a female role, and that therefore in accordance with Huli custom (*mana*) it is appropriate and expected that she will clean pig's intestines before their eventual consumption:

Table 3.3 Distributive profile of socio-dramatic play roles (SPR)[1]

	Post-colonial Adult male									Traditional Adult male							Traditional Adult female							
	Politician	Government officials	Drivers	Police	Anthropologist/assistant	Trade store owner	Hospital personnel	Road contract labourers	Sub-total	House building	Bridge building	Gardening	Hunting	Pig killing/cooking	Father	Miscellaneous	Mother	Gardening	Pig killing/cooking	Miscellaneous	Spirits	Animals	Babies/children	Sub-total
Rural Male	5[2]	11	9		<1[3]	5	<1	3	35	4	6	4	2	<1		3	4	4	3	2		<1	<1	19
Rural Female		<1	3		<1		2	<1	7		<1			<1								<1	<1	19
Rural Male (elicited)										4	<1	<1	6	4								1		16
Rural Female (elicited)										2			2						3					7
Urban Male	2								2	2		5		2	5	2	10					2	5	24
Urban Female	2						8		10						7		30	10	5	3	7	2	2	64

1 Calculated on the basis of 26 fantasy play episodes
2 All figures expressed as whole percentages
3 < represents less than 1%
4 Naturally occurring fantasy play episodes
5 Elicited fantasy play episodes

Example 3.6
Ts. 12: ll. 84–91

1	Handabe:		<u>*tini*</u> (.)° *halu pubelo dugu nguliya*
2			I'll pull out and give you (Hoyali) the (pig's) intestines to go
3			and wash
4			*i walidago°*
5		→	you are a woman
6	Hoyali:		° ↑ *ibe°*
7			me?
8	Handabe:		*°tini halu pu°*
9			go wash the (pig's) intestines

With regard then to conventional gender inflection in Huli, it is not simply that in pretend scenarios the 'underlying structure of logical if-then deductions' (Garvey 1993a:262) is maintained, but that play roles tend also to retain their standard gender associations irrespective of the gender category of the player.

Table 3.3 does more than simply display the various identities assumed by players across the play transcripts. It seeks to convey further the distributional frequencies for *gender* – male, female or undetermined – *location* – urban (Tari) or rural (Yaluba; see Chapter 2) – and *data type* – naturally occurring vs. elicited fantasy dialogue (boxed with a dotted line). The 'post-colonial' sector of Table 3.3 depicts roles that are deemed discontinuous with those that are known to have occurred in pre-colonial Huli. As a repertoire of role models, Table 3.3 provides a unique window onto the changing nature of social identities across Highlands societies from the particular perspective of mimetic dramatists such as children.

The principal findings in regard to Table 3.3 can be summarily given as follows:

1   *Rural-Urban*: in the rural (Yaluba) context the average role-per-person ratio in any social pretend engagement was 1.8, which was significantly lower than that for the urban (Tari) context, which yields a per-person ratio of 2.3. Now the compositional profile of male/female players respectively across the two areas is 76 per cent: 24 per cent (rural), and 78 per cent: 22 per cent (urban), a complete statistical flip-flop. However, a more fine-grained breakdown of roles per person across gender/locale lines in fact revealed no marked difference whatsoever between actors. Thus gender cannot alone account for the regional discrepancy in roles-per-person figures. Equally discounted in alternative computations was

the size of the fantasy play group and relative ages of the players. Rather, it appears as if in the urban context actors' scripts reflect their more diversified social ecology. This compels children to transform their identities more regularly within a drama than is the case for their rural counterparts. Given that Table 3.3 reveals rural children adopting post-colonial roles (42 per cent) at approximately the same rate as they adopt what we might loosely refer to as traditional roles (58 per cent), it is not the identities *per se* that control the number of transformations so much as developments in the story lines.

2 *Naturally occurring-elicited*: it is of some importance here that when given free reign to 'pretend to pretend' for a fieldworker children rarely enacted identities that were discontinuous with traditional roles. While on the one hand this signals a warning about reading results from such fabricated data, thus emphasising a point made above, on the other hand it discloses the peculiar sensitivities and expectations the children had about 'what might interest' the ethnographer.

3 *Male-female*: the highest percentage occurrence of female identities across both locales was the 'mother' role. This appears consistent with findings for same-gender actors in Western play groups. Apart from an also high incidence of hospital dramas, particularly notable was the enactment of 'spirit' characters in the Tari township. This, I believe, reflects regional variations in anxieties about supernatural attacks. Tari has a much larger and more cosmopolitan immigrant population than is the case for rural settings, which fuels Huli fears concerning 'outside' powers and sorcery. Without perhaps attempting to read too much into the frequency distributions, the single most dramatic feature of Table 3.3 is that while females clearly took on 'male' roles like father, house builders, vehicle drivers, policemen, and even 'anthropologist's assistant' Make-believe play script 3.1, we find no instances of boys adopting conventional 'female' roles. Once again this finding is quite consistent with those reached for Western actors in doctor–patient scripts, where boys invariably assumed 'male doctor', rather than 'patient/baby', identities (cf. Sachs 1987:180; Miller and Garvey 1984:124). In effect, Table 3.3 confirms a picture of entrenched gender inflection in pretence role taking with clear perceptions amongst the actors of what constitutes *prestigious emulation*.

Conclusion

Personative performances, such as that illustrated in Make-believe play script 3.1, are rarely intended as veridical mirrors or real-world documentaries. Rather they present as distorted, embellished, elliptical and exaggerated vignettes. History and experience are drawn upon and then heavily editorialised. Notwithstanding the truth of this oft-noted characterisation, Huli players do evince a concern with aesthetic integrity and authenticity in their 'voicing' of cultural roles. In the symbolic action of fantasy play, child actors instantiate and enact their understandings of the language–identity relationship. This is clearly demonstrated by the kinds of repair work performed by child conversationists. In their culturally shaped emulations, child pretenders index the centrality of voicing in caricature, as well as their cognition of the gender-inflected world of social roles. If these twin dimensions are considered as perhaps fundamental expressions of how roles present to children, then one might agree with Gadamer when he noted that in the reality of irreality is 'the recognition of the essence' (1975:103). Far from the Platonic view that artistic representations are 'inferior child[ren] born of inferior parents' (1974:ll. 603), it seems that at least in the above respects 'the being of representation is superior to the being of the material represented' (ibid.). And so we are returned to the kinds of issues discussed in the Introduction regarding the relationships between so-called copies and originals.

Chapters 2 and 3 are by no means intended as any kind of closure on the discussion of social pretend play. They are of necessity limited in scope, and merely attempt to provide a detailed and comparative view of a culturally specific case of what is possibly a universal form of child interaction. The issues broached are not exhaustive of the topic, the findings not mooted as necessarily final. Rather, they offer an opening onto the kind of complex theoretics encapsulated in the Western history of *mimesis*, *play* and *imagination*. Most centrally, double-play is at yet another tangent to the interrelationship between myth and make-believe. While much has been said in this chapter about the identities children enact and construct – and the manner in which they become mythologised within the play – there remains the broader canvas of which models outside the fantasy interaction itself might influence how children experience and comprehend their behaviour as play. Invoking genre shifts enables, even empowers, players to re-present one myth in terms of another; the narrative genre restructures what is in the process of being constituted by the primary fantasy script. But does this mythical register present a generic face, or is there some particular symbolic complex, some particular folklore figure, which permeates the cultural world of Huli children in a unique way? Between what 'stays' (*henene* – 'truth') and what passes into another body (*tingi* – 'pretend'), between mimesis and mythos, lie the liminal characters of the trickster and the antinomian ogre.

Chapter 4

The Ogre: A Melanesian Cyclop

In almost every race and people throughout the globe, traditions and legends
are to be found of monstrous and gigantic beings who were supposed to live in
caves, forests or mountains, to the terror of normal human beings.

Thompson 1968:129

In every culture we find ogres, and they have nothing to do with basic or non-
basic institutions . . . but rather the undeveloped infantile ego with its aggression,
identification and anxiety.

Roheim 1950:4–5

Introduction

As ubiquitous inhabitants of the *Weltmärchen* world, ogres, bogies, goblins
and other 'frightening figures' (Widdowson 1971) are emblems of imaginative processes which generate fiction as a modality of historical experience.
The magnification of monstrousness in which children and adults delight
rearranges the known to portray the unknown either in some mythic past
or in some verisimilitude of time. Needham has referred more generally to
such protean forms as 'synthetic images' (1978:41) in which a set of features
combines to constitute a complex that has, he argued, global distribution
and constancy. Such contrivances of the imagination, anthropologists have
long claimed, disclose a predisposition to abrogate constraint. Humans seek
to transcend the limits of reality by conjuring the impossible – images 'like
you can't imagine'. As products of the imaginative consciousness ogres
quintessentially embody what Coleridge (1906:161) talked of as 'poetic faith'
– the importance humans attach to willing others to suspend disbelief in
represesentations that are proclaimed as at the same time 'beyond belief'.
Myth producers, in which class this book has argued must be included
child pretenders, are seeking to purchase an immunity from convention,
and yet paradoxically the efficacy of their fiction depends on its power to
redescribe and remake their reality (Ricoeur 1978:123; Evans-Pritchard
1967:30).

Ogres as a topic of inquiry appear then uniquely equipped to address what van Baal identified as the singular challenge of myth – 'the fact that every myth confronts us with at least one event or situation which is physically or humanly impossible' (1977:165). They force us to confront a range of issues about culture and imagination hinted at in the two opening citations. Are such representations part of the universal stock of human pretences operative in social control contexts and exploited by caretakers? If they have a pan-cultural instantiation, does this signal some autonomous pre-cultural vector of the mind where 'fabricators, audiences, and analysts are bound together by common criteria of fantasy and by common imaginative predispositions' (Needham 1978:60)? Does the ogre embody a mythical archetype unaffected by culture, or contexts of performance? Or are they, as Roheim suggests, ultimately reflections of childhood psycho-dynamic processes?

While such questions portend precisely the kind of humanistic vision required to understand child pretence, and while, if somewhat apprehensively, forays are made towards providing some answers, 'ogrology' (to coin a term) impinges on the present project in quite specific ways. Myths, much as the make-believe play products of children, talk obliquely and in the language of symbols about the nature of being and of the universe. As imaginative exemplars they embed reality and irreality, fuse fact and fiction. Worlds are remade with their own spatial-temporal boundaries in 'contra-distinction' (Wagner 1978:33) to reality. What is there manufactured is what I have earlier referred to as a slippage between the 'what is', 'what was' and 'what if', where the declarative (it is) and subjunctive (as if it were) appear to qualify each other recursively. Such oral artefacts – whether adult narrative or child pretence – constantly move between these modalities. They inform us equally about the knowns of this world and about what can potentially be known. This feature of imaginal potentiality is what allows myths to wreak transformations as a sense-making exercise. In the formation of these mythic 'as–if' worlds the implicit proposal to pretend – to make believe the impossible – directly parallels the manner in which children constitute fictionality in their own socio-dramatic episodes. These kinds of homologies underscored the discussion in the Introduction of why 'pretence' and pretend play have serviced theoretic models of literary fiction. Myths encapsulate, if only silently, fantasy proposals of the 'let's pretend' type; adults and children reproduce their texts as forms of social action in remarkably similar fashion. Morever, as we have seen in the preceding chapters, the myth: make-believe relation is articulated by Huli children in the special ways in which they structure and mythologise their fictionalised play artefacts as *muthoi*, products of the mimetic process.

The acknowledged relationships between pretend play and myth – the forging of 'links between the exceptional and the ordinary' (Bruner 1990:47) – provide a general rationale for the present discussion. But this quest to defy imaginative construction is more than abstract rhetoric. As imparted by the refrain 'like you can't imagine' encountered in the epigraph to this book, this cognitive disposition is also in Huli a linguistic device which frames narrative content and delivery in both Huli myths (*bi te*) and make-believe play (see Chapter 2). This alone makes a profound statement about the incessant project of world reconstruction and understanding amongst Huli children. Beyond even these lines of connection ogres refract a model of pretence, in all its affective and moral dimensionality, which, along with the trickster, I shall argue scaffolds the frame-shifting of child pretenders themselves. Succinctly stated then, constructing an ethnography of fantasy play in Huli within an interpretative paradigm of mimesis and mythos is necessarily to engage the anthropophagous ogre *Baya Horo* and the trickster *Iba Tiri*.

This chapter, however, is not conceived as a contribution to the voluminous legacy of theory and materials on myth in anthropology, though where germane these are variously referenced. My concern in dealing with two of the most recurrent figures in world eschatology is in its own way a plea for the intrusion here of more child-focused consideration. It may be, as Turner proclaims, that the discursive instrument of myth brings 'members ... to an encounter with the ontological curvatures of their experience with others' (1978:7), but anthropology in general continues to remain oblivious to the 'other' as child. Children too often appear as uninvited and invisible performers, invisible audiences and invisible myth makers, 'as if' culture is only reinvented by and for adults. A study of bogeydom serves as a timely corrective to such oversights for many reasons, some of which have been broached above, and some of which are further explored below. Child images have a motility; they set in motion ideational diffusion across various sectors of the fantasy economy. The representations of child and adult are not only genetically related but surely mutually incorporative.

The traditional interest in ogres spans a number of disciplines. For some analysts ogres represent child-engendered projections of parenthood and innate destruction fantasies (Roheim 1950; Bettelheim 1975). For others they constitute a type of 'imaginary companion' (Mead 1934:150) or 'consensual imaginary figure' (Prentice et al. 1978 – eg. Easter Bunny, Sandman, Tooth Fairy) representing punishment, and a generalised (or culturally stereotyped) 'other' which controls and instructs. More recently pychologists' concern with such figures has been with the light they can shed on children's ability to distinguish systematically between fantasy and reality (Harris et al. 1991; Taylor et al. 1993), and thefore the role that fantasy plays in cognitive development. In this regard there are lessons here too for anthropologists engaged with problems about the factual/fictional status of narrative categories within the cultures they study. While it appears that very young children attribute reality status indiscriminately at first (Morison and Gardner 1978; cf. Emmison and Goldman 1997), their later understandings of the phenomenal status of these figures appear to vary under certain conditions with the emotional charge associated with that object. That is, children may become confused between the reality status of imagined entities because they provoke heightened affective responses so that they become unsure about the rules, or the application of the rules, that govern transformations between real and pretend. The argument to be pursued in this and the next chapter is that for Huli children the ogre *Baya Horo* stands to the trickster *Iba Tiri* as 'monster' to 'imaginary companion'. Both figures are emotionally charged but contraposed as representing negative and positive valances respectively (cf. Taylor et al. 1993). In this regard the figures do provide a special arena for rethinking our approach to the age-old problem of the 'trickster', but it is a reconceptualisation led entirely by the ethnographically etched character of their personae in this region.

Bogies and tricksters are thus types of transformational phenomena which 'play on the border-line between jest and earnest' (Huizinga 1955). Equally, the compositional form of such characters and their reinventions in narrative and quotidian discourse appear explicable by virtue of their infantile nature. Ogres resonate images of grotesqueness, size reversal, cannibalism, amoral and lawless behaviour. These optical and poetical illusions demand disbelief and have lead many an anthropological and folklore scholar (cf. Austin 1983) to proclaim that such fantasy traditions are inalienably rooted in, and predicated upon, cultural models of child imagination. Ogres, like tricksters, embody child voices. As narrativised identities, they 'put an adult mind in a child's heart and a child's eye in an adult head' (Pelton 1980:279). In this vein ogrology must seek to locate disjunctions and intersections between perceptions of historical fact and nursery fiction, between adult and child visions of the unimaginable, and thus between lofty drama and burlesque comedy.

Given what appears to be a significant cross-cultural incidence in beliefs about cannibal giants across Asia, Europe, Africa and India (cf. Beecher 1938; Motz 1982; Glenn 1971; Mondi 1983; Butterworth 1987; Page 1955; Aarne 1973) – often of the one-eyed variety as in the Greek tradition of Polyphemus, the Basque *Tartaro* or Greco-Turkish *Tepekózis* – it is surprising that our understanding of ogres, as perhaps a distinct sub-genre of demons, is so little developed either at the level of general anthropology or indeed at the level of Melanesian folklore. Seemingly unworthy of initial inclusion as a Jungian 'archetype' – a precultural 'psychologem' (Jung 1956:200) located in universal psychic structures – ogres appear to have suffered by comparison with the attention lavished on trickster figures. One explanation for this apparent neglect is that mythic traditions of ogres, though common, are not intellectually provocative. They lack descriptive thickness and are not associated with the narrative 'cycles' that typify other mythic characters. Leading on from this, ogres therefore speak to analysts in very mono-chromatic and unambiguous terms. That is, ogres are not perceived as living an antinomian existence, and do not present baffling or elusive arrays of masks, or complex symbolic roles. Lacking a pervasive liminality they fail to service the categorial or mediatorial models of analysts. Unlike the trickster's their logic of subversion is articulated not as a reflection of some profound existential dilemma – a therapeutic anamnesis – but simply as personalities wholly inimical to humans.

However, this seeming incapacity to confound classification is problem-atic when viewed in the context of Huli beliefs. On the one hand, the ogre profile is here as finely etched as any other in the folkloric pantheon such that the sheer breadth of tales and their thematic integration eclipses all other traditions in Huli culture. On the other hand, the very presence of the trickster in ogre epics compels us to accept that perhaps the intelligibility of both these figures is mutually interdependent. Cross-cultural findings that trickster-fixers are heroes who vanquish giants – 'Usually the creature is a "cannibal monster" (Ricketts 1965:336; cf. Street 1972:96, Radin 1956:166) – suggest their co-presence as mythic actors is perhaps more than pure coincidence.

In privileging a child-centric viewpoint of the nature and meaning of Huli ogrology I declare an avowed interest in how children experience such figures, through what ranges of cultural phenomena and with what implicit intentionalities these monsters are mimicked, invoked and reproduced. In this endeavour the resonant images of ogres are shown to extend beyond the confines of any ensemble of mythical texts or tales. Understanding involves the interlacing of ogre motifs across diverse fields such as proverb usage, child games, mourning laments and nursery rhymes. Furthermore, the argument is developed that the historical condition and humanity of Huli as make-believers is thrown into relief by contexualising their ogrology within local, regional and pan-cultural monster traditions.

In this last respect, the epigrammatic phrase 'Melanesian Cyclops' deliberately hints at a universality of leitmotif, a 'monster theme'

(Kluckhohn 1959; Bettelheim 1975), suggesting the kind of unity behind diversity that has long preoccupied anthropological studies of myth (cf. Fortes 1959; Lévi-Strauss 1955; LeRoy 1985). The argument is often made that tales talk similarly across the world. In this belief it has long been commonplace in anthropological works (eg. Kerényi 1956) to draw comparisons between bodies of data by importing, say, Greek myths. In adopting this strategy in the form of a literary device (indicated by < >) which indicates citation from Homer (1961), I had two purposes in mind. First, the quotations of Cyclopic poetry serve as a conversational backdrop that plays with ideas about ogre universals to enrich comprehension of the historical and fabled in Huli consciousness. This is not to reduce or annul culturally diverse traditions into a single irreducible monad. Rather it is an allusion to the common grounding of both the Greek and Huli ogre traditions in folktales for children. At another level it also resonates with the contrasting perspectives of Plato and Aristotle on mimesis (cf. Introduction), and the status of Homer as respectively dissembler of truth (Plato 1974:597), or prophet who 'taught other poets how to tell lies as they should be told' (Aristotle 1962:1460). In this vein the literary device signals an irony, for Cyclopean mythology, like that of Huli *Baya Horo* (hereafter BH), betrays processes of contamination whereby, in the constant seepage of ideas between folk tradition and epic narrative, individual traits come to assume the status of collective markers of identity. If 'Melanesian Cyclops' thereby invokes in readers a stereotype of one-eyed anthropophagous figures, how far have we become dupes of a post-Homeric heritage that all Cyclops, rather than just Polyphemus, are ocularly challenged?

Ogres in the Melanesian Literature

> < Cyclops: . . . These [sheep] I sacrifice to no one but myself – never to the gods – and to my belly, the greatest of divinities. To guzzle and eat day by day and to give oneself no pain..as for those who have passed laws and complicated men's lives, they can go hang. For my part, I shall not forgo giving pleasure to my heart – by eating you [Odysseus].>

Euripides 1994 ll. 330–40].

Much as has been argued for the mythic character *trickster* (cf. Beidelman 1980; Carroll 1984), ethnographers have tended to employ a global concept of *ogre* that indiscriminately covers a multitude of sometimes quite disparate figures. Synonyms like *demon, denizen, fiend, ghost, giant, spirit* or *monster* are used for almost any frightening or threatening figure irrespective of whether it has the defining attribute of being a 'human-eating giant' or not. Such literary practices have vitiated any attempt to establish ogres as a distinct analytical grouping. Furthermore, perhaps because the true cosmological import of ogres has not always been acknowledged, developed descriptions are few in number, tend to be largely anecdotal, and are rarely amplified in respect of other potential levels of ethnographic importance. Set against this lack of information, Table 4.1 presents an indicative listing of ogres noted in the Papua New Guinean literature. It is by no means an exhaustive enumeration of ogre citations, and other references from Melanesia which might easily be included would be the

Table 4.1 Selected reports of ogres in Papua New Guinea

Culture	Term – gloss used	Characteristics	Reference
Kyaka	*kwanambo* – cannibal ogre	Large tusks, lure children to their homes	Bulmer 1965:136, 154, 161
Mae Enga	? – demons	Long fangs, large penis, tall, hairy, one eye	Meggitt 1976:67, 80–1
Kewa	*remo* – ghosts, ogrelike	Sheathed long fangs, long hair	LeRoy 1985:88, 90
	kapa kalado – goblins	Long hair, half-man	Franklin & Franklin 1978:463
Bimin-Kushusmin	? – animal-man monsters	Portrayed to children in tales	Poole 1983:12
Daribi	*toro* – ogres	Hunt humans, suspend victims from trees until ripe	Wagner 1978:172
Umeda	*Yaut/Kwod* – ogres, fiend	Roles taken in Ida rituals	Gell 1975:165, 194–8
Duna	*auwepe* – giants	Giants, some with one eye, cut mothers' breasts	Haley 1993:78; Stürzenhofecker 1993:219; Modjeska (personal communication)
Huli	*baya horo/auwebe* – ogre	Sheathed tusks, one eye, giant size, ripens victims, eats parents, used in tales to children	Goldman 1983
Wola	*iybtit* – ogre	Grotesque, cassowary-like claws as nails, four eyes(?)	Sillitoe 1993:224

Dobu *Tokedokeket* – 'a horrid ogre of terrifying appearance' (Fortune 1963:270; cf. also Poignant 1967) – the Massim *Kuporu* (Seligman 1910:390) and the Sabarl *Katutubwai* – a 'monstrous cannibal ancestor' (Battagalia 1991:86) who appears as a pig. Notwithstanding such omissions, what Table 4.1 enables us to do is (1) to make a preliminary assessment of what kinds of discriminations might be made within the general category of fearsome figures; and (2) to broach the issue of whether there might exist some regional sub-tradition of ogrology.

From even the slender evidence available there appear to be at least three discriminable features of ogreship which either manifest as independent identities, or are fused in any single cultural representation. These are:

1 *pervasive*. They are omnipresent spiritual beings which are conceived to exert influence or control on human lives continually. They may be supplicated, nullified or scared off in various ways. Where such figures do not signify a distinct anthropophagic nuance they are perhaps best considered within the broader set of beliefs in forest and/or bush demons. Comparable entities in Huli are known simply as *tayenda dama* ('forest spirits': Glasse 1965:35).

2 *ritual*. They are representations which enact burlesque roles in rituals and which may or may not figure prominently in the culture's mythological pantheon. The *Yaut, Yautagwa, Sebuha* and *Kwod* characters in Umeda Ida rites (Gell 1975:194) are prime examples of this class. They generally act to instil fear in an audience, and most frequently exercise licensed aggression especially against children. The Huli ritual ogre is the *Kabugua* ('wrapped [*kabu*] one': cf. Figure 4.1), which was never mythologically underwritten and did not occupy a niche anywhere else in the theology. As is evident from Figures 4.1 and 4.2, the predominant decorative motif is black charcoal, black cassowary plumes, dark tangett leaves and a gourd mask. *Kabugua* carried sticks and made loud sounds by clunking pig bones against each other while proclaiming 'I have eaten bones, I have eaten flesh' (*kuni naru mbirini naru*). They wreaked disorder amongst children and women in Tege fertility dances.

3 *mytho*. These are figures which inhabit the realms of history and/or fantasy, and which are associated with defined oral traditions. The Huli identity *Baya Horo* falls into this category, as do the many types of Papua New Guinean ogres and ogresses alluded to in Chakravarti's (1974) initial overview of this topic.

With respect to mythological ogres, Chakravarti (ibid.) isolated a number of key dimensions to what he claimed was a uniform national type. The

Figure 4.1 *Kabugua* – Huli ritual ogre

Figure 4.2 *'Baya Horo* is coming'

ogre appears as a cannibalistic giant from an early epoch that threatened the continued existence of humankind. The ogre may assume (or transform to and from) exaggerated humanoid or animal form – e.g. pig, bird, dog, snake or sea-creature. It is often devoid of anatomical parts or has a peculiar cephalic or ocular configuration (ibid.: 13). Moreover, the ogre is invariably associated with meteorological phenomena such as rain, storm, lightning, thunder or earthquakes, which accompany or herald its presence. Ogres symbolise anarchy, untamed wilderness, an antithetical force against society, which threat is finally removed in epic confrontations with culture heroes and heroines.

Notwithstanding remarks that only surface glimpses of ethno-ogrologies are thus far available, there are some suggestive links between the macro picture drawn by Chakravarti (ibid.) for Papua New Guinea and some of the more regionally restricted noticings listed in Table 4.1. Ogrish features encompass at least some of the following key dimensions:

1 gigantic size;
2 association with meteorological forms;
3 long (sheathed) fangs;
4 ripening of victims;
5 association with children;
6 eating of humans;
7 one eye.

In the light of known linguistic, historical and cultural interrelationships among some of the societies included in Table 4.1, I suggest the tentative finding of a mythic sub-tradition of ogres across the Kewa, Mae Enga, Duna, Daribi and Huli. That is, these Highlands ogrologies constitute what von Sydow termed an 'oicotype' (1948:243), the isolation of a mythical form which, through fusion and adaptation within a specific milieu, assumes a distinct identity of its own. Setting aside for the moment questions about universal archetypes, the recurrent motif of long (sheathed) fangs merits further comment. One possible explanation is that the teeth hark back to Pleistocene megafauna and remains of creatures like *Protomnodon*, which had massive molars. Findings of such remains spawned stories of a prior 'monster' race. Another possibility is linked to the noted prevalence of 'ogres = pigs' across the southern and eastern areas of Papua New Guinea, even though the western Highlands ogres appear demonstrably anthropo-morphic. The most likely explanation for the aetiology of the fang motif is that it evidences a transformation ($\rightarrow$) in the ogre myth as it diffused throughout the region:

Ogre (pig) → Ogre (humanoid).

Even beyond the oft-noted symbolic and transactional convertibility of human: pig in this locale, there is other evidence which supports such a speculative thrust and which tempers counter-arguments that there is no more to these data than chance similitude.

For example, Chakravarti (1974:13,15) records a Mekeo folktale in which a brother inserts boar's tusks into his mouth to terrorise villagers before actually transforming into a monster pig. In somewhat parallel fashion, when Huli children play the game *Baya Horo Ibira* ('the ogre is coming': see 'Traditional Huli children's games' no.12, Chapter 1) they always represent the ogre by inserting two boar's tusks into their mouth (cf. Figure 4.2). More problematic, given the absence of any native rationale, is the question of why such teeth are often portrayed in narratives as having been 'sheathed'. This may relate to motivational themes of disguise – transformative states that typified, for example, 'vampire' traditions – or protection (ie. they are 'wrapped' until needed, like feathers and other items of adornment). Furthermore, one wonders whether sheathed fangs are symbolically like sheathed penes, both mediating elements, representing respectively asexual and sexual consumption. Given that Huli, certainly in figurative speech, draw an analogy between eating and having intercourse (cf. Goldman 1988:25, ll. 878–82) is the sheathing comparable, say, to the Winnebago Trickster's 'penis in a box' (Radin 1956)? Equally tantalising are the many resonances which this regional corpus has in terms of our knowledge of global ogre mythologies: these are the recurrent 'one-eyedness' – ease of destruction, bestial distortion, reflection of child-visions of adult visages? – gigantic size – McCarthy and Pfund report an eastern Highlands giant as 'so tall mountain moss grew on his head'(1973:22) – and mode of denouement – killed by young heroes who throw stones down the giant's mouth or spears into its eyes.

But going global with our monster motifs inevitably invites the kind of critique of unfounded speculation hurled against all such projects of vaguely Frazerian proportions. The pan-cultural existence of beliefs in ogres – from the Greek *scythian arimaspi* or *cyclopes* to the Scandanavian and Germanic giants – and indigenous histories that reflect an earlier epoch of cave-dwellers as in Huli and Daribi (Wagner 1978:71), will always prompt conjecture as products of coincidence, diffusion, archetypal patterns or some 'genetic encoding of narrative patterns' (cf. Stinton 1979:435). Nevertheless, common to Western ogrologies is a set of beliefs in primeval figures of an historically early time that in function and appearance are seemingly continuous with those briefly sketched above, and which, on all available scholarly indications, appear to have eastern derivations. In this vein, Motz's (1982) comparison of Germanic giants in folklore and Eddic mythology adumbrates a set of characteristics that serves well as an apt introduction to the Huli materials. These ogres are never 'wholly vanquished but present an ever-present threat' (ibid.:78) through subterranean imprisonment. In addition to having features (1), (2) and (6) listed above they also present as:

8   living outside communities;
9   associated with stones;
10   having peculiar head/eye forms;
11   having family social structures;
12   creators of landscape;
13   having a preordained defeat;
14   cave-dwellers

Let us then at this juncture take a reality check. The ogre emerges from the above very much as a synthetic image, a cultural representation drawn from a seemingly finite permutation of factors – a 'phenomenal conjunction' (Needham 1978:60) – disclosing psychic foundations certainly in part related to interaction with children. Beyond any regional motif phylum subsist pan-cultural commonalities in thematic structure and iconology. In the context of such ogre faiths the hoary question remains of how to explain the apparent incidence of similar belief patterns, in different places and at different times, when transmission seems at first glance unlikely. In this endeavour ogrologies need first to be fully contextualised within fields of social action where their meanings are reinvented and displayed, for 'it is not enough to study folk-tales as tales only. It is also necessary to make oneself familiar with the use of folk-tales, their life in tradition' (von Sydow 1948:44).

Baya Horo: What's in a Name?

The Huli perceive *Baya Horo* to constitute a type of *dama* – a general class of spirits of which some are ancestral progenitors, some ubiquitous presences, some specific to ritual forms, and all represent potential sources of danger. Informants consistently presented understandings of this ogre as an historically real race from an epoch predating all other *dama* and all major ritual activity. In the cycle of aetiological tales (Table 4.2) known as 'source/origin stories' (*tene te*), we find no interaction with any other spirit,

Table 4.2 Historical Cycle of Ogre Texts

Ref.	Personnel	Location	Plot abstract
Ts. 1 2(m)[1] #[2]	Garua & Mabili clans	Mbiduba, Lebani	BH kills Mabi Mabiya (Mabili). Garua (Tibi Tibiya), aided by non-cannibal BH daughters and Mabiya's relatives, kill all BH. [BH are invited to a ritual celebration (*peda*) and deceived by 'daughters' who set alight wood and stones that cause all BH to implode. Daughters flee to Nogoli.]
Ts. 2(m)	Pipini Dinga	Mt Ilu, Nogoli	Regenerated BH kills Pipini Yadinga, son of one of the BH daughters who had fled to Nogoli. The BH 'daughters' kill the BH. [BH enticed with food and as he cooks they cut him in half.]
Ts. 3(m)	Palindali, Paliwayali	Mt Marago	Regenerated BH captures a young victim which he wraps and leaves on top of a nut tree. Another young boy foils his plan and forces BH to Duna side where he turns to stone. [The young boy substitutes a stone for the victim, fooling BH, who is then further enticed to follow a long rope to Duna side.]
Ts. 4(m)	Hambu Puli,	Waralo,Hambuali Mt Ibira	Regenerated BH travels to Waralo (Hambuali) and kills a boy. Hambu Puli attempts to kill BH but he runs away. BH returns and kills five brothers. The last siblings, Biango Peli and his sister Gurubu Aguali, resolve to revenge their kin and kill BH. [Gurubu Aguali entices BH who is shot by Biango Peli (cf. Frankel 1986: 41).]
Ts. 5a 5b(m)	Dog, man	Gulupu, Daberanda	Regenerated BH takes a human bride. The bride's father's dog goes to Tombe and constructs a hideaway in an Areca tree where it and the father can watch BH's movements. BH returns to consume them and follows their path along Ayena river. As BH climbs the tree the dog and man hurl hot stones down his mouth. BH returns home and imprisons both his wife and another

Table 4.2 Historical Cycle of Ogre Texts (*continued*)

Ref.	Personnel	Location	Plot abstract
			woman.They escape and eventually entomb him. [Two women lure BH down a hole in Daberanda and then close the hole with large stones and hardwood logs.]
Ts. 6(*m*)³	Dala Pari	Hanapo Dorege, Mt Kare	Regenerated BH lands at Kare and wreaks havoc in tandem with the python Dala Pari. Huguru, son of Hogote, finally ties the python's jaw to prevent further wrongdoing.
Ts. 7(*m*)	Gindabu Gindame Daga Tinali Gugu Ibalime	Lagabe (Mogra Pugua)	BH woman, Gindabu Gindame, assumes identity of Gugu Ibalime and tricks her boyfriend, Daga Tinali, into shooting her and throwing her into the river. Her brothers, Hiribi Diwi and Nduali, find her and revive her. The boyfriend discovers the deception and throws the BH woman down a sinkhole closing the hole with large stones. He finds his real partner who eventually kills him in revenge. [The woman stuffs a pig with hot stones which blind the man when he attempts to cut the pig so that she is able to kill him.]

1	(*m/f*)	male/female narrators
2	#	sung performance
3		non-traditional addition

though ogres are perceived to exist on the boundary of man and *dama* (*agali damala tuni*), where 'man' signifies the earliest human progenitors. Importantly, and quite unlike even the trickster *Iba Tiri*, *Baya Horo* is not implicated as an ancestor in any genealogical charter. Ogres belonged to an epoch which is interpreted as bounded or closed off from the beginnings of human settlement and clan social organisation. The giant dynasty was obliterated in the remote past but, as will become clear, nevertheless represents a latent source of potential danger for future Huli generations.

The epithet *Baya Horo* is suitably constructed as an anthropophagous appellation betraying both some of the defining characteristics of the ogre, and some of the interpretative problems that have plagued analysis of pantheistic identities in Huli theology. The name is constructed of the terms *baya* (3-Past-'kill/hit') + *horo* ('to inter'). In Huli myths and folktales we find these terms (the morphs of which are shown in bold in Figure 4.3)

Baya Horo				
A Generic Huli terms:				
Baya	**Horo**	*Naba*	**Bayaga**	*Horo*
Bayaga	**Horo**	*Nabaya*	*Balu*	*Nana*
Baya	**Horo**	*Nabaliya*	*Balu*	*Nabono*
Balu	*Nolene*	*Nabene*	*Balu*	*Nolene*
Bayaga	*Nalu*	*Nabene*	*Horo*	*Nabu*
Bayaga	*Balu*	*Nolene*	*Nalu*	*Nabiya*

B Generic Huli cognates of Duna terms:	
Auwebe	*Papuna Nabene*
Hulu Auwebe	*Ayege Dabali* (F)
Auwebe Auwanda	*Dawene Mope*

C Individual ogre names:			
Nali	*Horali*	*Baruna*	*Naruna*
Nangu Nana	*Bauwi Nana*	*Kewago*	*Ewago*
Girabo	*Yuni*	*Girabo*	*Hini*
Girabo	*Galuni*	*Girabo*	*Gauni*
Tauwanda	*Tauwa*	*Handara*	*Wabara*
Ariba	*Tauwa*	*Ula*	*Uwane*
Palindali	*Paliwayali*	*Urubua Aba*	*Tiyabe*
Gindabu (M)	*Gindame* (F)	*Nogobe*	*Gelo*
Gili Gelali			

Figure 4.3 Ogre nomenclature

poetically embellished through various forms of non-conventional reduplication or verbal inflection, much as already discussed for child speech play in Chapter 1. Most frequently the name is collocated with some equally contrived form of the verb 'consume/ingest' (*na*) to produce a prototypical epithetical string of:

Kill [*ba*] + Inter [*horo*] + Consume [*na*].

In many cases, as Figure 4.3 reveals, the same anthropophagous morphemes occur in individual ogre names (eg. *Nangu Nana*). Where this is not the case, most other appellations in Figure 4.3 (C) form part of rhyming dyadic or triadic sets exhibiting degrees of phonological similarity (as underlined below) in the component lexemes. For example:

(Figure 4.3 (C)

       Palind<u>ali</u> : *<u>Pali</u>wayali*   *Hand<u>ara</u>* : *Wab<u>ara</u>*

(Appendix 1, – Ts. 2:ll. 79–84)

       Girabo Yu<u>ni</u> Hi<u>ni</u> Gau<u>ni</u>   *Da<u>wa</u>nda <u>Tauwa</u>* : *Ariba <u>Tauwa</u>*

The occurrence of the names in Figure 4.3 (B) indicates, as is explained more fully below, the Huli belief that the historical origins of BH lie in Duna territory. *Auwebe* (Appendix 1, Ts. 1: ll. 4,15 and Ts. 2: ll. 72,293), which is commonly employed by narrators in the Huli region, is clearly cognate with Duna *Auwepe* (Haley 1993:80), as is *Dawene Mope* with the Duna *Dana Mope* (Modjeska: personal communication) that in its literal usage refers to the fossilised bones of BH.

Beyond the semantic encoding of anthropophagy in the BH appellations, and indeed the continuities in synonym structure these sustain with names elsewhere in the fantasy economy, lie further layers of symbolic meaning. Indeed, the valency of BH as a negative moral foil in Huli child psyche is partially revealed by the terminological relationships the tag sustains with other similarly constituted names in Huli cosmology. We begin thereby to articulate the links between names, games and scaffolding pantheistic figures. I have in mind here the infamous figure of *Baya Baya* (Glasse 1965:46; Frankel 1986:23; Goldman 1983:116). Baya (BB) now refers both to a set of rites which formed part of a large fertility cycle known as *dindi pongo* ('knot of the earth') and to a young Duna boy who in the recent past was inadvertently killed. Various parts of the mythology of BB were ritually invoked (involving, it is claimed, child sacrifice) to regenerate (*gini*) land and people, and supposedly to provoke the dark period (*mbingi*) which heralds the fecund ash fallout (*da pindu*: 'goods of the sky'). The anatomical parts of BB are believed to have been variously distributed among Huli clans in accordance with a well-known schema partially reproduced below:

Huli clan name	Body part	
Tiba	*tibini*	Eighths
Wida	*wi*	Penis
Ayago	*ayuni*	Spleen
Tiri	*tini*	Intestines
Hiwa	*himuni*	Abdomen
Hambuali	*hambuni*	Lips
Halengo	*halene*	Ears

We can see that the initial phonological shape of a body part lexeme is also shared by the clan appellation (marked in bold), so that in recitation the two form a rhyming pair of terms based on assonance or alliteration. The point that has re-emerged time and again throughout the expositions of Huli materials is the sense in which their experience of history, a part of their experience of culture itself, is mediated through the creative imagination and poetic portraiture of fictionality. History is as it is because it is good to say it that way – it presents as partially a soundscape of truth. Narrative codifications are founded on aesthetic engineering and speech play irrespective of the fact/fantasy status of its knowledge content.

Now whatever historical importance BB had in pre-contact Huli cosmology, most observers agree that accounts have now been overlaid with Christian doctrines that promote identification between Christ and BB (incarnate innocence and sacrifice), and between Christ's mother and BB's mother. Most probably this syncretism has altered too the manner in which the term BB has been both (mis)understood and used. Thus Frankel noted 'Bayebaye means "perfect"'(1986:23), no doubt persuaded by the homonymy between the lexeme *baya* ('good') and the name *Baya[e]*. However, not only is the emphatic form of 'good' in Huli *baya bayele*, but on this interpretative principle one might otherwise be persuaded to render *Baya Horo* as akin to the stereotypical Australian greeting of 'good (*baya*) day (*horo*)' – an odd epithet for a cannibal monster who wilfully transgresses rules of conduct, not to mention grammatical word order between noun and adjective in the language! More likely, the term *Baya Baya* reproduces the notion of 'killed (*baya*) killed (*baya*)', an intransitive counterpoise to the transitive 'killed' reflected in *Baya Horo*. The death and destruction symbolised by the ogre are here set against the death and creative regeneration symbolised by the Duna boy; the terminological reflection of this semantic relatedness is the mutual incorporation of the single lexeme *Baya*. The identities are similar and yet different. The failure to remain sensitive to such delicacies of translation may explain why those working ideological transformations of Huli traditions in terms of Christian doctrine did not seize the possibility of recasting *Baya Horo* as the 'devil', a common fate that befell many early European ogres.

The above argument is of course based on an implicit assumption that, in the generation of character names, such semantic considerations may be encoded so as to establish relationships between cosmologically axiomatic figures. What other evidence is there that might support such a premise? If the history of anthropological analyses of myth teaches us anything it is that myths at some level define a logic of oppositions. Given that all scholars (cf. Lévi-Strauss 1963; LeRoy 1985) of myth have invariably identified the dual symbolic categories of 'life and death' as *the* fundamental antinomy of human existence – along with allied transformational themes of rebirth, restoration and regeneration – the natural antithesis of '*Baya*'-based characters in Huli would be those which trade on the name 'water/fluid' (*iba*), the elixir of human life *par excellence*. And indeed *the* culture hero and trickster in Huli is named *Iba Tiri* ('water fool'). Significantly both *Baya Horo* and *Iba Tiri* (hereafter IT) share features not common to any other spirit in the pantheon: (1) they are the subject of both historical and fictional tales; (2) they co-occur in stories relating epic struggles as opposed forces; (3) they have well-developed characteristics and psyches; (4) they are associated with narrative 'cycles' (as for example in the English 'Jack cycle' of stories); and (5) they alone are represented in both proverbs and children's games – that is, they alone have permeated everyday Huli discourse. One might thus suggest that the contracted relationships between BH and BB are both opposed and balanced by those contracted between the schizophrenic egos of IT as respectively destructive buffoon and creative culture hero, explained more fully in the next chapter.

Other narrative characters whose positive identity is marked by *Iba* are *Iba Mulu Lunguya* (the Huli 'superman' described below), *Iba Gurubuniya* and *Iba Gurugu* (other minor narrative heroes). In this regard, one must also include both *Iba Giya/Iba Wiliaba/Iba Dagia* – the terms of reference (cf. Goldman 1983:326) used for bachelor cult (*Haroli*) initiates whose spiritual and bodily health critically depended on the ingestion of bespelled water – and *Ibago Wali* – the name of the woman who turned the bow around so that men could use it properly (cf. Goldman 1983:232). The oppositions of Figure 4.4 further throw into relief the symbolic association of trickster with cultural renewal, as the horizontal passage from death to life is also seen by Huli as historically one of 'disappearance/destruction' to 'appearance/existence' (cf. Chakravarti 1974:12).

Suffice it to remark at this stage that IT, as seems to be the case across cultures which have trickster figures (cf. Pelton 1980:255), is associated with

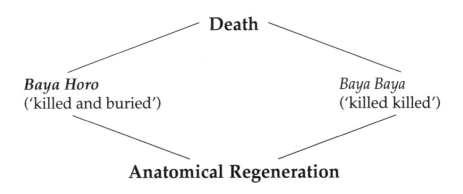

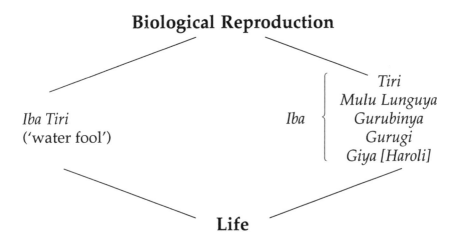

Figure 4.4 Ogre and trickster symbolism

phallicism and the creation of sexual mores in Huli culture (cf. Goldman 1983:223, 1995). Its symbolic efficacy is then very much one rooted in *biological reproduction* – a 'symbol of the procreating power' (Radin 1956:146). By contrast, both BH and BB appear as 'asexual' figures whose powers of rebirth (in the sense of spontaneous recreation of form, mitosis or fertile remains) are based on *anatomical regeneration*. This contrast is perhaps further signalled by the previously mentioned symbolic apposition between sheathed fangs and hidden penes. The opposition between *Baya* and *Iba* figures may be phrased as that between two types of creativity as much as between life and death. These findings support the previously made point that our understanding of Huli ogres is dependent on the cultural significance attached to Huli tricksters and other identities in the cosmological pantheon. Figure 4.4 thus explicates the sense in which the synthetic images of ogres and tricksters represent a primal symbolic complex as a property of imaginative consciousness in Huli.

Succinctly put, the ogre looks very much at this stage like an antagonistic, immoral force in the universe, opposed by the trickster and thus ultimately inimical to humans. We know too, foreshadowing further discussion below, that the ogre is mimicked in child play and games, that children as young as 4 are able to recount ogre stories, and that children use the trickster appellation in their fantasy play teasing. We are left in no doubt that as juxtaposed moral identities this primal symbolic complex of ogre/trickster is one that is internalised in some part by child pretenders. From the data presented above Baya Horo is, in name alone, the ultimate child bogy.

Baya Horo: **The Narrativised Identity**

> But it is all pretend, of course, and this explains why some narrative features grow larger than life.
>
> LeRoy 1985:25

The Huli terminologically mark a distinction between historical talk, *bi tene/ tene te* (talk (*bi*)/account (*te*) + source/origin (*tene*)), and fictional talk, *bi te* (talk + account) that superficially appears to parallel similar distinctions drawn among the Kewa (*ramani: lidi*: LeRoy 1985), Duna (*pikono: hapiapo tse*: Stürzenhofecker 1993; Haley 1993), Daribi (*namu: po*: Wagner 1978) and many other Highlands societies. Huli consciousness of BH is very much grounded in the ensemble of narratives and evidential landscape associated with these traditions. However, such emic categories, as appears the case across folklore cultures, have the capacity to confound ready classification as 'fact' and 'fiction' for both indigenes, where unanimity on genre rubric may be unimportant, and indeed analysts alike (cf. Needham 1978:54). In the context of Huli oral tradition, this appears related to the profound insight that 'from historical speech fictional speech will later emerge' (*tene te mani mo bi te holebira*). What this implies is that the two domains are not relatively autonomous but are mutually referential, mutually implicative, mutually incorporative, and mutually instantiated in any single narrative. The same events and even personae can occur across the two categories with an oscillation between what we ordinarily gloss as fiction and non-fiction. This lack of genre discreteness implies then that the bifurcated categories are better thought of as indications of how the information in any narrative should be understood. Very much as we noted in the Introduction, and has been argued by literary theorists like Searle (1975) and Ariel (1984), the terms denote not a property of some text but rather an attitudinal or propositional stance of *pretence* or *non-pretence* to be taken towards a set of discourses. For both narrator and audience there are conventional cues which signal how such information is to be processed in respect of these modalities of appreciation.

As a general rule *tene te* tend to be spatially and temporally (see Table 4.2) contextualised in terms of place names, visible evidence markers like landscape features (Appendix 1, Ts. 1: l. 18), and may interweave genea-logical information (*malu*) such as ancestral or clan names in the account. By contrast *bi te* are rarely anchored to real geography but rather incoporate pre-formulated sets of names referencing fabled places, rivers and partic-ipants. These genre transformation markers are additional to conventions like openings and closings which of themselves may indicate the inform-ational intentions of the narrator. Both types of tale can be delivered either in a relatively unembellished prose, or in their most stylistically appreciated form in a distinctive melodic recitation known as *bi mo*, 'good style'. They tend to be sung at night in the company of other adults and children irrespective of age. Poetic conventions include parallel repetition, context-specific synonym substitutions, and the framing of story events and actions in cellular structures that are marked by metanarrative forms of the inflected verb 'say', as discussed previously in Chapter 2.

An indication of the process of poetic fictionalisation can be gained by comparing the narrative modes of Transcripts 1 and 2 (Appendix 1), which are ostensibly a single aetiological account of the origins of *Baya Horo* for Huli. Both versions were recounted by the same story-teller. The first was in essence a practice run delivered in front of an audience as a check on the accuracy and sequence of events to be related, much as is the case among the Daribi (Wagner 1978:11). What is represented as 20 lines of text in Ts. 1 takes up 112 lines of text in Ts. 2. This is entirely attributable to embellish-ment with conventionalised synonym sets (*kai*: see Chapter 1) where an ordinary-language lexeme may have several poetic analogues (preceded by → in the following list):

Ts. 2: ll. 3–10,36	*tia* (possum)	→	*yagi ainya, limbu ainya, limbawi ainya, homa haguanda*
Ts. 2: ll. 11,23,27	*hana* (moon)	→	*hiru waya, ega hombene, daga hana*
Ts. 2: ll. 46–55	*manda* (hair)	→	*mbalu duni, hondo duni, dabiale duni, wandiba duni, hundube duni*

| Ts. 2: ll. 209–12 | *dibu* (dawn) | → | *iba gurubu, bane, banewa* |
| Ts. 2: ll. 265–70 | *danda* (bow) | → | *dingi, wara, waralu* |

Significantly, the narrator constantly switches between the location of events as referenced to existing clans (Ts. 2:ll.144–58) and place names:

| Ts. 2: ll. 39–40 | Mbiduba, Baluba, Payena, Pele, Dale |
| Ts. 2: ll. 309–22 | Komi, Komiabu, Galoma, Baria, Yubi, Galuma |

and events located in 'fantasy land' as denoted by widely known kai sets used with features like banks (*tigida*), valleys (*pango*), rivers (*iba*), mountains (*hari*), bridges (*togo*) and cleared grounds (*hama*):

Ts. 2: ll. 58–68, 115–16,133–8	Umili, Tombeli, Yaguali, Yawe, Yalinga, Yalima, Hinini, Lumuni, Daiba, Dedaiba
Ts. 2: ll. 171–9	Duwane, Dunduwane, Wania Mai, Bebenani, Aiolame, Gendolame, Auwi Yuli, Pingi Yuli
Ts. 2: ll. 235–9	Dendeba, Paleda, Yawa, Yalinga, Yalima

This fusion of what is to be taken as having actually happened, and what is to be taken as poetic embellishment, does not present interpretative problems for an audience who know from the appearance of certain names, and the redundant facts to which they refer, that these are 'as-if' propositional statements. Importantly then, an historically true tale (like that of Appendix 1, Ts. 1–2) can in Huli, and within the context of a sung performance, have its 'facts' embellished by inclusion of non-factual referents and events from a stock fantasy landscape. The narrative, like the figures of the ogre and trickster, presents to children as a constantly transformational artefact moving between truth as 'what stays' (*henene*) and pretence as what temporarily is embodied (*tingi*). The myth, its performance and its figures, are structurally homologous with the frame shifting that typifies child fantasy play.

Because so much of the performativity of ogres as a fusion of fact and fantasy is enveloped then by conventions which are embedded in narrative processes and performances, we are compelled to examine how ogres are constructed in Huli oral literature. Many of the data on which this analysis of BH is based thus consist of a loose ensemble of texts, collected over a period of two decades, which have in common that they involve in some way ogres, ogresses and ogrillons. Those peceived as predominantly about an historical cycle of events are listed in Table 4.2, while those which consensually presented as fiction are given in Table 4.3. The tables show that ogres interact with a host of characters some of which are exclusive to the imaginative world of *bi te* (Figure 4.5 (d–i)), and some of which, like BH, are cross-genre (Figure 4.5 (a–c)) in type. For example, Bebogo Wane Pandime (c) is frequently implicated in aetiological accounts of Haroli (Goldman 1983:325). Only the narratively recurrent and major figures have been listed in Figure 4.5.

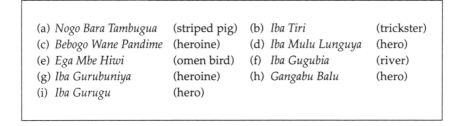

(a) *Nogo Bara Tambugua*	(striped pig)	(b) *Iba Tiri*	(trickster)
(c) *Bebogo Wane Pandime*	(heroine)	(d) *Iba Mulu Lunguya*	(hero)
(e) *Ega Mbe Hiwi*	(omen bird)	(f) *Iba Gugubia*	(river)
(g) *Iba Gurubuniya*	(heroine)	(h) *Gangabu Balu*	(hero)
(i) *Iba Gurugu*	(hero)		

Figure 4.5 Major *bi te* characters

'Beyond Belief': Narrative Conventions and Imagination

How then do Huli construct ogres as narratively encoded presences which transcend the perceptive limits of audiences? This larger-than-life figure is here set against the 'other' in a contrastive relation that is privative, not equipollent; the amalgam is one of positively defined features unique to ogres and attributes which are based on the absence of humanoid properties, much as Homer articulated Cyclopean existence. Many of the tales in which ogres appear incorporate recurrent story motifs. Two examples follow:

1 Story themes may relate how a sequence of people, often related as close family members or siblings, encounter misadventures when seeking to discover what harm befell one of them. This morphological theme corresponds to Propp's (1968) Function 1: 'One of the members of a family is absent from home.' The plot allows for the last and youngest sibling, or orphaned child/children, to exact revenge on the agent of death – often a BH – before reviving the slain victims. As is evident from the plot abstracts of Tables 4.2–4.3, *Baya Horo* are depicted as easily duped oafs. Lacking the trickster's subtle cunning, they are frequently

Table 4.3 Fictional texts of *Baya Horo*

Ref.	Personnel	Location	Plot abstract
Ts. 8(*m*)[1]	Hogorene Giwi	Lebani	While en route to collect oil in Lebani each one of five brothers is in turn accosted by the ogrillon Hogerene Giwi, who invites them to stay in his house. While asleep they are disembowelled. The fifth and youngest of the brothers eventually finds the dead bodies and kills Hogorene Giwi. With water, possum intestines and *nigi* (Laportea sp.) leaves he revives his brothers. [He entices Hogorene Giwi to the forest to collect grubs and then entraps him between two halves of a split log. A large fire is lit and Baya Horo implodes.]
Ts. 9(*f*)	Mandi Pubu Mbuli Pubu	–	Mbuli Pubu chances upon a BH who had prepared pig meat and intestines and had stuffed them down into the neck part of his head which he had temporarily removed from his body. Mbuli, who sees this from his hiding place, removes the meat before BH reconnected his head and returns to Mandi. On a subsequent occasion Mandi follows his brother to obtain his own meat but is caught and eaten by the BH.
Ts. 10a(*c*)[2]	–	–	A father is killed by BH while out looking for his Nogo Bara Tambugua. His wife searches for him and is also killed and eaten by the same BH. The orphaned children collect small lizards and insects and when BH comes to kill the children the insects shout and scare him away.
Ts. 10b(*f*)	–	–	As for Ts. 10a with the following changes: the pig swallows the parents' heads and regurgitates them in front of the two daughters, telling them to collect the lizards, grasshopers, cockroaches, worms and frogs.
Ts. 11 (*c*)	EMH[3]	–	An old man finds a large egg at the top of a pandanus tree which turns into a

Table 4.3 Fictional texts of *Baya Horo* (*continued*)

Ref.	Personnel	Location	Plot abstract
			boy the next morning. The boy later befriends a BH woman who leads him to BH land. While there the boy meets an old woman who gives him a parcel (*hubuane*) with the injunction not to eat the BH food. The boy escapes and the BH kills and cooks the old woman instead.
Ts. 12 (*m*)#	IML⁴/IT⁵	–	Five BH brothers are fighting over some nuts and IML kills one of the BH. The relatives of BH perform divination and two BH find IML. Each holds onto one side of his hair to pull him apart. But two IT intercede to rescue him and the BH go away. The two IT revive IML with water, pigs' liver and intestines, ginger and *nigi* (*Laportea* sp.) leaves.
Ts. 13(*c*)	–	–	BH woman entices each one of five brothers in turn to prepare a death platform for her supposedly dead husband, who then kills and eats them in succession. The fifth brother digs a large burial hole and throws both the BH woman and her husband into it.
Ts. 14(*m*)	NBT⁶/ Iba Gugubia	–	A father follows his lost NBT and is killed by a BH. His wife searches for him and gives her two children a magic parcel (*hubuane*) to be used if BH should come to their house while she is away. The BH kills her, cuts off her breasts, which he inserts into a bamboo, and makes his way to the children's house to feed them the flesh. Each time he attempts to catch the children they unwrap the parcel, place it under their armpit, and transform themselves into birds before flying off into the trees.
Ts. 15(*f*)#	BWP⁷/Iba Gurugu	–	Four sisters abuse their fifth and youngest sister BWP. BH entices each one of the four sisters in succession with pig meat and then kills them. Aided by Iba Gurugu, the fifth sister tricks BH by telling him at the lower end of the

Table 4.3 Fictional texts of *Baya Horo* (*continued*)

Ref.	Personnel	Location	Plot abstract
			valley people are cooking food, and she then pushes BH down a hill. Iba Gurugu transforms into IML and they marry.
Ts. 16(*m*)	BWP/IML EMH/Iba Gugubia/ IT	–	IML meets the poor BWP, who has no relatives or house or garden. He takes her back to his mother's place and she works hard building house and gardens. IML becomes angry with her and goes off to Obena to attend a celebration (*mali*). IML's mother and BWP follow him, but they are attacked by Obena, and they fight for five days. BWP takes out her parcel (*hubuane*) and pays compensation before returning home with IML's mother. The mother dies and is buried by BWP, who then shares the funeral (*homanego*) pigs with relatives and IT. BH arives and tells her they are going off together. She destroys all gardens, houses and personal belongings and cuts off her fifth finger in grief. BH kills and eats her. IML discovers what happened and in despair attempts suicide before changing into a bird.
Ts. 17(*m*)#	IT/IML EMH	–	Darama Ginu, a small boy full of sores, is abused by his brother every day. The older brother goes to a Mali in Obena and locks Darama Ginu in the house. The boy manages to extricate himself and chances upon BWP. BWP cares for him, does all the work, kills a pig and gives some to IT. Darama Ginu claims he is unable to work on account of his sores, so BWP prepares men's decorations and shows him how to change into IML by entering and exiting red and black lakes respectively. His brother returns with a BH woman; both abuse him as before. But IML and BWP run away together.

Table 4.3 Fictional texts of *Baya Horo* (*continued*)

Ref.	Personnel	Location	Plot abstract
Ts. 18(*m*)#	IML/BWP	–	IML steals some pandanus nuts from the gardens of BH. There is a fight and IML is helped by BWP's relatives, who destroy the BH.
Ts. 19(*m*)#	IML/IT/IG⁸ Gurubuniya	–	IML is staying with his old mother Bauwa Dundame. While he is gone BH arrives, abducts her and kills her. The body floats in the flooded rivers and drifts to IT's place. IML hears about what has happened and recovers his mother's body. While there he meets Iba Gurubuniya (IG) and they perform divination (*toro*) to discover the culprit BH. IG entices BH into the gardens, where IML kills him. But the Pipiya Buawaya bird tells the BH relatives what has transpired and they search out IML and fight for three days. They shoot IG and IML kills two BH in revenge. He obtains pig's liver, water and some *nigi* (Laportea sp.) leaves and revives IG. BH groups lie in wait for IML, IG and their pig (*buru tamia ainya*). When BH try to kill IML the pig dashes them to the ground, throws one into a hole, and consumes the other.
Ts. 20(*c*)	–	–	Two men in the forest are cutting wood and hunting possum. They are joined by a BH who eats all the possums himself while the men are cleaning out the intestines. On the next occasion they make BH clean the intestines and consume the excreta.

1 (*m/f*) male/female narrators
2 (*c*) child narrator
3 EMH Ega Mbe Hiwi
4 IML Iba Mulu Lunguya
5 IT Iba Tiri
6 NBT Nogo Bara Tambugua
7 BWP Bebogo Wane Pandime
8 IG Iba Gurubuniya

enticed or deceived by various food forms – as in the Polyphemus tale – so that their downfall is portrayed as a reflection of their state of greed for human flesh and pig. The ritualised dialogue frequently proceeds by locating the pursuit, rescue and denouement in the land of the ogres (cf. Dundes 1964:282).

2 Transformations of people into birds or inanimate landscape features, or of disfigured persons into beautiful heroes and heroines, are also recurrent motifs in Huli tales along with interdiction–violation–consequence sequences (cf. LeRoy 1985). This may be effectuated by the ubiquitous magic parcel (*hubuane*), or by passing through black and red lakes respectively, where red (as in the bachelor cult wig) signals the highest pinnacle of achievement.

Such themes are interwoven then with standard narrative techniques aimed at enhancing dramatic excitement and describing what is explicitly presented as 'beyond description'. For example, pre-formulated interrogative sequences (like that of Text 4.1) invariably presage an arrival of *Baya Horo*. This may take the form of some representation of interior conversation by a central character, much like the verbal formula associated with the Western hero Superman – 'Is it a bird? Is it a plane? Is it a rocket? No, it's Superman!'

Text 4.1
Ts. 16: Appendix 1
Informant: Kadia (Koma clan), Yaluba 1977

---

1 *O biagoreni beraria haburalu*
2 while sitting there a sun shower came
3 *dambe dayele gemboria ogoria mialu dai dai bini lama hendeni*
4 it's been seen the raindrops were taken from the wild bamboo leaves which
5 dried up again
6 *edele nadele gemboria mialu dai dai bini lama hendeni*
7 it's been seen the raindrops were taken from the wild bamboo leaves which
8 dried up again
9 *dawi dayago hugulu yunini wini mialu dai dai bini*
10 the raindrops were taken from the wild bamboo leaves which dried up
11 again
12 *ani biyagola nde*
13 it was like that and then
14 *agile agi handarobe*

15 what will I see?
16 *waba gabua handarobe*
17 will I see a wild pig?
18 *dodo andi handarobe*
19 will I see an eagle?
20 *habolima handarobe*
21 will I see a cassowary?
22 *Balu Nolene Nabene igini handarobe*
23 will I see the son of Baya Horo?

In ll. 1–13 a sense of expectation and tension is built up in the audience that they are about to witness the entry of the ogre, indicated by the familiar rain and sun shower, and the image of raindrops being taken from leaves, which giants are known to do. This impending presence is further dramatised by the pre-formatted sequence of rhetorical questions that follow in ll. 14–23. In addition to the above, there are a number of canonical devices Huli poets rely on to convey the truth of ogres as 'the truth of our imagination' (Bettelheim 1975:117). For the most part, they exhibit quite striking similarity to those used by Homer (1961:145) to frame his picture of Cyclopean identity.

Bracketing Devices

> \<He then picked up a huge stone, with which he closed the entrance. It was a mighty slab, such as you couldn't have budged from the ground.\>

> Homer 1961:145

Most typically descriptive information is bracketed by a repeated phrase which functions as an explicit solicitation to suspend disbelief (cf. Appendix 1, Ts. 2: ll. 284, 354, 363):

```
... ogo(bi)alebe        toba         hea
this + like + IGV    ignorant    be-3-PTST
[the like of which one is ignorant of]
like you can't imagine
```

directly paralleling the use of 'explicit fantasy proposals' used by children when initiating their make-believe play episodes. So whatever structural similarities may subsist between non-verbal games and the 'motifemes' (Dundes 1964) of verbal folklore, there are clearly continuities in the way adults and children pattern fictional episodes, whether playful or serious.

One example of how this technique is deployed – as it is in the above Homeric extract – is given below. Text 4.2 depicts Iba Mulu Lunguya, the Huli male *par excellence*, whose appearance is always portrayed as 'beyond' known ideals of beauty. The text is complemented by one describing extreme female beauty, previously presented as an introductory citation to this book:

Text 4.2
Field notes
Informant: Giame, Yaluba 1993

---

uyuguria handa tagi halu heria
While they were looking outside
gulu babu gulu barabu gulu pilipe pili logobe o lama igiri mbira ibiya
One boy came blowing these pan pipes
igiri ibiyaria ai ibiyabe toba hayagola
As the boy came she didn't know who was coming
wali biago ibu gi howa handalu heria igiri ale la tago tago howa nabi layago
When she saw him she was frightened because this boy was not like other boys

→ *unduni hundu mandaru ogobialebe toba hea layago*
  With a wig coiffure like you can't imagine
→ *ulu babu gulu barabu gulu ogoalebe toba hea layago*
  With cordyline leaves like you can't imagine
→ *honagaga lagoli uru ogoalebe toba hea laya*
  With brown cassowary feathers fixed on his wig like a kneecap on a knee, such as you can't imagine
pulu yabe kindiru ogoalebe toba hea laya
With a flapping bag decoration like you can't imagine
geni ge haleru ogoalebe toba hea laya
With leg bands on the legs like you can't imagine
pagabua mano gu gau learu ogoalebe toba hea laya
With the apron ends making sounds like that made by pigs when moving, like you can't imagine
gelabo mandibu gugu ndibu learu ogoalebe toba hea laya
With the apron sitting tightly on each thigh like you can't imagine
agali igini ale tago tago nabi ibiniya laya
A person like this man's son couldn't be mentioned in the same breath as others, and he came
agali igini handaya howa nabiya laya
It wasn't possible even to look at this man's son
Iba Mulu Lungiya agali igini ndo

Iba Mulu Lungiya was not like any man's son
walirume bi labe naheaya
It wasn't possible even for women to talk to him
igiri hegene aube toba hea
This was a clever man like you can't imagine
amu daramabi biagoria dugu yalu tagira ibiyagola igiri labona agali iginila paliaba
loa nabi nahea
When he came out of the red lake he was an utterly amazing man such
that you couldn't tell another person to go and sleep with him

Iba Mulu Lunguya is depicted as having a full complement of decorative dress items but all in a state of such excellence as to defy imagination. Not only is he in a league of his own, but so exalted as to render women dumbstruck and men reticent to approach or stay with him. The character is drawn then in terms of outward physical appearance rather than inner mental states or dispositions. Importantly, Huli folktale figures are not sketched by detailing stereotypical behaviour patterns in terms of enumerative lists of deeds or the championing of causes or ideologies. Their bodies betray their moralities as much as their deeds speak volumes about their quality of mind. In this context, 'like you can't imagine' indexes how Huli myth makers, be they adult or child pretenders, reproduce their imaginative products as evasive fantasies (Needham 1978:60) – reflecting dispositions to exceed limitations, to suspend disbelief, to intimate the 'larger-than-life' dimensions to their pretenceful products.

Negated Normality

<And what a formidable monster he was. No one would have taken him for a man who ate bread like ourselves.>

Homer 1961:144

Working in tandem with such explicit disbelief markers are statements, invariably couched in the negative (cf. Austin 1983), which portray the abnormality of figures by rendering impossible certain behaviours which in the normal course of things should present no problems. For example, in Appendix 1, Ts. 2: l. 271, Tibiya declares that his mortal weapons are incapable of killing *Baya Horo*:

Baya   *babenahego*
Baya Horo   kill + NEG + ABIL + EMPH
It's not possible to kill *Baya Horo*

Ordinary people cannot talk to, sleep with, or be included (*tago*) or mentioned (*la tago*) in the same company as supermen like Iba Mulu Lunguya (see Text 4.2):

Table 4.3, Ts. 19

→ *agali   iginiale   tago tago nabi   ibiniya   laya*
man son + like mix mix NEG + do-STSTM come-RP say-3-PST
[Like this man's son one can't mix and he came it is said]
this wasn't like any ordinary man's son and he came it is said

. . .

honogagaru mani gudi layagola
cassowary feathers flow down the back of his (Iba Mulu Lunguya) neck
→ *agali igini la tago howa nabi*
he cannot be referred to as like any ordinary man's son

Table 4.3, Ts. 17

igiri labona agali iginila paliaba loa nabi
this impossible boy, an ordinary person couldn't say to him 'Let's sleep together'

These 'others' are set apart as interactionally unequal with ordinary Huli; they cannot be conversed with, are not genealogically derived from mortal origins:

Table 4.3, Ts. 18

→ *Gongodale lame Togome lame walime gime bini ndo*
his (IML) mothers Gongodale and Togome were not from a woman's hands
[born of another kind of woman]
ilu hali yule bini nu dambale Gabialu ilu hali yule bini mbira biarume
they used to make bags and aprons from the flying fox bones from Gabialu
→ *walirume   bi   labenaheya*
women + ERG   talk   say + NEG + ABIL + PEV
it was impossible for women to talk to him

and cannot be caught like normal prey:

Table 4.3, Ts. 15

Iba Mulu Lunguya

. . .

→   *balu minalu mina ore nabiya laya laro*
    it was impossible to hit, catch or hold him

The larger-than-life character of any persona may thus be indicated by statements which overtly deny comparison with humans in terms of either their own identity, or aspects of their social life, such as the pigs in the *Baya Horo* ecology:

Table 4.3, Ts. 17

→   *agali nogo ndo*
    not (like) a man's (human) pig
    ne gayeneru gibi mbira ede biagoria karara ngarara laga bialu
    with enormous tusks it was shouting and scowling there

Positive Abnormality

<we were going to find ourselves face to face with some being of colossal strength and ferocity, to whom the law of man and god meant nothing.>

Homer 1961:145

In apposition to what I have called 'negated normality' – in which conventionality is explicitly denied – the narrator may, conversely, positively indicate the 'extraordinary' either by means of the content contained in the characterisations, or by incorporation of hyperbolic terms like *hiriribi* ('frighteningly/amazing'), *kulu mege* ('intimidating'), *gibi* ('enormous/ incredible'), or *labona* ('extraordinary': cf. Text 4.2):

Table 4.3, Ts. 17

→   *igiri labona agali iginila paliaba loa nabi*
    This boy (IML) capable of amazing feats, it wasn't possible to ask him to sleep with you

→   *igiri labona gibiore gudu mamu pagabua ere dambeleru*
    this amazing incredible boy (IML) with shell necklace and pigs' tails on
    his apron

Table 4.3, Ts. 8

emene biago ndo agali ale bunia hale piyagoni
BH was not (now) small but had transformed into the size of a man
→   *timbini gibi Baya Horo nabaya agali ibini hiriribi*
    a big enormous ogre, a frightening real humaniod

Significantly, in comparisons made between not-human (ogre) and human
the ogre may itself be used as a rhetorical gauge for portraying relative
size or 'otherwordly' status. In the following extract Iba Mulu Lunguya is
portrayed as 'ogre-like':

Table 4.3, Ts. 18

Iba Mulu Lunguya agali igini ndo
IML was there, not like a man's son
Auwebedege mbaluego
he seemed like an ogre (in size)

Statements of Effect

<With a great din he cast this [bundle] down inside the cavern, giving us such
a fright that we hastily retreated to an inner recess . . . the booming voice and
the very sight of the monster filled us with panic.>

Homer 1961:146

Somewhat differently, a redactor may indicate the nature of some super-
normal character by describing the effects produced by their presence or
actions; that, for example, they instil fear (*gi*) confusion (*purugu*: Appendix
1, Ts.3: l. 61), induce extreme shyness (*yurigi*) or cause the land or animals
to shake and move. As for the Cyclops Polyphemus so for Baya Horo:

Text 4.3
Table 4.3, Ts. 19

Baya Horo came down
ega hinana urume ega ayuba urume lama agini pulipuli piyagola
the birds were flapping around frightened
Gurubi yari Gedene yari Garobi yari mbira biarume unu Wabia i dindi yagi hangu piya
the cassowaries from Gurubi, Gedene and Garobi went down to Wabia side
irabe gabua biarume kau laua
the wild pigs shouted too
Girabo Yuni ge kulu layago
Girabo Yuni's (ogre) footsteps made thundering sounds
nogombi lepage puya urume emama bialu piai heneni
all the snakes moved and went away
dindi emama bini
the ground shook

From a comparative consideration of the above devices and texts we gain an insight into both how Huli construct their unbelievable worlds and figures as 'like you can't imagine', and what continuities subsist here with the narrative conventions used by children in their fantasy play speech. In all of these respects ogres are etched in the same fashion as Huli heroes and heroines. The incidence of credibility markers and the predominance of negativity are rhetorical strategies which throw into relief the comparative discontinuity between human and non-human existences, between civilised and barbarian cultures, and between utopian and entropic worlds. These are the critical contrasts which underlie and motivate descriptions based on negative assertions. And indeed it is this poetic formula which so atypically characterises Homer's portrait of the Cyclopic world: 'even his positive assertions are recapitulations of statements asserted in the negative. The Cyclopes have no *themis* (state law); they put their faith in the *undying* gods; they *neither* plant *nor* plough, but everything grows *unplanted* and *unploughed*' (Austin 1983:23).

Cyclopean Figures, Ecology, Polity and Psyche

Attributes and Anthropophagy

The process of fleshing out the specific character of *Baya Horo* is one which will intentionally move between mythic texts and wider embodiments in cultural forms like proverbs, song, games and nursery rhymes. Most Huli when asked to describe ogres can proffer a routine verbal formula (*pureremo*) not dissimilar in content to that of Text 4.4, which provides a useful introduction to the principal make-up of Huli ogres. Everything that relates to the way in which ogres speak to children is contained in the text:

Text 4.4
Informant: Alembo (Pi clan), Tari 1993

1	*Baya Horo*
2	Baya Horo
3	*Balu Nana igini*
4	Balu Nana's son
5	*Balu Nabono igini*
6	Balu Nabono's son
7	*Waya Hegene mendego pu laga*
8	white feathers one will flap
9	*mendego hea laga*
10	one will stand up
11	*Balu Nolene ne timane agayaguame hubua bi ibiniyago*
12	Balu Nolene with teeth bound with rope cloth and bared out he came
13	*Pu talu talu bima*
14	raining and shining
15	*Haburalu bima*
16	raining and shining
17	*Ginali pogo pogo lama*
18	raining and shining
19	*Dawi yunini wini miya*
20	on the leaves of the Dawi bamboo (rain drops) have been taken
21	*Dayago yunini wini miya*
22	on the leaves of the bamboo rain drops have been taken
23	*Hugulu yunini wini miya*
24	on the leaves of this tree rain drops have been taken
25	*Egele yunini wini miya*
26	on the leaves of this tree rain drops have been taken
27	*Au lama ibalu penego*
28	saying like this he came and went
29	*Ogonime bo yalu ibiragola*
30	this one killed and brought it
31	*I ainya balu nayada*
32	he killed and ate my mother
33	*I aba balu nayadago*

34 he killed and ate my father
35 *I ainya anini bo yalu piyadabe*
36 my mother where did he kill and carry her away
37 *Iba abi tigida*
38 to the banks of Abi river
39 *Ebolo tigida*
40 to the banks of Ebolo
41 *Kulu tigida*
42 to the banks of Kulu
43 *Kaliabu tigida*
44 to the banks of Kaliabu
45 *ibu ainya bo yalu puwa Bayaga Horome*
46 he killed and carried his mother away, Baya Horo
47 *Bo yalu ayu ibirabe*
48 having killed is he bringing her now?
49 *Yawi ibirabe hondole bedo lowa*
50 is he bringing her tomorrow, I am waiting to see it is said
51 *ogoni i ainyanaga bayene kodo kodo lara*
52 your mother's thigh is sizzling (in the bamboo on the fire)
53 *abeyene kodo kodo lara*
54 the side of the stomach meat is sizzling
55 *kuabeyane kodo kodo lara lalu*
56 the rib meat is sizzling it is said
57 *ibu ainyanaga andu pugu wowa*
58 his mother's breast has been cut off
59 *wandari igiri emene biago nelo mialu howa*
60 he gave those things to little children to eat
61 *bo yalu piaga lene*
62 he used to kill and carry off like this it is said
63 *Uru abiyene hendedo*
64 I saw his Dugube axe
65 *Bayaga Balu Nolenenaga ulu abiyene hendedo*
66 I saw the Dugube axe of Bayaga Balu Nolene
67 *Waya hegene hendedo*
68 I saw the white feather
69 *Tabagua tilini hendedo*
70 I saw his moustache and hair (*kai*)
71 *Migulini hendedo*
72 I saw his killing axe
73 *waneigini dugu biragola ani laga*
74 when the children are crying it used to be said like that

Following the variant rhyming ogre names (ll. 1–6), l. 7 (see also l. 67) references the decorative marker by which Huli audiences recognise ogre identities. The white sulphur crested cockatoo feathers, one of which flaps around, parallels the associations made between ribbon-tail feathers and the trickster *Iba Tiri*. In tales, mention of this emblematic motif is sequentially followed by other ogre accoutrements and icons:

Text 4.5
Table 4.3, Ts. 16

→   *abuale gewale urume*
    (BH) with cockatoo feathers in his hair
    ira mane buru lalu heane handaya
    with tops of trees chopped long and big
    ede ibaruagoni agibe laya
→   so who is coming over there?
    o biagoria iraga haya ne gayene ugu aga urume kabubi
    he (BH) climbed up with his canine teeth bound with bark cloth
    pongonia duria pira homale togole
    with five or ten flies dying scattered (around its mouth)

Ogres carry special weapons (Text 4.4: ll. 63–6, 71), the terms (ie. *migulini, uru abiyene*) for which seem always to match those (cf. Goldman 1983:68) used stereotypically to depict 'foreign' peoples collectively referred to as Dugube. Ogres, like 'outside' cultures, represent dangerous lines of power. In Text 4.5 reference is made to a mouth around which are clustered flies thus indicating remains of putrefying human flesh, and emphasising the ogre's human-eating habits. This is reinforced both in Text 4.4 (l. 11) and in Text 4.5, which make mention of long sheathed fangs, discussed previously, typical also of the Kewa ogre (LeRoy 1985:90) and suggestive of a gaping, voracious maw. It is this image and its symbolism which are dramatically evoked in the mimetic play of children in the game 'the ogre is coming' (cf. Chapter 1, List of Traditional Huli Games no.12). Typically, in tales this motif is poetically developed with *kai* sets of string names (*tobai–nabai–nabale*):

Ne	*gayene*	*diwi*	*aga urume*	*kabu*	*biniya*
Tooth	canine	string (*Trimeniaceae*)	covering those + INST	wrapped	done-RP+EV

with those string coverings they (teeth) are wrapped
tobai aga urume kabu biniya
nabai aga urume kabu biniya
nabale aga urume kabu biniya

The metereological sign of ogres – rain showers through which the sun shines (*haburalu*) and raindrops taken from leaves (Text 4.4: ll. 19–26) – is described in Text 4.4: ll. 13–18 (see also Text 4.1: ll. 1–2) and is consistent with cross-cultural ogre characterisations. One thinks here too of Hesiod's Cyclopes as personified storm elements who supplied Zeus with his thunderbolts. As amongst the Duna (Stürzenhofecker 1993), Huli ogres kill parents (Text 4.4: ll. 29–50), and in particular mothers, by first cutting off their breasts. In this regard BH are not just dormant figures inhabiting some fairy-tale world. They are employed, as Text 4.4: l. 73 makes clear, to frighten young children so that they cease crying; 'if you don't stop crying BH will come and feed you your mother's breasts.' Within the context of narrative performances, they thus parallel Bimin-Kuskusmin monster tales which 'are told at night around the flickering hearth to frighten unruly children' (Poole 1983:12).

There is little doubt then that the ogre conveys a vision of control analogously encapsulated in Western frightening figures like the 'bogy-man' or 'little green monster' used to coerce, frighten or cajole children into obedience. But unlike the culturally engendered fiction of Datagaliwabe (cf. Goldman 1995), the external threat does not symbolise that of an authority figure punishing misdemeanours. The fiction as transformed history is not primarily a vehicle for policing operations. However, because the ogre quite fundamentally frame shifts as a being who is between fact and fiction it stands apart too from imaginary figures or companions like the Sand Man, Jack Frost, Easter Bunny, Man in the Moon, Tooth Fairy, or Father Chistmas, who most often are invested solely with a 'second-world' reality (Prentice et al. 1978).

The cannibalistic theme is developed by depicting what anatomical parts are inserted into the bamboo tubes for roasting (Text 4.4: ll. 51–8), the sizzling sounds (*kodo kodo*) which will be heard as they cook, and the manner in which they will be served up as food to the children (l. 59). Much of the ethnography here resonates with themes inherent in the Jack cycle of stories in Western folklore and the giant whose signature refrain is 'Fe Fi Fo Fum I smell the blood of an Englishman.' Typically, ogre victims are carried back to the BH abodes, caves or houses, where they are either dismembered or ripened (cf. Wagner 1978:172 on Toro ogres among the Daribi) by continual feeding with cucumber (*bambo*: *cucumis sativus*) before they are consumed. This equivalence of 'humans = ogre food' has a number of resonances in Huli culture. Cucumber is recognised as a food type associated with the earliest epoch of Huli history, which again temporally dislocates BH from the 'time of man' (*agalinaga*). Equally, cucumbers, like *mandi* leaves (*Euphorbiaceae*: see Chapter 1), are believed to grow in the land where dead spirits go – *Humbirini*. What is brought together in Huli thought here is two paramount lines of association. First is the 'otherworldly' status of BH existence and cannibalism, and perceptions of 'outside/marginal' domains like Humbirini and Dugube. Second is the allied conjunction of death, females (human and BH) and *mandi* leaves; as Gillison (1993) has recently remarked, myths here instantiate a debate about gendered propositions. Thus in women's wailing laments (*kiabu dugu*) people are talked about as descending to *humbirini* to pick cucumber. Similarly Huli women – the praise analogue of which is *mandi wali* (cf. Goldman 1983:259) – may figuratively allude to their impending death in ordinary conversation, mythical narratives or death laments with the statement that they 'will soon be picking *mandi* leaves':

Table 4.3, Ts. 16

Wai Wayeli Angaru Gigaru Lebo Lebani mandi mulebero
In Wai Wayeli Angaru Gigaru Lebo Lebani (Humbirini) I'll pick *mandi*

The Ogrish Body

<*And we came to the land of the Cyclopes, a fierce , uncivilised people.*>

Homer 1961:142

The insulation of cannibalism within an earlier historical epoch, and projected as a practice belonging to the 'other', is of course a common cultural phenomenon (Arens 1979). But such images of pre-civilisation existence are dual: cannibalism is at once something anathema to humans and an expression or embodiment of 'strength'. These resonances impinge directly on children because they are encoded in nursery rhymes used to promote child growth. In the following example, which is a rhyme made to a female baby from Dugube, the mother alludes to the anthropophagous associations of Dugube people, who are regarded as the source of all dangerous and powerful sorcery:

Nursery rhyme 4.1 – Yaluba 1993

→   *Ainyali balu naga ara wane*
    O mother, daughter of people who used to kill and eat

daughter of Hengeda, Pupigi, Pogai
→ *balu naga Hulu wane*
daughter of people who used to kill and eat

Such cannibalistic symbolism has its acme in the rhetorical depiction of BH, where various anatomical parts function as items of adornment, again emphasing the disjunctions between human and non-human that underpin Huli ogrology. The rhyme is the centrepiece of any ogre narrative and children as young as 4 are totally familiar with the composite elements of the ogre body. Everything we note about the invariant descriptive sequence harks back to the speech play games analysed in Chapter 1, to the analysis of body appellations as ludic materials in BT, and most particularly to the structuring poetic structures. The text is constructed on both (1) the striking physical resemblances of body parts to their decorative functions – the spleen as an axe, the omentum as a net bag, the trachea as a bow string (see the ogre identikit represented in Figure 4.6) – and (2) the marked assonance and alliteration between the anatomical terms and accoutrement terms (designated in bold):

tombene	*tangi*
stomach	(wears as a) cap
ayuni	*ayu yi*
spleen	(as an) axe he holds
nuni	*nu hene*
omentum	(as a) net bag carried
yabuni	*yandare yi*
anal passage	(as a) spear he holds
gibuni	*gi hondole*
trachea/oesophagus	(he wears as an) arm bracelet
gibuni (variant)	*dandu hibu he*
trachea/oesophagus	used as bow string

Huli adults understand these rhetorical devices to inscribe an imaginary, make-believe body. Their belief in the historical Baya Horo is not thus grounded in the specifics of an anthropophagous identity. Such embellishment is articulated as for the delight and delectation of children. It is then one more exemplar of the realisation of pretence as '(em)bodiment', which in both its symbolic and linguistic modalities is quintessentially playful in nature.

Much as Meggitt (1976:84) remarked for the Mae Enga ogre, apart from a set of invariant characteristics there is a host of attributes which appear

Figure 4.6 *Baya Horo* – A visual representation

to vary from story to story. Images of monstrousness are thus amplified and augmented by features such as those further included in the composite identikit of Figure 4.6. These can be briefly listed as follows.

1 *Long fingernails* (*gi gindiba lu*). These are analogously compared to arrows and employed to rip open bodies, or disembowel victims (similar to the image of Western witches). Huli ogresses in particular are described in this manner, as in Appendix 1, Ts. 2: ll. 244–5, where we may note that the ogress's name **Ginda**bu **Ginda**me contains suffixed forms of the reduplicated morph *ginda* ('nail').

2 *Gigantic size and height*. These are variously conveyed by images of hair/wigs extending over mountains (Appendix 1, Ts. 2: ll. 309–22):

<he [Polyphemus] reminded one rather of some wooded peak in the high hills>

Homer 1961:144

and by the use of whole tree tops as posterior coverings (see Text 4.6), pandanus leaves as front aprons (Appendix 1, Ts. 2: l. 324), and a whole *Arecaceae* tree as a spear –

<the Cyclops had a huge staff..it looked more like the mast of some black ship..that was the impression its length and thickness made on us>

Homer 1961:148

Text 4.6 Table 4.3, Ts. 19

Auwebe Auwanda igini udu Umili Tombeli Yaguali udurua howa
BH sons from Umili Tombeli and Yaguali
agali ndo biniyago
not like men
→ *biba Ayege homa yandare yalu*
carrying a whole Ayege tree as spear
→ *tauwa maiya mane payabu bialu*
wearing the top of a pandanus tree as a tangett

---

3 *Decorations*. These symbolise the 'wild/untamed': ogres often appear bedecked in black charcoal and with live dogs as ear-rings or substitute possum decorations (Appendix 1, Ts. 2: ll. 305–36; cf. Figure 4.6). This aggressive symbolism allows BH to stand as an emblematic marker of anything 'frightening' or 'dangerous'. For example, sharpened fence stakes

may metaphorically be described as like the removed jaw bones of ogres or, in a piece of paradoxical hyperbole, narrators may convey the 'beyond imagination' element of ogre identity by denying even the possibility of comparison to an ogre:

Table 4.3, Ts. 15

Baya Horo Nali Horali alendoya laya
not like a BH (but even worse)
embone uru dalu bogamabiya
his head shining and sharpened
pu kuabu tombe mandibu winiya laya
wearing a big string as his belt on his stomach

4 *One-eyedness.*

Appendix 1, Ts. 2: l. 88

Girabo Yuni Hini emarume de mbiyaore hearume
Girabo Yuni and Hini (BH) with one eye

As previously noted, ogres are often depicted as having peculiar ocular or cephalic arrangements. Individually named BH may be one-eyed (Appendix 1, Ts. 2: l. 88; cf. Figure 4.6), or lack eyes, nose, hands or arms. They may wear their wigs on one side, or have half a stomach, as commonly depicted in narratives told by children. Whilst it is clear from the corpus of tales collected that one-eyedness is not a generic feature of Baya Horo, nevertheless informants consistently acknowledged it as a recognisable physical characteristic of ogres.

But how does this sit with the asserted analogy with Cyclopes? The scholarly consensus (Page 1955; Glenn 1971; Mondi 1983) suggests that in the independent folk tradition of ogres, on which Homer drew for the Polyphemus tale, one-eyedness was not part of the original conception of the elemental Cyclopes. Greek vases and shards depicting Odysseus and Polyphemus do not consistently represent the latter as having only one eye. Notwithstanding the baffling omission by Homer of an explicit definition of Polyphemus as ocularly challenged, the post-Homeric reception of the tale wrought a wholesale change in what was generally understood as the prototypical make-up of Cyclopic figures. Homer's abbreviation and modification of a regional folktale, and one that I feel was clearly part of nursery lore as much as mythic history, itself generated changes in perceptions of historical fact. Whilst Homeric commentators have thus attempted to explain this ocular characteristic as variously associated with the manner in which Polyphemus is overcome, or even as a reflection of its Eastern origins in *vajra* (Butterworth 1987), the Huli incidence appears consistent with systematic forms of disfigurement within the culture as well as within pan-cultural traditions of ogrology (eg. 'one-leg' beings in Azande: cf. Evans-Pritchard 1967:29).

What is common to both Homer and Huli is the type of diachronic transformation wrought by creative narrative on folk-tradition and history. The condition of one-eyedness does not properly belong to *Baya Horo* as historical figures, or generally to BH as folktale creations, though most probably the contamination between traditions may yet develop this physical feature as a generic characteristic. More pointedly, what was intended as fictional elaboration for children diffuses back into 'fact' for adults, realising a bi-directional flow of influences between realms of child pretence and non-pretence.

Cyclopic Ecology

<And we came to the land of the Cyclopes, a fierce, uncivilised people who never lift a hand to plant or plough but put their trust in Providence. All the crops they require spring up unsown and untilled, wheat and barley and the vines whose generous clusters give them wine when ripened for them by the timely rains.>

Homer 1961:142

Certainly one of the most puzzling and seemingly contradictory aspects to Huli ogrology is the objective depiction of the ogres' land as a paradise landscape, a veritable 'Garden of Eden'. This otherworldly environment is benign, well-ordered and excessively fertile. We are never informed, for example, that BH are horticulturalists (that they have *agorai*) since in this land of plenty they appear not to have to do anything to subsist. Pigs, abodes and BH themselves are presented as outsize and the dominating landscape colour is black (*mindi*), signifying density of growth. Not only do trees bend (*ba hene*) under the weight of fruit, but legs disappear into thick piles of fallen leaves, and bats normally active at night come in the daytime to pick fruit, so confused are they by the sheer darkness of superabundant (*balu*) growth:

Appendix 1, Ts. 2: ll. 233–36

→ *Gayumba uru dalu mindibi ya howa ka*
    The *gayumba* (cordyline) was so thick it looked black
    Wayali tigu uru nde ega Dendeba Peleda iluru hewadago lau laya ya howa ka
    There were bananas there and there were flying foxes in Dendeda and
    Paleda places flapping around in the daytime

The key to understanding this narrative logic lies in the Huli idealisation of the past, a 'golden age' within their historical consciousness. Thus while on the one hand *Baya Horo* symbolise nature in its inhuman, bestial and predatory aspects, they also hark back to a bygone era of plenty. Theirs is a pre-civilisation utopia depicted as the negation of all that is recognisably human; the tension is created between this idyllic paradise and the entropy since human habitation. Frankel has also referred to a 'past era of effortless perfection' (1986:98,110) in reference to the origins of fire. The BH landscape represents a refracted vision of Huli experience, and the frustrated desire to reclaim this era was channelled previously through land fertility rites (cf. Goldman and Ballard 1998). In this regard Huli and Homer part company, for while the Cyclopean paradise reflected the benevolence of a grateful Zeus (Mondi 1983:23), the paradise of *Baya Horo* certainly appears as a conflation of ideas about 'golden ages' and cannibal giants.

Cyclopean Polity and Psyche

<The Cyclopes have no assemblies for the making of laws, nor any settled customs, but live in hollow caverns in the mountain heights, where each man is lawgiver to his children and his wives, and nobody cares a jot for his neighbour.>

Homer 1961:142

Like the Greek Cyclopes, in the often indistinct world of *Baya Horo* there appears no public *themistes* (state law), for this is a society lacking any social organisation beyond kinship relations. Although not all BH are cannibalistic it is an anarchic polity in which fathers eat daughters and grandchildren, and are themselves often killed by family members such as 'daughters' (Appendix 1, Ts. 1-2):

<Limb by limb he tore them to pieces to make his meal..the Cyclopes had filled his great belly with this meal of human flesh.>

Homer 1961:147

Irrespective of the type of tale collected, the motivational *raison d'être* of Huli ogres is Euripidean in nature – to satisfy their lust for human flesh (cf. Appendix 1, Ts. 1: l. 7):

Table 4.2, Ts.3

agali bo nana ibaga bialu haga henego au buwa
(BH) was going around looking for man to kill and eat
agali waga bialu bo nalu agali hangu tai bialunaga henego
searching to kill and eat, looking only for man

Significantly, in some of the historical tales this motive is linked to the necessity for human sacrifice to counter the infertility of land:

Appendix 1, Ts. 2: ll. 110–12

Auwebe Auwanda igini dindi ko hayagola gini bule bo yalu piyagoni
The BH's sons' land was bad and so to straighten it they killed and carried the body back

This may be indicative perhaps of a subsequent overlaying onto the ogre folk tradition of beliefs and/or practices about the relationship between ground and 'blood', common also in Duna. In the mythical data collected there is no mention of any involvement of ogres with acts of incest or indeed any behaviour which has sexual overtones. The antithetical morality of BH is fundamentally asexual, which is confronted and opposed by the sexual potency of the culture hero Iba Tiri, the ally of humans.

History, Gender and Childhood in Huli Ogrology

<The Cyclopes . . . live in hollow caves in the mountain heights.>

Homer 1961:142

Appendix 1, – Ts. 1: ll. 17–20

Baya Horome bo yalu piyagola libu ede ege kabani anda puwa hayagoni
Baya Horo had killed him and taken him inside the cave, over there.
Ege anda biagoni ayu ngago unugura ha
That cave is there now, over there

The mythic saturation of fantasy worlds by BH is matched by the extensive 'cycle' of historical tales recounting the travels and events surrounding ogres. The uniqueness of this tradition in Huli history lies not only in the existence of such a cycle of tales, but also in the fact that this earliest of eras was brought to a closure by the total eradication of all BH. Despite this period being portrayed as a veritable Eden, the historical passage is one of renewal, in which out of destruction is created the present world (cf. Figure 4.4). Unlike any other pantheistic spirit BH ceased to influence or interact with Huli beyond this period and were furthermore never implicated in Huli genealogies. Pre-dating all ritual activity, they are generally thought of as originating in Duna, though in effect this means no more than that they inhabited land to the north-west of Yaluba.

The history of BH as presented in Table 4.2 exemplifies a 'big-bang' theory. As narrated in Appendix 1, Ts. 1–2, BH were blown up at Mt Mbiduba by their daughters in alliance with progenitors of Garua and Mabili clans. From parts of the exploding heads various auto-regenerations occurred throughout the Huli region, as shown in Figure 4.7. The motif of fertile heads is one consonant with ogre traditions elsewhere (cf. Motz 1982), and indicates the catabolic nature of BH, a trait often also associated with the mythic personage of tricksters. All subsequent BH are either killed or imprisoned in subterranean holes from which they continue to present a latent threat – 'we say they will come out later' (Appendix 1, Ts. 2: l. 375). The evidential landscape of this cosmological event includes the burnt long-house posts, areca trees, caves (Appendix 1, Ts. 1: ll. 17–20), holes where BH are entombed, and large stones which are said to be the fossilised remains of BH.

Very much as is the case with its moral foil *Iba Tiri*, the symbolic meanings of *Baya Horo* ramify through many levels of Huli childhood, finding representation both in games and verbal practices. Huli adults draw a loose association between things which bite/consume one and their origins in this first cataclysmic event. As told to children, the sparks generated by the explosion became large red ants (*Aya Haraba*) which bite, whilst other sparks became fleas (*tede*), lice (*kua*), bugs (*gaiyamo*) and mosquitoes (*hina bibi*), all of which 'eat' people:

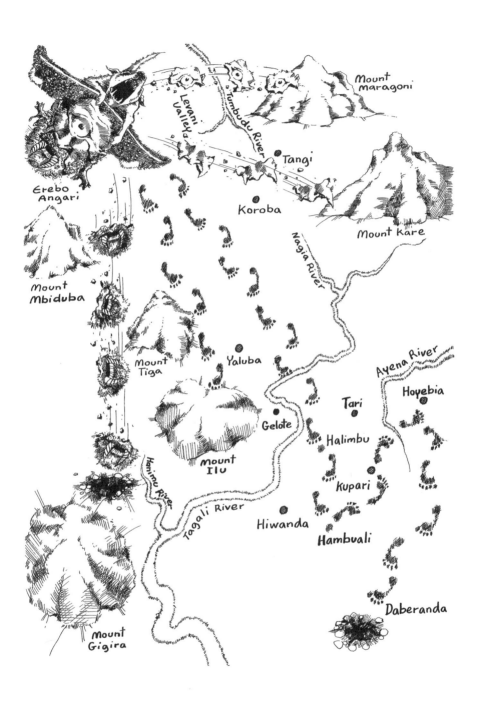

Figure 4.7 Historical travels of *Baya Horo* – a folk map

Informant: Alembo (Pi clan)
Tari – August 1993

Bayaga Horo ibu dele pene mo mogo buwa anda hene ogo damene
sparks gathered together and grew into those things
di de lalu porogo laga biyago ibu uruni bunia haga bini
the sparks that scattered became those things
tandagabi damenego o Bayaga Horo ibu neda lowa
anything which causes pain or bites we say are the teeth of Baya Horo

From the same explosion the remnant bones became large boulders known as *Dawene Mope*, which were kept in caves or transported on platforms across Lebani, Mogoropugua and parts of Duna by Kuni and Hugini clans during land fertility rituals. Such pre-contact rites express the kind of meanings depicted in Figure 4.4 concerning the positive associations made between life, anatomical regeneration and the 'golden age'.

Importantly, much of this folklore tradition of ogres is encoded in sayings which convey both the general sense of ogres as frightening, gluttonous figures – the consumptive imagery of ogreship – and specific events surrounding individual ogre personalities which provide allegorical resources. For example, children who simply sit and cry for food without doing anything are often reprimanded with the retort that they are like *Baya Horo*. Haley (personal communication) reports a similar scenario in Duna, where children will make faces and say *'no auwepemo*: I'm like an auwepe [BH: see Figure 4.3(B)].' The following restricted selection of proverbial forms encapsulates many of the ogre themes discussed above:

1   *Hogarene Giwi harebe*
    Are you becoming Hogarene Giwi?
    [Said to a person who pinches another to see if she/he is awake. Recalls Table 4.3, Ts. 8, in which the ogre Hogorene Giwi used to pinch his victims to ensure they were asleep before disembowelling them.]

2   *Ogo agi bere ibi dayadabe hondole ya handarebe*
    What are doing, checking whether I am ripe?
    [Said to a person who feels you over as if he/she is acting like a Baya Horo to see whether you are ready for eating.]

3   *Dawene Mope ngebe?*
    Are you Dawene Mope?
    [Said to a person who does not move. The saying makes an analogy with the fossilised bones of BH, which were so heavy and immovable they had to be carried on a stretcher by many men.]

4a   *Mandi pububi ti ngu ogobidege*
     Grubs on the Mandi leaf and the smelly excreta are the same thing

4b   *Mandi pubu mbuli pubula tumu tumu ogobi degego*
     These two types of grubs smell the same (so don't look for something else)
     [Said to a person who ignores what is in front of her/him and looks for
     other things. Recalls the moral of Table 4.3, Ts. 9, involving Mandi Pubu
     and Mbuli Pubu.]

A measure of the singular importance of both the ogre and trickster in
child culture is, as previously described, the fact that they are the subject
of much mimetic play. In addition to the various games in which players
dress up as BH (cf. Plate 4.6) to frighten other children, their anthropophagic
predilection is also the theme of *Dugulano Begelano* (cf. the list of 'Traditional
Huli children's games' (28) in Chapter 1) the only child game to have an
attached origin story. The game involves a number of children who take
turns to be 'cooked in ashes', recalling a well-known ogre tale in which
ogrillons attempted to cook human children for the first time.

From this vast landscape of ogre-inflected phenomena there appear few
areas of Huli life untouched by this dominating tradition. The data firmly
indicate that, at least for the Huli, ogres present an ethnographic thickness
and symbolic complexity that in many ways goes to the core of metaphysical
thought in this culture. Though I have here said little about the nature of
gender in relation to BH other than to point out that there are ogres, ogresses
and ogrillons which figure in the tales summarily listed in Tables 4.2–3,
there is evidence of conflaton between the ogrology and the prevailing
ideology of femininity. Male myths and everyday conversation may utilise
a standard set of derogatory terms and phrases for women which reference
them as female ogres. The following text phrases the appellative set in terms
of rhetorical interdictions:

Informant: Alembo (Pi clan)
Tari – August 1993

1   *Mandi yu puguabi wali lole(ni)*
2   red leaves of the *mandi* (Acalypha) tree, don't call women by this name
3   *Gerere anga wanga wali lole(ni)*
4   the *gerere* (pandanus) nut leaves will move like when women weave with
5   needles, don't call women by this name
6   *Tawa manana wali lole(ni)*

7   the dried tops of this pandanus, don't call women by this name
8   *Palia anda anda wali lole(ni)*
9   she sleeps from house to house, don't say that is woman
10 *Hariga pamiale wali lole(ni)*
11 she roams about on the road, don't say that is woman
12 *Damberali/emberali wali nahangalu hene*
13 the asparagus (*tiabu*) woman never plants

The association with BH follows from the belief that ogresses used to eat the *mandi* leaves mentioned in l. 1, and used to employ the pandanus leaves mentioned in l. 6 for dancing and celebrations (cf. Appendix 1, Ts. 2: ll. 323–6), so that these statements convey a form of ideological derogation. Furthermore, appellations such as those contained in ll. 3–7 are themselves substitute terms of reference for *Baya Horo* women, often deployed in narrative accounts.

The antipathic nature of Huli ogres as anthropophagous beings becomes a malleable resource for invoking 'poetic faith' in the visions of the unimaginable generated by both narrative drama and comedy. Whether these 'primordial characters' (Needham 1978) and symbolic complexes ultimately defy the diluting power of cultural relativism is not a question which, to my mind, is in the context of this book one urgently in need of an answer. More important is the recognition due to to the fact that this folkloric tradition scaffolds for children their experience and understanding of pretend play. Children are audiences for the ogre tales from birth. Now while not every detail of the tradition may be known by every child in every age bracket, certainly by the time they are seasoned pretenders Huli children are conversant with the framework of their indigenous ogrology. The ogre, like the trickster to be considered in the next chapter, simultaneously inhabits imaginative literature and sacred history, thus projecting a model of agency grounded in a seeming capacity to frame shift between these phenomenal domains. This makes them special occupants of children's worlds, and special exemplars of pretendership. The very fictionality of Baya Horo comes to serve as a metaphor of and for ludic activity replicated in the myth-making and myth-telling activities of their own fantasy play. By such means the socio-dramatic creations become infused with sacredness; moreover, the fictions become for the children their modality of historical experience.

As historically constituted identities, ogres heighten perceived boundaries between the human and non-human, civilised and barbarian, male and female, and utopian and entropic worlds. Ogres represent a culturally unique protean pool of symbolic resources, constantly transformed by the ongoing dialogue between fantasy and reality that narrative agents instantiate. In this welter of meanings there appear clear structural parallels with the manner in which adult and child construct their make-believe worlds. Equally, the factive and fabricated ogre models a moral universe for both child and adult. They are the ultimate icons of nefarious deeds, of evil, and of the latent threat of destructive forces within the universe. A child-centric perspective on ogrology thus helps us reconfigure the homologous relations between the way in which adults relate to their mythology and the way children relate to their mimetic products. But there is more to this set of parallels than mere homology. The mythic relations instantiate diffusionary processes between truth and pretence and between child and adult – the relationships are mutually incorporative, mutually referential, and mutually implicative.

Chapter 5

The Trickster: A Melanesian Enantiomorph

'Well, it's no use *your* talking about waking him,' said Tweedledum, 'when you're only one of the things in his dream. You know very well you're not real.'

Carroll 1960:239

Introduction

Few other areas of anthropological discourse display quite the same kind of ritualised openings and prose devices as those employed by authors who have addressed 'tricksters'. It is as if these mythical and mercurial personages seduce their narrators into reproducing images imbued with effusions of mythopoeic energy. Like some hierophantic gatekeeper, the ethnographer seems irresistibly compelled to preface the treatment of tricksters by initially disclosing two central truths. First, the 'trickster' is a universal folklore figure which, unlike any other character in myth, has uniquely engaged anthropological attention (Radin 1956:ix; Lowie 1909:432; Wallace 1966:23; Pelton 1980:1; Griswold 1983:669; Abrahams 1968:193; Abrams 1977:151; Leary 1982:57; Carroll 1984:105; Street 1972:82; Babcock-Abrahams 1975:158). Second, and with conceptual disquiet as well as delight, they report that trickster figures invariably present as a conjunction of confounding identities – ultimate hero, consummate hoaxer.

We are alerted then to the point that tricksters, like child fantasy players, are transformative agents. Their mythical *raison d'être* is as a refracted image of cultural humour, of deceit as a disjunction between appearance and reality, and of history as how much of the world came to be the way it is. The purpose of this chapter is to explore the multi-dimensional ways in which Huli children experience the trickster *Iba Tiri* (IT). The argument pursued here is that the trickster both represents an opposed model of agency to that of the ogre – primarily one with a positive valency and one that appears to constitute the trickster as a culturally standardised 'imaginary companion' (hereafter IC) – as well as a figure that, like the ogre, frame shifts between fact and fantasy. The trickster scaffolds the way children conceptualise and experience socio-dramatic play. It is an embodiment of authoritative and authorial voices of pretendership, a projection of culturally shaped self-images through which children come to understand the playful 'other'. This is the mask that speaks about the permanence of illusion in child imagination. With respect to both this child-centric perspective, and the hypothesis of the trickster as IC, the discussion offers a somewhat different interpretative slant on a topic of traditional concern to anthropology. We need first of all then to overview briefly what anthropologists have had to say about these figures.

The literary heritage on tricksters shows analysts transfixed by the need to capture the essence of this synthetic image by means of rhetorical coinage – they speak no differently to the voices which generate such representations in the cultures they study. The trickster is thus variously portrayed as 'lord of the liminal' (Griswold 1983:670), 'demon of deception' (Goldman 1995), 'super-shaman' (Campbell 1971:275), a 'cocksure contradictor of contradiction' (Pelton 1980:165), 'masquerader and marauder' (Abrahams 1968:201), 'trickster-fixers' (Ricketts 1965:327), 'benefactor and buffoon' (Radin 1956:124), 'subhuman and superhuman' (Jung 1956:203) and 'culture hero and capricious hoaxer' (Street 1972:95; Babcock-Abrahams 1975:162). For anthropologists, tricksters have yielded symbolic play material *par excellence*. And yet beneath the now famous attempts to capture a creature slavishly driven by gastronomic and priapic appetites:

> loutish, lustful, puffed up with boasts and lies, ravenous for foolery and food, yet managing always to draw order from ordure, (Pelton 1980:1)

> creator and destroyer, giver and negator, he who dupes and is always duped himself, (Radin 1956:x)

> monster of depravity: liar, cheat, lecher, murderer; vain, greedy, treacherous, ungrateful, a poltroon, a braggart ... recklessness, impetuosity, puckish irresponsibility, (Evans-Pritchard 1967:28)

lies an enmeshment with problems of historical, comparative and epistemological proportions both general to anthropology and specific to this mythical domain. So scholastically influential and weighty has been the baggage of trickster studies that one remains almost oblivious to the need to pause and think again about the question posed some years ago by Pelton: 'just what does it mean to study the trickster in any particular culture?' (1980:14). Is the Huli trickster IT to be viewed as no more than a new embodiment of an archetype? Do findings about its regional instantiation in mythic tapestries ultimately disclose what Radin (1956) contended was the irreducible 'psychological' nature of tricksters' existence?

The literary career of trickster has been one marked by a predilection to dissolve and explain away (cf. Carroll 1981; Babcock-Abrahams 1975) the coexistence of seemingly opposite characteristics – the trickster as the epitome of incongruity. This intolerance of contradiction – to think of the trickster as a 'scattered' (Basso 1988) self – was fused with a doctrinal adherence to 'evolutionary' dogma. Thus the 'trickster–transformer–culture hero' realised a developmental trajectory that was also a gauge of the social progress of cultures which possessed such mythic personages. For example, the folklorist Brinton (1896) argued that the trickster's divinity preceded, and was later corrupted by, his ignoble duplicity, a thesis successively challenged by Boas (1898), Lowie (1909), Radin (1956) and Ricketts (1965). These later analysts forcefully argued that this thesis was intrinsically flawed and that the evolutionary privileging of 'the divine one' did violence to known ethnographic facts. Various incarnations of these counter-theses appeared, vacillating between the following positions: (1) that the identities of tricksters as variously 'benefactor and buffoon' (Radin 1956:125) were indissolubly fused in cultural representations; (2) that the trickster as 'fool' (Radin 1956:164; Ricketts 1965) was somehow primordial and evidenced by the morpho-semantic ubiquity of 'fool' in trickster appellations; or (3) that the ethnographic data suggested a converse evolutionary continuum of tricksters from fool to fool–hero to a gradual separation of these identities, sometimes loosely claimed as covariant with levels of subsistence economy (Ricketts 1965:328; Lowie 1909:433).

Although these interpretative probes appear in hindsight somewhat antiquated, if not sterile, it is nevertheless curious how far, and how late, writers from other disciplines embraced the seriousness of these explanations. For example, Abrams (1977) and Abrams and Sutton-Smith (1977) have suggested that the developmental complexity of Western children's trickster stories (about such characters as Bugs Bunny, Br'er-Rabbit, Road-runner or the Gingerbread Man) provide a genetic mirror of the 'logical sophistication/pattern' (Abrams 1977:145; Abrams and Sutton-Smith 1977:53,47) of tricksters across cultures – basically, that people get the trickster they deserve given the state of their cultural advancement. One recoils here not simply at the fanciful and long-critiqued equivalence of 'primitive = child', even allowing for an element of infantile regressiveness in trickster profiles, but perhaps too at the naivety of wholesale reliance on Bugs Bunny as a cultural gauge mechanism.

Notwithstanding these reservations, all of the above commentaries betray a more fundamental set of premises about the ontological nature of tricksters, which, to borrow some terms from the discourse on sexual identity, cluster around either an *essentialist* or a *constructionist* posture. The former viewpoint variously adumbrates a Jungian pathology that the trickster manifests a mythical archetype, an 'autonomous psyche' (Layard 1958), pre-cultural, pre-representational and unaffected by the specific types of performativity associated with this personage within a cultural environment. The trickster is said, with an unusual unanimity of voice, to objectify a transcendent 'self/psyche' in its full technicolour of distortion, paradox and projected angst (Pelton 1980:160; Basso 1988:304; Abrahams 1968:194; Radin 1956:150; Evans-Pritchard 1967:30; Ricketts 1965:347). While clearly not always expressed in the Jungian cant of 'rudimentary undifferentiated consciousness', 'shadows' or 'objectified memory', the explicit or implicit assumption of some psychic universal nevertheless underpins the comparability of 'tricksters' across cosmologies and oral traditions. Although these etiologies are variously mooted as forms of 'symbolic pattern' (Pelton 1980:16), 'underlying logics' (Carroll 1981), 'imaginative structures/primordial features' (Needham 1978:60–5) or simply 'human nature' (Street 1972:104), they all tacitly accept the Lévi-Straussian 'problem' (1955:204) of the similarity of world myths. In its more diluted form the essentialist stance seeks to distance itself from any immobilisation of the trickster image by suggesting instead the idea of a trickster identity as no more than a 'search device', a probe heuristically capable of enlarging and altering the common architecture but always sensitive to cultural particulars. In simple terms, the 'trickster' is about flow and fluidity, not fixity.

The constuctionist vision is merely the hoary chestnut of cultural relativism, with its emphases on 'irreducible particulars' and the analyst as comparative 'encyclopedist'. In their role as anthropological thought police it was Beidelman (1980), and later Carroll (1984), who argued vehemently against adopting the obfuscatory rubric 'trickster'. Such practices as lumping together Bugs Bunny, Taugi, Maui, Anansi, Hermes, Loki, Ture, etc., should be forsaken for a more pedestrian case-by-case study. Like it or hate it, history has not been kind to such arguments in the context of trickster scholarship, partly because of a paradigmatic shift back to the type of humanistic anthropology in which similarities rather than differences are dwelled upon. Cries of contextual disembowelment have been drowned out by the clamour for commonsensical indications of continuity and homology in trickster mythologies.

Apart from such methodological wranglings, trickster scholarship has also bequeathed an impressive array of messages, interpretations and findings about this persona as a narrativised identity. Two major strands can be identified as follows:

1 Very much in the functionalist vein, the argument is made that the
   trickster allows for the expression of sublimated – 'beneath the layer of
   convention and consciousness' (Evans-Pritchard 1967:30) – desires. This
   mythically articulated and celebrated subversion – the trickster as the
   spirit of infraction – enables vicarious breaches of an accepted order to
   occur within the quiescent realm of imagination. Succinctly put, the
   theory suggests that the trickster allows adults (and children?) to take
   pleasure in behaviour which convention categorises as anti-social. Under
   this 'release-valve' theory (Abrahams 1968:195; Kerényi 1956:185;
   Abrams 1977:153; Turner 1968; Makarius 1970:66; cf. Babcock-Abrahams
   1975:183) the trickster functions as a cog in socialisation programmes
   foregrounding the adaptive potential of nonsense and playfulness
   (Abrams and Sutton-Smith 1977).

2 In a more structuralist vein, others have sought to identify basic
   structures in respect to what trickster myths are and do. Most analysts
   defer to the notion that tricksters have a marginal/liminal status – either
   outside or 'between' spheres. Such visions operate to mediate, evade or
   resolve existential dilemmas, often through symbolic inversion (Carroll
   1981; Lévi-Strauss 1955; Beidelman 1980:32). The trickster then embraces
   a conceptual reflection on, and apprehension of, a mode of existential
   being; it exudes a veritable 'mythology of the human condition' (Eliade
   1969:157). *Homo religiosus* thus engenders tricksters as a metasocial
   commentary, a way of talking about ourselves, but always in a satiric,
   ironic and comedic (Pelton 1980:266; Radin 1956:151; Evans-Pritchard
   1967:22) vein. As was noted above, tricksters here represent not simply
   an epiphany, but an entelechy of self-images that reflect transformative
   powers to change 'meaningless into meaningful' (Radin 1956:196; Street
   1972:101) or the 'undifferentiated into differentiated' (Douglas 1966).
   The trickster myth as symbol becomes enabled, as well as empowered,
   as 'therapeutic anamnesis' (Pelton 1980:275; Jung 1956:204).

Given the above it may seem almost wishful thinking to assume that
much in the way of anything novel could be said about the topic of
tricksters. And yet it is hardly an acute observation to remark that talk about
this 'archaic *speculum mentis*' (Radin 1956:x) has proceeded apace with little
reference to child actors or to trickster occurrences among Papua New
Guinean cultures. Without doubt this is attributable both to the late
historical development of mythical analysis in the region and to the extreme
paucity of materials disclosing personae comparable with the finely etched
profiles found, say, in North America and Africa. The agenda of this chapter,
as detailed above, is first to examine the evidence for a tradition of trickster

mythology in the Highlands region. Second, and against the above backdrop of ideas about tricksters as external projections of self-images, I want to moot the notion that trickster constitutes a type of 'imaginary comforter-companion' (Mead 1934; Myers 1976; Taylor et al. 1993), with its unique species of irrationality and its unique capacity among pantheistic figures to '*frame-shift*' between reality and make-believe.

Fools, Pools and Tools

'Yes indeed,' so he says, 'it is on this account that the people call me Wakjunkaga, the foolish one! They are right . . . Correctly indeed am I named Wakdjunkaga, the foolish one!'

Radin 1956:134–5

On the evidence presented in Table 5.1 the prolonged and somewhat overdue incubation of the Western Highlands trickster would appear to be at an end. This tradition among a congeries of linguistically related and

Table 5.1 Highlands tricksters of Papua New Guinea

Culture	Term-gloss used	Mythic personage	Reference
a Kewa	*Ipakeala – ipa* (water) + *keala* *Ipakeali – ipa* (water) + *keali* (madman)	Trickster Trickster	LeRoy 1985:182 Josephides (personal communication)
b Wola	*Iybitt – iyb* (water) + *tit* (fool)	Ogre (?)	Sillitoe 1993:224
c Duna	*Yu/Ipa T[s]iri – yu/ipa* (water) + *tiri* (fool)	Trickster	Goldman 1983:224; Haley 1993 Stürzenhofecker 1993
d Huli	*Iba Tiri – Iba* (water) + *tiri* (fool)	Trickster	Goldman 1983, 1995
e Ipili	*Ipa Titi – Ipa* (water) + *titi* (fool)	Trickster	Biersack 1995
f Wiru	*Uelali – Siri/Tiri – Ue* (water) + *ali* (man)	Trickster	Strathern (personal communication)

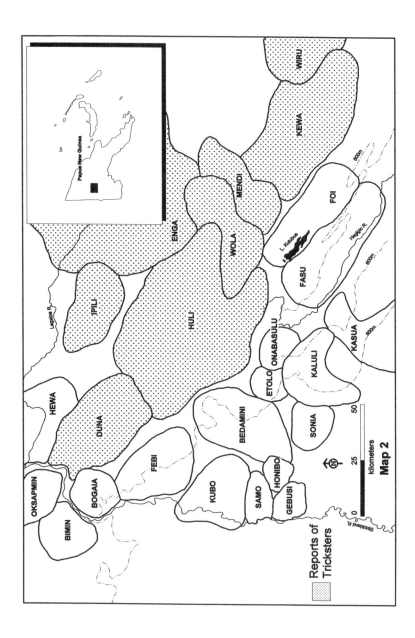

Figure 5.1 Reports of tricksters in the western highlands of Papua New Guinea

historically interacting societies surely stands comparison with the textbook cases from West Africa and North America. As depicted in Figure 5.1, the trickster genre cuts a transverse swathe through the Southern Highlands region bordered to the north by Ok, and to the south-west by the Bosavi regional complex.

The generic trickster appellations (a–e) in Table 5.1 reveal a strikingly similar agglutinative logic. In other words, the names are all constructed as combinations of 'water' and 'fool':

$$\text{Water } [iba] + \text{Fool } [tiri]$$

The initial word 'water' (*Iba*) is cognate for language stock members (a,c,d,e), and the second term 'fool' (b–f) clearly occurs as related variations of *siri*/*tiri*/*tit*. So whatever the epidemiology of this mythic figure here, in crossing known language families – (b,c and d) are not part of the West Central family to which (a,d and e) belong – it has nevertheless retained its nominal constitution. Now even accepting that the ethnographic descriptions of these seemingly comparable identities are unequally developed across our member cultures – and a nominalistic position in which only the name is shared appears untenable – there are at least two compelling questions that need to be addressed with respect to the above finding:

1 To recast Lévi-Strauss's (1955:220; cf. Carroll 1981:302) inquiry as to why the coyote or raven invariably incarnates trickster throughout North America, I pose the question of 'Why is the trickster here regionally conceived as a "waterman" and/or a "fool"?'
2 What other symbolic complexes have diffused with trickster myths across the region, and thus, on the available evidence, what major discontinuities subsist in the culturally specific shapings of trickster identities?

It would of course be quite wrong to infer anything from the nominal priority of 'fool' in trickster designations about the historical/developmental primacy of 'buffoon' over 'hero' in these Highlands cultures. Nevertheless, it is equally perhaps not mere chance that these playful associations are predominant and underscore everyday conversational usages of trickster names. Certainly for the Huli, this superhuman minder and his mythically chronicled acts are not of the type that mortals could even approximate. This chasm between what a human, as opposed to a trickster-fixer, can achieve precludes any possibility that the trickster name might be used to reference some sort of mortal 'hero'. When people in Huli designate others as 'tricksters' they always reference disorderly presentation and behaviour.

This negative pole is eminently replicable by any earthly transgressor (cf. Frankel 1986:51,58; Goldman 1983:225–7, 1988:73). Importantly then, from among the many modalities of identity that the trickster discloses or manifests for each of these cultures, it is the 'tragic' – marginal, low-status, mentally or physically impaired (cf. Makarius 1970) – and 'comic' – clown, fool, jokester, poltroon – textures alone which provide the default settings for how Huli use and experience IT. These nuances are encoded in the epithetical role of IT in the discourse of jokes, negative assessments, insults and abuse. The name surfaces in conversation alluding to shame, to uneven dress or deportment, and to people who make irrelevant contributions or flout speech norms (Goldman 1983, 1995). Trickster as selfish buffoon compulsively acts in violation of the 'most fundamental social values' (Basso 1988:292).

Elsewhere (Goldman 1983:271, 1993:247-8) I have provided numerous dispute text examples of insult speech from women to men, and men to men (but note never from women to women, or men to women) where males are disparaged by reference to their 'female'-like constitution, disordered presentation, speech and IT status:

[Two women ridiculing their brother for being a weak individual]

Kibime:	*o biago wali ialego =*
	that one (Hanai) is a woman like me
	/He is a woman not a real man/
Dagome: →	*= unugo yamo Iba Tiri*
	that one (Hanai) is a nothing, an Iba Tiri

(Goldman 1993:247–8, 369–70)

In the above text female interlocutors use irony to assimilate the identity of a male to that of a derisory class of 'womenlike' men, and ultimately to IT. Hanai is emasculated; he is a man-less person incapable of worthy words or actions. The conventional imagery of the trickster is invoked as an institutionalised symbol of disorder.

But so entrenched and ubiquitous is this cultural stereotype of deviancy that even children as young as 3 and 4 are thoroughly versed in the ethnography of using his name in ritualised insults. The following two text examples from naturally occurring play episodes, in addition to the one presented as Example 1.4, indicate not only the acceptance of a gendered trickster, but also how early in the developmental and enculturative process IT comes to fuse notions of idiocy and playfulness:

Example 5.1
Ts. 6 Tape 4: 156–248
Players: Dara (boy, 5–6 yrs) and Dagiwa (boy, 5 yrs)

[Dagiwa and Dara play 'Butterfly Ainya Abala'; see 'Introduced games observed at Yaluba' (3) in Chapter 1]

Dagiwa:		*outi ndo*
		I'm not out
Dara:		*OU:TI*
		you are out
Dagiwa:		*AI HONDO HA HENDE*
		you wait, you'll see
Dara:		*GEME HAYI HARI*
		you stepped over it
Dagiwa:		( ) *i au bedogo laro*
		I did it like this I am saying
Dara:	→	*AH* (.) *ogoni wulebere* (.) *dama tiri*
		ah – you were going to put your foot here, you Iba Tiri

Example 5.2
Ts. 19, Tape 6:15–204
Players: Dagiwa, Marina (girl, 9–10 yrs), Nabili (girl, 10–11 yrs)

[The three players are engaged in constructing small replica houses out of twigs and weeds.]

Dagiwa:	((pretends he is carrying a pig on a stick for a funeral payment and begins to chant the appropriate song genre *Nogo U*))
	ale ho:: ale ho:: ale ho::
Nabili:	*i mbirali homaragola larebe*
	did someone die and that's why you are singing that?
Dagiwa:	*e* (4.1) *ale ho:: ale ho:: ale ho::*
Nabili:	>*O AGILE LALU KA*<
	what are you going on about?
	Iba Tiri ↑ *harebe*

> →   are you becoming Iba Tiri
>   *mbirali homo ngagola lagago*
>   we only used to sing that when someone is dead

Even without further in-depth knowledge of the trickster profile, it is evident from these texts that children's understandings of IT encapsulate notions of infraction, subversion, or contra-normative behaviour such as lying and deviancy. The trickster represents a culturally given framework of meanings by which to reference unacceptable 'others' in play contexts. It is difficult to assess to what extent similar conversational usages occur within the societies named in Table 5.1, but Sillitoe, to take one example, notes for the Wola that 'in banter someone may refer to another whose actions or thoughts they think are silly as an *iybtit*, "twit" or "idiot"' (1993:225). If then we are able to contextualise the appellative 'fool', this still leaves the residual problem of 'water'.

Iba Tiri's abode is revealed in the formulaic speech routines that occur as narrative devices in trickster myths precisely as was the case for the ogre. We learn not only about his address, but about the deceptive calling card of 'noises' (cf. Sillitoe 1993:224) all significantly produced by aquatic animals like eels, fish, the 'swish' of grass-skirts made from swamp grass, or ritual rattles from crayfish. All resonate with aquatic symbolism:

> Iba Tiri is along the banks of Bembe river/along the banks of Baralu/along the banks of Tuya/along the banks of Tumane/along the banks of Golia/along the banks of Ayele/the ends of his string-apron are uneven/the points of his three-pronged arrow are uneven/his ribbon-tail feathers are all on one side/ he makes a noise like a grass skirt and we used to say (think) it was pig/he makes a noise like fish and we used to say it was pig/he makes a noise like an eel and we used to say it was pig/he makes a noise like a Dugube rattle and we used to say it was pig/he makes a noise like a cricket and we used to say it was pig. (cf. Goldman 1983:225)

We are introduced to a figure that deceives people into thinking there is another presence, which resonates with the idea of the disjunction between appearance and reality. The chemistry of the trickster is the alchemy of pretence. Moreover, the tricksters' trademark body is codified above as 'dishevelled' – uneven dress, uneven accoutrements, uneven decoration.

In respect to water, here too occupation of this prime piece of cosmological real estate appears less the result of some opportunistic shuffling of sacred space than a profoundly intended design. Indeed the literary legacy of trickster studies reveals that 'water' as a residential address has been mortgaged from the twin banks of liminality and antinomy. There are good reasons why IT is a 'water'-fool, which reflect the symbolic 'betwixt and between' nature of such fluid abodes in world mythology. Certainly for all these Highlands cultures water manifests the type of creative/destructive forces that interpreters (cf. Babcock-Abrahams 1975:160; Carroll 1981, 1984) of tricksterhood have suggested is the quintessential dynamic of this personage. In the form of rivers, lakes, streams, pools and rain, water represents a constant source of danger and illness, as well as a necessary nutrient for human and ecological survival. In Huli this was dramatically signalled in the closing rites of the Tege fertility cycle known as *Iba Paya* ('water closed in'). An entwined penis and vagina were buried in a hole in the ground to enrich the ground's fertility; the coda of the associated spell included the line 'let them have intercourse and sleep: *mo tanga haga buwa palelalu*'. The ritual symbolically brought together concepts about fluidity and fertility.

Thus on the one hand we find tricksters portrayed in this region as malevolent aquatic inhabitants – residents of pools, rivers, ditches, sink-holes, etc. – capable, as explained below, of causing death. On the other hand, they constitute cosmic minders who provide, protect and play with elements like fire and water. So that while our regional trickster does not present as some theriomorph in the tradition of 'spider' (Azande, Asanti, Hausa), 'fox' (Toba), 'hare' (Kaguru, North American Indians), 'coyote, raven and hyena' (North America) or 'snake' (north-east New Guinea) – thus presenting a semiotic conundrum like the Lévi-Straussian (1955:221) 'carrion-eating' coyote – it nevertheless appears to retain its role as a cog in the theoretic machine of mediation. The enmeshment of trickster with water appears as both a regional and universal diacritic which we need to trace carefully through the ethnography.

Drownings and other misadventures continue to be attributed to IT, just as in the past water-based illnesses in children such as constipation (*pai haragola*) or diarrhoea (*ti lama*) were considered capable of being influenced by this trickster. Traditionally, these conditions were relieved by oblations of pig and performances of the *Tiri Yagia* rite, in which men mimicked this spirit in pantomimic performances. As makers of pure comic theatre the performers would terminate their pretences by chasing and frightening children. The fact that this was the only occasion on which there was direct mimetic representation of a deity, for and on behalf of children, speaks significantly about the ludic resonances of Huli tricksters. But we know too that water is also, in its natural or bespelled forms, the elixir of life used widely for human sustenance and ritual purification. Most commonly in myths lakes constitute entrances to gardens of Eden, or mediums of transformation by which the ordinary or marginal actor is changed into some superhuman agent (see Text 4.2). As was pointed out in the previous chapter, these aquatic values are terminologically encoded in Huli in 'water' (*iba*) based names of heroes/heroines – **Iba** Mulu Lunguya, **Iba** Gurubuniya, **Iba** Gurugu, **Ibago** Wali (see Figure 4.5), and important cult names like that of the bachelor Haroli – **Iba** Giya (water + given [contracted form of *ngiya*: 3rd-PST-give]), **Iba** Wiliaba (water + bog iris) or **Iba** Dagia (water + platform). Such opposed aquatic valences seem partially duplicated in the antinomian constitution of the name 'water-fool', echoing Lévi-Strauss's findings that in mediating between life and death (see Figure 4.4) the trickster retains a duality – 'namely an ambiguous and equivocal character' (1955:223).

How all of this more directly impinges on children is partly revealed by the further layers to the regional articulation of this spirit, which explain why the forwarding address is c/o 'water'. Iba Tiri is frequently portrayed as 'playing' with water by alternatively damming and releasing the flow of water at the head of rivers, often precipitating flooding. This 'childlike' behaviour is seen as a 'model' of and for the children's game *Iba Paya Dugua* ('water + close + open'; see 'Traditional Huli children's games' (26) in Chapter 1). In all of these respects the trickster's spheres of influence establish links between cosmos and personal body, both of which may experience too much or too little water. But in line with what appears as their universally conceived role as cosmic mechanics, tricksters are equally agents who assign, align and alleviate natural forces such as the weather, seasons or rainfall. These cosmic plumbers regulate nature in both its ordered and disordered states (Ricketts 1965). In this vein references to the involvement of this culture-hero with the element 'water' are legion in the literature (Radin 1956:166; Street 1972:83; Evans-Pritchard 1967:32–40; Basso 1988:297; Abrahams 1968:194) disclosing what Pelton (1980:267) succinctly described as a form of socialising and anti-entropic energy. Moreover, waterways appear also to constitute 'marginal' or 'liminal' space. They lie at the boundaries of community, residence and social interaction so that tricksters' 'solitary' (Carroll 1981:309, 1984:115) existence is one lived out not *among* humans but at the *periphery*.

There are two further critical aspects to the trickster's watery persona that prove illuminating. First, pushing the comparison with Radin's seminal materials, all of the above cosmological notions are, as Babcock-Abrahams (1975) reminds us, readings one makes of the Winnebago figure of Wakdjunkaga. Episodes from this mythic cycle all involve the trickster at, with or in water, and as creating navigable waterways (ibid.:176–7). Second, in abode as well as interactional space, the trickster occupies an interstitial position between *sky* and *earth* very much in the mould of Lévi-Strauss's

(1955) symbolic intermediary. As described elsewhere, and as appears to be the case for Duna and Ipili (cf. Biersack 1995:20; Modjeska 1977:96; Haley 1993:32), the Huli trickster regulates the smooth flow of rain. All the waters in Huli 'have their confluence in a tree known as Ira Hale. These waters are cleaned by the *dama* Iba Tiri and bound with cane. They are believed to rise up to a mythical place in the sky called Daluyeli from where the waters fall as rain: Daluyeli *pu tara* – "the people in Daluyeli are urinating"' (Goldman 1983:119). What the trickster enables then through his centripetal plumbing is a cosmological house whose floors (earth) and roof (sky) are conceptually as well as constructionally integrated, precisely as amongst the Legba (Pelton 1980:74) and Ashanti (ibid.:2) of Africa.

This hydraulic engineer's job of keeping the earth together was critically acknowledged in previous earth fertility rituals (*Dindi Pongo*). Importantly, the trickster's travelling tool kit is the 'axe' (*ayu*), and it is significant that in Huli individual trickster names like Muguali, Amini, Lebe, Herebe (cf. Table 5.2 below) are also praise lexemes for axes which function as synonyms in the types of parallel repetition found in sung myths:

Table 4.3: Ts. 16

i	*abanaga*	*ayu*	*paluni*	*arabe*		
my	father's	axe	legacy	where		
Where is my father's legacy about axes						
→	*muguale*	*paluni*	*araba*			
where is my father's legacy about axes						
→	*lebe harebe*	*paluni*	*arebe*	*laya*	*lama*	*hendene*
Where is my father's legacy about axes						

Furthermore, unaccountable losses of axe heads were often blamed on IT. A victim would first present an offering of pig meat to the trickster before making *lagoya* (a profane divination form) to locate the missing axe head. If the axe was found then the pig meat was retrieved as a form of 'trickback'. In other words, humans interacted with tricksters along symmetrical lines of deceit, as illustrated by the story of (Appendix 2, Ts.3).

To appreciate further the status of the trickster as cosmic mediator 'between above and below' we need to examine how the sky represents a locus of spirituality and good fortune for Huli. The 'sky-place' (*Daluyanda*) is inhabited by unnamed beings collectively referenced as 'the sky-people' (*Daluyeli*). Perforated cloud formations (*gili gili biama polebira* – cloud decorations) are said to be the garden mounds of these sky beings, just as rain is sometimes phrased as their urine, wind noises their activities, and thunder the sound of marching 'sky-beings'. Notwithstanding an aura of fictionality surrounding such beliefs in Huli, almost anything that falls from the sky is described as '*Daluyeli's* pigs'. In tales the sky-people are frequently described as providing possum to ancestors and humans. Such benefaction explains why children are said to be like these paragons of virtue. They lack 'bad thoughts', just as in *Daluyanda* 'it isn't possible to do bad things' (*edo bulene nawi*). Particularly significant here is the belief that a person who tells a much admired narrative is said to be making a 'bridge' to the sky land (*ibu Daluyanda togo wialu pene*) for himself/herself – conceptualised as creating a pathway for his/her eventual residence amongst *Daluyeli*. Glasse, commenting on this desirable celestial address, noted that Huli often sighed 'Oh, to quit this life and go to Dalugeli' (Glasse 1965:30).

Much of what comes to people on earth does so by having fallen from 'above'. These important associations attached to 'sky' augment the beneficent status of the trickster. All of these kinds of mythic enmeshment with 'water' provide a skein of related conceptions that go some way towards answering the question of why in this region the trickster incarnates as a 'waterman and/or fool'. It would of course be erroneous to assume that in sharing a name the cultures of Table 5.1 (a–f) share the same monolithic structure of cosmological knowledge. However, we can ask what associated symbolic and mythic complexes appear to be associated with Western Highlands tricksters.

Throwing some caution to the wind, there is evidence that many of the protean waterman's traits and stories diffuse as total packages. That is, in their culturally instantiated form, higher-order relationships between motifs/themes are retained in the process of cultural transmission. I refer here to the frequently cited claim that hero-tricksters engage in 'freeing the world from monsters, ogres and giants' (Radin 1956:166; Street 1972:96; Evans-Pritchard 1967:93,108; Basso 1988:296–7; Abrams 1977:145; Carroll 1981:305; Ricketts 1965:327,342; Eliade 1969:157). Now when we overlay the selected ethnographic reports of Table 5.1 onto Table 4.1, it is clear that where we find the trickster we tend also to find the ogre as an inalienable mythic cohort or enemy. Irrespective of the pan-cultural manifestation of this pairing, I believe there is good regional evidence to substantiate the claim made in the previous chapter that we confront here a distinct oicotype – a mythic complex that through diffusion and adaptation within a specific milieu has assumed a quite distinct identity, though one clearly comparable with trickster complexes found elsewhere.

The co-presence of these figures as epic protagonists, where the trickster operates either independently or as an ally of human ancestors, compels us to accept perhaps that the intelligibility of ogres and tricksters is mutually interdependent. We need not rehearse here the supporting arguments given previously other than to restate that the organisational structure of symbolic opposition between life and death (Figure 4.4) is predicated on the unique and overarching pantheistic opposition between 'trickster' and 'ogre'. Death, as encoded in names morphologically based on *Baya* ('dead/killed'), has its natural antithesis in characters which trade on the name *Iba* ('water/ fluid'), the life fluid. They are unique pantheistic figures in respect of their narrative cycles, the degree to which their identities are finely etched, and the manner in which they interface with child culture and games.

The trickster and ogre have a pre-cosmic, ahistorical primordiality; they existed in a world that pre-dated human civilisation. This universe, while mythically depicted as some pre-cultural utopia, a golden age, was also bestial, predatory and baleful. The ogre race was inimical to any continued habitation by humankind until their fictionalised annihilation by the cultural companion the 'trickster'. The trickster enables renewal by mediating the passage from 'death/destruction' to 'appearance/existence'. The contrast between trickster and ogre is symbolically that between two forms of creative and transformational energy: biological reproduction and anatomical regeneration. While the Huli articulate an ideology of entropy since the close of the paradise epoch, the trickster nevertheless remains an anti-entropic force within the cosmos – 'Iba Tiri . . . is a force for both life and death' (Clark 1993:753).

How much or how little of the above nexus of mythic properties inheres in the narrativised trickster identities across these cultures in the area is difficult to assess at this stage. No doubt while the essential mosaic remains constant other elements have moved around but configure differently in different areas. For example, common to the Huli, Duna, Wola and Wiru is the idea that tricksters fire arrows into people, causing pain and necessitating special curative rites. Strathern (personal communication) reports that among the Wiru the 'waterman' can be manipulated by sorcerers who control his 'pools', which appears to draw a link with the importance of divination in West African trickster mythology. The Kewa personage, however, appears to fall more into the mould of a shape/skin-shifter, as further discussed in the next section. Most problematic of all is the status of the Wola *iybtit*, who appears in both our ogre and trickster tables. Although writers have referred (perhaps loosely?) to tricksters as morally ambivalent, often ogrish in nature – 'at various times he is clown, fool, jokester, initiate, culture hero, even ogre' (Abrahams 1968:194) – there is no evidence of a coalescence in one personage of anthropophagons being and divine guardian. In all other respects – association with fig trees, insults, deceptive appearance and help in fights – the Wola *iybtit* is a prototypical trickster. It remains to be seen then what links obtain between this Western Highlands complex and culture-hero traditions like that of Kilibob-Manup in Northeast New Guinea (Pomponio et al. 1994). Beyond these macro issues in comparative mythology, what we carry forward from the above exposition is the sense that there is nothing incidental about the trickster in children's lives. Their being is intimately one that is tied to cosmological states and figures as external and influential agencies. The question to be addressed, however, is in what particular respects the trickster models children's pretence.

Enantiomorphs and their 'Skins'

> Tricksters . . . often have a two-fold physical nature and/or a 'double' and are associated with mirrors. Most noticeably, the trickster tends to be of uncertain sexual status.
>
> Babcock-Abrahams 1975:159

The Huli IT is a spirit pervaded by a relentless dualism, as if his inner and outer selves were iconic markers of his duplicity, his 'double-dealing activities' (Layard 1957:107; Goldman 1983:226; LeRoy 1985:189; Pelton 1980:37), and perhaps too his antinomian embodiment of creative/destructive forces. In these respects he reflects a paradigmatic trickster identity. As noted above, IT does not present here as a theriomorph or herpetanthromorph (part-human, part-snake), and only rarely is he a metamorph. But there is good evidence to suggest that we are dealing more properly with enantiomorphic (mirror-image) forms in the tradition, say, of Tweedledee and Tweedledum. If one accepts this line of interpretation then important issues are broached about the relationships between tricksters and ICs. As the psychological literature informs us (cf. Myers 1976; Taylor et al. 1993), ICs are themselves linked to fantasy twins, mirror dreams and decentration processes. Whilst we do not as yet know how far enantiomorphicity is a diacritical trait of other regional tricksters, it is comparable with 'twin' manifestations in North America (eg. flesh and stump: Radin 1956) or, for example, the depiction of the Winnebago trickster Wakdjunkaga's right and left hand fighting each other (ibid.).

The metaphorical idioms of Huli deceit and its 'doubleness' – an IT has 'two minds and two talks' – have been explored elsewhere (cf. Goldman 1983:226–8, 1993:243–8). It is sufficient here to remark then that as the paragon of pretence, the ontological being of IT reflects a pan-cultural opposition between the truth as 'one' and the lie as 'two' ('two-timing', 'double-dealing', 'forked-tongue', 'double-cross', 'two-faced'). Perhaps also there is encoded an understanding of pretence as simulating dual identity. The earlier contrasted metaphysics of truth as something which 'stays', contrasted with pretence as a transitory embodiment, resonates well with the idiomatic opposition of the straight/single and contradictory/dual. In the following discussion I restrict myself to looking at specific realisations of this physical and linguistic embodiment of duality.

This Melanesian Bill and Ben is always ritually represented as two identical personages in spells, myths, tales and songs, so that tricksters' names invariably occur as rhyming pairs:

Individual trickster names

Yug**uale**	Dab**uale**	Mug**uali***	Dab**uali**
E**labe**	Ke**labe**	**Kedo**	Geng**edo**
Mini	A**mini***	Wan**goba**	Mem**eba**
Lube	Pu**lube**	**Giyu**	Wan**giyu**
Gina	An**gina**	**Dangi** Luluya	**Dangi** Walaba
I**bale**	I**bira**	**Wayu**	Dong**ayu**
Kai	Ka**labe**	Yo**le**	Yu**rigi**
Yorobi	**Yolenda**	**Nibe**	Dind**ibe**
Yorobinda	**Yuriginda**	**Lebe***	Har**ebe***

* Also denotes praise terms for 'axe'

This kind of appellative pairing, while not unique within Huli naming traditions, is rarely found with such extensiveness. But there is a high degree of indeterminateness about the gender-inflected nature of the identities. Some Huli maintain the names denote male and female counterparts (Goldman 1983:226; cf. Sillitoe 1993:225), and yet in many of the myths from which they have been taken both ITs appear unambiguously male. Beyond invoking explanations of religious dualism, it may be (as Layard 1958:28 argued for the Winnebago figure) that the Huli trickster is hermaphroditic. However, I can find no evidence in Huli indicating sexual transformations from male to female analogous with the Winnebago trickster. Most probably there is a merging here of the symbolic importance of duality in its myriad forms, as well as an overlaying by principles ubiquitous in the poetic ecology which, as I have had occasion to note previously, generates and shapes Huli history.

This dualism that is a universally acclaimed physical and mental trait of tricksters has a number of other expressions in Huli. In the *Tiri Yagia*

Figure 5.2 Ritual representation of *Iba Tiri*

pantomime there are always two ITs represented, each of whom wears a decorated water-gourd mask (cf. Figure 5.2). The mask betrays, as all masks do, a passing into the body of another, an overlaying of identity on which pretence is predicated. In narratives, while a single trickster is known to have two long white ribbon-tail (*Astrapia mayeri*) feathers cascading from his head, a trickster pair can appear contrasted in that one is adorned with black-billed sicklebill feathers (*Dreparnornis albertisii*) and the other with the ribbon-tail feathers. This respective colour opposition of black; white here recalls Babcock-Abrahams's (1975:160) finding of a symbolic reflection of creative/destructive, life/death binarisms. Indeed black is associated in Huli with death, danger and destruction, much as was noted for ogre figures. So whatever symbolic attributes the trickster might display in respect of an ordered cosmos, his body more loudly proclaims instit utionalised disorder – not the 'positive/hero' but rather the 'negative poltroon'.

LeRoy's (1985:188) analysis of the Kewa skin-changer is insightful in the above respect. The 'hero' persona is confined to sacred contexts while his 'other' skin discloses itself in the mundane domestic sphere, as if the bad skin were merely a disguise over the true essence. Not only does the trickster 'follow the "principle of motley" in dress' (Babcock-Abrahams 1975:159; Makarius 1970:66) – his uneven aprons, arrow points, feathers, etc. – but his body encapsulates almost every form of clownish eccentricity, physical impairment and impoverishment (Frankel 1986:51,58,97). The presentational face of IT is deceptive and cosmetic only, for while his body proclaims one message his actions, and perhaps his alter ego, may proclaim another: '"Contrariwise," added the one marked "DEE"' (Carroll 1960:229).

The message exuded by the Huli trickster's narrativised self is essentially that appearances are only skin deep. If IT's constitution is that of 'skin on skin', then for children, who both tell and listen to trickster stories, he is experienced as a quintessential pretender. Such meanings about the disjunction between reality and appearance, about the world as trans-formative in nature, find further expression in gnomic forms such as proverbs and sayings. For example, the related notions that 'one shouldn't judge a book by its cover', or that 'every cloud has a silver lining', are paralleled in such Huli adages as:

Dalinaga dabu dabu bayele wiagago
The things that belong to a Dali (IT) also used to be kept in good order
[Don't insult people who appear bad because their things can be good and appearances are deceptive.]

The outer skin is an expression of the radical untidiness in the world, the anarchistic aspect of self (Abrahams 1968:194; Pelton 1980:252). The Huli employ a specialised idiom for earthly counterparts of the 'trickster poor-man' (LeRoy 1985) known as *Dali* (see Goldman 1983:225,271, and Text 5.1: l. 10 below) which can be used for either males or females. Such people are often described as 'flying around eating *hungu* fruit (a worthless inedible fruit)' (Frankel 1986:58), or 'playing worthless drums of *Piper* wood inside drains' (*gana habane hungi yu tabage yaga*). It is used to disparage others who in dress, demeanour or display fail to accord with conventional standards of acceptability. Precisely as LeRoy (1985:175) found to be the case for the Kewa trickster, one of the most referenced physical attributes of *Dali* status is unkempt hair – knotted (*gili*), crooked (*wangoya*), small (*gindiya*), or missing and uneven (*ilu nanabiya*). Like the English folklore trickster Merlin, IT can present then as highly mercurial and indeterminate. He may be understood as young, old, ageless, long-haired, or in stories as a hero bedecked in fine feathers and decorations. Most essentially IT shows 'an ability to disperse and disguise' (Babcock-Abrahams 1975:159; Basso 1988:302).

Now while on the one hand this merely evidences the trickster's deceptive constitution – his indulgence in audio-visual trickery – on the other hand it theoretically aligns him with consensual imaginary companions. For example, in war when one side is numerically outnumbered, the superior side is understood nevertheless to see an equal number of opposed warriors, which are in fact made up of otherwise invisible IT. Moreover, tricksters are said to warn people of approaching enemies by signs or presences in dreams. Irrespective of age or gender, IT very much acts, both anthropologists and indigenes tell us, in the interests of his 'children' (cf. Ricketts 1965:343; Basso 1988:297). In neighbouring Duna, the trickster seems also a familiar spirit – 'the Iba Tiri speaks to me' (Haley 1996:282) – who behaves in the mould of a personal medium.

The concept of an imaginary companion is not one Huli express knowledge of, or familiarity with, and I have been unable to find a single instance of the phenomenon among Huli children. Given that recent research indicates that as many as 65% of Western pre-school children have ICs (Taylor et al. 1993; Prentice et al. 1978), such absence might appear noteworthy. And yet the Huli trickster appears to serve precisely the same functions, and materialises with the same complex of psychological associations – twin fantasies, positive valency, externalised self-images – common to Western children's ICs. The argument that I am making here is that just as it is good for psychologists to experiment with ICs as an index of children's ability to discriminate between fantasy and reality (Taylor et al. 1993), so Huli children also play with precisely the same boundaries to their culturally formatted and consensual IC, the trickster IT. If it is appropriate for psychologists to conjecture about the relationship between the incidence of ICs and understandings of fact: fictional distinctions, then it seems equally appropriate to suggest that the trickster may similarly promote decentration processes in Huli children. With this line of interpretation the study of tricksters returns to Radin's (1956) notion of the irreducible 'psychological' existence of such identities. We do not, however, need to pursue the issue of reality discrimination, because the experience of IT is a glorying in infraction of boundaries for its own sake, and for what it communicates about pretendership and pretence. There are here intriguing lines of analysis that open up by positing the trickster as an IC, given the indexical relationship between beliefs in ICs and performance in tests on emotional adjustment or fantasy–reality understanding, levels of fantasy play involvement, and the general role of pretence in cognitive development. Equally, however, given the parlous state of interest in pretend play, we are a long way from any preliminary stipulation of gross cultural differences in levels of child fantasy play.

Huli children confront a trickster capable of corporeal deceit by transformation into animal or even human guises. The deceptive body, as cultural hero and hoaxer, opposes as thesis and antithesis. There is a representation of licensed buffoonery, a mythically articulated logic of subversion which is morally denigrated but nevertheless appeals and delights. Entertainment partakes here of what Simmel called the 'vitality' (1964:315) of an order constantly gnawed at and disturbed by imbalance. The profile of intelligence and intentionality embedded in the narrative texts (cf. Goldman 1998) I collected is one of unpredictable inventiveness. The pretence or trick is the key motif by which IT overcomes and is in turn subdued or eliminated. No stable insights are provided as to the ultimate goals or fulfilments of the trickster beyond that of immediate self-gratification. His actions lack premeditation. As I have noted elsewhere, 'the psychology lacks depth in respect to introspection about the paradoxes of his "self" or any pensive preoccupation over the lack of deference to a moral code of responsibility ... unlike the Kalapalo trickster (Basso 1988), IT simply is' (Goldman 1995:134–5). This is an intelligence profile which reflects less any uncertainty or flux in Huli history than an objectification of pretence as reflective of the ongoingness of the world. Through trickster myths children gain entrance into a world where pretence can be fatal or fun. The collage of self that is IT is the shared subjective reality of pretendership as a modality of being. As a symbolic projection, IT represents a playful pretender 'other', which informs children about, and 'socialises' (Prentice et al. 1978) them into, understandings of pretenceful being and behaviours. It is an image of a figure that frame shifts as both a pretend player and a serious player in the non-pretend universe. The contention is that this is the infantile face of tricksters, a model of agency in whose image Huli children see themselves and are seen by others.

When children employ the trickster epithet in their talk it is invoked in the heat of the moment. It does not proclaim or portend any permanent status or rank attribution. Being called an IT implies no lasting loss of status, for, like the pretence act itself, it leaves no lasting residue on personal landscapes. The immunity IT seems to purchase from any permanent moral turpitude is as it were conferred on those who use his name, and who are named in his image. These pretenceful overtones are further institutionalised in a number of children's games specifically played and named after this 'second-skin' figure. For example, in *Iba Tiri Ge Koya* (the 'deceiving legs of IT'; 'Traditional Huli children's games' (14) in Chapter 1), a child takes a blade of grass and progressively transforms its representational shape from a figure N to a figure X to give the impression or two legs. The game plays on the trickster's nuanced corporeal deception. Scatological meanings, prominent in cross-cultural trickster mythology, seem particularly to the fore in the cat's-cradle 'Iba Tiri's excreta' ('Traditional Huli cat's cradles' (z) in Chapter 1), where the player makes the string represent a pretenceful enactment by an imagined trickster. The social persona radiated by the trickster is thus accentuated as one of playful, non-malevolent subterfuge. The playing and the naming are yet further instantiations of the way children, as has been argued throughout this book, both conceptualise and act out their pretence against the supportive backcloth of myth. Whether this is always present in the mind or not does not vitiate the point that the model underscores their very being as fantasy players. It is a model that is embedded not just in child games, but in the whole panoply of stories, proverbs and conversational routines that are part of the everyday world of Huli children. It is a model that can always be deferred to, as well as referred to. Like the trickster who moves between the mundane and the magical, child pretenders move *between mimesis and muthos*.

But what ethnographic facts give credence to Huli beliefs, alluded to above, that generically they are the trickster's 'children'?

Paradigms of Pretence and Imagination

> Myths treat of origins but derive from transitions..myths relate how one state of affairs became another: how chaos became cosmos; how immortals became mortal . . . how androgynous beings became men and women.
>
> Turner 1968:576

Without doubt the single most recurrent leitmotif in trickster mythology is the Promethean theme of some primordial theft of 'fire' (Ricketts 1965:334). Central to such narratives are ideas about the socialisation of earth, the domestication of women's power, and a beneficence to human culture that is more often an accidental by-product of immorality than the intended achievement of some cultural emissary (Evans-Pritchard 1967:32; Radin 1956:166; Basso 1988:297; Carroll 1984:117, 1981:309). In Huli, as Clark (1993) perceptively noted, it is the uninhibited concupiscence of the trickster which both is causally related to culture origins, and constitutes this spirit's centrality in cosmology. In this respect Ricketts unveiled a thematic progression in such stories that charts an initial journey, followed by some episode of outwitting by deceit, a theft of fire, and a resultant cost to humanity. Importantly, there is a presupposition in this body of mythology that transcendent supernatural powers are somehow minatory and inimical to humans. In effect, the pre-human world was ogrish in nature.

Now while the names of central figures change in the various versions of the Huli theft-of-fire myth the details remain remarkably constant. Thus Frankel (1986:97–8) has recounted how IT followed his brother and received food cooked by the heat of an ancestress's genitals before copulating with this woman and stealing fire. He explicitly details the fact that humankind's lot was to be forever reliant on the burdensome toil of using friction cane to make fire. In the theft-of-fire myths I collected (cf. Goldman 1998) an 'asexual past' (Clark 1993:753) is foregrounded, female genitalia are described as inherently 'hot', and the trickster is depicted as a transformer of meaningless into meaningful by giving humankind 'fire', and by cutting fingers and toes from amorphous flesh. But again there is no explicit disclosure of the trickster's state-of-mind as that of a wilful benefactor. The myths detail how IT is implicated in the creation of landscape, recognisable human anatomy, and the whole lore of Huli sexuality including menstruation and traditional post-marital rites. The trickster is projected as a cultural choreographer who determines the blueprint of human sociality and sexuality. He thereby empowers humans with reproductive potentiality; he puts the efficacy of sex at their disposal. Like tricksters everywhere, IT has a Priapus-like symbolism, but his sexuality is imbued with an enduring nuance of fun not fear. For children 'sexuality' has yet to take on the nuances of anxiety associated with traditional adolescent culture.

Iba Tiri's penis, like that of Wakdjunkaga, is exaggerated; it mediates between spirit and others in analogous fashion to the probing incisors of ogres. It is often invoked in spells as a fertility/procreative symbol. In one sense the 'phallus is trickster's double and alter ego' (Kerényi 1956:182), seemingly endowed with its own agency. In the Winnebago cycle Wakdjunkaga's penis is coiled in a box, enters tree hollows, is sent across waters, and engenders plant life. Although by no means deserving of being regarded as a myth cycle, there are a number of strikingly comparable stock episodes (see Appendix 2, Ts. 3) in Huli (as well as Daribi) which, like 'beads on a string' (Evans-Pritchard 1967:33), are capable of being rethreaded in different combinations. The phallus may glow like 'fire' (Appendix 2, Ts. 3:ll. 14–22, 32–8), assume the form of a 'bridge' (Ts. 3:ll. 64–74), and exhibit an insouciant sexual appetite. In Appendix 2, Ts. 3, IT's fire is lit by the fuel of a woman's grass skirt (ll. 24–8), and the constant bellow action of 'blowing' (l. 12) or pouring liquid has the effect of sexual stimulation. The Huli trickster is an inveterate masturbator (l. 99), and the image of this is the staple of adult insults:

> Kibime (Female): *Iba Tiri wi ebere gidama ibaga biyago*
> He (Hanai) is an Iba Tiri and masturbating everywhere.
> (Goldman 1993:248)

Invariably, as is chronicled in the narrative (ll. 87–112), the trickster gets as good as he gives so that IT appears as both villain and victim, victor and vanquished. The trickster plays as much as he is played with, though never as a pretence collaborator.

But for all these levels of continuity between Huli and Winnebago tricksters, there are gross discontinuities in the developmental make-up of the identities. Huli myths do not chart a progression from an inchoate, 'pre-Copernican' (Douglas 1966:80) form or world to increasing self-awareness and differentiation: the actions and events do not betray a soul-journey or 'psychic pilgrimage' (Layard 1957:109; Ricketts 1965:333). Iba Tiri comes with a full complement of insatiable sexual and gustatory desires. His life style is confined to making love, making war, and making pretence for the sheer fun of it. The narrativised self and psyche are thus, by comparison with other trickster traditions, diffuse. Though disposed to committing shameful acts IT is not *per se* shameless, and in Ts. 3: l. 106 – where the trickster's hand continues to be placed on a female breast which he thought was a piece of fruit – he 'ends up in an embarrassing position' (Carroll 1984:119). In fact the trickster is very much a cultural stereotype of the 'shamed' (*taga*) individual whose physiological and/or figurative posture of 'bent/lowered/stooped head' draws an analogy in the culture with the bent branches of the tall Yuluba pine tree (*Araucariaceae*) which IT is credited with having planted. Such meanings are encapsulated in idiomatic speech forms such as :

Taga halu Iba Tiri Yuluba gai leneyagoni
[I didn't shame you only Iba Tiri bends the branches of the Yuluba tree]

The intelligence profile disclosed in Huli myths is of a person at the mercy of his passions and impulses. The accoutrements of axe and penis speak volumes about the gendered constitution of the Huli trickster – the male voice is mythically privileged. There is no euhemeristic slant to this tradition, no cultus, and little interest in rationalising the trickster's behaviour as some self-conscious awakening. His actions are very much 'in your face' and have an autotelic appeal: 'We are moving in a world of imagination . . . fiction imposes itself on experience' (Evans-Pritchard 1967:25).

The trickster emerges from the above discussion as at once 'child' and 'parent' to its creators. As an imaginary companion he is invariably summoned to the aid of protagonists in epic duels against anthropophagous monsters; he drains personal and social landscapes; he provides codes of social conduct (mana); and he is associated with introducing fig trees (*poge*: Text 5.1:l. 12), Yuluba trees (Text 5.1: ll. 31–6), and the health of pig bristles (Text 5.1: ll. 14,28,38), as expressed in this well-known adage:

> → *Iba Tirime   agalinaga   nogo   iridege   **gini   biagago***
> Iba Tiri   men   pigs   hair   **customarily straightened**
> Iba Tiri used to **straighten** the pig's hairs for men
> *Agalime   ogodagua   au   bule*
> men   like this   how   do
> But how can man do this for another?
> [A proverbial form used to complain about another person who is attempting to perform a task for someone else. The speaker implies that one cannot always help others since only IT can do the impossible.]

Recalling the discussion in the Introduction about the semantic equivalences that inhere in the tonally contrasted lexemes of *gíni* ('to straighten, tidy') and *gìni* ('to play') – both metaphorically and morphologically grounded in 'hand' (*gi*) – we might meaningfully assert that the Huli trickster is a handy companion who fixes as he plays. In this role as pre-eminent helper IT always had a privileged right to first cuts of pig meat (Text 5.1: l. 40). In stories one thus invariably finds a conversational episode in which the trickster rhetorically questions a pig owner about his/her intended distribution of meat – 'With whom are you sharing?':

Field notes

The woman (*mandina*) singed the hairs of the pigs and called all the Iba Tiri from the valleys of Bambi, Bambiya and Baralu. Smoke covered the whole place. She cooked and cut up the meat and left the meat and intestines there and came back to heat the stones . . . she left strips of meat for Iba Tiri Giyu, Wangiyu, Lube and Pulebe

Iba Tiri giyu wangiyu ema lube pulebe ema ai ila ailabe lene lama agini

Then the Iba Tiri Giyu Wangiyu and Lube Pulebe asked 'With whom are you going to share the meat?'

A profound and synoptic insight into the Huli trickster–benefactor is provided by Text 5.1 in which the informant, Alembo, skilfully blends standardised speech forms and prose to capture the ethnographic essence of IT:

Text 5.1 : Huli concepts of Iba Tiri
Informant: Alembo (Pi clan) – Tari 1993

1   *Iba Tiri Muguali Dabualila o mbira*
2   the Iba Tiris Muguali and Dabuali are one (pair)
3   *Iba Tiri Nibe Dindibela mende*
4   the Iba Tiris Nibe and Dindibe are another
5   *o Iba Tiri biaru manda gogora uru ai leago*
6   those Iba Tiri with long hair falling down
7   *dali gibi li hea gebi li hea tingini iri hea*
8   this Dali with hands, legs and body full of hair
9   *daliore holebira dali Iba Tiri ibugua*
10 he'll be a real Dali, this Iba Tiri
11 *poge uru hangagane*
12 he used to plant fig trees
13 *nogo uru harubiragane*
14 he used to look after pigs
15 *waneigini emeneru turu hagane*
16 he used to make children happy
17 *Iba Tiri ibu manda gogora uru yula daibi*
18 Iba Tiri his long hair is falling back
19 *ibu payebu uru yula hea*
20 his tangett will be sticking out
21 *o Iba Tiri ibunaga biabe biridagoni*
22 Iba Tiri's work that you did

23 *waneigini karu dagala*
24 count the children
25 *ira hengedaru dagala*
26 count the trees
27 *nogo karu dagala*
28 count the pigs
29 *au bigi biama*
30 it used to be done like that
31 *ira Yuluba mbira unu hearu*
32 the Yuluba trees are there
33 *Iba Tirinaga hengene ira Yuluba mbaria unu hearuni*
34 Iba Tiri planted those for himself
35 *Yuluba yulo wiaruni Iba Tirime yulo wini au laramaligo*
36 those Yuluba tree branches go and up and down and we said Iba Tiri bent
37 those
38 *nogo iriniru dagalaga iraru dagalaga*
39 he used to count the pig's hairs and the trees
40 *o Iba Tirinaga nogo maburabane podo dela laga*
41 we used to cut the neck fat and burn it for Iba Tiri

While adumbrating all the familiar cultural resonances of this personage – mirror-image name pairing (ll. 1–4), a dishevelled hairy appearance (ll. 5–10, 17–20) – the text also identifies a further axiomatic link between trickster and children (ll. 15–16, 23–4). By saying the trickster 'used to make children happy' Alembo invokes the panoramic landscape of ludic phenomena – of games, string-figures, comedic actors, clown personae, etc. – I have been considering in this chapter. He is a figure of fun but also a figure responsible both for the health of pigs and infants – he 'counts the children' (l. 24). Children are ultimately his creation and benefaction as the cultural progenitor who gave humankind 'sexuality'. The work that caregivers do is in this sense 'Iba Tiri's work' (l. 22); they are the handmaidens of the trickster, in whose image their life is defined. In this illuminating passage we come finally to an appreciation of why Huli are all the children of IT.

This raises again the quite fundamental question of the nature, and appropriate levels of understanding, of child-centricity in trickster traditions. Beyond the evidential data detailed within we might pose the simple question: 'For whom are the myths and stories told?' Though hidden, muted and somewhat undeveloped, the literature yields at least one consistent response – 'children' (Evans-Pritchard 1967:18,31; Pelton 1980:67; Street 1972:85; Radin 1956:196; Beidelman 1980:33–5). One cannot help but think that perhaps such anecdotal noticings betray a misplaced priority in articulating symbolic models without reference to child perspectives. That is, regardless of the trickster's progenitorial and minder roles, his clownish and comedic masks, the tales' 'childish and childlike' (Layard 1956:107; Jung 1956:202; Evans-Pritchard 1967:28; Abrahams 1968:196) character embraces an ethno-ludiology. It is one that moves between sacred history and imaginative literature. From the child's viewpoint, the tales are propaedeutic instruments which sensitise them to an 'imaginary universe impregnated by sacredness' (Eliade 1969:157).

In this vein the non-literality of the trickster is best analysed as part of a broader inquiry into the cultural shaping of imagination. With authorial unanimity, commentators have variously remarked over the years that this protean character instantiates a sense of imaginative process (Evans-Pritchard 1967; Needham 1978; Pelton 1980; Beidelman 1980). In this regard the trickster inhabits a virtual reality, a cyberspace in which alternative and convincing environments replicate reality and yet are not of that reality. This 'frame' creates its own texture of expectations and interpretative rules. For children, IT scaffolds their own transitions between reality and make-believe, between the fundamental and the foolish: he stands as the *paradigm of pretence*. Their world-building ventures manipulate context specific space–time continuums as they *frame shift* in the fashion of the liminal lord IT. Their mode of symbolic behaviour is thus played out against the supportive context of folklore performance, as children becomes mythologising agents creating their own sacred history and contrafactual worlds. Irrespective of other abstract themes we anthropologists like to read into trickster mythology, for Huli children the experience of the trickster is ultimately one in the alchemy of pretence.

But however appealing the argument that the trickster serves as a 'symbol of the transforming power of human imagination' (Pelton 1980:256) – an image and apprehension of imagination itself – saying it does not of course make it so. This chapter has been about showing what kinds of evidence could be adduced to support the claim of the trickster's scaffolding function. But the Huli do not present, and should not be seen as, a unique or anomalous case in these respects. Among the Dogon, for example, child play is mythologised as directly replicating and emanating from their trickster Ogo-Yurugu (Pelton 1980). The transformative capacity of play is reflected in their cosmogony, which bears the impress of the trickster's creative forces precisely as among the Huli. The trickster emerges from the above as reflecting a consciousness and concern with cosmological questions. It is a vision impregnated by the complementarity of creative/destructive forces of and at 'play': 'Lifetime is a child at play, moving pieces in a game. Kingship belongs to the child' (Heraclitus 1979: Fragment 94). Perhaps as a concluding comment we need to go back again to this

Heraclitean fragment, commonly cited by play analysts and previously quoted in my Introduction. It makes reference to a world that reflects the back-and-forth movements of a 'game'. The elemental transformations of the cosmos are like the reversals we find symbolised in trickster and child fantasy play. Children are 'kings' of the universe because, like tricksters, they control transformations between reality and make-believe 'like you can't imagine'.

Afterword

The game is a distorted (but recognisable) mirror of
reality, just as reality is a distorted mirror of fantasy.

Fine 1983:153

This book was furnished as a contribution to our knowledge of the ways
in which pretend play opens a unique window onto the imaginal life of
Huli children. In this project of understanding, play is perceived at its points
of disjunction and intersection with the wider fantasy economy. The
meanings of such play are thus never limited by or to the behaviour itself.
In their 'as-if' vignettes, pretenders are constructing, experiencing and
implementing their models of the world, models which are always culturally encumbered and inflected. There can be no denying a renewed curiosity
among analysts about pretending and about the nature of its connections
to play, mimesis and the imagining mind. The viewpoint forwarded here
has been that these connections are multi-layered and revealed symbolically.
The socio-dramatic child emerges as a social poet who, as part historian,
part redactor and part mimetician, continually forges links between the
ordinary and the exceptional. In this slippage between the 'what was', 'what
is', and 'what might be', children tread a linguistic pathway between
simulation and mythologisation. But their *muthoi*, as products of the
emulative process, present visions which are 'shaped afresh', visions drawn
not just from their experiential history but from images of pretenceful being
as instantiated in narrative forms.

While this is a perspective that emphasises the transformative (cf.
Schwartzman 1978) nature of pretend behaviour, it does not entail a
commitment to enjoin some Platonic discourse about originals and copies,
to adopt a bifurcated-worlds model of reality vs. fantasy, or to predicate
the analysis of social pretence on a given, pre-formed 'adult' culture. Indeed,
these kinds of implications, and the discourse in which they are most often
framed, appear quite alien to the play metaphysics of Huli. Most certainly
their concept of pretending is semantically analogous with our notions of
(im)personation, embodiment, corporealisation and *passing into another body*. But
this is a body with illusive and impermanent dimensions, which draws a
boundary with the 'real' that is less one between two worlds than between
two modalities of being in the world. Child play is not defined as an 'other'
contraposed with 'work', but as a transformative state juxtaposed with

'truth' as something that 'stays'. The real is what is etched on the landscape, the pretend is what fails to make a lasting impression.

As the body (*tingi*) materialises pretending (*tingi*), so the hand (*gi(ni)*) is the metonymic instrument with which play (*gìni*) is exercised. Pretence, as embodied voice, mediates then between mimesis and mythos, just as the hand manages the transition between the playing (*gìni*) self, and the self as played out, as realising a 'commensurate' (*gíni*) state of alignment. This nexus of meanings is at the heart of Huli ethno-ludology. It is one in which the corporeal trope brings play and pretence, body and hand, self and 'other' into dramatic relief as most fully a philosophy of pretence as being. In this skein of profundity can be located at least one answer, albeit from a Huli perspective, to the Nietzschian question (see Introduction) of 'What role does this performing being play in general being?' (Vaihinger 1924). This is as it should be, for in the imaginative play routines of children we encounter issues of realism and verisimilitude, of referentiality and illusion, and abstractly of the priority of the word in the accomplishment and commerce of fictional representation. An ethnography of pretend play must inevitably encompass a viewpoint on these philosophically enmeshed issues.

I have been concerned in this book to etch what children understand about their own fantasy play, how this becomes a resource in their playing, and more broadly how this behaviour is experienced. The idea that through their mythical artefacts child pretenders are brought to an encounter 'with the ontological curvatures of their experience with others and with their own reflexive solitudes' (Turner 1978:7) appeals. But in what does this experience of others consist? While child dramatists are authors of, as well as actors in, their fictions, others present as interlocutors who collaboratively and cooperatively help process representations. The imaginal products of these child pretenders do not simply reflect socio-genetic origins, they also service the very ways in which child actors jointly structure their understandings and knowledge. The institutional form of double-play, wherein a text which documents a given experience is further reconstituted as a narrative text that stands alongside, is simultaneously enacted, and establishes intertextual relations between, is one among many lines of connection that have unpacked the ties between myth and child make-believe in this book. What this implies is that the two domains are not relatively autonomous, but are mutually referential, mutually implicative, mutually incorporative, and mutually instantiated in any single pretence engagement.

Against this broader backcloth of folklore I have tried to identify several other lines of connection that articulate this myth–make-believe relation:

child games, caretaker–child interaction, and the shared patterning by structuring poetic structures. All of these infuse the life-worlds of Huli children with an understanding of human behaviour as 'storied'. No doubt further explorations might be undertaken into, for example, topics such as dreams, though in Huli a person never reveals a dream for fear of impending misfortune. The perspective I have on the chapters that compose this study is that they represent selective lines of articulation, sacred sites in the ethnographic geography of pretence. Their connections and disconnections merely capture the rhizomatic configuration of pretence itself.

So while on the one hand these data strongly supported the viewpoint of pretence as the passageway between mimesis and mythos, as a loquacious conduit of transformational activity, on the other hand they also revealed the possibility of perhaps identifying more definitively the experience of pretence as mythically constructed. Huli narratives are a fusion of sacred history and imaginative literature. Like make-believe play, they talk in the language of symbols to remake worlds by constantly shifting between the real and irreal. It is this property of imaginal potentiality that allows myths to make transformations as a sense-making exercise. On one level then, myth and make-believe play are structurally homologous patterns of frame shifting. But *muthoi* as discourse also solicit others to collaborate with their implicit proposals to pretend, just like child pretenders in their fantasy interaction. Adults and children reproduce their versions of social action then in remarkably similar ways.

In all of the above respects, pretence plays with the borders between historical fact and nursery fiction, between lofty drama and burlesque comedy, and between adult and child visions of the unimaginable. To pose the question 'How can a study of fantasy play become a theory-building part of anthropology?' is surely to remain blissfully myopic to issues of symbolism, of identity and of intercultural universals. Equally, it is to remain oblivious to some of the central philosophical questions discussed in the Introduction about the role of imagination in human existence, the ontological status of representations, and the aesthetic constitution of imaginal products. In this vein, *Child's Play* is part of the growing clamour from within anthropology that responds to such questions as 'Why child?' with 'Why adult?' While the ethnographic demonstration is never easy, sufficient materials have been provided to indicate real diffusionary processes between adult and child dimensions of the culture. It is not just that these myth makers engender artefacts that are mutually incorporative of each other's visions and images, but that they are both centrally predicated on the role, nature and function of renamings as quintessential pretenceful acts, as core tranformational media.

These central arguments contain in themselves the rationale for an ethnography of child pretending being compelled to articulate such behaviour against the broader vista of fantasy in the culture. Without doubt the topic of pretence has remained a psychological oasis, only occasionally engaging the attention of linguists, philosophers, literary theorists or mainstream anthropology. Much as I have critiqued methodological paradigms which fail to recognise that in naturally occurring play children of all ages may cooperate, and in ways which highlight how fleeting such episodes may be, all the fine-grained analyses of Chapters 2 and 3 seem to point to the conclusion that Huli child play, in its communicative fundamentals, is no different to that reported for Western children. The luxury of a full-length ethnography of this topic affords one, however, an opportunity of unmasking the cultural face in whose image pretenders pretend. Along this tangent I see the chapters on the ogre and trickster as pivotal.

Given the manner in which these identities permeate the world of child games, play and speech, it may appear tempting to express succinctly the primal symbolic complex they represent as simply that of 'good vs. evil'. They pose and present as moral foils in both mythical and ludic domains. Nevertheless, their significance for the present project lies elsewhere. Unlike any other pantheistic deity or spirit, they alone are mimicked by children, they alone compose proverbial forms, they alone come with narrative cycles, and they alone have personae poetically embellished and anatomically defined. Like the content and form of baby-talk, they speak to their audiences in the language of metaphor. They are both special occupants in children's worlds, and special exemplars of pretendership. They materialise the dual identity of 'skin on skin'. Without rehearsing all the arguments expressed previously, their very being for children is as frame shifters, the ultimate face of pretendership. They circumscribe again relations between myth and make-believe, and the freedom from constraint in images 'like you can't imagine'.

In the same way then that humans are the 'children' of the trickster, the experience of other co-players is the experience of co-tricksters. The mask held by the child on the front cover is the mask of Iba Tiri, the symbol of the permanence of illusion in the world. In their pretence routines children enact their symbolic roles as 'lords of the universe'.

Appendix 1

Transcript 1

Narrator: Mugu Ndi – Mogorapugua 1993
Prose recitation prior to sung performance
Tape A: 000–061

1 *O Agali mbira udu piya tia bo gaiya biyagola*
2 One man went to kill possum during the dry season
3 *Tia bo pialu heria o Auwebe*
4 While he was there killing possum Auwebe (BH came)
5 *Tibiya Mabiyala libu udu pu hearia agali waga bima ibiya agali ibini o bedama*
6 *ale mbirago ibu tia waga bialu heria*
7 While Tibiya and Mabiya were there, BH came looking for man, real men like
8 us sitting here while one of them was looking for possum
9 *O biago pialu heria Tibiya Mabiyalame o biago bo yalu piya*
10 That one, while they had gone, Tibiya and Mabiya, BH killed him (Mabiya)
11 and carried him away
12 *Agali biago Auwebeme bo yalu piyagola*
13 That man (Mabiya), Auwebe killed and carried off
14 *Nguarialu ai agi nguarialu libu ede ege kabane anda pu wa hayagoni*
15 To search him out, but how can he be found (Tibiya asked himself)? They had
16 gone to the cave
17 *Baya Horome bo yalu piyagola libu ede ege kabani anda puwa hayagoni*
18 Baya Horo had killed him and taken him inside the cave, over there.
19 *Ege anda biagoni ayu ngago unugura ha*
20 That cave is there now, over there

Transcript 2

Sung performance
Tape A: 063–11

[Passage breaks have been inserted in the text to help the reader recognise either major changes in story theme or statement. At some junctures only the English translation lines appear. This was done both in the interests of brevity and because the literal Huli has not been remarked upon in the body of the book].

1   *Mabi Mabiyala Tibi Tibiyala nde udu heneya*
2   Mabiya and Tibiya were there
3   *Tia balu udu pu heneya laya lama agini*
4   They had gone to kill possum it's said like it was said
5   *Yagi Ainyaru balu edena peneya*
6   To kill Yagi Ainya (possum) they had gone over there
7   *Limbu Ainya*
8   To kill Limbu Ainya
9   *Limbawi Ainyaru balu nde tayenda edena ubade heneya*
10   And Limbawi Ainya they had gone to the forest over there
11   *Ai labo piyeria nde Hiru Waya hombene dayaria*
12   While they had gone the moon was shining
13   *Nde Be ira udu bayagola*
14   Reflecting light off the Be (*Gramineae*) tree
15   *Bara ira udu bayagola*
16   Reflecting light off the Bara (*Rutaceae*)
17   *Bebogo ira*
18   The Bebogo (*Euphorbiaceae*) tree
19   *Hibili ira*
20   Hibili tree
21   *Haiyama ira udu bayagola lama hendene*
22   Reflecting light off the Haiyama tree it's been seen it's been said
23   *Ega hombene dayagola*
24   The full moon was shining
25   Mabi Mabiya said to Tibi Tibiya, 'You stay' and Mabi Mabiya went it's said
26   like that
27   *Daga hana dayagoria*
28   The moon was shining there
29   *Homa hagunda kirame hia ha layaru*
30   There were two Homa Haguanda (Mountain cuscus) possums shouting there
31   *Udu Yagi Ainya mbira udu ha layua*
32   One Yagi Ainya (possum) there also shouted
33   *Limbu Ainya*

34   Limbu Ainya
35   *Limbawi Ainya mbira udu ha layua*
36   Limbawi Ainya shouted
37   *Homa Haguanda ogoria ha layua lama agini*
38   And Homa Haguanda shouted it's been said like that

39   In Mbiduba, Baluba, Payena they were shouting and going from tree to tree
40   In Pele and Dale they were shouting and going from tree to tree
41   When the possums were shouting Tibi Tibiya was down there and Mabi
42   Mabiya climbed up it's said like that
43   He shot the Haguanda in the chest with an Aya Kopi arrow it's said like that
44   With one shot only
45   The possum took the arrow out and climbed down the tree
46   While Tibi Tibiya was over there the possum held Mabi Mabiya

47   *Udu mbalu duni hubi leneya*
48   He pulled him towards him by the hair
49   *Hondo duni hubi leneya*
50   Pulled him by the hair
51   *Dabiale duni hubi leneya*
52   Pulled him by the hair
53   *Wandiba duni hubi leneya*
54   Pulled him by the hair
55   *Hundube duni liange leneya*
56   Pulled him back and forth by the hair

57   Mabiya shouted to Tibi Tibya, 'I am being held'.

58   *Umili ema biya*
59   Umili land was shaking
60   *Tombeli ema biya*
61   Tombeli land was shaking
62   *Yaguali ema biya*
63   Yaguali land was shaking

64   'I am being held' Mabiya shouted
65   Yawe Yalinga Yalima was shaking
66   Hinini Lumini was shaking
67   Daiba Dedaiba was shaking
68   Nigibalu Dagibalu was shaking
69   While the moon was shining he was shouting and the land was shaking
70   Tibi Tibiya had gone but Mabi Mabiya was being held it's been said like that

71   *Auwebe udu Nagu Nana Auwi Nana emarume*

72   Those Auwebe Nagu Nana and Auwi Nana

73   *Auwianda igini emarume emo duguaya*
74   In Auwi those sons took out the cold ashes (figurative for the death of Mabi
75   Mabiya caused by the possum which had assumed the humanoid form of
76   Baya Horo)
77   *Ngubi Anda iginirume emo duguaya*
78   In Ngubi Anda the sons have taken out the cold ashes
79   *Girabo Yuni Hini Guani emarume*
80   Girabo Yuni and Hini Guani
81   *Guani Galuni emarume*
82   Guani Galuni
83   *Dawanda Tauwa Ariba Tauwa Angane emarume*
84   Dawanda Tauwa and Ariba Tauwa Angane
85   *Ula Uwane emarume lama hendene*
86   Ula Uwane it's been seen it's been said
87   *Girabo Yuni Hini emarume de mbiyaore hearume*
88   Girabo Yuni Hini those with one eye

89   They held the hairs of Hiabi Hiaba (Mabi Mabiya) and
90   *guni dambe dene yi urume*
91   they were holding the points of the knives
92   *gambe dambe dene yi urume*
93   holding the point of the knives
94   *garai gambe dene . . .*
95   holding the point of the knives

96   and making preparations it's been said like that
97   Girabo Yuni Hini (Baya Horo) those, it's been seen it's said, held onto Mabi
98   Mabiya properly
99   They killed and carried him

100 *Awenda iraga haya*
101 They climbed to Awenda
102 *Taweni anda iraga haya*
103 They climbed to Taweni
104 *Ngubi Anda iraga haya*
105 They climbed to Ngubi Anda
106 *Daralanda iraga haya lama hendene*
107 They climbed to Daralanda it's been seen it's been said

108 In Bebenani don't let the smoke come out, in Bebenani, Goraiyene, Gendolame,
109 Dara Walu there was muddy water
110 *Auwebe Auwanda igini dindi ko hayagola gini bule bo yalu piyagoni*

111 The Baya Horo's sons' land was bad and so to straighten it they killed and
112 carried the body back

113 In Tibi Tibiya's place they were shouting
114 Umili is shaking
115 Yaguali is shaking
116 Yagobia is shaking
117 My brother is being held Tibiya said
118 The places with *nigi* (leaves) and *dagi* (ferns) plants were shaking
119 Hinini Lumini were shaking
120 Dai Daidere were shaking
121 In those places everyone came outside it's been seen it's said
122 The sons from Tobia river were ready
123 The sons from Yagobia were ready
124 The sons from the places with *nigi* (leaves) and *dagi* (ferns) were ready and
125 they were there in little groups
126 Tibi Tibiya said to them, 'Mabi Mabiya has gone' it was said like that
127 'The sons of Auwebe Auwanda have killed him and gone and I will go and
128 see them'
129 The men with the shields were
130 *nainya ha nina ha lina ha uduna ha edona ha*
131 here, there, up there, down there and everywhere
132 rushing into their own groups

133 *Umili igiri gi ndole emama bira*
134 The boys from Umili their wrist bands were moving
135 *Yaguali igiri gi ndole emama bira*
136 The boys from Yaguali their wrist bands were moving

137 The brown cassowary decorations are untied there the boys from Iba Dobia
138 and Yagobia scattered off into groups it's been seen it's been said
139 Tibi Tibiya was still shouting and they were still gathering outside it's been
140 seen it's been said

141 *Edena ibu tagiria piyeria o yagi Tibi Tibiyahanda ibu tagiria piyeria*
142 On that side they were gathering outside and on this side, Tibi Tibiya side,
143 they were gathering outside
144 *Garu Pepo, Garu Wagira, Haga Dolo, Bibi Ayege, Gu Tàni*
145 Garua clan, Wagira clan, Dolo clan, Ganimu clan, Tàni clan
146 They were gathering into groups
147 *Daga Gengi, Daga Baria, Wabulu Diliya, Kiralabe, Mugu Haya* (from *Iba Tiri*)
148 were gathering too
149 *Ayu Hugu, Kara Kora, Hidi Ariya, Kulu Auwali, Be Aya*
150 Huguni clan, Kora clan (Duna), Ariya clan (Duna), Auwali clan (Duna) Aya

151 clan (Duna) were there

152 Auwi and Ogobi, Porebi and Urubi were there for Tibi Tibiya
153 Anoigini Mbuli Mbaguale Hogale they were on Tibi Tibiya's side
154 And they gathered at Yariabi and Yarianda it's been seen it's been said
155 It's been seen it's said they were there ready
156 Tibi Tibiya got all the men from this side
157 And over on that side where Mabi Mabiya was he got men it's been seen it's
158 been said
159 The owners of the body they had come outside it's been seen it's been said
160 Au Tiri, Guriya Mabu, Dawene Golia, Au Lalala clans,
161 Hoga Hibu, Yali Gimbu, Yali Gewange clans had come outside and were
162 gathering together
163 Dawene Golia too, it's been seen it's been said
164 Those from Mbuli Mbaguale Hogale too were ready it's been seen it's been
165 said
166 Those from Hewali Yaguali Pongoli too were ready there it's been seen it's
167 been said
168 Those from Burabia and Tanabia, from Ole Imamu Angai creeks were ready.
169 All these men were got together in groups and they stepped over Tiri
170 mushrooms (figurative for moved with speed)
171 In Baya Horo Duwane land they chopped wood and set alight fires
172 In Dundanane land they chopped wood and set alight fires

173 Those things belonging to Auwebe
174 They are getting in the places Wania Mai
175 Getting in Bebenani
176 Getting in Aiolame
177 Getting in Gendolame
178 Getting in Auwi Yuli
179 Getting in Pinigi Yuli and setting alight

180 Nothing was wasted and they said, 'Now kill one funeral pig' and they went
181 in groups it's been seen it's said
182 *Mburu pagabua mbira Anoigininaga*
183 From Anoigini place one white pig
184 *Mbulubi gula*
185 The pig's forehead decorated in spots from Mbulibi
186 *Mbaguale gula*
187 The pig's forehead decorated in spots from Mbaguale
188 *Yariabi gula*
189 The pig's forehead decorated in spots from Yariabi
190 With the killing stick made to dissapear (they used to hide the stick after ritual
191 death)

192 *Diwabi gula*
193 The pig's forehead decorated in spots from Diwabi
194 *Dimane gula*
195 The pig's forehead decorated in spots from Dimane
196 With the killing stick made to disappear it's been seen it's said

197 Tibi Tibiya said, 'I have killed a funeral pig for Mabiya now and I am going to
198 see where he (Mabi Mabiya) went' and he killed and carried away one mother
199 pig
200 The moon was shining on the ground as he went it's been seen it's said
201 They all scattered in groups while the moon was shining on the Bara tree
202 While the moon was shing on the Bebogo tree
203 While there was a full moon
204 They killed and carried pieces of pig to all the places it's been seen it's been
205 said
206 Tibi Tibiya, while the moon was shining said, 'There is nobody there' (when
207 he went to where Mabiya was killed)
208 When the morning broke he went off it's been seen it's said

209 *Iba gurubu dibiyagola*
210 It was dawn
211 *Bane ede banewa biyagola*
212 It was dawn
213 He came there and said, 'Who is going to stay there?' All right, it's been seen
214 it's been said
215 He was looking around it's been seen it's been said.

216 *Aulu poroli mbira o biagoria berenya*
217 A rat was sitting there
218 *Wai mbira o biagoria bereneya*
219 A rat was sitting there
220 *Haria walia holane wariabe mbira o biagoria bereneya*
221 To show the way a rat was sitting there
222 *Erene gili uru bayuabi*
223 With decorated tail
224 *Galimuli uru bayuabi*
225 With good dots on its skin that was said

226 The rat looked over there, looked at Tibi Tibiya, looked at the road ahead, and
227 went over there it's been seen it's said
228 The rat continued to look back at Tibi Tibiya
229 Tibi Tibiya followed the rat and went off down there.

230 There were *gi gulu* plants and gardens

231 *Baya gulu mabu ha ya howa ka*
232 There were *baya gulu* plants
233 *Gayumba uru dalu mindibi ya howa ka*
234 The *gayumba* (cordyline) was so thick it looked black
235 *Wayali tigu uru nde ega Dendeba Peleda iluru hewadago lau laya ya howa ka*
236 There were bananas there and there were flying foxes in Dendeda and Paleda
237 places flapping around in the daytime
238 *Ede Yawa Yalinga Yalima anga balu ha ya howa ka*
239 In Yawa Yalinga Yalima there were plenty of pandanus it's been said like that

240 Alright well Tibi Tibiya came there to the land of Auwebe
241 The daughters of Baya Horo with rib cages it's been seen it's said
242 Gindabu Gindame was wearing grass skirts where the rope was around the
243 ribs (ie. so large were they that the grass skirt started up at the rib area)
244 Man's intestines that used to be cleaned by nails
245 The nails were like an Ayu Kopi arrow (large), like they were glued there
246 There was one girl shining like the sun at dawn (*iba gurubuni*)
247 shining like dawn (*dibu*), shining like dawn (*bana*).

248 *Yagobi iba tigiru do kelelo hearia*
249 The ferns from Yagobi are planted on the hair in rows
250 *Yaguali iba tigiru do kelelo hearia*
251 The plants from Yaguali are planted on the hair in rows

252 While she was sitting there they came up to that place it's been said like that
253 She said, 'How did you come here? Tibi Tibiya how did you come here?'
254 'Mabi Mabiya is dead there' (he responded)
255 'Garua Tibiya why did you come here?' (she said)
256 'I was going around and I came in search of my brother' (he said)
257 'Well let's cook pig' (she said) and then the two of them prepared leaves for
258 cooking there
259 That girl cut the leaves and flattened the leaves for cooking
260 'It's not possible to kill my father' she said
261 'The stones which are planted are over there' it's been seen it's said
262 'There is nothing there but bare stones and you can't go over there.'

263 *Ibabuda*
264 With weakness
265 *Dingi inaga ibabuda*
266 My bow and arrow are weak
267 *Wai inaga wara ibabuda*
268 My weapons of war are weak
269 *Waralu inaga ibabudago*
270 My weapons of war are weak

271 *Baya babenahego*
272 It's not possible to kill Baya Horo

273 'You look at where they are sleeping' she said
274 They went there and then they came back
275 'You go and make Mali Dawe dance' she said
276 'You call the boys from Umbili Tombeli Yaguali
277 All the relatives, both Tibi Tibiya and Mabi Mabiya will make Dawe
278 The Depe Halebe cult house, the casuarina trees split them like debris from
279 Iba Gurubuni creek.'
280 Like the debris from Yagobia, Dabi Hale and Mbodoba creeks
281 The split logs were prepared and left around the long house
282 The Tibiya and Mabiya people made Dawe (*Dawe dibuwa*)
283 *Wandari biarume nogo ege dugualu orabe toba howa*
284 Those girls for the pig kill got the stones, so many like you can't imagine
285 They got the leaves and ferns, they killed pigs, and shared and ate
286 Umbili and Tombeli's sons their wrist bracelets were shaking (from eating so
287 much)
288 After finishing they made Dawe
289 The Baya Horo up there said, 'Our daughters are making Dawe, killing pig,
290 having Dawe so let's go
291 We'll do Ogo Peda (dance).'
292 *Auwebe damene udu Girabu Yuni emarume*
293 Auwebe's relatives Girabu Yuni
294 *Hini emarume*
295 Hini
296 *Gauni emarume*
297 Gauni
298 *Galuni emarume*
299 Galuni

300 They prepared the tops of the pandanus tree whole and used it as an apron
301 All the sons and relatives of Baya Horo came and were everywhere in the
302 house
303 'They (daughters) are carrying the lights' BH said to themselves it's been seen
304 it was said

305 *Biangoro hale haria*
306 The live dogs were used as ear-rings
307 *Ki kau lalu*
308 They (dogs) were shouting
309 *Manda halene ede Komi o Komiabu o*
310 The ends of the wigs extended to Komi and Komiabu
311 *Komiabu ede baruni paga heneya*

312 In Komiabu the ends extended over the sides at the highest peak
313 *Galomani paga heneya*
314 At the highest peak in Galoma
315 *Manda Mindi ede Baria*
316 The black wigs in Baria
317 *Baria mbira baruni paga heneya*
318 They were over the sides of the peaks of Baria
319 *Baya nde manda mindi halene edona edona leneyago*
320 All right the ends of the wigs were there and there it was said
321 *Ede Yubini ede Galomani lowa paga hea urume*
322 They were on top of Yubi and Galoma

323 They were having Mali Yagia dances there
324 The Tauwa (pandanus) nut leaves were broken and worn as aprons
325 'I am doing Peda dance' (*peda hangaro*) they said
326 They were wearing leaves in big heaps
327 *Biangoru hale haria*
328 Dogs as earings
329 *Galowabe pongo lowa*
330 Some dogs were used as Galowabe (straight possum tail in middle of wig)
331 Where they were tied it made them lively
332 The ear-rings were shouting, shouting
333 *Oyarume ki gau layua*
334 Those dogs were shouting
335 *Waiyurume ki kau layua*
336 Those dogs were shouting

337 They came inside and were doing Peda dance it's been seen it's said.

338 *I waneme hale amu yara*
339 'My daughters are holding the lights
340 *Degele amu yara*
341 They are holding lights' (BH shouted)
342 *Pabula amu birago*
343 They were shining
344 *Payola amu birago layagola*
345 They were shining

346 They (BH) didn't see the house had been set alight
347 They didn't see the people going around setting everything on fire
348 Those lights made a crackling sound in that valley it's been seen it's said
349 Everywhere lights were held, and Tibi Tibiya set everything on fire in all the
350 places
351 They held lights as far as Mbiduba and Galoma

352 In Dindi Mondo the fire came out and stopped
353 *Dindi o biago dalu orabe toba hea*
354 Everything was destroyed like you can't imagine
355 Pele Dale was scorched, Baya Pere Tagane and further was scorched
356 The fire came as far as Gau Noma it's been seen it's said
357 That land was completely burnt

358 'O daughters (*mamali mama*) my ears are burning, burning'
359 Girabu Yuni was burning, Auwebe Hini was burning, Gauni was burning and
360 Galuni was burning
361 'I am on fire' they said
362 *Auwebe biago dalu orabe toba hayagola*
363 Baya Horo were burnt like you can't imagine
364 The head that was burnt exploded and from that explosion one piece went
365 down to Iba Tumbudu (Duna) to the middle of the water there
366 It's been seen and said that Baya Horo were completely killed and burnt

367 Tibi Tibiya is Garua clan at Yemia Dola down to Guteria creek
368 Mabi Mabiya is Mabili on the side of the Nagia and their lands are adjacent
369 Now when they meet on the banks of Gu Teria Tibi Tibiya pulls the hair from
370 side to side and says, 'Brother brother, the Baya Horo killed you and I went to
371 save you'
372 From that time the Baya Horo were all killed and and they are locked in the
373 hole
374 *Auwe tagira polebira lene*
375 We say they will come out later

Appendix 2

Informant: Alembo (Pi clan) – Tari 1993
Prose recitation

---

1 *Wandari kira biraya*
2 Two girls were there
3 *wandari kira beraria Gambe Pogorabu haya*
4 while they were there Gambe Pogorabu (hereafter GP) was there too
5 *gambe pogorabu ira pu laya*
6 he blew on the fire (to extinguish it)
7 *ira pu ira pu ira pu wandari biago labo ira delayagola*
8 he kept blowing and those two girls kept on lighting the fire
9 *pu layagola delayagola pu layagola*
10 when he blew on it then they relighted it
11 *o biago do do ibu huwai wia wiabo hungo bule ndo*
12 they kept on blowing on the embers but it didn't make a flame
13 *'ainya ogodege agile iradabe'*
14 'mother, what kind of firewood is this' (they said to themselves)
15 *Gambe Pogorabunaga gidinidabe laya*
16 'is this the penis tip of GP?'
17 *delaya ndo nabule nabule agua biya*
18 they lit the fire but it wasn't working, what happened?
19 *Gambe Pogorabu agua biya*
20 what did GP do?
21 *unu biagoha hui la howa wiabo*
22 it (ie.penis) continued to glow at the bottom of the fire
23 *ogome hurua bagadago layagola hurua delaya*
24 with this grass skirt it might burn so they burnt the grass skirt
25 *hungu kulu laya*
26 then it made a large flame
27 *hurua delayagome hungu kulu laya*
28 when the grass skirt was set on fire then the fire flared up
29 *labo de lo paleribi delowa hina guyule lowa biyagola*
30 they made fire and slept and then tried to cook sweet potato
31 *ndo ogo labo libu hina guyareni agi*

32   'no you two why are you cooking sweet potato?' (GP said to himself)
33   *ibu gidini nimu lamiya*
34   then he pulled back his penis
35   *o biago gidini huai lo winiyago Gambe Pogorabunaga*
36   the fire that was glowing was his penis
37   *nimu lamiyagola ibu naiguria yamialu piarua*
38   he took his penis and disappeared
39   *halu mbira Gambe Pogorabu nai haya*
40   one day GP was over there
41   *ai hayagola tomo tai biya*
42   he was looking for food
43   *tomo dawaya*
44   they (two girls) were cooking food
45   *dawale bialu berebira Gambe Pogorabu ege hiraya*
46   while they were trying to cook GP heated a stone
47   *ega hirayagola tue tue tue layagola*
48   when heating it made this sound 'tue'
49   *hungu kulu laya*
50   then made a flame
51   *Gambe Pogorabunaga o biago tomo dawalenaga yamialu heria iba odaribi*
52   for GP's things and food they poured water on it
53   *dawaribi tabaribi Gambe Pogorabunaga gidini gidini biago yamiagola tomo biago*
54   *bibahende gange haya*
55   they picked the stones and cooked but he pulled his penis back and everything
56   was left raw and uncooked
57   *gange halu wa halu piribi*
58   the food was raw and they left it and went off
59   *ai agua biya*
60   'what's happened?' (they said to themselves)
61   *ai nde mini purugu leadago hondo ha*
62   their minds were totally confused, but wait
63   *Gambe Pogorabu tagira ibinigo edene halu mbira piya*
64   GP came outside once and went
65   *Iba Gugubiahanda iba li timbuni timbuni timbuni piya*
66   the river Gugubia was really very high
67   *ibali biagoria togo homane ogoroia howa edego dagua dibade howa wuwa biraya*
68   so he (GP) cut and put a bridge there from one side to the other
69   *wua bereria wandari biago labo pole pialu berebiguria*
70   while sitting there the two girls were going to cross the bridge
71   *Gambe Pogorabu iba hanuniore heria ogo labo libu togo domaribi ibu Gambe*
72   *Pogorabunaga gidini biago gia lamiya gidini togo winiyago iba togo*
73   while in the middle of the brige GP said, 'You two are crossing the bridge'
74   and withdrew his penis
75   *ira homane biago gia lamiyagola*

76   he pulled the stick (ie.penis) back

77   *ogo labo unu ibani tau la haya*

78   the two (girls) fell into the river and made a big splash

79   *ogolabo pilayahandala piribi ai agua biba*

80   seeing that they had fallen into the river 'So what shall we do?' (they asked

81   themsleves)

82   *Gambe Pogorabu halu mbira nde hinagari*

83   one day GP was hungry

84   *o biago dege biama ibaga bialu bereberia*

85   he was going around doing those things (tricks)

86   *unurua geromiore e kigo ndili nduli wiaria handaya*

87   he saw a branch with two very heavy Geromi fruit on it

88   *ma e li ndili ndulu laya*

89   there were four branches there

90   *Gambe Pogorabu o biago nde bayuaore biyadago*

91   GP thought that was good

92   *nde o biago dege biama ibaga biagago doliya lowa*

93   he was going around and he said (to himself) 'I'll pick them'

94   *nu hanalu irigi halu heria*

95   with his string bag he climbed up

96   *geromi biagoria yenia hayagola*

97   he was hanging on the Geromi branch

98   *Gambe Pogorabu giduwa haga biago o kegonibe*

99   they said, 'GP are you the one who used to masturbate?'

100   *unu biago libunaga andu yenia haridago*

101   that was their breasts that he was trying to hold onto

102   *Gambe Pogorabu pu laya*

103   and they told GP 'go'

104   *ai agua biya andu biagoria yenia ho heria Gambe Pogorabu gi mo taga hama puabo*

105   *haya*

106   while he was holding on his hand continued to acquire shame there

107   *Gambe Pogorabu o Iba Tiri larimago*

108   Gambe Pogorabu is Iba Tiri

109   *tini wali ugume hagobi agali ogome hagobi buwa*

110   he used to trick women and men

111   *Gambe Pograbubaba wali baba hagi bigi bigi biradagoni*

112   GP and people used to trick each other

Bibliography

Aarne, A. (1973), *The Types of the Folktale*, Helsinki: Helsingin Liikek Irjapaino.

Abrahams, R. (1968), 'Trickster, the Outrageous Hero', in T. Coffin (ed.), *American Folklore*, Washington DC: US Information Agency, pp. 193–201.

Abrams, D. (1977), 'A Developmental Analysis of the Trickster from Folklore', in P. Stevens (ed.), *Studies in the Anthropology of Play: Papers in Memory of B. Allan Tindall*, New York: Leisure Press, pp. 145–54.

——, and Sutton-Smith, B. (1977), 'The Development of the Trickster in Children's Narrative', *Journal of American Folklore*, vol. 40, pp. 29–47.

Adams, C. (1980), 'Distinctive Features of Play and Games: A Folk Model from Southern Africa', in H.B. Schartzman (ed.), *Play and Culture*, New York: Leisure Press, pp. 150–62.

Ammar, H. (1954), *Growing Up in an Egyptian Village*, London: Routledge and Kegan Paul.

Anderson, M. (1986), 'Cultural Concatenation of Deceit and Secrecy', in R.W. Mitchell and N.S. Thompson (eds), *Deception: Perspectives on Human and Non-human Deceit*, Albany NY: Suny Press, pp. 323–48.

Arens, W. (1979), *The Man-Eating Myth: Anthropology and Anthropophagy*, Oxford: Oxford University Press.

Ariel, S. (1984), 'Locutions and Illocutions in Make-Believe Play', *Journal of Pragmatics*, vol. 8, pp. 221–40.

——, and Sever, I. (1980), 'Play in the Desert and Play in the Town: On Play Activities of Bedouin Arab Children', in H.B. Schwartzman (ed.), *Play and Culture*, New York: Leisure Press, pp. 164–75.

Aristotle (1936), *Problems*, trans. W.S. Hett, Cambridge MA: Harvard University Press.

—— (1962), *The Politics*, trans. T. Sinclair, Harmondsworth: Penguin.

—— (1982), *Poetics*, trans. J. Hutton, New York: W.W.Norton.

Austerlitz, R. (1956), 'Gilyak Nursery Words', *Word*, vol. 12, pp. 260–79.

Austin, J.L. (1961), *Philosophical Papers*, Oxford: Clarendon Press.

Austin, N. (1983), 'Odysseus and the Cyclopes: Who is Who?', in C. Rubino and C. Shelmerdine (eds), *Approaches to Homer*, Austin TX: University of Texas Press, pp. 3–37.

Auwärter, M. (1986), 'Development of Communicative Skills: The Construction of Fictional Reality in Children's Play', in J. Cook-Gumperz, W. Corsaro and J. Streeck (eds), *Children's Worlds and Children's Language*, Amsterdam: Mouton de Gruyter, pp. 205–30.

van Baal, J. (1977), 'Review of D. Sperber, *Le Symbolism en général'*, *Bijdragen tot de Taal, Land-en Volkenkunde*, vol. 133, pp. 163–5.

Babcock-Abrahams, B. (1975), 'A Tolerated Margin of Mess: The Trickster and his Tales Reconsidered', *Journal of the Folklore Institute*, vol. 11, pp. 147–86.

Bakhtin, M. (1981), *The Dialogic Imagination*, Austin TX: University of Texas Press.

Ballard, C. (1995a), 'Death of a Great Land', Unpublished PhD dissertion, Canberra: Australian National University.

—— (1995b), 'Bibliography of Materials on the Huli, Duna and Ipili Peoples', in A. Biersack (ed.), *Papuan Borderlands: Huli, Duna, and Ipili Perspectives on the Papua New Guinea Highlands*, Ann Arbor: University of Michigan Press, pp. 401–17.

Bamberg, M. (1983), 'Metaphor and Play Interaction in Children', in F.E. Manning (ed.), *The World of Play*, New York: Leisure Press, pp. 127–43.

Basso, E. (1988), 'The Trickster's Scattered Self', *Anthropological Linguistics*, vol. 30, no. 3/4, pp. 292–308.

Bateson, G. (1955), 'A Theory of Play and Fantasy', *Psychiatric Research Reports*, vol. 2, pp. 39–51.

—— (1971), 'The Message "This is Play"', in R. Herron and B. Sutton-Smith (eds), *Child's Play*, New York: J.Wiley and Sons, pp. 261–6.

Battagalia, D. (1991), 'Punishing the Yams: Leadership and Gender Ambivalence on Sabarl Island', in M. Godelier and M. Strathern (eds), *Big Men and Great Men: Personification of Power in Melanesia*, Cambridge: Cambridge University Press, pp. 83–96.

Beecher, L. (1938), 'The Stories of the Kikuyu', *Africa*, vol. 11, pp. 80–7.

Beidelman, T. (1980), 'The Moral Imagination of the Kaguru: Some Thoughts on Trickster, Translation and Comparative Analysis', *American Ethnologist*, vol. 7, pp. 27–42.

Benjamin, W. (1979), 'Doctrine of the Similar', *New German Critique*, vol. 17, pp. 65–8.

Berger, P. and Luckman, T. (1966), *The Social Construction of Reality*, Harmondsworth: Penguin.

Berlyne, D. (1969), 'Laughter, Humour and Play', in G. Lindzey and E. Arnson (eds), *Handbook of Social Psychology*, Reading MA: Addison-Wesley, vol. 3, pp. 795–852.

Benthall, J. (1992), 'Child-Focused Research', *Anthropology Today*, vol. 8, no. 2, pp. 23–5.

Bettelheim, B. (1975), *The Uses of Enchantment: The Meaning and Importance of Fairytales*, New York: Alfred A. Knopf.

Biersack, A. (1995), 'Introduction', in A. Biersack (ed.), *Papuan Borderlands: Huli, Duna, and Ipili Perspectives on the Papua New Guinea Highlands*, Ann Arbor: University of Michigan Press, pp. 1–54.

Black, B. (1992), 'Negotiating Social Pretend Play: Communication Differences Related to Social Status and Sex', *Merill-Palmer Quarterly*, vol. 38, pp. 212–32.

Blount, B. (1977), 'Ethnography and Caretaker–Child Interaction', in C. Snow and C. Ferguson (eds), *Talking to Children*, Cambridge: Cambridge University Press, pp. 297–308.

Boas, F. (1898), 'Introduction', in J. Teit, *Traditions of the Thompson River Indians, Memoirs of the American Folklore Society*, vol. 66, pp. 1–18.

Boggs, S. (1978), 'The Development of Verbal Disputing in Part-Hawaiian Children', *Language in Society*, vol. 7, pp. 325–44.

Bornstein, M. and Tamis-LeMonda, C. (1995), 'Parent–Child Symbolic Play: Three Theories in Search of an Effect', *Developmental Review*, vol. 15, pp. 382–400.

Brenneis, D. (1988), 'Language and Disputing', *Annual Review of Anthropology*, vol. 17, pp. 221–37.

—— and Lein, L. (1977), 'You Fruithead: A Sociolingistic Approach to Dispute Settlement', in S. Ervin-Tripp and C. Mitchell-Kernan (eds), *Child Discourse*, New York: Academic Press, pp. 49–65.

Bretherton, I. (1984), 'Representing the Social World in Symbolic Play: Reality and Fantasy', in I. Bretherton (ed.), *Symbolic Play: The Development of Social Understanding*, New York: Academic Press, pp. 3–41.

—— (1989), 'Pretense: The Form and Function of Make-Believe Play', *Developmental Review*, vol. 9, pp. 383–401.

Brinton, D. (1896), *Myths of the New World*, Philadelphia: David McKay.

Brown, R. (1977), 'Introduction', in C. Snow and C. Ferguson (eds), *Talking to Children*, Cambridge: Cambridge University Press, pp. 1–27.

Bruner, J. (1983), *Child's Talk: Learning to Use Language*, Oxford: Oxford University Press.

—— (1990), *Acts of Meaning*, Cambridge MA: Harvard University Press.

Bulmer, R. (1965), 'The Kyaka of the Western Highlands', in P. Lawrence and M. Meggitt (eds), *Gods, Ghosts and Men in Melanesia*, Melbourne: Oxford University Press, pp. 132–61.

Burke, K. (1969), *A Grammar of Motives*, Berkeley CA: University of California Press.

Burridge, K. (1957), 'A Tangu Game', *Man*, vol. 57, pp. 88–9.

Butterworth, E. (1987), 'The Tales Odysseus told Alkinoos, and an Akkadian Seal', in K. Atchity (ed.), *Critical Essays on Homer*, Boston: G.K. Hall, pp. 181–6.

Bynon, J. (1968), 'Berber Nursery Language', *Transactions of the Philological Society*, vol. 36, pp. 107–61.

—— (1977), 'The Derivational Process Relating Berber Nursery Words to their Counterparts in Normal Inter-adult Speech', in C. Snow and C. Ferguson (eds), *Talking to Children*, Cambridge: Cambridge University Press, pp. 255–69.

Callois, R. (1961), *Man, Play and Games*, New York: Free Press of Glencoe.

Campbell, J. (1968), *The Hero with a Thousand Faces*, Princeton NJ: Princeton University Press.

—— (1971), *The Masks of God: Primitive Mythology*, New York: Viking Press.

Carroll, L. (1960), *Through The Looking Glass*, New York: Clarkson N.Potter.

Carroll, M. (1981), 'Lévi-Strauss, Freud, and the Trickster: A New Perspective upon an old Problem', *American Ethnologist*, vol. 8, pp. 301–13.

—— (1984), 'The Trickster as Selfish Buffoon and Culture Hero', *Ethos*, vol. 12, no. 2, pp. 105–31.

Casagrande, J. (1948), 'Commanche Baby Language', *International Journal of American Linguistics*, vol. 14, pp. 11–14.

Casey, E. (1976), *Imagining: A Phenomenological Study*, Bloomington: Indiana University Press.

Castelfranchi, C. and Poggi, I. (1994), 'Lying as Pretending to Give Information', in H. Parret (ed.), *Pretending to Communicate*, New York: Walter de Gruyter, pp. 276–91.

Chakravarti, P. (1974), 'The Ogre-Killing Child: A Major Theme of Papua New Guinea Folklore', *Gigibori*, vol. 1, no. 1, pp. 12–20.

Chick, G. and Donlon, J. (1992), 'Going Out on a Limn: Geertz Deep Play: Notes on the Balinese Cockfight and the Anthropological Study of Play', *Play and Culture*, vol. 5, pp. 233–44.

Christie, J. (1982), 'Play: To Train or not to Train?', in J. Loy (ed.), *The Paradoxes of Play*, New York: Leisure Press, pp. 122–9.

Clark, J. (1993), 'Gold, Sex and Pollution: Male Illness and Myth at Mt Kare, Papua New Guinea', *American Ethnologist*, vol. 20, no. 4, pp. 743–58.

Coleridge, S. (1906), *Biographia Literaria*, London: J.M. Dent.

Conquergood, D. (1989), 'Poetics, Play, Process, and Power: The Performative Turn in Anthropology', *Text and Performance Quarterly*, vol. 1, pp. 82–95.

Corsaro, W. (1983), 'Script Recognition, Articulation and Expansion in Children's Role Play', *Discourse Processes*, vol. 6, pp. 1–19.

—— (1992), 'Interpretive Reproduction in Children's Peer Cultures', *Social Psychology Quarterly*, vol. 55, no. 2, pp. 16–77.

—— and Streeck, J. (1986), 'Studying Children's Worlds: Methodological Issues', in J. Cook-Gumperz, W. Corsaro and J. Streeck (eds), *Children's Worlds and Children's Language*, Amsterdam: Mouton de Gruyter, pp. 13–35.

Crawford, J. (1970), 'Cocopa Baby Talk', *International Journal of American Linguistics*, vol. 36, pp. 9–13.

Currie, G. (1990), *The Nature of Fiction*, Cambridge: Cambridge University Press.

Dansky, J. (1980), 'Make-Believe: A Mediator of the Relationship between Play and Associative Fluency', *Child Development*, vol. 51, pp. 576–9.

Dennett, C. (1987), *The Intentional Stance*, Bradform Books: MIT Press.

Derrida, J. (1981), *Disseminations*, Chicago: University of Chicago Press.

Dil, A. (1975), 'Bengali Baby Talk', *Word*, vol. 27, pp. 11–27.

Dixon, W. and Shore, C. (1993), 'Language Style Dimensions and Symbolic Play', *Play Theory and Research*, vol. 1, no. 4, pp. 259–69.

Douglas, M. (1966), *Purity and Danger*, London: Routledge & Kegan Paul.

Doyle, A., Doehring, P., Tessier, O., and de Lorimier, S. (1992), 'Transitions in Children's Play: A Sequential Analysis of States Preceding and Following Social Pretense', *Developmental Psychology*, vol. 28, no. 1, pp. 137–44.

Duncan, R. (1995), 'Piaget and Vygotsky Revisited: Dialogue or Assimilation?', *Developmental Review*, vol. 15, pp. 458–72.

Dundes, A. (1964), 'On Game Morphology: A Study of the Structure of Non-Verbal Folklore', *New York Folklore Quarterly*, vol. 20, pp. 276–88.

—— (1974), 'Comment', *Current Anthropology*, vol. 15, pp. 134–5.

Dunn, J. and Dale, N. (1984), 'I a Daddy: 2-Year-Olds' Collaboration in Joint Pretend with Sibling and Mother', in I. Bretherton (ed.), *Symbolic Play: The Development of Social Understanding*, London: Academic Press, pp. 131–57.

Duveen, G. and Lloyd, B. (1988), 'Gender as an Influence in the Development of Scripted Pretend Play', *British Journal of Developmental Psychology*, vol. 6, pp. 89–95.

Ebbeck, F. (1973), 'Learning from Play in Other Cultures', in J. Frost (ed.), *Revisiting Early Childhood Education*, New York: J. Wiley & Sons, pp. 321–6.

Ehrmann, J. (1968), '*Homo Ludens* Revisited', *Yale French Studies*, vol. 41, pp. 31–57.

Eifermann, R. (1971), *Determinants of Children's Games Styles*, Jerusalem: Israel Academy of Science.

Eliade, M. (1969), *The Quest: History and Meaning in Religion*, Chicago: University of Chicago Press.

El'konin, D. (1966), 'Symbolics and its Functions in the Play of Children', *Soviet Education*, vol. 8, pp. 35–41.

Ellen, R.F. (1977), 'Anatomical Classification and the Semiotics of the Body', in J. Blacking (ed.), *The Anthropology of the Body*, London: Academic Press, pp. 333–73.

Ellis, M. (1973), *Why People Play*, Englewood Cliffs NJ: Prentice Hall.

Emmison, M. and Goldman, L.R. (1996), 'What's That You Said Sooty? Puppets, Parlance and Pretence', *Language and Communication*, vol. 16, pp. 17–35.

—— (1997),'The *Sooty Show* Laid Bear: Children, Puppets and Make-Believe', *Childhood*, vol. 4, no. 3, pp. 325–42.

Erikson, E. (1950), *Childhood and Society*, New York: Norton.

Ervin-Tripp, S. and Strage, A. (1985), 'Parent–Child Discourse', in T.A. van Dijk (ed.), *Handbook of Discourse Analysis*, vol. 3, pp. 65–77.

Euripides (1994), *Cyclops, Alcestis, Medea*, trans. D. Kovacs, Cambridge MA: Harvard University Press.

Evans-Pritchard, E. (1967), *The Zande Trickster*, Oxford: Oxford University Press.

Farver, J. M. and Howes, C. (1993), 'Cultural Differences in American and Mexican Mother–Child Pretend Play', *Merill-Palmer Quarterly*, vol. 39, no. 3, pp. 344–58.

Farver, J.M., Kim, Y. and Lee, T. (1995), 'Cultural Differenrces in Korean and Anglo-American Preschoolers' Social Interaction and Play Behaviours', *Merrill-Palmer Quarterly*, vol. 66, pp. 1088–99.

Fein, G. (1975), 'A Transformational Analysis of Pretending', *Developmental Psychology*, vol. 11, no. 3, pp. 291–6.

—— (1979), 'Play and the Acquisition of Symbols', in L. Katz (ed.), *Current Topics in Early Childhood Education*, Norwood NJ: Ablex, vol. 11, pp. 195–225.

—— (1981), 'Pretend Play in Childhood: An Integrative Review', *Child Development*, vol. 52, pp. 1095–118.

—— (1987), 'Creativity and Consciousness', in D. Görlitz and J.F. Wohlwill (eds), *Curiosity, Imagination and Play*, Hillsdale NJ: Lawrence Erlbaum, pp. 282–304.

—— (1989), 'Mind, Meaning, and Affect: Proposals for a Theory of Pretense', *Developmental Review*, vol. 9, pp. 345–63.

—— and Fryer, M. (1995), 'Maternal Contributions to Early Symbolic Play Competence', *Developmental Review*, vol. 15, pp. 367–81.

—— and Glaubman, R. (1993), 'Commentary', *Human Development*, vol. 36, pp. 247–52.

Feitelson, D. (1959), 'Some Aspects of the Social Life of Kurdish Jews', *Jewish Journal of Sociology*, vol. 1, pp. 201–16.

—— (1977), 'Cross-Cultural Studies of Representational Play', in B. Tizard and D. Harvey (eds), *Biology of Play*, Philadelphia: J.B. Lippincott, pp. 6–14.

Fenson, L. (1984), 'Developmental Trends for Action and Speech in Pretend Play', in I. Bretherton (ed.), *Symbolic Play: The Development of Social Understanding*, New York: Academic Press, pp. 249–70.

Ferguson, C. (1964), 'Baby Talk in Six Languages', *American Anthropologist*, vol. 66, pp. 103–14.

—— (1977), 'Baby Talk as a Simplified Register', in C. Snow and C. Ferguson (eds), *Talking to Children*, Cambridge: Cambridge University Press, pp. 209–35.

Fernandez, J. (1974), 'The Mission of Metaphor in Expressive Culture', *Current Anthropology*, vol. 15, pp. 119–33.

Field, T., de Stefano, L. and Koewler, J. (1982), 'Fantasy Play of Toddlers and Preschoolers', *Developmental Psychology*, vol. 18, no. 4, pp. 503–8.

Fine, G.A. (1983), *Shared Fantasy: Role-Playing Games as Social Worlds*, Chicago: University of Chicago Press.

Fineman, J. (1962), 'Observations on the Development of Imaginative Play in Early Childhood', *Journal of Child Psychiatry*, vol. 1, pp. 167–81.

Fink, E. (1968), 'The Oasis of Happiness: Toward an Ontology of Play', *Yale French Studies*, vol. 41, pp. 19–30.

Fish, S. (1980), *Is There a Text in the Class?*, Cambridge MA: Harvard University Press.

Flavell, J., Flavell, E. and Green, F. (1987), 'Young Children's Knowledge about the Apparent–Real and Pretend–Real Distinctions', *Developmental Psychology*, vol. 23, pp. 816–22.

Flavell, J., Green, F. and Flavell, E. (1986), 'Development of Knowledge about the Appearance–Reality Distinction', *Monographs of the Society for Research into Child Development*, vol. 51, no. 1.

Forbes, D. and Yablick, G. (1984), 'The Organisation of Dramatic Content in Children's Fantasy Play', in F. Kessel and A. Göncü (eds), *Analysing Children's Play Dialogues: New Directions for Child Development*, San Francisco: Jossey-Bass, no. 25, pp. 23–36.

Forbes, D., Katz, M. and Paul, B. (1986), 'Frame Talk: A Dramatistic Analysis of Children's Fantasy Play', in E. Mueller and C. Cooper (eds), *Process and Outcome in Peer Relationships*, New York: Academic Press, pp. 249–65.

Fortes, M. (1959), *Oedipus and Job in West African Religion*, Cambridge: Cambridge University Press.

—— (1970), 'Social and Psychological Aspects of Education in Taleland', in J. Middleton (ed.), *From Child to Adult*, New York: Natural History Press, pp. 14–74.

Fortune, R. (1963), *Sorcerers of Dobu: The Social Anthropology of the Dobu Islanders of the Western Pacific*, New York: E.P. Dutton.

Forys, S. and McCune-Nicolich, L. (1984), 'Shared Pretend: Sociodramatic Play at 3 Years of Age', in I. Bretherton (ed.), *Symbolic Play: The Development of Social Understanding*, New York: Academic Press, pp. 156–91.

Frank, A.W. (1981), 'Pooh Talk: Formulating Children's Conversational Troubles', *Semiotica*, vol. 37, pp. 109–20.

Frankel, S. (1986), *The Huli Response to Illness*, Cambridge: Cambridge University Press.

Franklin, K. and Franklin, J. (1978), 'A Kewa Dictionary', *Pacific Linguistics* Series C, no. 53, Canberra: ANU Press.

Freud, S. (1959), 'Writers and Daydreaming', J. Strachey (ed.), *The Standard Edition of the Complete Psychological Works of S. Freud 1906–8*, vol. 9, London: Hogarth.

—— (1961), *Beyond the Pleasure Principle*, New York: Norton.

Furth, H.G. (1996), *Desire for Society: Children's Knowledge as Social Imagination*, New York: Plenum Press.

—— and Kane, S. (1992), 'Children Constructing Society: A New Perspective on Children at Play', in H. McGurk (ed.), *Childhood Social Development: Contemporary Perspectives*, Hove: Lawrence Erlbaum, pp. 149–73.

Gadamer, H. G. (1975), *Truth and Method*, London: Sheed and Ward.

Garvey, C. (1974), 'Some Properties of Social Play', *Merrill-Palmer Quarterly*, vol. 20, pp. 163–80.

—— (1990), 'The Modals of Necessity and Obligation in Children's Pretend Play', in *Play and Culture*, vol. 3, pp. 206–18.

—— (1993a), 'Diversity in the Conversational Repertoire: The Case of Conflicts and Social Pretending', *Cognition and Instruction*, vol. 11, pp. 251–64.

—— (1993b), 'Commentary', *Human Development*, vol. 36, pp. 235–40.

—— and Berndt, R. (1977), 'The Organisation of Pretend Play', *JSAS Catalog of Selected Documents in Psychology*, vol. 7.

—— and Kramer, T. (1989), 'The Language of Social Pretend', *Developmental Review*, vol. 9, pp. 364–82.

Geertz, C. (1972), 'Deep Play: Notes on the Balinese Cockfight', *Daedalus*, pp. 1–37.

Gell, A. (1975), *Metamorphosis of the Cassowaries: Umeda Society, Language and Ritual*, London: Athlone Press.

Giffen, H. (1984), 'The Coordination of Meaning in the Creation of Shared Make-Believe Reality', in I. Bretherton (ed.), *Symbolic Play: The Development of Social Understanding*, New York: Academic Press, pp. 73–100.

Gillison, G. (1993), *Between Culture and Fantasy: A New Guinea Highlands Mythology*, Chicago: University of Chicago Press.

Gilsenan, M. (1976), 'Lying, Honour and Contradiction', in B. Kapferer (ed.), *Transaction and Meaning: Directions in the Anthropology of Exchange and Symbolic Behaviour*, Philadelphia: Institute for the Study of Human Issues, pp. 191–219.

Glasse, R. (1965), 'The Huli of the Southern Highlands', in P. Lawrence and M. Meggitt (eds), *Gods, Ghosts and Men in Melanesia*, Melbourne: Oxford University Press, pp. 27–49.

—— (1968), *Huli of Papua: A Cognatic Descent System*, Paris: Mouton.

—— (1987), 'Huli Names and Meaning', *Ethnology*, vol. 26, pp. 201–8.

Glenn, J. (1971), 'The Polyphemus Folktale and Homer's Kyklôpeia', *Transactions and Proceedings of the American Philological Association*, vol. 102, pp. 133–81.

Goffman, E. (1974), *Frame Analysis*, New York: Harper & Row.

Goldman, L.R. (1979), 'Kelote: An Important Huli Ritual Ground', *Oral History*, vol. 7, no. 4, pp. 14–18.

—— (1980), 'Speech Categories and the Study of Disputes', *Oceania*, vol. 50, no. 3, pp. 209–27.

—— (1983), *Talk Never Dies: The Language of Huli Disputes*, London: Tavistock.

—— (1986a), 'Anatomical Terms in Huli: Names and Games', *Mankind*, vol. 16, no. 3, pp. 190–208.

—— (1986b), 'A Case of "Questions" and a Question of "Case"', *Text*, vol. 6, no. 4, pp. 349–92.

—— (1986c), 'The Presentational Style of Women in Huli Disputes', *Pacific Linguistics: Papers in New Guinea Linguistics*, vol. A–70, pp. 213–89.

—— (1987), 'Ethnographic Interpretations of Parent–Child Discourse in Huli', *Journal of Child Language*, vol. 14, no. 3, pp. 447–66.

—— (1988), *Premarital Sex Cases among the Huli: A Comparison between Traditional and Village Court Styles*, Oceania Monograph 34, University of Sydney.

—— (1991), 'Review of B. Schieffelin, *Language Socialisation of Kaluli Children*', *Language in Society*, vol. 20, no. 4, pp. 663–8.

—— (1993), *The Culture of Coincidence: Accident and Absolute Liability in Huli*, Oxford: Oxford University Press.

—— (1995), 'The Depths of Deception: Cultural Schemas of Illusion in Huli', in A. Biersack (ed.), *Papuan Borderlands: Huli, Duna, and Ipili Perspectives on the Papua New Guinea Highlands*, Ann Arbor: University of Michigan Press, pp.111–38.

—— (1998), 'A Huli Trickster for all Seasons', in L. Goldman and C. Ballard (eds), *Fluid Ontologies: Myth, Ritual and Philosophy in the Western Highlands*, Westport CN: Greenwood Press.

—— and Ballard, C. (1998) (eds), *Fluid Ontologies: Myth, Ritual and Philosophy in the Western Highlands*, Westport CN: Greenwood Press.

—— Duffield, G. and Ballard, C. (1998), 'Fire, Water, and Flux', in L. Goldman and C. Ballard (eds), *Fluid Ontologies: Myth, Ritual and Philosophy in the Western Highlands*, Westport CN: Greenwood Press.

——, and Emmison, E. (1995), 'Make-Believe Play among Huli Children: Performance, Myth and Imagination', *Ethnology*, vol. 24, pp. 225–55.

—— and Emmison, E. (1996), 'Fantasy and Double-Play among Huli Children of Papua New Guinea', *Text*, vol. 15, pp. 43–60.

Golomb, C. (1977), 'Symbolic Play: The Role of Substitutions in Pretence and Puzzle Games', *British Journal of Educational Psychology*, vol. 47, pp. 175–86.

—— and Cornelius, C. (1977), 'Symbolic Play and its Cognitive Significance', *Developmental Psychology*, vol. 13, no. 3, pp. 246–52.

Goodwin, M. (1988), 'Cooperation and Competition across Girls' Play Activities', in A.D. Todd and S. Fisher (eds), *Gender and Discourse: The Power of Talk*, Norwood NJ: Ablex, pp. 55–94.

—— and Goodwin, C. (1987), 'Children's Arguing', in S. Philips, S. Steele and C. Tanz (eds), *Language, Gender and Sex in Comparative Perspective*, Cambridge: Cambridge University Press, pp. 200–46.

Göncü, A. (1989), 'Models and Features of Pretense', *Developmental Review*, vol. 9, pp. 341–4.

—— (1993), 'Development of Intersubjectivity in Social Pretend Play', *Human Development*, vol. 36, pp. 185–93.

—— and Kessel, F. (1984), 'Children's Play: A Contextual-Functional Perspective', in F. Kessel and A. Göncü (eds), *Analysing Children's Play Dialogues: New Directions for Child Development*, San Francisco: Jossey-Bass, no. 25, pp. 5–22.

Gordon, D. (1993), 'The Inhibition of Pretend Play and its Implications for Development', *Human Development*, vol. 36, pp. 215–36.

Görlitz, D. and Wohlwill, J.F. (1987) (eds), *Curiosity, Imagination and Play*, Hillsdale NJ: Lawrence Erlbaum.

Griswold, W. (1983), 'The Devil's Techniques: Cultural Legitimation and Social Change', *American Sociological Review*, vol. 48, pp. 668–80.

Groos, K. (1901), *The Play of Man*, New York: Appleton.

Gulick, L. (1898), *A Philosophy of Play*, New York: Scribners.

Haight, W. and Miller, P. (1992), 'The Development of Everyday Pretend Play: A Longitudinal Study of Mother's Participation', *Merill-Palmer Quarterly*, vol. 38, pp. 331–49.

Haley, N. (1993), 'Altered Texts and Contexts: Narrative, History and Identity among the Duna', Unpublished Honours thesis, Macquarie University.

—— (1996), 'Revisioning the Past, Remembering the Future: Duna Accounts of the World's End', *Oceania*, vol. 66, pp. 278–85.

Hall, G. (1906), *Youth*, New York: Appleton.

Harris, P. (1991), 'The Work of the Imagination', in A. Whiten (ed.), *Natural Theories of Mind*, Oxford: Blackwell, pp. 283–304.

——, Brown, E., Marriott, C., Whittall, S. and Harmer, S. (1991), 'Monsters, Ghosts and Witches: Testing the Limits of the Fantasy–Reality Distinction in Young Children', *British Journal of Developmental Psychology*, vol. 9, pp. 105–23.

—— and Kavanaugh, R. (1993), 'Young Children's Understanding of Pretense', *Monographs of the Society for Research into Child Development*, vol. 58, no. 231.

—— Kavanaugh, R. and Meredith, M. (1994), 'Young Children's Comprehension of Pretend Episodes: The Integration of Successive Actions', *Child Development*, vol. 65, pp. 16–30.

Heraclitus (1979), *The Art and Thought of Heraclitus: An Edition of the Fragments with Translation and Commentary*, ed. and trans. C. Kahn, Cambridge: Cambridge University Press.

Hides, J. (1936), *Papuan Wonderland*, London and Glasgow: Blackie & Son.

Hogbin, I. (1946), 'A New Guinea Childhood: From Weaning until the Eighth Year in Wogeo', *Oceania*, vol. 16, pp. 275–96.

Homer (1961), *The Odyssey*, trans. E.V. Rieu, Harmondsworth: Penguin.

Howes, C. (1985), 'Sharing Fantasy: Social Pretend Play in Toddlers', *Child Development*, vol. 56, pp. 1253–8.

Hoyle, S.M. (1989), 'Forms and Footings in Boys' Sportcasting', *Text*, vol. 9, no. 2, pp. 153–73.

Hudson, J. and Nelson, K. (1984), 'Play with Language: Overextensions as Analogies', *Journal of Child Language*, vol. 11, pp. 337–46.

Huizinga, J. (1955), *Homo Ludens: A Study of the Play-Element in Culture*, Boston: Beacon Press.

Hume, D. (1951), *A Treatise of Human Nature*, London: J.M. Dent.

Hymes, D. (1964), *Language in Culture and Society*, New York: Harper & Row.

Jakobson, R. (1962), 'Why "Mama" and "Papa"?', *Selected Writings*, vol. 1, pp. 21–2.

Johnson, J. (1990), 'The Role of Play in Cognitive Development', in E. Klugman and S. Smilansky (eds), *Children's Play and Learning*, New York: Teachers College Press, pp. 213–34.

Jolly, A. (1988), 'The Evolution of Purpose', in R.W. Byrne and A. Whiten (eds), *Machiavellian Intelligence*, Oxford: Clarendon Press, pp. 263–378.

Jung, C. G. (1956), 'On the Psychology of the Trickster Figure', in P. Radin, *The Trickster: A Study in American Indian Mythology*, London: Routledge & Kegan Paul, pp. 195–211.

Kane, S. and Furth, H. (1993), 'Children Constructing Social Reality: A Frame Analysis of Social Pretend Play', *Human Development*, vol. 36, pp. 199–214.

Kearney, R. (1988), *The Wake of Imagination*, London: Hutchinson.

Kelkar, A. (1964), 'Marathi Baby Talk', *Word*, vol. 20, pp. 40–54.

Kelly-Byrne, D. (1984), 'Text and Context: Fabling in a Relationship', in F. Kessel and A. Göncü (eds), *Analysing Children's Play Dialogues: New Directions for Child Development*, San Francisco: Jossey-Bass, no. 25, pp. 37–51.

Kerényi, K. (1956), 'The Trickster in Relation to Greek Mythology', in P. Radin, *The Trickster: A Study in American Indian Mythology*, London: Routledge & Kegan Paul, pp. 195–211.

Kessen, W. (1983), 'The Child and Other Cultural Inventions', in F.S. Kessel and A. Siegel (eds), *The Child and Other Cultural Inventions*, New York: Praeger, pp. 26–39.

Kirshenblatt-Gimblett, B. (1976), 'Directions for Future Research', in B. Kirshenblatt-Gimblett (ed.), *Speech Play*, Philadelphia: University of Pennsylvania Press, pp. 175–7.

Klinger, E. (1969), 'Development of Imaginative Behaviour: Implications of Play for a Theory of Fantasy', *Psychological Bulletin*, vol. 74, no. 4, pp. 277–98.

Kluckhohn, C. (1959), 'Recurrent Themes in Myth and Mythology', *Daedalus: Journal of the American Academy of Arts and Sciences*, vol. 88, pp. 269–79.

Kyratzis, A. (1992), 'Gender Differences in the Use of Persuasive Justification in Children's Pretend Play', in K. Hall, M. Bucholtz and B. Moonwomon (eds), *Locating Power*, Berkeley CA: University of California Press, pp. 80–92.

Laboratory of Comparative Human Cognition (1979), 'Cross-Cultural Psychology's Challenge to our Ideas of Children and Development', *American Psychologist*, vol. 34, no. 10, pp. 827–33.

LaFrenière, P. (1988), 'The Ontogeny of Tactical Deception', in R.W. Byrne and A. Whiten (eds), *Machiavellian Intelligence*, Oxford: Oxford University Press, pp. 238–52.

Lakoff, G. and Johnson, M. (1980), *Metaphors We Live By*, Chicago: University of Chicago Press.

Lancy, D. (1996), *Playing on the Mother-Ground: Cultural Routines for Children's Development*, New York: Guildford Press.

Layard, J. (1957), 'Critical Notice on *The Trickster* by Paul Radin', *Journal of Analytical Psychology*, vol. 2, pp. 106–11.

—— (1958), 'Note on the Autonomous Psyche and the Ambivalence of the Trickster Concept', *Journal of Analytic Psychology*, vol. 3, pp. 21–8.

Lazarus, M. (1883), *Concerning the Fascination of Play*, Berlin: Dummler.

Leary, J. (1982), 'A Trickster in Everyday Life', in J.W. Loy (ed.), *The Paradoxes of Play*, New York: Leisure Press, pp. 57–64.

Lein, L. and Brenneis, D. (1978), 'Children's Disputes in Three Speech Communities', *Language in Society*, vol. 7, pp. 299–323.

LeRoy, J. (1985), *Fabricated World: An Interpretation of Kewa Tales*, Vancouver: University of British Columbia Press.

Leslie, A. (1987), 'Pretence and Representation: The Origins of "Theory of Mind"', *Psychological Review*, vol. 94, pp. 412–26.

—— (1994), 'Pretending and Believing: Issues in the Theory of ToMM', *Cognition*, vol. 50, pp. 211–38.

LeVine, R. (1980), 'Anthropology and Child Development', in C.M. Super and S. Harkness (eds), *Anthropological Perspectives on Child Development: New Directions for Child Development*, vol. 8, San Francisco: Jossey-Bass, pp. 71–86.

—— and LeVine, B. (1963), 'Nyansongo: A Gusii Community in Kenya', in B. Whiting (ed.), *Six Cultures: Studies of Child Rearing*, New York: J. Wiley & Sons, pp. 18–82.

Lévi-Strauss, C. (1955), 'The Structural Study of Myth', *Journal of American Folklore*, vol. 68, pp. 428–55.

—— (1963), *Structural Anthropology*, New York: Basic Books.

Lewis, G. (1974), 'Gnau Anatomy and Vocabulary for Illness', *Oceania*, vol. 45, pp. 50–78.

Lieberman, J. (1977), *Playfulness: Its Relationship to Imagination and Creativity*, New York: Academic Press.

Lillard, A. (1993a), 'Young Children's Conceptualisation of Pretense: Action or Mental Representaion State?', *Child Development*, vol. 64, pp. 372–86.

—— (1993b), 'Pretend Play Skills and the Child's Theory of Mind', *Child Development*, vol. 64, pp. 348–71.

Lloyd, B. and Goodwin, R. (1995), 'Let's Pretend: Casting the Characters and Setting the Scene', *British Journal of Developmental Psychology*, vol. 13, no. 2, pp. 61–70.

Lodge, K.R. (1979), 'The Use of the Past Tense in Games of Pretend', *Journal of Child Language*, vol. 6, pp. 365–9.

Lowes, J. (1927), *The Road to Xanadu: A Study in the Ways of the Imagination*, Boston: Houghton Mifflin.

Lowie, R. (1909), 'The Hero-Trickster Discussion', *Journal of American Folklore*, vol. 22, pp. 431–3.

Makarius, L. (1970), 'Ritual Clowns and Symbolic Behaviour', *Diogenes*, vol. 69, pp. 44–73.

Mandler, J. (1983), 'Representation', in J. Flavell and E. Markman (eds), *Cognitive Development: Handbook of Child Psychology*, New York: J. Wiley & Sons, vol. 11, pp. 420–91.

Marrelli, J. (1994), 'On Non-Serious Talk: Some Cross-Cultural Remarks on the (Un)importance of (Not) Being Earnest', in H. Parret (ed.), *Pretending to Communicate*, New York: Walter de Gruyter, pp. 254–73.

Martlew, M., Connolly, K. and McCleod, C. (1978), 'Language Use, Role and Context in a Five-Year-Old', *Journal of Child Language*, vol. 5, pp. 81–99.

Mathews, W. (1977), 'Modes of Transformation in the Initiation of Fantasy Play', *Developmental Psychology*, vol. 13, no. 3, pp. 212–16.

Maynard, D. (1985), 'How Children Start Arguments', *Language in Society*, vol. 14, pp. 1–30.

McCarthy, J. and Pfund, K. (1973), *Legends of Papua New Guinea*, Sydney: Rigby.

McCune-Nicolich, L. (1977), 'Beyond Sensorimotor Intelligence: Assessment of Symbolic Maturity through Analysis of Pretend Play', *Merill-Palmer Quarterly*, vol. 23, no. 2, pp. 89–99.

—— (1981), 'Toward Symbolic Functioning: Structure of Early Pretend Games and Potential Parallels with Language', *Child Development*, vol. 52, pp. 785–97.

McLaughlin, M. (1984), *Conversation*, London: Sage.

McTear, M. (1985), *Children's Conversations*, New York: Oxford University Press.

Mead, G. H. (1934), *Mind, Self and Society*, Chicago: University of Chicago Press.

Mead, M. (1930), *Growing Up in New Guinea*, New York: Morrow.

Meggitt, M. (1976), 'A Duplicity of Demons: Sexual and Familial Roles Expressed in Western Enga Stories', in P. Brown and G. Buchbinder (eds), *Man and Woman in the New Guinea Highlands*, Special Publication of the American Anthropological Association, no. 8, pp. 67–89.

Mendelsohn, E., Robinson, S., Gardner, H. and Winner, E. (1984), 'Are Preschoolers' Renamings Intentional Category Violations?', *Developmental Psychology*, vol. 20, no. 2, pp. 187–92.

Merlan, F. and Rumsey, A. (1991), *Ku Waru: Language and Segmentary Politics in the Western Nebilyer Valley, Papua New Guinea*, Cambridge: Cambridge University Press.

Miller, P. and Garvey, C. (1984), 'Mother–Baby Role Play: Its Origins in Social Support', in I. Bretherton (ed.), *Symbolic Play: The Development of Social Understanding*, New York: Academic Press, pp. 101–30.

Millar, S. (1968), *The Psychology of Play*, Harmondsworth: Penguin.

Miller, S. (1974), 'The Playful, the Crazy, and the Nature of Pretense', in E. Norbeck (ed.), *The Anthropological Study of Human Play, Rice University Studies*, vol. 60, pp. 31–51.

Milne, A.A. (1926), *Winnie the Pooh*, London: Methuen.

Mitchell, R. (1986), 'A Framework for Discussing Deception', in R. Mitchell and N. Thompson (eds), *Deception: Perspectives on Human and Nonhuman Deceit*, Albany NY: Suny Press, pp. 3–40.

Modjeska, C. (1977), 'Production Among the Duna', Unpublished PhD thesis, Canberra: Australian National University.

Mondi, R. (1983), 'The Homeric Cyclopes: Folktale, Tradition and Theme', *Transactions and Proceedings of the American Philological Association*, vol. 113, pp. 17–38.

Mook, B. (1994), 'Therapeutic Play: From Interpretation to Intervention', in J. Hellendoorn, R. van der Kooij and B. Sutton-Smith (eds), *Play and Intervention*, Albany NY: Suny Press, pp. 39–52.

Morison, P and Gardner, H. (1978), 'Dragons and Dinosaurs: The Child's Capacity to Differentiate Fantasy from Reality', *Child Development*, vol. 49, pp. 642–8.

Motz, L. (1982), 'Giants in Folklore and Mythology: A New Approach', *Folklore*, vol. 93, no. 1, pp. 70–84.

Myers, W. (1976), 'Imaginary Companions, Fantasy Twins, Mirror Dreams, and Depersonalisation', *Psychoanalytic Quarterly*, vol. 45, pp. 503–24.

Needham, R. (1978), *Primordial Characters*, Charlottesville VA: University Press of Virginia.

Nelson, K. and Seidman, S. (1984), 'Playing with Scripts', in I. Bretherton (ed.), *Symbolic Play: The Development of Social Understanding*, New York: Academic Press, pp. 45–71.

New, R. (1994), 'Child's Play – *Una Cosa Naturale*: An Italian Perspective', in J. Roopnarine, J. Johnson, and F. Hooper (eds), *Children's Play in Diverse Perspectives*, Albany NY: Suny Press, pp. 123–47.

Norbeck, E. (1974), 'The Anthropological Study of Human Play', in E. Norbeck (ed.), *The Anthropological Study of Human Play, Rice University Studies*, vol. 60, no. 3, pp. 1–8.

Ochs, E. (1982), 'Talking to Children in Western Samoa', *Language in Society*, vol. 11, pp. 50–78.

O'Connell, B. and Bretherton, I. (1984), ' Toddlers' Play, Alone and with Mother. The Role of Maternal Guidance', in I. Bretherton (ed.), *Symbolic Play: The Development of Social Understanding*, New York: Academic Press, pp. 337–68.

Overton, W. and Jackson, J. (1973), 'The Representation of Imagined Objects in Action Sequences: A Developmental Study', *Child Development*, vol. 44, pp. 309–14.

Page, D. (1955), *The Homeric Odyssey*, Westport CN: Greenwood Press.

Palmer, G. and Jankowiak, W. (1996), 'Performance and Imagination: Toward an Anthropology of the Spectacular and Mundane', *Cultural Anthropology*, vol. 11, pp. 225–58.

Pan, H. (1994), 'Children's Play in Taiwan', in J. Roopnarine, J. Johnson and F. Hooper (eds), *Children's Play in Diverse Perspectives*, Albany NY: Suny Press, pp. 31–50.

Patrick, G. (1916), *The Psychology of Relaxation*, Boston: Houghton Mifflin.

Paulme, D. (1977), 'The Impossible Imitation in African Trickster Tales', in B. Lindfors (ed.), *Forms of Folklore in Africa*, Austin TX: University of Texas Press, pp. 64–103.

Pawley, A. (1992), 'Kalam Pandanus Language: An Old New Guinea Experiment in Language Engineering', in T. Dutton, M. Ross and D. Tryon (eds), *The Language Game: Papers in Memory of Donald C. Laycock, Pacific Linguistics*, no. 110, pp. 313–34.

Pelton, R. (1980), *The Trickster in West Africa: A Study of Mythic Irony and Sacred Delight*, Berkeley CA: University of California Press.

Pepler, D. and Rubin, K. (1982), 'Introduction', in D. Pepler and K. Rubin (eds), *The Play of Children: Current Theory and Research*, New York: S. Karger, pp. 1–3.

Perner, J. (1991), *Understanding the Representational Mind*, Cambridge MA: MIT Press.

Peterson, C. and Siegal, M. (1995), 'Deafness, Conversation and Theory of Mind', *Journal of Child Psychology and Psychiatry*, vol. 36, no. 3, pp. 459–74.

Philostratus (1912), *The Life of Apollonius of Tyana*, trans. F.C. Conybeare, London: William Heinemann.

Piaget, J. (1962), *Play, Dreams, and Imitation in Childhood*, New York: Norton.

Plato (1970), *The Laws*, trans. D.J. Saunders, Harmondsworth: Penguin.

—— (1974), *The Republic*, trans. D. Lee, Harmondsworth: Penguin.

Poignant, R. (1967), *Oceanic Mythology*, London: Paul Hamlyn.

Pomponio, A., Counts, D. and Harding, T. (1994) (eds), *Children of Kilibob: Creation, Cosmos and Culture in Northeast New Guinea, Pacific Studies*, vol. 4.

Poole, F. (1983), 'Cannibals, Tricksters, and Witches: Anthropophagic Images among Bimin-kuskusmin', in P. Brown and D. Tuzin (eds), *The Ethnography of Cannibalism*, Washington DC: Society of Psychological Anthropology.

Prentice, N., Manosevitz, M. and Hubbs, L. (1978), 'Imaginary Figures of Early Childhood: Santa Claus, Easter Bunny, and the Tooth Fairy', *American Journal of Orthopsychiatry*, vol. 48, no. 4, pp. 618–27.

Propp, V. (1968), *Morphology of the Folktale*, Austin TX: University of Texas Press.

Radin, P. (1956), *The Trickster*, London: Routledge & Kegan Paul.

Rapp, U. (1984), 'Simulation and Imagination: Mimesis as Play', in M. Spariosu (ed.), *Mimesis in Contemporary Theory*, Philadelphia: John Benjamins, pp. 141–71.

Ratner, N. and Bruner, J. (1978), 'Games, Social Exchange and the Acquisition of Language', *Journal of Child Language*, vol. 5, pp. 391–401.

Raum, O. (1940), *Chaga Childhood*, London: Oxford University Press.

Richards, I. (1960), *Coleridge on Imagination*, Bloomington: Indiana University Press.

Ricketts, M.L. (1965), 'The North American Indian Trickster', *History of Religions*, vol. 5, pp. 327–50.

Ricoeur, P. (1978), 'The Function of Fiction in Shaping Reality', *Man and World*, vol. 12, no. 2, pp. 123–41.

—— (1994), 'Imagination in Discourse and Action', in G. Robinson and J. Rundell (eds), *Rethinking Imagination*, London: Routledge, pp. 118–35.

Robinson, C. and Jackson, R. (1993), 'The Relationship between Parents' Christmas Gifts and Piaget's Stages of Pretend Play and Games-with-Rules Play', *Play Theory and Research*, vol. 1, no. 2, pp. 141–52.

Roheim, R. (1950), *Psychoanalysis and Anthropology: Culture, Personality and the Unconscious*, New York: International Universities Press.

Rubin, K. (1980), 'Fantasy Play: Its Role in the Development of Social Skills and Social Cognition', in K. Rubin (ed.), *Children's Play: New Directions for Child Development*, San Francisco: Jossey-Bass, vol. 9, pp. 69–85.

—— Fein, G. and Vandenberg, B. (1983), 'Play', in E. Hetherington (ed.), *Handbook of Child Psychology: Socialisation, Personality, and Social Development*, New York: J. Wiley & Sons, vol. 4, pp. 693–774.

Rubin, S. and Wolf, D. (1979), 'The Development of Maybe: The Evolution of Social Roles into Narrative Roles', in E. Winner and H. Gardner (eds), *Fact, Fiction, and Fantasy in Childhood*, San Francisco: Jossey-Bass, pp. 15–28.

Rūķe-Draviņa, V. (1977), 'Modifications of Speech Addressed to Young Children in Latvian', in C. Snow and C. Ferguson (eds), *Talking to Children*, Cambridge: Cambridge University Press, pp. 237–53.

Ryle, G. (1949), *The Concept of Mind*, London: Hutchinson.

—— (1973), 'Conversation with Gilbert Ryle', in B. Magee, *Modern British Philosophy*, St Albans, Herts: Paladin, pp. 128–45.

Sabar, Y. (1974), 'Nursery Rhymes and Baby Words in the Jewish Neo-Aramaic Dialect of Zakho (Iraq)', *Journal of the American Oriental Society*, vol. 94, pp. 329–36.

Sachs, J. (1987), 'Preschool Boys' and Girls' Language Use in Pretend Play', in S. Philips, S. Steele and C. Tanz (eds), *Language, Gender, and Sex in Comparative Perspective*, New York: Cambridge University Press, pp. 178–88.

—— Goldman, J. and Chaillé, C. (1985), 'Narratives in Preschoolers' Sociodramatic Play: The Role of Knowledge and Communicative Competence', in L. Galda and A. Pellegrini (eds), *Play, Language and Stories: The Development of Children's Literate Behaviour*, Norwood NJ: Ablex, pp. 45–61.

Sanches, M. and Kirshenblatt-Gimblett, B. (1976), 'Children's Traditional Speech Play and Child Language', in B. Kirshenblatt-Gimblett (ed.), *Speech Play*, Philadelphia PA: University of Pennsylvania Press, pp. 65–110.

Sarbin, T. (1966), 'Role Enactment', in B. Biddle and E. Thomas (eds), *Role Theory: Concepts and Research*, New York: J. Wiley & Sons, pp. 195–200.

Sartre, J.-P. (1950), *The Psychology of Imagination*, London: Rider.

Sawyer, K. (1995), 'A Developmental Model of Heteroglossic Improvisation in Children's Fantasy Play', in N. Mandell (ed.), *Sociological Studies of Children*, vol. 7, pp. 127–53.

Scarlett, W. and Wolf, D. (1979), 'When it's Only Make-Believe: The Construction of a Boundary between Fantasy and Reality in Storytelling', in E. Winner and

H. Gardner (eds), *Fact, Fiction, and Fantasy in Childhood*, San Francisco: Jossey-Bass, pp. 29–40.

Schank, R. and Abelson, R. (1977), *Scripts, Plans, Goals and Understanding*, Hillsdale NJ: Lawrence Erlbaum.

Schegloff, E. and Sacks, H. (1973), 'Opening up Closings', *Semiotica*, vol. 8, pp. 289–327.

Schieffelin, B. (1979), 'Getting it Together: An Ethnographic Approach to the Study of Communicative Competence', in E. Ochs and B. Schieffelin (eds), *Developmental Pragmatics*, New York: Academic Press, pp. 73–108.

—— (1990), *The Give and Take of Everyday Life: Language Socialisation of Kaluli Children*, Cambridge: Cambridge University Press.

Schiller, F. (1875), *Essays, Aesthetical and Philosophical*, London: George Bell.

—— (1954), *On the Aesthetic Education of Man*, London: Routledge & Kegan Paul.

Schwartzman, H.B. (1970), 'Children's Play: A Sideways Glance at Make-Believe', in D. Lancy and B. Allan Tindall (eds), *The Study of Play: Problems and Prospects*, New York: Leisure Press, pp. 208–15.

—— (1976), 'The Anthropological Study of Children's Play', *Annual Review of Anthropology*, vol. 5, pp. 289–328.

—— (1978), *Transformations: The Anthropology of Children's Play*, New York: Plenum Press.

—— (1982), 'Play and Metaphor', in J. Loy (ed.), *The Paradoxes of Play*, New York: Leisure Press, pp. 25–33.

—— (1983), 'Child-Structured Play', in F. Manning (ed.), *The World of Play*, New York: Leisure Press, pp. 200–14.

—— (1984), 'Imaginative Play: Deficit or Difference', in T. Yawky and A. Pellegrini (eds), *Child's Play: Developmental and Applied*, Hillsdale NJ: Lawrence Erlbaum, pp. 49–62.

—— (1991), 'Imagining Play', *Play and Culture*, vol. 4, pp. 214–22.

Searle, J. (1975), 'The Logical Status of Fictional Discourse', *New Literary History*, vol. 6, pp. 329–58.

Seligman, C. (1910), *The Melanesians of British New Guinea*, Cambridge: Cambridge University Press.

Sillitoe, P. (1993), 'Forest and Demons in the Papua New Guinea Highlands', *Australian Journal of Anthropology*, vol. 4, no. 3, pp. 220–32.

Simmel, G. (1964), *Sociology*, trans. K. Wolff, New York: Free Press.

Singer, J. (1973), *The Child's World of Make-Believe*, New York: Academic Press.

Singer, D. and Singer, J. (1977), *Partners in Play*, New York: Harper & Row.

Smilansky, S. (1968), *The Effects of Sociodramatic Play on Disadvantaged Preschool Children*, New York: Wiley & Sons.

—— (1990), 'Sociodramatic Play: Its Relevance to Behaviour and Achievement in School', in E. Klugman and S. Smilansky (eds), *Children's Play and Learning*, New York: Teachers College Press, pp. 18–42.

Smith, P. (1977), 'Social and Fantasy Play in Young Children', in B. Tizard and D. Harvey (eds), *Biology of Play: Clinics in Developmental Medicine*, London: W. Heinemann Medical Books, vol. 62, pp. 123–45.

Snow, C. (1977), 'Mothers' Speech Research', in C. Snow and C. Ferguson (eds), *Talking to Children*, Cambridge: Cambridge University Press, pp. 31–49.

—— (1979), 'Conversations with Children', in P. Fletcher and M. Garman (eds), *Language Acquisition*, Cambridge: Cambridge University Press, pp. 363–75.

—— and Ferguson, C. (1977) (eds), *Talking to Children*, Cambridge: Cambridge University Press.

Spariosu, M. (1982), *Literature, Mimesis and Play*, Germany: Tübingen.

Spencer, H. (1873), *Principles of Psychology*, New York: Appleton.

Stambak, M. and Sinclair, H. (1993), *Pretend Play among 3-Year-Olds*, Hillsdale NJ: Lawrence Erlbaum.

Stinton, T. (1979), 'Phaedrus and Folklore: An Old Problem Restated', *Classical Quarterly*, vol. 29, pp. 432–5.

Stone, G.P. (1971), 'The Play of Little Children', in R. Herron and B. Sutton-Smith (eds), *Child's Play*, New York: J. Wiley & Sons, pp. 4–14.

Strathern, A. (1975), 'Veiled Speech in Mt Hagen', in M. Bloch (ed.), *Political Language and Oratory in Traditional Society*, New York: Academic Press, pp. 185–203.

Strawson, P.F. (1970), 'Imagination and Perception', in L. Foster and J.W. Swanson (eds), *Experience and Theory*, Amherst MA: University of Massachusetts Press, pp. 31–54.

Street, B. (1972), 'The Trickster Theme: Winnebago and Azande', in A. Singer and B. Street (eds), *Zande Themes*, Oxford: Blackwell, pp. 82–104.

Stross, B. (1975), 'Metaphor in the Speech Play of Tzeltal Children', *Anthropological Linguistics*, vol. 17, pp. 305–23.

Stürzenhofecker, G. (1993), 'Times Enmeshed: Gender, Space, and History among the Duna', Unpublished PhD thesis, University of Pittsburgh.

Sutton-Smith, B. (1967), 'The Role of Play in Cognitive Development', *Young Children*, vol. 6, pp. 364–9.

—— (1972), *The Folkgames of Children*, Austin TX: University of Texas Press.

—— (1982), 'Paradigms of Pretense', in J. Loy (ed.), *The Paradoxes of Play*, New York: Leisure Press, pp. 76–85.

—— (1984), 'Text and Context in Imaginative Play and the Social Sciences', in F. Kessel and A. Göncü (eds), *Analysing Children's Play Dialogues: New Directions for Child Development*, San Francisco: Jossey-Bass, no. 25, pp. 53–70.

—— (1994), 'Paradigms of Intervention', in J. Hellendoorn, R. van der Kooij and B. Sutton-Smith (eds), *Play and Intervention*, Albany NY: Suny Press, pp. 3–21.

—— and Magee, M. (1989), 'Reversible Childhood', *Play and Culture*, vol. 2, pp. 52–63.

von Sydow, C. (1948), *Selected Papers on Folklore*, Copenhagen: Rosenkilde and Bagger.

Taussig, M. (1993), *Mimesis and Alterity: A Particular History of the Senses*, New York: Routledge & Kegan Paul.

Taylor, M. and Flavell, J.H. (1984), 'Seeing and Believing: Children's Understanding of the Distinction between Appearance and Reality', *Child Development*, vol. 55, pp. 1710–20.

Taylor, M., Cartwright, B. and Carlson, M. (1993), 'A Developmental Investigation of Children's Imaginary Companions', *Developmental Psychology*, vol. 29, no. 2, pp. 276–85.

Thompson, C. (1968), *The Mystery and Lore of Monsters*, New York: University Books.

Toren, C. (1993), 'Making History: The Significance of Childhood Cognition for a Comparative Anthropology of Mind', *Man* (NS), vol. 28, pp. 461–78.

Turner, V. (1968), 'Myth and Symbol', in D. Sills (ed.), *International Encyclopedia of Social Sciences*, New York: Macmillan and Free Press, pp. 576–82.

—— (1974), 'Liminal to Liminoid, in Play, Flow, and Ritual: An Essay in Comparative Symbology', *Rice University Studies*, vol. 60, pp. 53–92.

—— (1978), 'Foreword', in R. Wagner, *Lethal Speech*, Ithaca NY: Cornell University Press, pp. 5–8.

Vaihinger, H. (1924), *The Philosophy of 'As If'*, London: Routledge & Kegan Paul.

Verba, M. (1987), 'Construction and Sharing of Meanings in Pretend Play among Young Children', in D. Görlitz and J.F. Wohlwill (eds), *Curiosity, Imagination and Play*, Hillsdale NJ: Lawrence Erlbaum, pp. 1–29.

—— (1993), 'Cooperative Formats in Pretend Play among Young Children', *Cognition and Instruction*, vol. 11, no. 4, pp. 265–80.

Vygotsky, L. (1966), 'Play and its Role in the Mental Development of the Child', *Soviet Psychology*, vol. 5, pp. 6–18.

Wagner, R. (1978), *Lethal Speech*, Ithaca NY: Cornell University Press.

Walker-Andrews, A. and Harris, P. (1993), 'Young Children's Comprehension of Pretend Causal Sequences', *Developmental Psychology*, vol. 29, no. 5, pp. 915–21.

Wallace, A. (1966), *Religion: An Anthropological View*, New York: Random House.

Walton, K. (1990), *Mimesis as Make-Believe*, Cambridge MA: Harvard University Press.

Wartofsky, M. (1983), 'The Child's Construction of the World and the World's Construction of the Child: From Historical Epistemology to Historical Psychology', in F. Kessel and A. Siegel (eds), *The Child and Other Cultural Inventions*, New York: Praeger, pp. 188–215.

Watson, M. (1986), 'Commentary', in J. Flavell, F. Green and E. Flavell, 'Development of Knowledge about the Appearance–Reality Distinction', *Monographs of the Society for Research into Child Development*, vol. 51, no. 1, pp. 70–6.

Werner, H. and Kaplan, B. (1963), *Symbolic Formation*, New York: Wiley & Sons.

Whiten, A. and Byrne, R.W. (1988), 'The Machiavellian Intelligence Hypothesis: Editorial', in R.W. Byrne and A. Whiten (eds), *Machiavellian Intelligence*, Oxford: Oxford University Press, pp. 1–11.

Widdowson, J. (1971), 'The Bogeyman: Some Preliminary Observations on Frightening Figures', *Folklore*, vol. 82, pp. 99–115.

Winner, E. and Gardner, H. (1979), 'Editors' Notes: Investigations of the Imaginative Realm', in E. Winner and H. Gardner (eds), *Fact, Fiction, and Fantasy in Childhood*, San Francisco: Jossey-Bass, pp. vii–xii.

——, McCarthy, M., Kleinman, S. and Gardner, H. (1979), 'First Metaphors', in E. Winner and H. Gardner (eds), *Fact, Fiction, and Fantasy in Childhood*, San Francisco: Jossey-Bass, pp. 29–41.

Winnicott, D. (1971), *Playing and Reality*, New York: Basic Books.

Wolf, D. and Gardner, H. (1978), 'Style and Sequence in Early Symbolic Play', in M. Franklin and N. Smith (eds), *Early Sybolization*, Hillsdale NJ: Lawrence Erlbaum, pp. 17–25.

—— and Pusch, J. (1985), 'The Origins of Autonomous Texts in Play Boundaries', in L. Galda and A. Pellegrini (eds), *Play, Language and Stories: The Development of Children's Literate Behaviour*, Norwood NJ: Ablex, pp. 64–77.

Woolley, J. (1995), 'The Fictional Mind: Young Children's Understanding of Imagination, Pretense, and Dreams', *Developmental Review*, vol. 15, pp. 172–211.

Index